Democracy, Society and the Governance
of Security

The promoti   is-
persed and ta   n-
governmenta   do
we know abo   o-
moted in thi   ng
advanced an   nd
Dupont brin   on
our understa   v-
ernance. Off   at
democratic ti   ti-
tutions and t   rs
in this volum   ir-
ical example   of
criminology,

JENNIFER WC   n-
tre for Securi   k,
Australian N   o-
ordinator of t

BENOÎT DUP(té
de Montréal,   ne
Police: Le Ca   of
Policing the L

Democracy, Society and the Governance of Security

Edited by

Jennifer Wood and Benoît Dupont

CAMBRIDGE
UNIVERSITY PRESS

CAMBRIDGE UNIVERSITY PRESS
Cambridge, New York, Melbourne, Madrid, Cape Town, Singapore, São Paulo

Cambridge University Press
The Edinburgh Building, Cambridge CB2 2RU, UK

Published in the United States of America by Cambridge University Press,
New York

www.cambridge.org
Information on this title: www.cambridge.org/9780521616423

First published 2006

Printed in the United Kingdom at the University Press, Cambridge

A catalogue record for this book is available from the British Library

ISBN-13 978-0-521-85092-6 hardback
ISBN-10 0-521-85092-4 hardback
ISBN-13 978-0-521-61642-3 paperback
ISBN-10 0-521-61642-5 paperback

Contents

vi   Contents

Contributors

SCOTT BURRIS, Professor, Beasley School of Law, Temple University and Senior Associate, Johns Hopkins Bloomburg School of Public Health

ADAM CRAWFORD, Professor and Director, Centre for Criminal Justice Studies, University of Leeds

BENOÎT DUPONT, Assistant Professor, International Centre for Comparative Criminology, Université de Montréal

ANDREW GOLDSMITH, Professor, School of Law, Flinders University

LES JOHNSTON, Professor and Research Director, Institute of Criminal Justice Studies, University of Portsmouth

IAN LOADER, Professor of Criminology and Director of the Oxford Centre for Criminology, University of Oxford

PETER K. MANNING, Brooks Chair of Policing and Criminal Justice, College of Criminal Justice, Northeastern University

MONIQUE MARKS, Research Fellow, Security 21: International Centre for Security and Justice, Regulatory Institutions Network (RegNet), Research School of Social Sciences, Australian National University

CLIFFORD SHEARING, Professor, Regulatory Institutions Network (RegNet), Research School of Social Sciences, Australian National University

NEIL WALKER, Professor of European Law, Law Department, European University Institute

JENNIFER WOOD, Research Fellow, Security 21: International Centre for Security and Justice, Regulatory Institutions Network (RegNet), Research School of Social Sciences, Australian National University

Foreword

This is a timely book that echoes important developments occurring in other fields. Pluralism in law is now an important trend in legal theory. The 'anchored pluralism' for which this collection of essays is arguing may also become a thread running through various innovative approaches to the theory and practice of security.

The book has a theoretical and a pragmatic focus and it succeeds in many things. I will mention four of these. First, it is a welcome exercise in conceptual analysis, as it tries to spell out the meaning of a new set of joint notions – governance, node, pluralism and the governance of security, just to mention a few – that are taking an increasing place in theoretical discourse. The authors make a convincing case that these concepts are the building blocks of a robust perspective that future research will have to take into account.

Second, the essays go far beyond definitional issues and the explanatory power of their key notions is truly put to the test. One such key notion, which is approached from different angles in the book, is that of 'nodal governance'. This notion implies that power flows from a nexus of connected – but not necessarily co-ordinated – agents rather than from a single well. Despite its trendy garb, nodal governance may prove to be a useful tool, as it allows us to overcome two obstacles to building a new paradigm for reflecting upon the exercise of power. First, thinking about power and its potential effects has been hindered by the centripetal–centrifugal polarity. Either power accumulates in a single locus, according to the traditional *centralization* model, or it is dispersed, in accord with the no less ancient *decentralization* model. What is common to both of these models is that they view power as a single kind of stuff – the force of the state – that is either put in one place or tucked in several corners. What they fail to capture is that it makes little difference whether all the ministries are located in one capital or spread out over the whole territory, as long as they remain *state* ministries. Not only does the idea of nodal governance escape from the *one-centre/no-centre* pseudo-alternative, but, more crucially, it does away with the *single stuff* mythology: depending on its agent, power can be public, private, hybrid or yet uncategorized. Getting rid of the single stuff mythology also means moving beyond the second obstacle to thinking lucidly about power. This monumental obstacle, still very much insurmountable in countries that have experienced centralized government, is *statocentricity*. Statocentricity does not only rest on the belief that all power is governmental; it also asserts that all valid discourse on power must be grounded in things political. Just as theology was the sole fount of religious thought in the West when there was only one religion, political theory claims to encompass all knowledge on power when force is vested exclusively in the state.

Third, the authors of the various chapters in this book have a normative outlook and they do not claim to be above pragmatics. A normative focus can be variously interpreted. At the least, it implies arguing for what ought to be done. This book takes a much bolder approach and dares to pronounce on moral issues. In this time and age when moral discourse is proffered in a key more consonant with angry elevator music than a Bach cantata, a genuine voice is a welcome sound, even if it is dissonant. Finally, it must be stressed that the various authors of this book are engaged in a vigorous debate, an activity less placid than dialogue and now more needed. Although united by the urgency to think anew about security, these writers have healthy disagreements on basic issues. Writing a foreword to this stimulating collection is frustrating because one has to keep from jumping into the fray. But not for long, as all readers of this book will feel.

JEAN-PAUL BRODEUR

Acknowledgements

As with any collection, there are many individuals who have made essential contributions 'behind the scenes'. We would first like to acknowledge some members of our broader intellectual community, both near and far, whom we have had the privilege of engaging with and learning from on a regular basis. Our colleagues from the Regulatory Institutions Network (RegNet) have inspired us to look beyond our disciplinary boundaries, not only to explore connections with broader transformations in the fields of governance and regulation, but to be concerned about what they mean for the fair and equitable distribution of security outcomes for all human beings. We would in particular like to acknowledge the invaluable contributions of John Braithwaite, Peter Drahos, Jenny Fleming and Peter Grabosky. We are also very grateful to Nina Leijon, whose research and administrative support was central in making this project happen. In Montreal, colleagues from the International Centre for Comparative Criminology (CICC) provided us with another source of inspiration and discussion over the meaning of security and the various morphologies it might take. Here, Jean-Paul Brodeur, Maurice Cusson and Mylène Jaccoud deserve a special mention.

We have also had the honour of working with practitioners and scholars from different parts of globe. Our participation in the Project for Safe and Just Communities (PSJC) in Argentina continues to be near to our hearts, and has opened up our eyes to the challenges of democratic transformation in social, political and economic contexts that are profoundly different from our own. Special thanks to Enrique Font for allowing us to be included, in the modest ways that we can, in his pursuit of forms of security governance that privilege human rights. We would also like to acknowledge the generous financial support of the Canadian International Development Agency as well as the support of the Centre for International Studies, University of Toronto in managing the PSJC.

We have also benefited greatly from collaborative projects devoted to research and innovation in the field of security with which we are currently involved in Australia and Canada. These projects have been made possible by grants from the Australian Research Council (LP0346987; LP0348682) as well as from the Social Science and Humanities Research Council of Canada (410-2004-1637) and the Quebec Research Fund for Society and Culture (2004-NC-20738).

Finally, we should like to thank Shannon Dallas and Valerie Dupont for their continued loving support of our work.

Introduction
Understanding the governance of security

Jennifer Wood and Benoît Dupont

This collection of essays has an explanatory as well as a normative focus. On the one hand it tries to establish and clarify what it is that we know, as well as that which we don't know (at least very well), about the ways in which 'security' is thought about and promoted within diverse empirical contexts. Based on what we know, and recognizing what we don't know, this book shares some key concerns about how the advancement and protection of democratic values is being threatened or compromised by contemporary arrangements for security governance. In light of such worries, various theoretical and practical ideas for ways forward are argued, and in some cases vehemently so, by contributors to this volume.

What we, as editors, hoped for in preparing this book was to provide more structure to the 'friendly dialogue' that has been occurring between those advancing different descriptions and explanations of what has been happening and/or those offering different assessments of what is at stake for the future of democracy and what to do about it. In reading the chapters herein it will become clear that there is more agreement about what has been happening than there is about what to do about it. None the less, there remain important differences in the ways in which scholars describe and explain contemporary developments, reflecting their use of different conceptual and analytical tools. In this way, the book is intended in part to provide an opportunity for 'taking stock' of similarities and differences in scholarly opinion. While the themes and issues raised in this collection are undoubtedly complex, and probably raise more questions than provide more answers, the idea for the book itself emerged from the stance that we (and hopefully others) share that 'superior explanatory theory (ordered propositions about the way the world is) and superior normative theory (ordered propositions about the way the world ought to be) arise from an explicit commitment to integrating explanatory and normative theory' (Braithwaite 2002a: ix–x). If this book has made but a modest contribution to this 'integration' enterprise, it will have achieved its core purpose.

This introductory chapter is intended primarily to establish the core explanatory themes of this collection, leaving a consideration of normative issues and agendas to the concluding chapter. Presumably, the best place to start is with the one conceptual pillar that supports all the various chapters, which is the notion of the 'governance of security'. The term 'governance' in this context refers to conscious attempts to shape and influence the conduct of individuals, groups and wide populations in furtherance of a particular objective – in this case, 'security'. It can be similarly described, just as Shearing does in this volume, as 'shaping the flow of events' (Parker and Braithwaite 2003). The key theoretical influence on the term is Foucault's notion of 'government', which refers essentially to the 'right disposition of things, arranged so as to lead to a convenient end' (1991: 93). In line with the Foucauldian claim that 'political theory attends too much to institutions, and too little to practices' (Gordon 1991), to govern means 'to structure the possible field of action of others' (Foucault 1982: 220 cited in Simon 1997: 174).

Notwithstanding the theoretical (and hence potentially off-putting) nature of the term 'governance', it can and has been utilized to make the very practical point that collective goods, like 'security', are promoted by a range of institutions including, but not limited to, those of the state and its military and criminal justice organizations. The chapters in this book illustrate this 'plurality' through various empirical examples and cases, such as the participation of 'commercial military service providers' at the transnational level (Johnston), the establishment of inter-agency networks in anti-terrorist efforts (Manning), the 'marketization' of public policing (including patrol) and forms of 'enclosure' such as 'gated communities' and privately owned shopping malls (Crawford).

While the contributors to this volume agree that pluralism is a general trend, the ways in which they describe, explain and assess this plurality differ. The contributions by Shearing, Johnston, Burris and Wood promote a 'nodal governance' approach (Johnston and Shearing 2003; Shearing and Wood 2003b; Burris 2004; Drahos 2004; Burris et al. 2005), one which 'refuses to give conceptual priority to any particular locus of power' (Johnston, this volume: 34). While the term 'nodal governance' is relatively new in its usage (see Kempa et al. 1999 for an early conceptualization) its intellectual origins can be traced to the work of Shearing and Stenning (1981; 1983; 1985) some two decades ago on the rise of 'private governments' (Macaulay 1986), defined by Shearing as 'non-state entities that operate not simply as providers of governance on behalf of state agencies but as auspices of governance in their own right' (this volume: 11). For the past two decades Shearing has been arguing, with increased vigour, that scholars must move out of a 'state-centred view

of governance', which he sees as a 'particularly tenacious paradigm' that
'needs to be eclipsed' (13). He adds, '[t]his is so not simply because
this ... view of the world is preventing us from developing an understanding of the world that captures what has been taking place, but because it
is limiting normative thinking' (13). More recently, Shearing, along with
others, has suggested that a 'nodal conception' of governance provides a
means of breaking out of this paradigm. 'Just what the role of the state is
and how it does or does not relate to other nodes should be an empirical
question and not one to be decided *a priori* on the basis of conceptual
claims such as those of Hobbes and Weber' (27).

A 'node', Burris summarizes (2004: 341), is 'a site of governance
exhibiting four essential characteristics:
• Ways of thinking (*mentalities*) about the matters that the node has
  emerged to govern;
• Methods (*technologies*) for exerting influence over the course of events
  at issue;
• *Resources* to support the operation of the node and the exertion of
  influence; and
• An *institutional structure*'.

As both Johnston and Wood point out, the general line of empirical
inquiry that Shearing advocates has to date been pursued in ways that
focus largely (but not exclusively) on the 'mentalities' and associated
'technologies' of different governance nodes. This has led to the identification of, and distinction between, 'risk-based thought and action'
(Johnston, this volume: 35) – seen to reside 'naturally' in corporate governance (Johnston and Shearing 2003: 76) – and a 'punishment mentality'
seen as deeply embedded in the practices of criminal justice institutions
(Johnston and Shearing 2003). In his chapter on transnational security governance Johnston seeks to move beyond such a depiction of
ideal typical nodes to explore ways in which, and the extent to which,
proactive (risk-based) and coercive military technologies are melded.
For example, 'governments are now turning to contractors for operational services that either require or make more likely their use of
force' (44). In recognizing this complex 'mixing' of ways of thinking
and acting within and across nodes, Dupont points out that the language of 'privatization' 'restricts the transformation of the security field
to a dichotomous and simplistic analytical framework impervious to
the infinite combinations possible ... Hence, the continuum approach,
with the "public" and the "private" at each end, and various unpredictable combinations of pluralization and commodification in its middle, seems more appropriate to depicting the current situation' (this
volume: 87).

Both Manning and Dupont place more conceptual emphasis on 'networks' of security governance, and seek to advance our understanding of how networks are constituted in particular time- and space-specific contexts. Similar to Johnston's critique of ideal typical descriptions, both of these authors see the formation of networks in terms of continuous, iterative and more or less temporary processes carried out by a range of security actors (nodes) according to different positions of power. Based on two case studies of American anti-terrorist activities (the 2002 Salt Lake City Olympics and the 2004 Democratic National Convention in Boston), Manning echoes Johnston in arguing that risk-based thinking differs across the local, state and federal agencies that come together to manage terrorist threats. 'Risk' and 'security', he argues, are 'imagined' and constructed by agencies according to their own 'tacit knowledge' and established ways of acting on particular problems. He contrasts, for instance, the risk-orientation of local police with that of federal agencies like the Federal Bureau of Investigation. Whereas the police (due to their primarily reactive capacity) imagine risk according to categories of crimes and criminal sanctions – what Simon would describe as the 'governing through crime' approach (1997) – federal agencies deploy a more future-oriented, long-term perspective centred on an 'intelligence-based' perspective. Manning's study reminds us that established ways of acting on problems – organizational 'habits' as it were – shape ways of thinking; 'the objects of concern, what is seen, are sustained by the practices that have developed over time to detect them' (82). Furthermore, 'networks' are best seen not in terms of crystallized structures, but as more or less temporary hubs of practice. '"Network" is a metaphor ... that does not assume shared aims', but does assume behavioural interchange and practices that 'intersect to form a consistent concrete system of action' (54).

Manning's work points to the need for further research – that deploys a range of methodologies, including ethnography (as he has done) – on the highly site-specific and contingent nature of network formation. Dupont makes a similar point in his study of how governance 'auspices' and 'providers' (Bayley and Shearing 2001) engage in 'power struggles' with one another (and even within their own organizations) as they seek to 'jockey' for important positions in the field of security delivery. Based on data collected for an 'oral history' project sponsored by the Australian Institute of Criminology, Dupont looks at what police commissioners (both active and retired) had to say about those actors in the security field with whom they engaged, aligned with or contested, namely political actors, unions, the media and community groups. The comments of commissioners revealed 'how their field of possible actions was shaped or constrained' (this volume: 96) by these actors. He further examines 'how police commissioners exercised their agency and manoeuvred through this field' (97). Dupont contends that the power plays engaged in by commissioners involved 'accumulating', 'investing' and 'trading' different forms of what Bourdieu (1986) describes as 'capital' (economic, political, cultural, social and symbolic) in order to promote their particular organizational interests. Such power struggles are geared towards a 'broader tacit outcome', where the public police are the central and most 'professional' guarantor of security, an outcome that others have similarly observed in the power struggles of police unions (Fleming et al. in press).

Notwithstanding such power struggles, some contend that the public police do, by their very nature, possess a rather 'sacred' status and cannot be seen simply as 'one node among many' (Crawford, this volume: 137). Consistently with Dupont's analysis, Crawford examines ways in which different policing and security providers relate to and engage with one another in a 'mixed economy'. A key dimension of this mixed economy is the development of a 'second tier of policing and security [that] has mushroomed sometimes blind to, at other times in conflict or competition with, and at yet other times hand in hand with or steered by, state policing' (111). He sees this second tier as of a very different character to that of state policing which 'occupies a residual position, one which is both symbolically and normatively different from other forms of security provision' (112).

Crawford deploys the conceptual framework of 'club goods' in unravelling the strategies of particular interest groups – either residential or commercial – in their quest for additional security. His analysis shows that the pursuit of privileged access to security depends as much on private providers as on the capture of public goods such as policing, and their enclosure to the benefit of mini-sovereignties. 'Security clubs' engage in 'power struggles', as Dupont would put it. 'They can use state policing as a background asset, sometimes drawing it into the foreground for symbolic or instrumental purposes. In so doing, they can exploit its general, all-encompassing and sacred mandate' (Crawford, this volume: 136).

Marks and Goldsmith make a similar point about the 'residual' character of state governance. They argue that notwithstanding the democratic potential of community-based governance structures (which must be assessed very carefully), the state is, philosophically and practically speaking, best placed to manage and deliver security in an equitable manner and in accordance with universal normative standards. Drawing from the South African experience, they view the rise of private security as a 'supplement' to inadequate state-provided security, implying that 'large lacunae of unpoliced space' remain (this volume: 158). They further add that '[w]here state protective services have been unreliable or absent, community reliance upon the alternatives will almost always, we suggest, reflect necessity rather than unimpeded free choice or a freely chosen preference with a realistic possibility of *exit* or *voice*' (163; italics in original). For those who do subsist in 'unpoliced space', it is the state that is 'best placed in terms of capacity, legitimacy and effectiveness to provide equitable policing services' (139–40).

Marks and Goldsmith's view is supported by Loader and Walker's contention that 'the state's place in producing the public good of security is both necessary and virtuous' (this volume: 167). From an instrumental perspective they argue that the 'security of any individual depends in some significant fashion upon the security of others, and thus that the very idea of "private security" is oxymoronic' (Loader 1997b). They explain that the 'objective security situation' of an individual is optimized only if one's own self-protection measures are complemented by the security-producing activities of a range of citizens, groups and agencies that can so contribute. In addition to this instrumental dimension of security, they also argue that there is a social dimension: 'The individual, in order to *feel* confident in his or her ability to pursue his or her ends without interference, must feel reasonably secure that the conditions for the effective and ongoing realization of his or her objective security are themselves reasonably secure' (Loader and Walker, this volume: 186). Furthermore, Loader and Walker argue that security has a 'constitutive' dimension. The pursuit of security both reflects and constitutes a 'we feeling' based in a form of 'political community' bound by its 'affective commitment to put things in common'. They suggest that it is states, or their 'functional equivalents', that are best placed to engage in 'instrumental ordering work *and* in the work of cultural production of social identity' (193).

This stance that states are a 'necessary virtue' (Loader and Walker, this volume) in the production of security for all must be tempered by an awareness, and concrete empirical assessment, of those 'vices' that have concerned state sceptics over the years. As Loader and Walker concede, '[t]he state *can* be and often has been a physical and psychological bully. It *is* prone to meddling, to interfering where it is not wanted. It *does* take sides, and in so doing packs the hardest punch. It *will* tend towards stupidity' (183). While Marks and Goldsmith contend that states, in Loader and Walker's words, are 'indispensable to any project concerned with optimizing the human good of security' (183), they acknowledge 'there are clear transformation deficits' in the democratization of South African policing. What is required is to 'understand why police continue to act in ways that are undemocratic and to think about ways to promote speedier change within these organizations' (Marks and Goldsmith, this volume: 144).

They add that such an agenda must involve a sophisticated appreciation of police culture.

As we write this introductory chapter we find ourselves creeping into the realm of the normative. States may be seen as 'necessary' as much as 'virtuous', and in this way, essential to any conceptualization of democratic security governance. If one accepts this call for a cautiously optimistic 'state-centredness', one need not, however, assume that non-state forms of governance do not, or could not, have the capacity, legitimacy and effectiveness to enhance or enrich the delivery of 'public security' so conceived. In addition to Marks and Goldsmith, Loader and Walker make this point in their call for an 'anchored pluralism' (this volume: 194). This is a point taken up more explicitly by Burris, who explores the implications of both state-centred and nodal governance approaches to the transformation of security governance in accordance with public health outcomes.

Burris is concerned not only with the health consequences of crime and insecurity, but also with the vices of criminal justice institutions and practices in terms of ways in which health outcomes are compromised by the pursuit of security outcomes. While physical and emotional 'costs' of crime victimization are obvious, '[t]he means used to prevent and punish crime also have dramatic health consequences' (this volume: 198). For example, the use of imprisonment can lead to the development of prison populations that have high rates of rape and violence as well as high incidences of communicable disease. Also, some law enforcement practices of police can actually undermine the opportunities for drug users to deal with their addictions such as attending syringe exchanges, which could thereby increase their chances of engaging in risky behaviour. At the same time, the institutions of police, courts and corrections can be seen as promoters of health outcomes. For instance, '[c]riminalization of drug use makes the criminal justice system, from the police officer through the court or drug court to the prison, a player in the provision of drug treatment' (200). As another example, he suggests that 'the deinstitutionalization of the mentally ill combined with a lack of health services has left prisons to care for patients who would once have been in the psychiatric treatment system' (200). In this vein, he explores ways in which a state-centred approach would involve efforts to both minimize the health-related harms of criminal justice institutions as well as maximize their health-related benefits, with the proviso that '[t]he standard state institutions of police, courts and prisons are necessary but not sufficient to the governance of security' (206).

Burris' discussion reminds us of the importance of clearly setting out the criteria against which established institutions and practices of security

8   *Jennifer Wood and Benoît Dupont*

governance can be assessed. For him, the health consequences of security practices are paramount, but say for Crawford, it is those broader patterns of inclusions and exclusions generated by the delivery of 'club goods' that inform his explanatory work. In her chapter on innovating in the field of security, Wood argues that the future of research and innovation in the governance of security should be guided by a much more systematic and robust explanatory and normative agenda, one that serves to unite scholars and practitioners, such as the contributors to this volume, in a common quest to enhance our understanding of what is happening in the governance of security, what its outcomes are in relation to the delivery and distribution of particular 'goods', and what to do about the harmful outcomes that threaten the very protection of democratic values in the communities and societies in which we live. This multi-pronged agenda would consist firstly of a rich set of explanatory lines of inquiry that deploy a range of qualitative and quantitative methodologies in answering new questions in interesting ways, or even asking old questions in new ways. Secondly, it would involve establishing a clear set of criteria against which we are conducting a normative assessment. This would allow us to make explicit those normative issues that we are bringing to the fore (e.g. the negative outcomes for disadvantaged and marginalized populations) as well as those which we are neglecting (e.g. the deleterious effects on health of criminal justice practices). Such an assessment would then inform the design and implementation of innovations – such as models, policies, programs and practices – aimed at addressing what we discover to be 'democratic deficits', 'transformation deficits', or general 'governance deficits' in the time- and space-specific contexts within which we are working.

Within this overall approach to research and innovation in the governance of security, projects could be developed with various degrees of narrowness or breadth in regard to that which is the central object of inquiry. Such a project could centre specifically, for example, on what is happening in public policing, even though the research orientation that Wood promotes is one that supports Shearing's call for better maps of the 'mentalities', 'institutions', 'technologies' and 'practices' of state and non-state nodes. On the other hand, projects could be devised that map nodal relations and the 'networks' they constitute, consistent with the work of Manning and Dupont. Of course, such projects on the governance of security can easily become projects on the governance of health, as the work of Burris reminds us. 'Security' is indeed a 'wicked issue' (Clarke and Stewart 1997), one that is thought about and acted on by a range of governance institutions regardless of their primary mandate.

This brings us to a question that we have skirted around in the above discussions. What is 'security'? As Manning reminds us, 'security' is 'imagined' (Wood and Shearing in press). Buzan and Wæver similarly contend that 'security' is not an objective state of affairs, but a 'speech act' (Wæver 1995; Buzan et al. 1998); '[it] is not of interest as a sign that refers to something more real; the utterance *itself* is the act' (Wæver 1995: 55). For them, 'securitization' is a process of social construction involving those who carry out the speech act ('securitizing actors') who articulate an existential threat to a 'referent object' (Buzan et al. 1998). Traditionally, studies in areas like the sociology of policing or international relations have centred on the state as the primary 'referent object'. This, however, is shifting. In some circles, *human beings*, and in some cases, the environment and the planet are now emerging as the central referent objects in processes of 'securitization'. In the 'human security' movement,

[t]hinking about security broadened from an exclusive concern with the security of the state to a concern with the security of the people. Along with this shift came the notion that states ought not to be the sole or main referent of security. People's interests or the interests of humanity, as a collective, become the focus. In this way, security becomes an all-encompassing condition in which individual citizens live in freedom, peace and safety and participate fully in the process of governance. They enjoy the protection of fundamental rights, have access to resources and the basic necessities of life, including health and education, and inhabit an environment that is not injurious to their health and well-being. (Ginwala, in Commission on Human Security 2003: 3)

Burris' chapter provocatively leads us towards a 'health security', and, more broadly, a 'human security' paradigm (see generally UNDP 1994: 27–8 and Commission on Human Security, 2003) and Marks and Goldsmith's chapter acknowledges 'the inextricable link between security and development' (this volume: 151). Shearing's chapter implicitly 'securitizes' poverty and structural inequity and alludes to the need for a more rigorous 'dialectic' between 'state-centric' and 'human-centric' notions of security (Kerr 2003). This book, however, will not satisfy readers interested in a comprehensive engagement with new discourses and practices of securitization, a task which is too ambitious for a single collection of essays. Rather, we have attempted to establish some conceptual parameters, similar to what Bayley and Shearing did in their analysis of the future of policing, where they clarified that 'the scope of our discussion is bigger than the breadbox of the police but smaller than the elephant of social control' (1996: 586). In a similar vein, we would stipulate that the discussions contained herein can be understood as bigger than the breadbox of 'governing through crime' (Simon 1997), but smaller than the elephant of, say, 'governing through development'. In the end, perhaps what is most important is to recognize that the concepts and language we use shape to a large extent what is 'thinkable' as either an explanatory line of inquiry or as a means of engaging normatively. Indeed, as Shearing reminds us, 'ways of seeing are always also ways of not seeing' (this volume: 12).

1   Reflections on the refusal to acknowledge private governments

Clifford Shearing

> . . . the writing is on the wall if we refer to historical experience, according to which there is no oppression that is not met with resistance. As for the social and political outcomes of this resistance, uncertainty and experimentation are the only possible assessments, as the process of change muddles through the collective experience of rage, conflict, struggle, hope, failure, and compromise.   (Castells 2000: 128)

Introduction

There has been, among many scholars and practitioners, a steadfast refusal to acknowledge the existence of what Macaulay, many years ago, recognized as 'private governments' (that is, non-state entities that operate not simply as providers of governance on behalf of state agencies but as auspices of governance in their own right) (Macaulay 1986). These governments, like state governments, authorize and direct activities intended to shape the flow of events (Parker and Braithwaite 2003) so as to promote various governmental outcomes – in distinguishing between auspices and providers of governance I am drawing on Bayley and Shearing (2001). Private governments that engage in steering the flow of events to promote security are, like states, auspices that engage in '[purposive strategies] involving the initiation of techniques which are intended to offer guarantees of security' (Johnston 2000b: 10).

Private governments are now ubiquitous. More importantly, what they do has shaped, and continues to shape, the world fundamentally and dramatically. While what they do sometimes has benefits that are consistent with the broad values of other constituencies, they are motivated by partisan objectives that are intended to promote 'common goods' (Shearing and Wood 2003a). In saying this I do not want to suggest that state governments do not advance partisan interests. They do. Indeed they do so by definition. Governments are formed by groups that promote particular sets of policies designed to support and respond to the objectives and concerns of particular constituencies. This is true irrespective of whether they are democratically elected or not.

Private governments and their governance, as I have noted, constitute a truly global phenomenon. Yet, they are barely acknowledged by scholars, policy analysts or politicians as auspices of governance. There is what might be thought of as a widespread conspiracy of silence to avoid acknowledging what is there for all to see – an emperor's new clothes phenomenon of global proportions. We have all been given, and most of us willingly wear, lenses that exclude private governments from our reality.

Even when these governments are pointed out, and even when this pointing gets some attention, the 'reality' that is brought briefly into view is soon put out of the line of sight again as we adjust our spectacles as quickly as possible to ensure that what was seen will disappear.

To illustrate, let me provide an example with which I have had some involvement. Some years ago, Stenning and I argued that a fundamental feature of the governance-of-security landscape (and governance more generally) was the emergence of 'mass private property' (Shearing and Stenning 1981; 1983). By this we meant privately owned property, ordered by private governments, to which 'the public' often had easy access. We argued that these territories were ordered by corporate governments in line with their corporate objectives. One consequence of this, we argued, was a shift in these domains from a state-defined concern with violations of law (crime) to concerns with loss. One of our central intentions was to show how the growth of private security provided evidence for the emergence of private auspices of governance who governed in ways that enhanced their profit. While the articles in which this argument was advanced have become relatively well known, the arguments about the emergence of corporate governance that were central to them have not received much sustained attention. The focus instead has been on the argument that the growth of private security has been facilitated by the growth of mass private property.

Kuhn, also many years ago, identified this phenomenon of intentional collective blindness (or what might be better thought of as myopia) and provided an account for it (Kuhn 1967). He argued that our scientific theories (and world-views generally) constitute paradigms that not only provide accounts and explanations but also constitute the worlds they explain (see also Foucault 1988). Paradigms bring worlds into view. Paradigms, Kuhn argued, are ways of seeing the world that exclude from view those parts of the world that do not fit their ambit. Smith (1987) has expressed this well by saying that ways of seeing are always also ways of not seeing.

In doing this, paradigms (and the world-views that often underlie them) protect themselves by making 'invisible' evidence that refutes their standpoint. Eventually, Kuhn argued, as evidence that falls outside a paradigm's way of seeing mounts up, there is a shattering of a paradigm and the birth of a new one that comprehends the 'new' world by including what had been excluded. In due course this new paradigm acts in similar self-serving ways to exclude phenomena that challenge its understandings.

As the history of science has made clear, the support for a particular paradigm that makes truth claims about the world is often as much political and social as it is scientific. Foucault makes a similar point when he talks about truth as being closely related to power. When the world is authorized through a claim of being a certain way, it benefits, and is supported by, those whose power to shape the world depends on it. An obvious, and now non-controversial, example was the Catholic Church's strong opposition to the ideas of early natural scientists who were making claims about the nature of the universe and life in it that challenged their world-view. As this history makes clear, one can, and often does, get in to serious trouble for challenging firmly entrenched, and politically supported, paradigms.

Associated with this is what Unger has called 'institutional fetishism'. Burris explicates this idea when he writes that:

we cling tenaciously to the belief that the contemporary array of institutions is the only one capable of producing a salubrious, prosperous, and democratic environment. Change must therefore begin with a different way of seeing the present. (Burris 2004: 340)

In this chapter I will argue that the state-centred view of governance that excludes, or at least obscures, private governments and continues to dominate our thinking has been, and continues to be, a particularly tenacious paradigm. For all its staying power, however, and indeed because of it, it is a paradigm that needs to be eclipsed. This is so not simply because this state-centred view of the world is preventing us from developing an understanding of the world that captures what has been taking place, but because it is limiting normative thinking. It is restricting our ability to comprehend and respond to the divisions that are being created in the world by limiting our awareness of the sources of these divisions and the options and opportunities available to challenge and, hopefully, reverse them.

It is these consequences that Castells flags in the passage with which this chapter opens. This passage follows a discussion by Castells of a global tragedy that is unfolding as a huge gulf emerges between a first world – or what might be better thought of as a super-first world – and a huge and growing 'Fourth World' of excluded persons. As a way of illustrating these developments, Castells focuses on the 'African tragedy'. He writes that:

a new world, the Fourth World, has emerged, made up of multiple black holes of social exclusion throughout the planet. The Fourth World comprises large areas of the globe, such as much of Sub-Saharan Africa, and impoverished rural areas of Latin America and Asia. But it is also present in literally every country, every city, in this new geography of social exclusion. It is formed of American inner-city ghettos, Spanish enclaves of mass youth unemployment, French *banlieus* warehousing North Africans, Japanese Yoseba quarters, incarcerated, prostituted, criminalized, brutalized, stigmatized, sick and illiterate persons. They are the majority in some areas, the minority in others, and a tiny minority in a few privileged contexts. But everywhere they are growing in number, and increasing in visibility, as the selective triage of informal capitalism, and the political breakdown of the welfare state, intensify social exclusion. (Castells 2000: 167–8)

In making this link between the planet and Africa Castells writes that:

It is precisely this selective articulation of elites and viable assets, together with the social exclusion of most people and the economic devaluation of most natural resources, that is specific to the newest expression of Africa's tragedy. (Castells 2000: 128)

While I was in the midst of writing this chapter, I walked up a small mountain near Cape Town to clear my head and to get some exercise. A little way from the top I stopped to take a breath. I turned around and there before me lay an iconic exemplar of the juxtaposition of worlds to which Castells has drawn our attention. On my right hand lay Pollsmoor Prison, where Nelson Mandela was imprisoned for some time. It looked surprisingly small given the large population gated within its walls. Not really surprising, of course, when one considers the huge overcrowding that characterizes South Africa's prisons – and prisons in most parts of the world (van Zyl Smit 2004). Alongside the prison, literally cheek by jowl, on my left lay another gated community – a golfing estate with perhaps no more than the number of residents of a handful of the common cells in Pollsmoor, yet taking up many times the space. This second gated community was all painted a vibrant green by grass doused with toxins to keep it beautiful. On my left an enclave of enormous luxury and privilege; on my right an enclave of brutality and poverty. The one 'fortified enclave' (Caldeira 2000) made up of poor, young, indigenous South Africans; the other made up of wealthy citizens of the world (who are as likely as not to be from Britain, Germany, Holland and the United States, to name just a few countries, as they are to be from South Africa). The one, part of Castells' Fourth World; the other, part of the complementary super-first-world. Not far from this as I cast my eyes further to the right was another gated community of residential houses, more closely packed.

Here too was an enclave of privilege, albeit much more modest – small homes, housing working people. As I saw it, my mind went back to the informal housing settlement that had been cleared to make way for this new enclave.

What I have just described is an emblematic picture of the new South Africa – a picture that at first glance does not look very different from the old South Africa. But it is, in significant ways. In the old South Africa the enclaves of privilege were not as international in character – the new colonialism of enclaves of global privilege was not as well developed. The divisions are similar but the make-up of the enclaves of privilege and the interests and resources that sustain them have changed significantly. Places like Cape Town – geographically beautiful parts of our planet – have been secured as places in the sun for the globally wealthy and mobile to retire, to holiday or simply to live permanently with an income from global investments. All this is made possible by flows of money and local cheap labour. As I looked from my privileged position on the mountain I was reminded that I was looking not simply at South Africa but at the 'new world order'. These two constituencies – simply the rich and the poor, the weak and the powerful – represent new 'planetary class interests' created by global forces that have destroyed 'our global loyalties' and 'forced states to begin to relinquish nationhood' (Monbiot 2003: 9).

As I write, the 2005 South African budget has been released to much acclaim, as a budget for everyone. It has been well received in the financial sections of the country's newspapers. It is a budget that at once includes tax cuts and increased budgets to state agencies. One of the most respected newspapers, the *Sunday Independent*, reports that:

Manuel [the Minister of Finance] announced tax cuts amounting to R10.6 billion. The main beneficiaries are individuals, big corporations and small businesses.

He also allocated an additional R23.3 billion to social grants, raising the total expenditure on grants over the next three years to R181.6 billion. (*Sunday Independent*, 27 February 2005, Business Report: 1)

Some taxes did go up – the 'sin taxes' on alcohol (except for traditional beer) and cigarettes. Fuel taxes also went up.

Azar Jammine, the chief economist at Econometrix is reported in the same article as saying that:

The government has reduced its deficit, borrowing, and interest payments on debt. The government has halved its interest payments, and now it is saving R30 billion per year. That money is being spent elsewhere. (*Sunday Independent*, 27 February 2005, Business Report: 1)

By world standards this is indeed an excellent budget, as is South Africa's economic performance generally, with relatively low inflation (4 per cent projected for 2005) and a projected growth in GDP for 2005 of 4.3 per cent. And yet there was a front-page article in the same issue of the *Sunday Independent* under the banner 'State warned to expect more violent protests.'

The People's Budget Campaign warned this week that the frustration of poor people was mounting and the government should not be surprised by more violent protests. (*Sunday Independent,* 27 February 2005: 1).

While South Africa is being seen more and more as a place of stability that can be relied upon by international investors, and as the super-first-world constituency feels more and more comfortable about creating its enclaves of privilege here, there remains Castells' fourth-world constituency – they experience and see a different reality.

At the heart of this divided world are private governments who manage these spaces of mass private property and privilege on behalf of their 'denizens' (Shearing and Wood 2003b) and who make the investments that support them. It is these governments, and their ways of steering the flow of events, that the state-focused paradigm, for all its usefulness, pushes into the background. In doing so it not only drives out of sight a critical set of direction and resources that are shaping the global divide to which Castells draws attention but also excludes non-state avenues of response.

Shifting a paradigm that has favoured the thinking and objectives of as many powerful interests, as the state-centred paradigm has, is not likely to be an easy task. If such a move is to be accomplished, as I believe it must if we are to have any hope of responding to the massive global challenges that face us across every realm of governance, it is essential that we understand the roots and the persuasive power of this paradigm at the level of ideas as well as socially and politically. My purpose in this chapter is to contribute to such an understanding.

The state-centred view

In February 2004 I attended a very informative conference near Cape Town that looked both back at the achievements within criminal justice of ten years of democracy and beyond them to the challenges and possibilities of the next ten years. The conference itself was held in a splendid gated venue on the coast – a venue that could have been anywhere in the super-first-world from St-Tropez to Phuket. Speaker after speaker at the meeting, which lasted two days, confirmed in one way or another their commitment to a state-centred paradigm. This is what had reigned during the first ten years of democracy in South Africa and this was what should frame the efforts to improve on South Africa's criminal justice system for the next ten years.

The culmination of this celebration of state governance (and systematic obscuring of private governments and governance) took place during the closing plenary session when a courageous South African Police Services legal officer suggested in a wonderfully poetic closing address, through well-chosen parables, that if South Africa was going to be transformed into a fair and equal country it would have to look beyond the state to private governance, not simply to understand the sources of many of the difficulties it faced, but more importantly the sources of the knowledge, capacity and resources that would be needed to tackle the challenges facing it. He was not thinking of the private governance that has been my focus to this point, but of how the huge number of South Africans in the Fourth World could, through the appropriate institutional arrangements, contribute to the transformation of South Africa through their resources and governance initiatives to steer the flow of events.

In his remarks he pointed specifically to the need for the state police, the South African Police Service, to recognize itself as one node among others that had the knowledge and capacity required to govern security effectively. In particular, he talked of the importance of paying attention to the knowledge and capacities, and most of all the direction, of the people of the Fourth World. The police, he said, did not have all the resources or all the answers required, and never would.

The responses to his remarks, other than silence, told an interesting story. What he was doing, it was argued, was drawing attention away from the importance of ensuring that the police and other government agencies had the resources they required. If they did not have these resources now, it was argued, it was either because the monies available stayed at the top of state bureaucracies and did not filter down to the bureaucrats who could get the job or because the state should be taxing its citizens more effectively.

How is it that a very reasoned and very sensible commentary by a very thoughtful practitioner would fall on such deaf ears? To use a remark from another session where a similar debate took place, why was it that recognizing the resources of the Fourth World and encouraging them to engage in private governance to direct and reshape their lives was seen as promoting 'ghetto justice'?

The logic that pervaded the speakers and commentaries at the conference, as far as I have been able to unpack it, is set out in the following four paragraphs:

The old South African government used its resources to establish a regime of exclusion known as apartheid. This was a legally based regime that used laws, in particular pass laws which required black South Africans to have approval to enter white areas, to create a social order based on racial inequality. These laws were effectively enforced by its agencies – the police, the courts and prisons. The apartheid government was overthrown by a process of struggle that culminated in democratic elections that have led to two successive democratically elected governments that have taken over the reins of state power and committed themselves to transforming the country so that the inequalities of apartheid are eliminated.

To do so it has quite properly begun with the obvious premise that there are many needs, particularly among poor South Africans (the legacy of apartheid) that must be addressed. This is what 'transformation' should accomplish. These needs are recognized in the Constitution which redefines them in terms of rights. Thus, for example, if there is a need for shelter there must be a right to shelter; if there is a need for water there must be a right to water; and so on. If the promise of these rights is to be realized there must be a duty attached to them. This duty falls on the South African state. The state has an obligation to see to it that these rights are turned into realities of provision. At this point the argument could go in several directions.

The direction taken is that for the state to accomplish its rights-duties it should devolve these duties to specific state agencies who are obligated to deliver on these responsibilities. Thus, for example, the police should be given the job of governing security, as security is a right that people have. These agencies should, in turn, devolve these duties to particular persons who are to be held accountable for delivery. An implicit assumption here is that if apartheid governments could have mobilized state agencies so effectively to do their bidding then these agencies should be able to do the same for post-apartheid governments provided that they are motivated to do so.

In order to ensure that government agencies understand just what they have to do, and just what the rights they are duty bound to deliver on are, there need to be institutional arrangements that enable them to hear the voice of local people – for example, Community Police Forums which are designed to allow citizens to express their views about what the police should be doing and to apprise them of their evaluations on how well they are doing whatever it is they should be doing. In addition, monitoring systems need to be established that will allow experts to make judgements on the extent to which state agencies are fulfilling their duties, for example, police complaint systems.

This obvious or common view – what Husserl calls a 'natural attitude' – does not fully understand either apartheid – which colluded with private governments of various sorts (Shearing and Berg, in press) – or the conditions necessary for creating a new and very different reality within South Africa or elsewhere.

Where does this deeply entrenched view come from? Why is it so firmly established? Why is it so robust, especially as there have been so many well-argued scholarly challenges (for example, by Latour and Foucault to name but two)? Why, if it does not fit very well at all with the South African reality either ten years ago or now, is it held to so firmly? This is not a particularly South African issue, and while the answer for South Africa does have some specifically South African features, it has more to do with what South Africans have inherited, and continue to adopt, in terms of mentalities, institutions, technologies and practices from elsewhere.

An important part of the answer I will provide has to do with understandings of governance and government that have deep European roots. Let me canvas some of these roots briefly with reference to the English political thinking of Hobbes and the German sociologist Weber.

Europeans have been engaged in a centuries-long process of state-building (and now superstate-building with the European Union) that has sought to reduce the diversity of auspices of governance. Maitland (1972 (1885)), writing near the end of the nineteenth century, described this process as one through which a single 'public peace' progressively 'swallowed up' multiple 'private peaces'. This has always been a project rather than a reality. The state-building project to which Maitland was referring had as one of its roots the Peace of Westphalia of 1648 – when the European system of independent, autonomous and sovereign states responsible for governing their territories was formally acknowledged as an ongoing political project. 'Westphalia', as Braithwaite and Drahos have noted, 'marked the most decisive shift in the locus of control over citizens from the domination by the Church and empires to domination by nation-states' (Braithwaite and Drahos 2000). Another of its taproots was the political philosophy of Thomas Hobbes – his *Leviathan* was first published in 1651.

The state-building project was a response to what might be thought of as an 'age of plural governance'. Hobbes referred to, and caricatured, plural governance as a 'state of nature' in which everyone was a law unto themselves and life was accordingly 'nasty, brutish and short'. While this did not describe, and was not intended as an empirical description of, plural governance it certainly discredited it as an undesirable state that should be transcended.

To bring an end to the anarchy of plural governance, Hobbes argued in support of a state-building project that would centralize governance within states. His equation of plural governance with the greed and violence of an imagined (and for many plausible) state of nature meant that he was able to present this as a civilizing project that would promote the accomplishment of shared collective ends – what is now often thought about as a public interest – to be realized in the face of individual self-interest.

This way of making up the world of governance has, as my introductory observations suggest, been so influential that it has become common sense. This conflict between individual and collective ends has been presented in a host of different ways. A revealing, and influential, formulation is Hardin's (1968) now classic statement of the 'tragedy of the commons'.

The 'rational' users of a commons . . . make demands on a resource until the expected benefits of his or her actions equal the expected costs. Because each user ignores costs imposed on others, individual decisions cumulate to a tragic overuse and potential destruction of an open-access commons. (Ostrom et al. 1999)

Ostrom et al. (1999), in citing Hardin, notes that he argued that solutions could be found in either the Hobbesian answer of a Leviathan or the free-market answer of Adam Smith (1998 (1776)). This dualism has been fundamental to recent debates about how best to promote collective ends in governance. On the one side are those who argue that plural governance in the form of markets, provided they are regulated so that they are 'free', far from creating a Hobbesian war of all against all, may be viewed as promoting public peace. Within this understanding, private peaces do not need to be swallowed but rather should be regulated so that they operate appropriately. On the other side are the Hobbesians, who argue for 'central government control of all common-pool resources' (Ostrom et al. 1999).

While the Smithian side of this argument continues to have currency, and this is certainly the case within South Africa, it is the Hobbesian one that rules when it comes to the question of transforming the governance of security and justice within South Africa, as the conference ethos made clear.

In explicating the Hobbesian argument a useful place to begin is with the concept of the 'commonweal'. The *Oxford English Dictionary* (1989) notes that the commonweal was 'properly two words: common well-being and refers to "the general good, public welfare and the prosperity of the community"'. Both the project of centralized state governance and the plural project of private governance through markets seek to promote the commonweal. They differ in how this should be accomplished – for a useful recent review of arguments on both sides, see Stiglitz (2003).

The central idea of the state-building project has been that states can, and should, aggregate individuals and group concerns and objectives to promote the commonweal (democracy is a way of creating legitimate governments that will do this). This coupling of states with the commonweal has been very tight and enduring. This is illustrated in the ideas of a 'commonwealth' which the *OED* defines as 'the whole body of the people, the body politic; a state, community'.

This idea of states aggregating multiple interests, through the metaphor of the body, is nicely illustrated on the frontispiece of the first edition of *Leviathan*. The frontispiece pictures a friendly giant standing behind, and over, a landscape. The body of the giant is made up of people – Maitland's 'private peaces' – that the Leviathan body incorporates. The idea is that the Leviathan acts for all these people whose preferences have been aggregated in him. For Hobbes this giant is not a tyrant but a legitimate ruler created with the consent of the people through a social contract that includes everyone (democratic governance is conceived of as a way of renewing this contract and the legitimacy that flows from it).

Again the image of the giant on the cover of the first edition is revealing. In the giant's left hand is a sceptre that symbolizes his legitimacy as the source of the commonweal; in his right, the sword through which he maintains the commonweal in the face of resistance to it. This commonweal holds across the territory that the Leviathan has mastery over – namely, the territory of states that the Westphalian project sought to recognize, constitute and protect.

In this concept, as in the Weberian concept that we will now consider, overwhelming force is critical. Sovereignty cannot be maintained without it. Order requires 'the terrour of some Power' as 'Covenants without the Sword, are but Words, and of no strength to secure a man at all' (Hobbes 1985 (1651): 223).

This idea of the Leviathan receives its most influential modern account in the writings of Max Weber (1958 (1919); 1978). Like Hobbes, Weber sees sovereignty as linked to a collective end (not simply a private economic need). The factual substance of this end is, for Weber, 'conceptually irrelevant'. What is critical for him is that a Leviathan, in the form of a state, dominates a territory as part of a Westphalian state system. For Weber, such domination can only be achieved through a legitimate monopoly of physical force. 'The state is considered the sole source of the "right" to use legitimate violence' (Weber 1958 (1919): 78). It is not the particular ends a state pursues that matter but its means, namely, physical force that is deployed legitimately.

It is around this point about the importance of states monopolizing the legitimate use of physical force that the Smithians and the

Hobbesians-Weberians can, and often do, find common ground. Free markets require that certain conditions of possibility exist and these, in turn, require a monopoly of force. Thus market-based solutions do not argue against a Leviathan but rather want to limit its role to supporting markets.

Within Weber's writings this normative idea – that states should be the vehicle for aggregating preference, and more importantly, that they can only effectively realize these preferences through establishing, and then maintaining, a legitimate monopoly of physical force – slides into a definitional statement that only 'political associations' that do realize such a monopoly should be considered to be states. This in turn is transformed into the empirical claim that states do monopolize legitimate force and that the state-building project has been realized.

Within this Hobbesian-Weberian paradigm the private realm is the governed realm (the realm over which the Leviathan rules) – it is not a realm of governance. This governed realm is governed by a single auspice, the state. This way of thinking turns an analytic blind eye to developments that do not conform to the Westphalian project. There is, and can conceptually be, no other way of producing a 'Common Benefit' or a 'Common Power' (Hobbes 1985 (1651): 227) than through state power and authority.

Like Maitland, Weber identifies a historical state-building process as a 'struggle of appropriation' (Weber 1958 (1919): 83) in which other 'political associations' (77) are swallowed up by states as they move to successfully monopolize force. In developing this line Weber argues that states have:

[e]xpropriated all autonomous functionaries of estates who formerly controlled these means [the use of force] in their own right. The state has taken their position and now stands in the top place. (83)

Within this view the governance of security, understood as the task of establishing and maintaining a monopoly of violence, is a foundational order that must be maintained if states are to remain on top.

Recent developments have demonstrated that this state-centred view can be successfully married with a Smithian view. This marriage, that is often located under the sign of neo-liberalism, argues that states can, and should, maintain their position as the sole auspice of governance while devolving provision to others. Neo-liberal thought sees states as being able legitimately to operate at a distance by retaining control over the steering of governance while devolving its rowing to others. A term that has been deployed to refer to states that govern in this way is the 'regulatory state' (Braithwaite 2000). In exploring the regulatory state we move beyond the mindset, outlined above, which still has not fully embraced these developments and, indeed, displays signs of resisting them in favour of a more centralized welfarist model (Dixon 2004; van der Spuy 2004).

The regulatory state

The central idea behind the development of the regulatory state is well captured in a quotation from E. S. Savas:

The word government is from a Greek word, which means 'to steer'. The job of government is to steer, not to row the boat. Delivering services is rowing, and government is not very good at rowing. (cited in Osborne and Gaebler 1993: 25)

Osborne and Gaebler writing in the early 1990s with the United States in mind argued that state governments had this to say:

Governance is the process by which we collectively solve our problems and meet our society's needs. Government is the instrument we use. The instrument is outdated, and the process of reinvention has begun. We do not need another New Deal, nor another Reagan Revolution. We need an American *perestroika*. (Osborne and Gaebler 1993: 24)

To realize this revolution, what was required, they argued, was 'entre-preneurial governance'. This was not something new. It was already happening all over the United States. It was important, however, to rec-ognize that these initiatives should be extended as deliberate government policy so that they constituted what has been called a 'revolution at the roots' (Eggers and O'Leary 1995).

In outlining the nature of entrepreneurial governance Osborne and Gaebler argued that entrepreneurship was not about taking risks but about recognizing and acting on opportunities – 'entrepreneurs do not seek risks, they seek opportunities' (1993: xx). This required agility. This was precisely what established governments do not have, they argued – they have a 'distinct ethos: slow, inefficient, impersonal' (14). This was no accident. Governments have been organized to operate in a top-down fashion. In saying this Osborne and Gaebler echoed Hayek (1944; 1960) in arguing that top-down government does not permit entrepreneurship because those 'at the top of the pyramid' do not have 'enough informa-tion to make informed decisions' (Osborne and Gaebler 1993: 15) about how to govern locally. What we have had traditionally, they argued, was governments that served citizens. What was needed were 'institutions that *empower* citizens rather than simply *serving* them' (Osborne and Gaebler 1993: 15).

Because successful, entrepreneurial businesses that know how to deliver services already exist there was, they argued, no need to create government mechanisms to do this. The task of governments was to mobilize these existing capacities. The same applies to citizens. Effective volunteers already exist. What governments needed to do was to mobilize them more effectively. So what needs to be reinvented was governments' ability to recognize this world of knowledge, capacity and resources and to make better use of it. To do this governments should, they argued, think of themselves more as businesses who contracted out tasks that they did not do well. They need to be 'thinking like owners: "If this were my money, would I spend it in this way?"' (Osborne and Gaebler 1993: 3)

This idea of governments directing rather than doing is nicely captured in two phrases: 'rule at a distance' (Rose and Miller 1992) and 'state-anchored pluralism' (Loader and Walker, this volume). Within this vision of governance governments are meta-regulators (Grabosky 1994) rather than direct regulators. This concept integrates the Weberian top-down state with the idea of governance through markets. Within this neo-liberal 'third way' (Osborne and Gaebler 1993; see also Giddens 1998; Stiglitz 2003), we, it is argued, should not choose between strong governments and strong markets but should create a form of governance that combines both. We can, and should, have it both ways. In Bayley and Shearing's (2001) language, state governments should remain 'auspices' of governance while devolving the 'provision' of governmental services to markets.

This 'neo-liberal' understanding of state governance seeks to bring back the idea that at the core of governance should be the injunction 'not to impede the course of things, but to ensure the play of natural and necessary modes of regulation, to make regulations which permit natural regulation to operate' (Gordon 1991: 17).

Within this mentality, people are to be 'governed through freedom' (Rose 1999) in the sense that power is to be exercised through encouraging persons to choose a particular course of action. Or in Reus-Smit's words, an important aspect of power is 'the ability to 'attract' voluntary compliance' (Reus-Smit 2004: 58). With this mode of governance the state becomes a 'composite reality' (Reus-Smit 2004: 103) made up of clusters of assemblages that cut across public–private spheres. State institutions become, in Johnston's terms, 'hybrid' entities (Johnston 1992) that 'glory in the blurring of the public and private and [do] not try to draw a disappearing line in the water' (Cleveland cited in

Osborne and Gaebler 1993: 43). Rose and Miller echo this when they write:

the political vocabulary structured by opposition between state and civil society, public and private, government and market, coercion and consent, sovereignty and autonomy and the like, does not adequately characterize the diverse ways in which rule is exercised in advanced liberal democracies . . . individuals are not merely subjects of power but play a part in its operations. (Rose and Miller 1992: 174)

States are seen as being strengthened, not weakened, within this model of governance. They enlarge their capacity to govern by 'us[ing] many different oarsmen' to implement their policies (Osborne and Gaebler 1993: 37). The regulatory state seeks to operationalize its 'programmes of government by influencing, allying with or co-opting resources that they do not directly control – banks, financial institutions, enterprises, trade unions, professions, bureaucracies, families and individuals' (Rose and Miller 1992: 189).

Drucker has put this nicely:

We do not face a 'withering away of the state'. On the contrary, we need a vigorous, a strong, and a very active government. But we do face a choice between a big but impotent government and a government that is strong because it confines itself to decision and direction and leaves the 'doing' to others.

[We need] a government that can and does govern. This is not a government that 'does'; it is not a government that 'administers'; it is a government that governs. (Drucker cited in Osborne and Gaebler 1993: 47–8)

In developing this idea of governing through partnerships Osborne and Gaebler are again instructive: 'The basic idea is to make public safety a community responsibility, rather than simply the responsibility of the professionals – the police. It transforms the police officer from an investigator and enforcer into a catalyst in the process of community self-help' (Osborne and Gaebler 1993: 50).

This way of understanding governance has proved very helpful in making sense of much that has happened within the governance of security (for a review, see, for example, Bayley and Shearing 2001). This 'convergence of a private and a public policing corporate sector' has created what O'Malley and Hutchinson term a 'police industry' (unpublished manuscript). These developments, as the writings of neo-Foucauldian scholars have made clear, have taken place across many domains of governance. Indeed, it is difficult to think of an arena of governance that cannot be used to illustrate these rule-at-distance developments.

The picture that emerges in these accounts is of a state, understood as precisely as Weber understood it, jealously guarding its sovereignty while devolving authority and functions to non-state locations where this suits its purposes. Within this concept, private governments are once again hidden from view. We have private governance, in the sense of private provision, but only public governments. The conspiracy of silence that deletes from view the very clear and consequential steering that corporate entities and other non-state governments engage in is maintained. Within this understanding, however, this conspiracy is on more slippery ground than it is when both direction and provision are conceived of as a direct state responsibility. It is a short step from contractual arrangements that enable states to devolve the messy business of rowing to others to circumstances in which these others are autonomous actors in their own right (Rose and Miller 1992).

Beyond a state-centred paradigm

The conclusion reached to this point is that the major theoretical and policy developments have eschewed a critical phenomenon that lies at the heart of a growing disparity of resources, that is facilitated by states, but where state government is no longer the only player with a lead role. The question this poses is: How are we to move theoretically to positions that recognize a diversity of governing auspices; that is, to positions that will recognize the role of state while at the same time recognizing, and bringing clearly and explicitly into the equation, the role of non-state auspices, as well as non-state providers of governance? This is a difficult question indeed, given the state-focused nature of the dominant positions.

As I have already suggested by citing the work of Castells so extensively, much has already been accomplished under the sign of networked governance. Recently Burris et al. (2005) have reviewed some of the theoretical possibilities and have endorsed the idea of 'nodal governance' as a possibility that is worth exploring. In this work they draw on earlier work that Johnston, Shearing and Wood have been pursuing, both separately and together (Shearing 2001a; Johnston and Shearing 2003; Shearing and Wood 2003a; 2003b). The focus on nodes seeks to emphasize that networks are dependent on the mentalities, technologies, institutional arrangements and resources of nodes, and that nodes and nodal assemblages should be a major focus of analyses of governance (Burris 2004).

Drahos has further argued that network resources are often brought together (but not integrated) through a 'type of node (termed a "super-structural" node) that does not integrate networks, but rather is a structure that brings together actors who represent networks in order to concentrate resources and technologies for the purpose of achieving a common goal. Super-structural nodes are the command centers of net-worked governance' (Drahos 2004: 405).

Burris writes of the way in which a nodal approach seeks to build on a networked one:

> The theory of nodal governance is intended to enrich network theory by focusing attention on and bringing more clarity to the internal characteristics of nodes and thus to the analysis of how power is actually created and exercised within a social system. While power is transmitted across networks, the actual points where knowledge and capacity are mobilized for transmission is the node. Given networks, nodal governance asks how local participation is organized and effectuated. (Burris 2004: 341; see also Johnston and Shearing 2003)

This nodal view accepts, indeed insists, that in Castells' words: 'A net-work, by definition, has nodes, not a centre' (Castells cited in Loader 2000).

Within a nodal governance framework not only is it 'sociologically implausible to seek to defend or resurrect a field constituted by one sole state provider' (Loader 2000: 324) but it is just as implausible to conceive of the state as the sole auspice of governance. Burris has recently argued that 'non-state actors have taken on the role of governing, not just other private entities but the state itself... The state is not necessarily either the chief guarantor or the chief threat' (Burris 2004: 339; see also Scott 2004). Braithwaite develops this idea: 'the corporatization of the world during the twentieth century... meant that the greatest regulatory capa-bilities lay with corporations themselves... by the mid-90s for the first time, a majority of the largest "economies" in the world were transna-tional corporations rather than states' (Braithwaite 2000: 229). The state, as Johnston and Shearing (2003) have argued, becomes one auspice and one provider among many. Given this, the task within a nodal framework is to go beyond this recognition and to map out the relationships between nodes as both auspices and providers. Just what the role of the state is and how it does or does not relate to other nodes should be an empirical question and not one to be decided a priori on the basis of conceptual claims such as those of Hobbes and Weber.

This is a task that Braithwaite and Drahos have begun in their mam-moth studies of business and intellectual property regulation (Braithwaite and Drahos 2000). In both these analyses they show not only the contin-uing importance of states as key players in today's nodal world but also the vital role that private governments are playing as they work on their own as well as with, and often through, states. In this work they highlight the roles currently being played in global governance by corporations,

NGOs and key individuals as well as by states and the variety of supra-state governing entities that have emerged.

In summing up their analysis, Braithwaite and Drahos argue that:

> our story of the globalization of regulation [and accordingly governance] is a story of domination. The global law-makers today are the men who run the largest corporations, the US, and the EC. Women, excluded national minorities and citizens of developing countries are the law-takers. The domination of North Atlantic business has given us, as Chomsky has put it: 'the rule of law for the weak, the rule of force for the strong; neo-liberalism for the weak, state power and intervention for the strong'. When the strong have wanted regulation, very often it has been to protect their monopoly; when they have wanted deregulation it has been to save them from paying for the burdens they inflict on ordinary citizens. Consequently, most citizens of the world – men and women, black and white – rightly want the opposite: deregulation of monopoly privilege and strengthened regulation to protect the community from the abuse of corporate power. (Braithwaite and Drahos 2000: 629)

This analysis has been extended by Drahos and Braithwaite (2002) and by Drahos alone (see, for example, Drahos 2004) in their analyses of intellectual property and how these laws have worked and are working to the benefit of the rich and the strong, and to the detriment of the weak and the poor.

What can be done?

One cannot help, after reviewing this and similar reviews of the development of nodal governance (see, for example, Stiglitz 2003), becoming pessimistic about the possibilities of responding to the fact that 'the sovereignty of big business over globalizing regulation [and indeed all governance] will continue to dominate' and that the 'weapons of the weak' are so easily overwhelmed. And yet it is precisely to these 'weapons' and their potential that we must turn. We have no alternative but to take the optimistic view that there are 'threads we can grasp' (Braithwaite and Drahos 2000: 629) that can, with care and ingenuity, be woven into a strong cord. In reflecting on the position he and Drahos took in *Global Business Regulation*, Braithwaite has expressed this cautious optimism as follows: 'We argue the strong mainly prevail over the weak, but there are actually quite a lot of opportunities for the weak to use ju-jitsu to turn the strength of the strong against the strong' (personal communication, 20 February 2005). The question is how to develop these ju-jitsu moves in ways that could help build a critical mass that might contribute to a turning of the tide. Fortunately, increasing numbers of people across the planet are learning this governance ju-jitsu and coming together in various forums to learn from each other and to combine their efforts. Monbiot talks of a growing global opposition movement that while full of conflicts and contradictory stances has, he believes optimistically, 'begun to present a mortal threat to the existing world order' (Monbiot 2003: 14). This struggle, he argues, is not about looking aspirationally to unifying values but is about the exercise of power. In a Foucauldian vein he argues that: 'Power . . . either forces the weaker person down or forces him out. Power is as intrinsic to human society as greed or fear: a world without power is a world without people. The question is not how we rid the world of power, but how the weak first reclaim that power and then hold it to account' (Monbiot 2003: 15). A very high aspiration indeed but one that none the less needs to be pursued. Drahos has conceptualized this idea as one that requires us to transform the way in which we think about democracy. It is not simply an arrangement that enables a wide variety of disparate interests to be aggregated within a single magical 'public interest' defined by some global-Leviathan, but a basis where bargaining can take place in forums where the voices of the weak count (Drahos 2002: 161–82). This turns Habermas somewhat on his head by arguing that what we need are not forums where power has been outlawed – because this is impossible – but ones where the weak develop and then sustain the power to bargain effectively.

One of the things challenged by the idea of 'democratic bargaining', and the position taken by Braithwaite and Drahos about exploring the ability of the weak to do better as bargainers, is the continued usefulness of the concept of 'the public interest'. What it questions is the usefulness in today's very diverse and fractured world of an aspiration that is founded on the idea that one can develop positions that will harmonize and integrate competing interests into an agreed single set of interests. To go back to the Hobbesian image of a giant made up of people and acting for them in ruling the landscape, the question the idea of democratic bargaining raises is whether this is still a sensible image – especially as it is now widely agreed that powerful interests so often can and do hijack the idea of a public interest for their own ends.

What the work of Braithwaite, Drahos and others suggests is that we should perhaps cease to place such a heavy normative burden on this idea, even as a convenient fiction, as this inevitably moves us towards the notion of a benign Leviathan – an idea that runs counter to the idea that a 'network, by definition, has nodes not a centre' (Castells cited in Loader 2000). Within a nodal governance framework we are likely to be better served by values such as fairness and equality with respect to access to resources. As useful as the chimera of a public interest has been politically, we should perhaps accept, albeit reluctantly, that its day as a useful normative concept may be over. If we do, we can begin to ask different questions to do with the most appropriate forums for pursuing the ju-jitsu skills necessary for successful democratic bargaining by hitherto weak constituencies.

Conclusion

This brings me back to the point in the outline I provided of a state-based framework that was so well established at the conference I attended, where I said that the option of assigning duties to the state and then to state officials to act directly to take action that would meet the very real needs of South Africans was not the only conceptual turn possible. Another turn that I have canvassed here is the neo-liberal turn of 'contractual governance' (Adam Crawford, personal communication, 20 October 2004). But neither is this, as I hope I made clear, a suitable move for responding to the chasm that divides the super-first-world and the Fourth World. The turn that I have been supporting here, and the turn that the notion of 'democratic bargaining' supports, is something much more radical. Yet it is at the same time eminently practical, as well as being exceedingly difficult, because as Monbiot has argued, potentially effective strategies will not be 'unopposed' and are likely as a result to be 'difficult and dangerous' (Monbiot 2003: 62).

What is required is the promotion of conditions that promote and support the construction of nodes, including super-structural nodes, that recognize and mobilize the resources of the weak in ways which strengthen their bargaining positions. For myself, in the contributions that I and others have sought to make towards this end, the focus has been on institutions and processes that enable a radical decentralization of governance, within limiting constitutional frameworks grounded in widely accepted values like human rights. At the heart of such possibilities is the issue of resources and how to acquire and then harness them. It is here, obviously, that the situation of the weak and the strong contrast most sharply – it is access to resources that makes the strong, strong and lack of access that makes the weak, weak.

It is not easy to imagine ju-jitsu moves to respond to this fundamental problem. Yet this is precisely what needs to be done. The weak can do, and do, much to contribute towards providing themselves with resources by donating their time. NGOs and others with access to donor funds also play a part. But none of this is enough. What is required is to find ways of channelling tax resources more directly into the hands of private governments of the weak. Bayley and Shearing sometime ago argued for the promotion of block funding to the institutions of the weak from states (Bayley and Shearing 2001). Arguing along similar lines, the Independent Commission on Policing for Northern Ireland argued that local policing boards should be able to raise taxes directly to promote enterprises that supported institutions of locally directed and provided policing.

A major block to these proposals and similar proposals in this and other arenas has been the very firm hold that states insist on maintaining over the direction of governance for the weak while, at the same time, routinely leaving the strong with plenty of legal space to engage in the very forms of governance they deny to the weak. While the people who support the 'state-must-do-it-all' argument outlined earlier do so with the best of intentions, it is precisely this argument that is contributing to a situation in which there is one set of rules for the strong and another for the weak. This two-rule stance is, of course, not simply a national one. It is globally pervasive. In drawing attention to this, Stiglitz, a Nobel laureate, one-time chair of the Clinton Council of Economic Advisors and Chief Economist at the World Bank, has commented recently on the gulf between what the United States says others should do and what it does to support its own constituencies: 'The medicine we dispensed abroad was, in important respects, not really the same stuff we drank at home' (Stiglitz 2003: 23).

I know only too well from personal experience (drawn from Argentina, Canada, the United Kingdom and South Africa) how difficult it is to per-suade states to make block grants available to poor communities to engage in their own governance, even though the ways the grants will be used is highly regulated so as to ensure that they abide by widely accepted stan-dards of governance, and even if what is done can be shown to contribute directly, and in ways that states find it difficult to do themselves, to state-endorsed agendas. The agencies within states that now own most of the tax monies allocated for service provision are very reluctant to let any of this go directly into the hands of poor, and hence weak, constituencies to fund private governments. No matter what governments say about their commitment to the provision of resources to the weak, they do not wish to trust the weak to direct their own affairs, even though this is precisely what they do, in effect, with respect to the strong.

This reluctance to let people outside of government agencies govern is very understandable from within a Hobbesian-Weberian framework where the public sphere is the sphere of governors and the private sphere is the sphere of the governed. Indeed, as Ghanaian scholar Armah argues, this probably has a much longer European lineage that goes back to Plato and Aristotle for whom government, by definition, is the exclusive domain of those with the capacity to rule (Armah 2005). This hierarchical stance sees governance as necessarily having a centre, a government, from which rule emanates.

A nodal conception rejects this view. Instead it concurs with Foucault that power is everywhere, not because it is everywhere but because it comes from everywhere (Foucault 1990). Within a nodal conception, nodes are always potentially governors and governed. It is this potential that the normative stance taken here seeks to realize more effectively for the weak (it has already been realized for the strong). This double standard, this principled refusal to grant the weak the tools of governance taken for granted by the strong is, to use a phrase from Monbiot, 'dampening public faith in democracy' (Monbiot 2003: 21).

And yet there is cause for some optimism. Monies can be released from a variety of sources, and institutions can be built that will responsibly and accountably administer these resources in ways that will allow the weak to direct their own affairs. Ways can be found that will enable the weak to decide how governmental services will provide for their own governance. And this can be done in ways that ensure that the resources used remain within communities. This can deepen democracy. We know a lot about how to do this. What we do not know enough about is how to get it done.

2 Transnational security governance

Les Johnston

Introduction: The nodal model of governance

Understanding shifts in governance is increasingly difficult. On the one hand, the state continues to play a substantial – some would say an expanding – role in governance. On the other hand, both governance, in general, and security governance, in particular, have experienced significant pluralization. In respect of the latter, available evidence suggests that commercial police outnumber state police by a ratio of almost two to one in Britain (Johnston 2000b), two to one in India (Kempa et al. 1999), between two and three to one in North America (Swol 1998; Rigakos and Greener 2000), five to one in Hong Kong (Johnston 2001b) and between five and seven to one in South Africa (Irish 1999). This pluralization or 'multilateralization' (Bayley and Shearing 2001) of security governance has been explained, primarily, in terms of the state's dispersal of functions to the non-state sector under neo-liberal conditions. Yet, that process has been far more complex than existing analogies ('core' versus 'peripheral' activities, or 'steering' versus 'rowing' functions) would suggest. For, alongside the devolution of state functions to non-state auspices, there has also been an emergence of new forms of governance outside state parameters (Elkins 1995; Shearing and Wood 2000).

Analogies such as 'steering' and 'rowing' (Osborne and Gaebler 1993), while providing useful descriptive insights into *some* governing objectives, remain limited. By focusing on the state's capacity to mobilize non-state agents in the (apparently successful) pursuit of (apparently singular) governing objectives, the analogy fails to do three things: to explore the contingent uncertainties of state action; to consider the competing objectives of governing agents; and to explore the extent to which, and the manner by which, governance is constituted in relations among plural agents.

In the light of such criticisms an alternative, nodal model of governance has been proposed (see, among others, Shearing 2001b; Johnston and Shearing 2003; Shearing and Wood 2003b; Dupont 2004; Cherney

2005; Shearing, this volume). Two aspects of the nodal approach are particularly important (Johnston and Shearing 2003). Firstly, the model refuses to give conceptual priority to any particular locus of power, seeing governance as a relationship contained within a shifting network of alliances rather than as a product of the realization of governing interests. Secondly, the model refuses to posit any correspondence between governing mentalities, the objectives, institutions and technologies associated with them, and determinate governmental 'outcomes'. In view of that, it is possible to ask whether the same mentality might, under different conditions, support normative programmes and substantive outcomes different from those with which it is 'normally' associated. One illustration of this thinking may be found in Bayley and Shearing's (1996) proposal to enable the poor to benefit from participation in markets for security. Another may be seen in projects that rework the risk paradigm in order to help deliver security and justice to poor people with the minimum use of pain (Johnston and Shearing 2003; Shearing and Johnston, 2005).

Two further things may be said about the nodal model. Firstly, despite refusing to prioritize any single source of power, it does not deny the state's role as a crucial site of governance. Proponents of the nodal model merely argue that with demonstrable evidence of nodal governance becoming more and more apparent, alternative opportunities may arise to transform networked relations in ways that could, under the right conditions, advance just and democratic outcomes. Secondly, under present-day conditions, the nodal model is better suited, than are state-centric models, to help us theorize 'optimal security'. An optimal system of security would be one in which security is neither quantitatively excessive (to the detriment of objectives other than security) nor qualitatively invasive (to the detriment of personal freedoms) and which satisfies conditions of collective accountability, effectiveness and justice (cf. Johnston 2000b: 180). One of the objectives of the optimal model would be to develop security as a collective good (Loader and Walker 2001). Though, in the past, the state was regarded as the exclusive repository of the collective good, that position is less and less tenable. Nowadays the state is one player – albeit a crucial one – in a network of governing agencies. A key challenge for democratic governance is to ensure that the actions of the various commercial and civil partners engaged in governance accord, as much as possible, with the collective good. That is not to underestimate the tensions that divide governing agents; it is merely to insist that there are no immutable contradictions between the objectives of commercial, civil and collective partners. Thus, as regards security governance, it is necessary to consider how, in a market economy, mechanisms can be established to ensure that the collective good is protected in security networks made up partly of commercial elements.

The nodal model also aims to be generic (in so far as it is applicable to the local, regional, national and transnational levels) and specific (in so far as it is concerned with the analysis of particular, empirically contingent processes and patterns of action). To date, most empirical discussion of the model has focused on security governance at the local, regional and national levels. Here, it has been observed that the pluralization of governing auspices and providers is characterized by risk-based thought and action – that is, with the proactive anticipation and management of security risks – both within and across the private and public sectors. These processes are two-edged. While risk-based technologies offer the opportunity for non-coercive forms of justice to be developed, sometimes they are *integrated* with coercive ones, to produce new security configurations or to reshape established ones. One example, at the domestic level, is the emergence of zero-tolerance modes of 'community policing' (see Johnston and Shearing 2003: chap. 6).

This chapter considers developments at the global level, our focus being on the extent to which the growth of transnational commercial security provides new opportunities for proactive (risk-based) and coercive technologies to be combined and recombined. The first section looks at the structure and activities of transnational commercial security. The next section explores the increased interpenetration of risk-based (commercial) and coercive (military) security. To some extent this development is part of a wider 'securitization' of society, the impact of which is evident at a number of levels. Thus, while at the global level, states debate their right to engage in 'anticipatory self-defence', domestic governments invoke the 'war against terror' in order to justify anticipatory security practices that may violate human rights. In considering this interpenetration of commercial (risk-based) and military (coercive) technologies we focus, specifically, on a single example: the growing importance of commercial 'military service providers'. The third, and final, section considers how useful the nodal model is in helping us to understand the development and significance of transnational commercial security. In order to address this issue we shall revisit some of the themes discussed in this Introduction and relate them to recent criticisms of the nodal model.

Transnational contract security: market structure and corporate activities

This section and the following one examine recent developments in commercial security at the transnational level.[1] As several authors have

---

[1] 'The term 'transnational corporation' refers to an economic entity operating in more than one country or a cluster of economic entities operating in two or more countries – whatever

previously noted (Shearing and Stenning 1987; South 1988; Johnston 1992), defining the term 'security' is fraught with difficulty. At the domestic level, confusion has arisen about the boundaries between 'in-house' and 'contract' security and about how to define 'security' functions when such functions are commonly 'embedded' in generic work tasks. This confusion is compounded at the transnational level. Here, under the ambit of 'security', one finds not only dedicated contract security companies (e.g. Securitas) but also companies offering, among other things, risk management services (e.g. Control Risks), business intelligence (e.g. Kroll) and military services (e.g. DynCorp). In addition, multi-functional 'services' companies (such as Serco and Sodexho) have penetrated the criminal justice, security and prison markets in countries like the UK and Australia. Given this complexity, there is little to be gained from engaging in lengthy discussion about the precise meaning of 'transnational commercial security'. For that reason our aim is merely to describe some of the most significant developments in a complex and rapidly changing field.

Research undertaken over a decade ago (Cunningham et al. 1990) valued the US commercial security market at around $37.9 billion (£21.3 billion)[2] in 1990. By comparison, the value of the aggregated markets for security products and services in 'Europe' (defined only as France, Germany, Italy, Spain and the UK) was estimated to be around £11.2 billion in 1992 (Narayan 1994). Bearing in mind that the latter figure excludes a significant number of countries, the combination of these figures would suggest that by the early 1990s the value of the world's two largest security markets was well in excess of £32.5 billion. A more recent estimation of the size of today's global security market[3] – excluding consulting and investigation services in the USA – cites a figure of about £60 billion with the US market accounting for one-third and the European market for more than two-fifths of that total. Significantly, the fastest growth rates – expected to rise to around 10–11 percent per annum – are to be found outside Europe and the USA.

At the transnational level the contract security industry is increasingly dominated by a small number of large companies. Typically, they

their legal form, whether in their home country or country of activity, and whether taken individually or collectively' (United Nations Economic and Social Council Commission on Human Rights 2003).

[2] Based on the average US dollar/pound sterling exchange rate between 1 January and 31 December 1990. Exchange rate data obtained from http://www.oanda.com/convert/fxhistory/ (accessed 26 October 2004).

[3] Data obtained from the Securitas website at http://www.securitasgroup.com/ (accessed 26 October 2004).

generate high revenues, growth and profit; engage in dynamic market activity through acquisitions, sales and joint ventures; and seek to penetrate new markets, an increasing number of which are overseas (Johnston 2000b). Writing in 1997 Thomas Berglund, the chief executive of Securitas, stated that 'the size of the market [was] no restriction . . . the amount we can grow . . . is more a question of our own energies' (cited in McIvor 1997). This comment proved to be apposite since it signalled the start of a rapid period of mergers and acquisitions among the major companies:

- In February 1999 Securitas acquired Pinkerton, a company which, some months earlier, had boasted about its 'aggressive acquisition program on high margin security businesses as well as growth by foreign expansion' (cited in Johnston 2000b: 28). The result of this acquisition was a company with 114,000 employees and a turnover that made it the world's largest security corporation. By combining the core activities of Securitas (alarms, cash-in-transit and guarding) with those of Pinkerton (pre-employment screening, risk assessment and integrated security systems) the acquisition resulted in a company with massive global reach.
- In May 2000, Group 4 and Falck (a major Danish security company providing security, fire and rescue services to government and the private sector) merged to form Group 4 Falck thus establishing the second largest security company in the world with 115,000 employees.
- In August 2000 Securitas acquired its US rival, Burns International Security Services.
- In May 2002 Group 4 Falck completed the acquisition of Wackenhut thereby gaining a foothold in the US security market.[4]
- In 2003 the United Technologies Corporation (USA) took over the UK-based guarding and alarms company Chubb.
- In February 2004 a merger was announced between Group 4 Falck and Securicor thus producing a company to rival Securitas as market leader in Europe and North America. The new company, Group 4 Securicor, which brought together the well-known brands of Group 4, Wackenhut and Securicor, operates in more than 100 countries and has around 340,000 employees. A company report produced when the merger was announced (*Creating a Global Leader in Security Services*) identified five areas of particularly high growth – many of them also areas of high political volatility. These included Central and South America; Central,

[4] This acquisition also had implications for the UK security market. Both the Wackenhut Corrections Corporation (as it was then called) and Group 4 Falck had major involvement in UK prison and asylum services. The Competition Commission approved the takeover believing it would not have any adverse effect on the UK market.

Western and Southern Africa; South-Eastern Europe; areas around the Gulf and North Africa (including Saudi Arabia, Yemen, Oman and parts of Iraq, Iran and Egypt); and areas of Asia (including India, Pakistan, Afghanistan, Mongolia, China and Indonesia).[5]

Transnational security companies undertake a wide range of functions. These range from conventional ones (such as guarding, cash-handling and alarm services, electronic security and the provision of integrated security systems) to more specialized ones linked to transnational governance (such as airline security, drugs-testing, surveillance, executive protection, facility hardening and the monitoring of populations engaged in travelling, tourism and migration). A particularly significant area of work involves anticipating business risks and minimizing the losses arising from them. One critical factor in this has been the commodification of information. Peter Manning noted some years ago that the US government, in co-operation with large corporations (many of them part of the defence industry), had broadened its definition of 'the national interest' to include industrial ideas with R&D potential (Manning 2000:183). Companies such as Control Risk, Kroll or Pinkerton (now part of Securitas) are particularly active in this field.

In recent years a particularly fruitful area for global security growth has been in the provision of custodial and related services. Commercial involvement in the control of so-called 'problem populations' is by no means new, the UK's immigration detention centres having been run first by Securicor then by Group 4 since 1970. In recent years, however, programmes such as the UK's Private Finance Initiative (PFI) – now being widely replicated overseas – have provided a new impetus to commercial involvement in the custodial system. While predictions made a decade ago about massive privatization on a global scale have not come to fruition, the industry grows steadily and continued expansion is likely.

In the USA 6.5% of federal and state prisoners are in private facilities, proportionally fewer than may be found in either the UK (9%) or Australia (almost 18%). However, with around 120,000 prisoners – almost twice as many as in 1990 – the USA has by far the largest number of private prisoners. The Corrections Corporation of America (CCA) which operates fifty-nine facilities in twenty states, controls almost half of the market (with over 58,000 beds). Most of the remainder is divided up between three major players: GEO (formerly Wackenhut Corrections Corporation) with 21%; MTC (Management & Training Corporation)

---

[5] Data obtained from the Group 4 Securicor website at http://www.group4securicor.com/merger_announcementv2.pdf (accessed 12 November 2004).

Table 2.1. *Operating and owning companies for private custodial and detention contracts in England and Wales*

Operating company	Owning company
Global Solutions (7)	Falck A/S (two with Carillion plc; one with Amey Assets Services)
UK Detention Services (5)	Sodexho UK, Royal Bank of Scotland, Interserve Project Services Ltd
Premier Prison Services Ltd (4)	Serco Group plc
Premier Detention Services (1)	Serco Group plc
Securicor Justice Services Ltd (1)	Group 4 Securicor, Innisfree Skanska UK, Costain plc

Source: Adapted from S. Nathan 2004.

with 9.2%; and the Correctional Services Corporation (CSC) with 6.3% (S. Nathan 2003).

Domination of the market by a few large companies is also evident in the UK. This was confirmed by evidence presented in a written parliamentary answer of May 2004 (reported in S. Nathan 2004) showing how the eighteen contracts so far awarded (eleven for custodial facilities and seven for immigration detention facilities) had been allocated (see Table 2.1).

The industry continues to undergo major restructuring, some of it – such as the recent transactions and legislative challenges involving Group 4 Falck, Global Solutions (the former's prison business), Wackenhut Corrections Corporation (now renamed GEO Group Inc.), Premier Prisons and Serco (a general service company) – being of Byzantine complexity (see Nathan 2004). Further confusion has followed Group 4 Falck's acquisition of Securicor, since part of that deal involves the company disposing of GSL. In this instance, however, the company is not being sold to a security firm but to two venture capital companies, Electra Partners Europe and Englefield Capita. The result will be that three companies, Group 4 Securicor (which, as we have said, operates in more than 100 countries), Sodexho (which operates in 76) and Serco (which employs around 35,000 people in Europe, the Middle East, North America and Asia Pacific), will remain the only genuinely transnational players in the custodial market. However, that position may alter in the future, Martin Narey, chief executive of the National Offender Management Service, having made it clear that US companies such as MTC, CSC and Cornell will be invited to bid for future UK contracts.

Many companies providing security services – whether contract or service companies – have links to wider security communities including those connected to aerospace, the military and the nuclear industry. Consider the example of Serco.[6] The company was established in 1929 as RCA Services Ltd, the UK subsidiary of the Radio Corporation of America. Originally, the company was involved in providing services to the growing cinema industry. However, in the early 1960s RCA won the contract for the Fylingdales Ballistic Missile Early Warning System. Later, in the 1980s, when the Ministry of Defence began contracting for the operation and maintenance of its facilities, it used Fylingdales as a model. Serco, as it was called from 1987, enjoyed rapid expansion through government outsourcing of contracts. Further impetus for expansion came through the PFI and PPP (Public–Private Partnership) initiative. The company now does 90 per cent of its business for the public sector and has contracts in education, health, transport, justice, defence and aerospace. In October 2004 a subsidiary (Premier Custodial Services) was awarded a five-year contract for electronic monitoring of offenders in England and Wales. In November 2004 Serco won a five-year contract to manage the Hessen prison service in Germany. The company also manages (with BNFL and Lockheed Martin) the UK Atomic Weapons Establishment.

Transnational contract security: the private military services industry

Though by no means a dedicated contract security company, Serco's activities span many different dimensions of 'security': from conventional domestic security concerns (the domain of 'criminal justice'), to matters of commercial, military and nuclear security. It is to the changing connections among the different dimensions of security that we now turn. Following past criticisms that 'private policing' was an under-researched area, a growing body of empirical research relating to the commercialization of domestic security is at last emerging (e.g. Rigakos 2002; Wakefield 2003). Some commentators have also suggested that domestic security, as well as being commercialized, is being subjected to increased militarization (Kraska and Kappeler 1997; Kraska 1999). Significantly, however, little attention has been paid to the commercialization of *military* security itself, an issue that is particularly important at the transnational level.

---

[6] Information obtained from Serco website at http://www.serco.com/default.asp (accessed 16 November 2004).

Companies and contracts

Corporate involvement in the provision of military and peacekeeping services is nothing new (Johnston 2000b). However, the 'war against terror' and the post-war 'reconstructions' of Afghanistan and Iraq have given major impetus to such involvement. Singer (2004a) divides the private military services industry (what he terms 'private military firms') into three sectors: military providers (often called 'private military companies' or PMCs) which provide combat and protection services; military consultant firms which provide advisory and training services; and military support firms which provide back-up services such as logistics, technical support and transportation.

Though it is virtually impossible to say how many companies offer military services, their number is significant and growing. Estimates of the number of overseas security personnel employed in Iraq range between 6,000 and 20,000, the best estimate probably lying somewhere in between. A recent report by the British American Security Information Council (Isenberg 2004) listed the UK company Global Risk Strategies as supplying the largest number (1,200), followed by Control Risks Group (750), Blackwater (600) and Triple Canopy (350). Locals also work on security contracts, the largest number (around 14,000) being employed by Erinys to guard pipelines and oilfields.

Contract values are high. In 2003 DynCorp received $50 million for Year 1 of a contract to create a new Iraqi police force.[7] The Erinys pipeline contract is valued at $100 million. Meteoric Tactical Solutions, has a £270,000 contract with the UK's Department for International Development providing bodyguards and drivers for its most senior official in Iraq. ArmorGroup is being paid £876,000 by the British Foreign Office to supply twenty security guards. However, the largest contract so far awarded went to Tim Spicer (formerly of Sandline International and infamous for his past involvement in Sierra Leone) whose new company, Aegis Defense Systems, received $293 million to co-ordinate all private security contractors in Iraq (Fisk and Carroll 2004; Isenberg 2004; Quirk 2004).

---

[7] The US Department of State's International Police Program Recruiting section has an on-line 'Information Source'. It says that DynCorp, on behalf of the Department of State's Bureau of International Narcotics and Law Enforcement Affairs, is seeking individuals with appropriate experience and expertise to participate in an international effort to re-establish police functions in post-conflict Iraq. Applicants should be 'active duty, retired or recently separated sworn police officers'. Police Advisors' salary is $120,632. Lodging, meals and transport are provided. The Department of State site lists opportunities in Iraq, Afghanistan, East Timor and Liberia. http://www.policemission.com/

One writer estimates that the annual revenues of British military service providers rose from £200 million before the Iraq War to £1 billion after it (Wilson 2004). However, there are important cost implications for government. It was originally anticipated that security would consume about 10 per cent of the $87 billion appropriated by the US Congress for Iraqi regeneration. Some are now estimating that total expenditure will be double or triple that amount (Kurlantzick 2003). Indirect costs have also to be considered. In Britain, the Ministry of Defence is reported to have asked security firms operating in Iraq to refrain from poaching its soldiers. A recent report revealed that 350 senior soldiers had applied for Premature Voluntary Release during a six-month period compared to only 499 over the previous twelve months (Brady 2004). Special forces, such as the Hereford-based SAS – coincidentally, Hereford is the home of a significant number of private military companies – are particularly badly hit. This situation is hardly surprising when companies employing ex-SAS and other Special Forces veterans can charge £1,000 per day for their services; and where ex-commandos can earn around seven times what their former colleagues are currently earning in Iraq (Corpwatch 2004).[8]

Particular concern has arisen in respect of two related issues. Are contracts awarded fairly and transparently? And do they offer value for money? The first issue raises questions about lobbying and undue political influence. In the USA a lobbying organisation, the International Peace Operations Association, actively supports the interests of some of the largest companies. Leading companies, such as DynCorp and MPRI, are also strategically based in northern Virginia. This not only gives them direct lobbying access to the Pentagon, but also enables them to recruit from senior Pentagon staff. A spokesman for MPRI – himself formerly head of the Pentagon's Defense Intelligence Agency – put the matter succinctly: 'We have more generals than the Pentagon' (cited in Kurlantzick 2003).

It is also alleged that, by virtue of their substantial donations to Republican causes, companies like DynCorp, Bechtel and Halliburton are able to mobilize political support for hawkish foreign policies (Krane 2004). Particular controversy has surrounded the giant energy services, engineering construction and logistics company, Halliburton (formerly run by Vice-President Dick Cheney). In 1991, after the Gulf War, Cheney, then

---

[8] Ethnic variations in award structures in Iraq are noteworthy. An ex-British commando working for a private military company can earn up to $20,000 per month. An ex-Nepali commando, doing the same job, will earn $1,500 and an ex-South African commando $1,000 (Corpwatch 2004).

Defense Secretary, commissioned a Halliburton company, KBR (Kellogg Brown & Root), to conduct a study of the benefits of military outsourcing. A year later KBR was awarded the first contract under the new Logistics Civil Augmentation Program (LOGCAP) allowing the Army to call on the company for field operation support (including combat, peacekeeping and humanitarian assistance). When the US joined NATO forces in the Balkans in 1995 KBR was deployed there. The company lost the second LOGCAP contract to DynCorp in 1997 when the General Accounting Office (GAO) reported that KBR had exceeded its estimates on the Balkan contract by 32 per cent. Despite this, KBR was awarded the third LOGCAP contract, renewable for ten years, in 2001. Under LOGCAP, companies respond to 'task orders' issued by the Army for services required. The company is paid a fee of 2 per cent above the cost of the service. Since these contracts are demand-led their value is open-ended and, as a result, there is neither an incentive for good nor a disincentive for bad service. By September 2003 KBR had been awarded sixty-seven task orders amounting to $2.2 billion, of which more than $2 billion was for Iraq. Subsequently, two Democratic congressmen have asked the GAO to investigate whether the US Agency for International Development and the Pentagon are circumventing government contracting procedures and favouring companies with links to the Bush administration (The Center for Public Integrity 2004).

In these circumstances there are serious doubts about whether contracts represent value for money. Further doubt is added by the opaque transnational subcontracting arrangements that drive service delivery. Neff and Price (2004) illustrate how costs are elevated by these and other means. In one alleged instance, Blackwater first added a 36 per cent mark-up plus its overhead costs to an invoice. Then it sent the bill to a Kuwaiti hotel (sic) company. That company, Regency Hotel, added on its costs for buying vehicles and weapons plus a profit element. The invoice was then forwarded to a German company (ESS) that cooks meals for the troops. ESS added its costs and profit and forwarded the bill to Halliburton. Halliburton added further overhead and profit before sending the bill to the Pentagon. The Defense Contract Audit Agency recently said that Halliburton could not document 42 per cent of a $4 billion invoice submitted to the Pentagon – much of it for subcontractors about whom Halliburton refuses to communicate on grounds of commercial confidentiality. Allegations that Halliburton has also been involved in financial abuses and 'kick-backs' eventually led to the company reimbursing government and the Pentagon suspending payment on some of its overcharged accounts. Despite this, Halliburton has continued to receive contracts from the Army (Hartung 2004: 3).

Concerns

Commercial involvement in the military is, of course, long established, with large companies such as Northrop Grumman having provided forces with communications, technology and weapons for decades. However, governments are now turning to contractors for operational services that either require or make more likely their use of force. Though this has been happening in 'peripheral' war zones, such as Sierra Leone, for over a decade, the role of private operatives has become especially critical in Iraq:

> We're talking about people using military training and weapons to carry out military functions within a war zone . . . Some refer to them as 'security guards'; but they aren't like security guys in the shopping mall . . . [providing] airport security in Baghdad doesn't mean watching bags go through the x-ray machine – it means hiring ex-Green Berets to defend the airport against mortar attack. (Singer cited in O'Neill 2004)

In Iraq private personnel have been called upon to provide security for the head of the Coalition Provisional Authority; escort supply convoys through hostile territory; and defend key locations in Baghdad's Green Zone (Barstow et al. 2004). They have also been used in the interrogation of prisoners. Particular controversy arose following the reports of abuses at Abu Ghraib Prison. Here, it transpired, twenty-seven of the thirty-seven interrogators belonged not to the US military, but to the Virginia-based private contractor, CACI International.[9] A further twenty-two linguists who assisted them were from the California-based company Titan International. Unlike the seven reservist guards who faced criminal trials as a result of their alleged indiscretions, however, these civilian employees are subject neither to military law nor to the Geneva Convention; and while, theoretically, they could be subjected to local prosecution – were a working criminal justice system to exist in Iraq – Paul Bremer, head of the CPA, had issued an order protecting contractors from such intervention during the previous year (Hurst 2004).

Several further concerns have been raised about the deployment of private operatives. Firstly, there has been criticism of the quality and character of recruits. Many South Africans are working in Iraq illegally, having breached new laws passed by the Pretoria government to control the export of mercenaries. Ex-military personnel employed to guard Baghdad Airport include Chileans, some of whom were trained under the Pinochet regime (Barstow et al. 2004; Fisk and Carroll 2004). There

---

[9] Subsequently, it came to light that CACI Productions, a subsidiary of CACI International, supplies ethics training videos to staff employed in the White House.

have also been allegations of gross impropriety (such as the DynCorp staff alleged to have been involved in a prostitution and rape scandal in Bosnia) and incompetence (such as the claim that Vinnell botched the task of training the Iraqi military so badly that the Jordanian army was called in to finish the job) (Hurst 2004).

Secondly, there are doubts about the efficacy of operational procedures. These include the lack of uniform rules of engagement; complaints from some guards about being put into combat situations without adequate weaponry, training or equipment; and reports of poor communication links with military commanders, where security guards have been stranded and left without reinforcements when under attack (Barstow et al. 2004).

Thirdly, contractual procedures make lines of authority and communication over-complex. Many security guards are hired as independent contractors by companies that are subcontractors of larger security companies. They, in turn, might be subcontractors of a prime contractor, which could have been hired by a United States agency. In reality, then, government authorities have little effective oversight of the companies on their payroll (Barstow et al. 2004).

Fourthly, it has been noted that the distinction between military ('soldiers') and civil ('guard') functions is increasingly fudged. The rules of engagement for private security contractors are ostensibly clear: guards can defend themselves but not engage in offensive action. Indeed, military legal experts have said that guards risk being treated as illegal combatants if they support military units in hostile engagements. However, two factors complicate this situation. First, as we have said, the Pentagon has relied, to an unprecedented degree, on security companies to guard convoys, senior officials and Coalition Authority facilities. Second, insurgents make no distinction between security guards and combat troops; and even if they chose to do so, the often-similar dress of soldiers and guards would make this problematic.

Finally, some of these concerns need to be considered in a broader context. The opacity of contractual processes and the fudging of civil–military distinctions are, in particular, linked to wider governance strategies. Both have, in effect, enabled states to evade public scrutiny of their actions in sensitive situations. This has been particularly apparent in the USA where Congress receives no notification of contracts worth less than $50 million and where the Pentagon admits it has no idea of how many workers it employs through private companies (Hartung 2004). As a result it has been possible for private guards to be deployed 'behind the backs' of Congress and the public – as was the case with their mobilization in the 'war against drugs' in Colombia.[10] A similar situation appears to be developing in the UK. In a recent interview a former Special Forces soldier claimed that Foreign Office and Ministry of Defence contracts for guarding British military facilities in Iraq were 'kept very quiet for political reasons'. A senior official from UK-based company Olive Security added said 'It's high time politicians were told exactly what we are having to do in Iraq, which is basically reconstructing it and doing the job British forces should be doing' (Nathan 2004). Despite the scale of deployment in Iraq, however, no effective system of regulation or vetting exists.[11]

The nodal model revisited

So far, it has been argued that risk-based technologies present us with both opportunities and dangers. On the one hand, they offer the prospect, under appropriate conditions, for security and justice to be delivered to people with the minimum use of pain (Johnston and Shearing 2003; Shearing and Johnston 2005). On the other hand, they can be integrated with coercive technologies to produce oppressive outcomes and to undermine just and democratic ('optimal') security provision. As we have seen in the previous section, some recent developments in transnational commercial security are indicative of the latter process. We now consider how useful the nodal model is in helping us to address the issue of transnational commercial security. In order to do this we shall revisit some of the themes discussed in our introduction and relate them to four specific criticisms of the nodal model made by Loader and Walker.[12]

Earlier we claimed that the nodal model is better suited than are state-centric models to help us theorize 'optimal security'. However, this does not mean that there is any essential normative connection between the latter and the nodal model. We emphasize this point because of Loader

---

[10] It is also worth bearing in mind that the 'body count' of security personnel killed in wars and other risky operations is more easily obscured from public scrutiny than would be the case with serving military personnel. Security guards killed while working for governments do not merit the symbolism of state recognition.

[11] In June 2004 guidelines were proposed for US contractors working in Iraq and for the US government offices supporting them. These were intended to provide 'an initial blueprint for eventual adoption of common contractor coordination and security rules for all nations providing contractors for the reconstruction of Iraq' (cited in Isenberg (2004: 9). There is, however, doubt that the regulatory organizations involved have the necessary co-ordination capacities required (Isenberg 2004: 138)

[12] Here, we draw upon two sources: Loader and Walker's (2004b) recent review of *Governing Security* (Johnston and Shearing 2003); and their chapter in this volume which provides a more general critique of the Security 21 project.

and Walker's first criticism: their allegation that a slippage occurs in *Governing Security* 'between its use as a descriptive/explanatory term and its development as a normative framework' (Loader and Walker 2004b: 224). To justify this claim they contrast an instance in the book where the term is used to *'describe'* the messier [empirical] configurations of security governance with one in which reference is made to the [normative] *'principles'* of nodal governance, the latter allegedly enabling its authors to advocate the concept as a means of making democratic security outcomes *'more thinkable'* (see Johnston and Shearing 2003: 18, 149 and 160 (italics added) respectively).

In one, albeit limited respect, this criticism is justified. It is certainly true that in the case cited – which involved a discussion of the Patten Commission – the word 'principles' was used, though the authors' intention in using it was to refer to the *conceptual* principles of the nodal model. However, one case of linguistic ambiguity hardly sanctions a 'normative' reading of the text as a whole. *Governing Security* cannot, justifiably, be read as a normative tract 'in favour' of nodal governance. The latter term is meant to elucidate important changes occurring in the sphere of governance, recognition of which might *facilitate* the 'thought-work' (the intended meaning of 'thinkable' in the above quotation) required to pursue given normative ends. Nodal governance is a theoretical concept describing an 'is', not a normative one promulgating an 'ought'. In that regard the concept is normatively neutral. Thus, while *Governing Security* argues that the nodal model can usefully be employed to facilitate practices of non-coercive local capacity governance, the same model can also be used to inform very different normative ends.

That the 'stick' of nodal governance can be 'bent' in a variety of different normative directions should be obvious from our previous discussion. In key areas of domestic and global policy transnational commercial security organizations now operate as governing nodes alongside other entities such as national governments, supranational authorities and NGOs. The expansion of the prison industry and the war in Iraq – together with the subsequent 'reconstruction' of that country – demonstrate that nodal processes can support coercive technologies just as easily as non-coercive ones. It is increasingly clear that today's strategists conceptualize warfare in a nodal-networked form. Firstly, they seek to co-ordinate military force through 'net-centric' methods such that the network 'becomes the weapon'. Secondly, they perceive the network in a non-territorial form. War is fought less through formal alliances between territorial nations and more through what Donald Rumsfeld has called 'floating coalitions that change and evolve'. Though, admittedly, Rumsfeld is referring to coalitions of countries here, it is increasingly the case that such coalitions include terrorist cells and transnational corporations – not least those offering military and security services.[13] Relations between coalition members may, of course, be contractual as well as diplomatic. Indeed, it is widely believed that al-Qaeda has, itself, used the services of private military companies.

We now turn to a second criticism made by Loader and Walker (this volume): that advocates of the nodal model operate with a conception of 'the state as idiot'; then, perversely, rely upon the state to provide key conditions of existence of nodal governance. Let us consider each of these points in turn. The assumption that the state is an 'idiot' derives, it is suggested, from proponents of the nodal model adopting two Hayekian propositions: that the state lacks the knowledge and capacity to deliver security to local communities; and that, in its efforts to do so, is prone to authoritarian tendencies. Two things may be said about this criticism. First, if the state is an 'idiot' the same is true of all complex organisations with multiple objectives. Johnston and Shearing's (2003) rejection of interest-based models of governance and their insistence that the relationship between mentalities, technologies and institutions is enabling rather than determining (cf. Hindess 1988) is intended, precisely, to confirm the conditional relationship between an agent's objectives and its accomplishments.

In order to illustrate what is at stake here, consider our previous discussion of relations between the US state and military service providers. Clearly, by developing these relations, the state sought to advance certain objectives, one of which was the desire to 'govern [war] at a distance' (Miller and Rose 1990). To a significant degree this objective seems to have been achieved. By devolving 'rowing' functions to the private military sector in the arenas of Afghanistan, Iraq and Colombia, the state was able to 'steer' operations against terrorism and drugs behind the backs of the public and its representatives. However, the pursuit of such strategic objectives, even when successfully accomplished, can also give rise to unforeseen and unintended consequences, the effects of which can be to undermine the very objectives that strategies of distanciation are meant to support. One example is given in Avant's (2003) account of MPRI's work in Bosnia. Here the company's ability to exploit contractual conditions enabled it to exert control over aspects of US foreign policy. In this case the strategy of distanciation, far from merely consolidating state power, also compromised it critically.

---

[13] See Duffield's analysis of 'war as a network enterprise' for a thought-provoking discussion of these issues. http://users.aber.ac.uk/cjm/globalsecurity/4war.htm (accessed 2 December 2004).

Instances such as this confirm two things. Firstly, our earlier claim that the 'steering and rowing' analogy fails to explore the contingent uncertainties of state action, fails to consider the competing objectives of governing agents and fails to recognize the plural constitution of governance is confirmed. Secondly, 'idiocy' – if one chooses to use that unfortunate term – is an inherent feature of governing practices rather than a particular characteristic of the state.

The second aspect of Loader and Walker's criticism is that advocates of the nodal model, having deemed the state an 'idiot' by virtue of its inability to know people's preferences, then call upon it to provide key conditions of existence of nodal governance. However, the fact that the state's restricted knowledge of people's preferences might limit its effective intervention in *some* areas or levels of activity does not preclude it from effective intervention in *all* areas or levels of activity. Thus, it is perfectly feasible under nodal conditions, to envisage the state laying down some general regulatory ('meta-authoritative') principles for security governance without having to 'know' the particular preferences of particular constituencies. In that respect, there is no inherent contradiction between 'nodalism' and 'meta-authority'. It is simply that, in our view, the former places significant empirical limitations on the potential accomplishments of the latter. At the transnational level, of course, there are further empirical limitations on the nation state's capacity to fulfil the role of regulatory 'meta-authority', an issue we return to when considering Loader and Walker's final criticism.

Loader and Walker's (2004b) third charge is that the authors of *Governing Security* too easily adopt a 'left-Hayekian' position born of unjustified pessimism about the governing potential of the state. It is certainly true that proponents of the nodal model are more pessimistic than their critics about the state's capacity to lead the fight for justice and security under neo-liberal conditions, not least in the transnational context. However, such pessimism is far from being the exclusive preserve of those who advocate that model. Drucker, in posing the question 'Who takes care of the Common Good?' observed that the unitary state's replacement by a new pluralism arose precisely 'because it could neither satisfy the needs of society nor perform the necessary tasks of community' (Drucker 1995: 95). Indeed, Loader and Walker (this volume) are themselves mindful of such concerns, not only recognizing the past 'chequered history' of public/ state authorities in advancing democratic politics, but also bemoaning the state's present-day 'impotence' to effect social justice. Inevitably, however, such recognition poses questions about the provenance of the state's general meta-authoritative role in security governance; and, ironically, mirroring their earlier criticism of *Governing Security*, we are left wondering whether such meta-authority is an (empirical) 'capacity' to be 'exercised' or a (normative) 'claim' to be invoked (see Loader and Walker 2004b: 224–5).

This tension between the normative and the empirical has implications beyond mere academic debate. We can all offer good normative reasons why it is desirable that liberal democratic states should fulfil key governance functions. The problem is that states are often unable – and may, indeed, be unwilling – to do so. Take the case of global peacekeeping. While Western states repeatedly refuse to commit significant numbers of their well-trained and well-equipped forces to peacekeeping roles, the world's poorest – and, in some cases, least democratic – countries are forced to shoulder the burden (Mason 2004). In July 2004 the largest global peacekeeping providers were Pakistan (8,544), Bangladesh (7,163), Nigeria (3,579), Ghana (3,341) and India (2,934). Among Western nations, the largest contributors were the UK (567), Canada (564), France (561), Ireland (479) and the USA (427). In view of this, reports – denied by official sources – that Kofi Annan, the UN Secretary-General, is exploring the possibility of employing private security to deal with the peacekeeping problem are hardly surprising (Deen 2004).

Our response to Loader and Walker's third criticism is, therefore, simple. It is one thing to invoke good normative reasons to justify why the state *should* exercise meta-authority over governance. It is another to make it happen. That is not to denigrate the state's legitimate authority. It is merely to affirm that under conditions where the state's governing capacity is problematic – something which is apparent at both domestic and transnational levels – one should explore a variety of auspices through which those same desired normative ends could be pursued.

Finally, let us turn to Loader and Walker's fourth criticism: that proponents of the nodal model fail both to address sufficiently the problem of security as 'a collective *or* public good' (Loader and Walker 2004b: 225; italics added) and the state's role (as 'meta-authority') in the pursuit of that good. There is some truth in each of these claims. Proponents of the nodal model have, indeed, said relatively little about security as a *public* good and, as a result, have placed limited emphasis on the state's meta-authoritative role. While these issues remain a crucial matter for debate, however, their relative absence from the nodal model is by no means an oversight. It is, in fact, a result of that model's attempt to refocus our understanding of the relationship between public and *collective* goods (or objectives), a distinction which has been lacking from previous analysis. As Shearing and Wood (2003a) argue, we need to move beyond the 'public–private dichotomy' to a better conceptualization of collective goods and objectives. In particular, it is necessary to recognize that as well as 'the public', many other collectivities with shared objectives and concerns engage in governance. On the one hand, proponents of nodal governance would concur with Loader and Walker that states should continue to explore regulatory strategies to retain authority over non-state providers where these affect public interests. On the other hand, they would also maintain that 'we should be working to promote both public and common goods and we should be mobilising both state and non-state auspices to do so' (Shearing and Wood 2003a: 221).

Though the debate about nodal governance has, so far, focused on issues of 'local capacity-building' within nation states the nodal model is also applicable to our assessment of security governance at the transnational level. There are both empirical and normative reasons for suggesting this. Empirically, it is clear that regulatory regimes of all types now operate on a nodal basis. At the domestic level, professional bodies, trade associations and insurance companies carry out regulatory functions, while at the global level equivalent activities are undertaken by bodies such as the IMF and the World Bank (Scott 2002). In the particular case of commercial security, it is also apparent that the limited success states have had in bringing about effective regulation at the domestic level (Button 2002) is nothing compared to the problems of achieving democratic governance at the transnational level (Nossal 2001; House of Commons 2002). In that context, strategies for the democratic governance of transnational commercial security are bound to involve both state and non-state auspices, something which is, at last, being recognized in proposals put forward by those advocating reform (e.g. Lilley 2000 sect. VIII).

Whether states could, collectively, exercise meta-authority over such putative transnational regulatory regimes is arguable. Realistically, however, were it to occur, it would be a minimalist form of meta-authority: one involving the establishment of minimal ground rules and constitutional constraints regarding what companies might legitimately do and how they might legitimately do it. Such a minimalist outcome is not only empirically unavoidable, it is also normatively beneficial. For in denying the conflation between 'collective' and 'public' goods and in demanding a more nuanced understanding of the relationship between public, common and private ones, proponents of the nodal model are suggesting two things: that subject to minimal public standards, democracy is better served the more 'local' it is; and that that normative agenda – whether at the local or transnational level – is best facilitated through an understanding of the nodal character of contemporary governance.

3 Two case studies of American anti-terrorism

Peter K. Manning

Introduction

The recent scholarly interest in terrorism and anti-terrorism as a social problem exemplifies how politics and political interests shape research. The most penetrating and lucid work is the Report of the 9/11 Commission (2004). Clearly, control of, and response to, terrorism is a question of relevance to police studies, to the governance of security, and speaks to the fragmentation and multiplicity of forms of social control. Simultaneously, the power of the state has grown (Cohen 1985; Garland 2001; Johnston and Shearing 2003). Contemporaneous studies of social control agents and agencies provide data that can connect organizational theories, the negative risks associated with terrorism, and observable police actions in respect to putative terrorism and/or anti-terrorism. The emerging role of private and public police and anti-terrorism preparations are particularly revealing of the changing shape of control because terrorist policing and anti-terrorist policing, with some exceptions, have previously been eschewed by Anglo-American police (Liang 1993; Manning 2003: 41–2). Implicit in these developments is the question of to what degree these preparations threaten democratic freedoms and civil liberties.

This chapter, drawing on ethnographic-evidence studies of organizational responses to terrorism, has three themes. The first theme is that contingencies imagined as negative risks are not shared within and across policing (regulatory) organizations. The second concerns the problems associated with assembling temporary organizational networks to defend an event, place, or group at risk. The third is identification of the practical issues that emerge in the course of policing such an event and how they, in turn, reflect the practices of the co-operating-competing organizations in the network. By echoing variations on these themes, I seek to explicate Crozier's foundational points concerning contingencies (he terms them 'uncertainties') and interactive dependencies within organizational networks (Crozier 1964; 1972; Crozier and Friedberg 1980). These contingencies reveal power relationships.

Data are derived from two case studies, the Winter Olympics in February 2002 in the Salt Lake City, Utah area (actually a regional event covering sites from the Ogden region in the north, to Park City in the east to West Valley in the west), and the Democratic National Convention held in July 2004 in Boston, Massachusetts.[1] My concern is to elucidate the relationships between the three themes and power. The day-to-day dynamics, although observed, are not presented here (see Decker et al. 2002; McDevitt and Farrell 2004). Let us first consider the relevance of organizational theory to the functions of a control network.

Organizational theory

Organizations must manage contingencies, matters that are neither factually closed, nor completely open-ended (Perrow 1984; Vaughan 1996: 81–2ff.). Associated with such contingencies are risks or imagined outcomes, judged in light of their consequences but always not fully known. These risks can be subjective, such as fear, dread or excitement, or objective, such as the damage done by hurricanes, mining disasters or floods, or something of both (Short 1984: 715). As both Short and Vaughan have described in great detail, the societal level of the acceptance of risk is closely and perhaps inextricably linked to the institutional mandate: 'The relationship between institutions and risk is reflexive, and causal relationships are therefore reciprocal' (Short 1984: 714). This means, in short, that institutions identify, dramatize, symbolize and publicize a selected range of contingencies which they are prepared to manage, and these in turn are those safeguards the citizenry in theory attributes to them (Douglas 1986). Deciding, allocating limited resources with authority requires, it would appear, 'satisficing' or making the best of a complex situation, rather than optimizing or seeking the single best solution (March and Simon 1958; Heimer 1985). Crozier and Friedberg (1980: 67), building on the earlier work of Burns and Stalker (1965) and Crozier (1964; 1972), argue that relations between organizations create interactive dependencies, in part based on the 'porosity and fluidity' of organizational boundaries and the 'difficulty, if not impossibility, of determining... a precise line of demarcation between what is 'internal' and what 'external'. This dependency is a cue to power relations (Heimer 1985: 412). Heimer's work in particular emphasizes the network she calls the information order as a cue to organizational dependencies. As a result of this pattern of dependency, regardless of the complexity

---

[1] Both were included in a new category, 'National Security Events', by the Office of Homeland Security.

of the environment, organizations create and dramatize their obligations, practices and resource use. This is the first of the themes of this chapter. A socially legitimated organizational mandate includes the principal contingency, associated strategies and tactics, and a rhetoric or explanatory framework for selectively dramatizing risk(s) (Hughes 1958; Vaughan 1996). Dramatizing a contingency consistently entails some form of internal audit or risk analysis.

While risk analysis has been freighted with mathematical and statistical approaches to technological and scientific risks, risk in practice is grounded in perceptions, tacit knowledge, assumptions and knowledge about matters that are negotiated between the public and the institution (Short 1984: 717). Contingencies are defined, constructed, responded to, typified and connected to the sanctioned means by which the control of those risks is to be accomplished (Manning 1992: 256). This proposition suggests the need for close analysis of practices rather than statistically based models of variable relationships (cf. any issue of the *Administrative Science Quarterly*). The study of organizational response to risk has benefited from important theoretically sophisticated ethnographically grounded works (Heimer 1985; 1987; Clarke 1989; Vaughan 1996; Espeland 1998; Hawkins 2003). They connect risks-as-defined-by with the organizational response to these risks through closely observed naturalistic materials. Clarke and Heimer have been extraordinarily sensitive to the contingencies of temporary, new and time-bound organizations, especially with respect to information and what Heimer (1985: 397) calls the 'information order'. Heimer highlights the second theme of this chapter, the problem not only of obtaining information, but also of processing and using it when the network is temporary, new or emerging. She argues that 'we must examine cases in which decision making procedures have not been made routine and in which there is some ambiguity about which information *should* be used in decision making' (Heimer 1985: 397). It is a question not only of information, but of how it is to be displayed in practice.

The third theme of the chapter is the nature of the organizational network. Networks are loose configurations with nodes of co-operation and competition bound together by some consistent exchanges, usually asymmetrical, as well as other commitments (Johnston and Shearing 2003). 'Network' is a metaphor that suggests an open-ended, incomplete set of connections of varying strength, density and quality (Bott 1971: 58). It does not assume shared aims, only transactions that intersect to form a concrete system of action (Crozier and Friedberg 1980: 127). Regulatory forces such as law, political authority and local traditions also shape networks.

Now, consider police organizations as a type of formalized and centralized interaction.[2] Police organizations, often considered as a unique form,
have transnational features. They are concerned with reacting to and regulating negative risks attached to property and life. Democratic policing
as practised in Anglo-American societies post-9/11 and the perspectives
of agencies on their mandate, chief contingency and associated practices
appear to be changing.[3] Dealing with terrorism and anti-terrorism intro-
duces new forms of organizational contingency and risks – threats and
actual damage to property and life that arise not from greed or lust, but
from beliefs, even altruism (e.g. suicide bombings). Although terrorism –
against the British and Indians, and as a form of self-help in the North
American West – was a part of frontier life, at least from the time of
the French and Indian Wars (Gurr et al. 1969; Fischer 1994) current
responses to terrorism and the politicization of 'national security' reveal
American naïvety and inexperience with terrorism, and tensions between
domestic and high (or security) policing, policing concerned with national
security itself.[4]

Organized response to uncertainty

As noted above, the primary concern, essential for organizational survival,
is defining and sustaining the nature of the organizational, collective,
contingency and associated negative risk(s) as it (or they) is embedded
within the formal structure of the organization. That is, organizations take
on those contingencies with negative consequences that cannot be fully
resolved factually nor stand as unanswerable because of their character,
the data required or the limits of present knowledge. Risk management

---

[2] Organizations are characterized by hierarchy, bounded interactions that are more dense
and concentrated within than outside the organization, and typically occupy an ecologi-
cal/spatial niche and a place within a hierarchy of other related organizations.
[3] See Maguire's (2002) empirical analysis of the stability of the structure and functions of
large police organizations in the United States.
[4] In addition, the experience of the members of Anglo-American policing systems (US,
UK, Canada, Australia and New Zealand), local, state and federal, has been primarily with known groups of terrorists who take responsibility for their threats and
bombings; with largely concealed bombs placed in public places (department stores,
parks); with groups which eschew of random, unannounced or suicide bombers; with
restricted symbolic targets with few actual deaths (not withstanding the damage to property as in the Manchester Marks and Spencer and London Harrods bombings); and
with domestic bombings and terrorist acts that are on the home ground rather than in
foreign or overseas locations such as military bases, embassies and ships at sea or in
port. Domestic anti-terrorist activities overlap with armies and special police units as
revealed in the policing of Northern Ireland and the Irish Republic (Ellison and Smyth
2000).

becomes institutionalized as a basic foundational set of practices. The task of control is reflexive in a powerful fashion, for social control agencies define and attempt to reduce risks experienced in society as a regulatory body as well as those risks that must be managed for the particular organization to maintain its mandate (Manning 1997: chaps. 4–5).

Organizational analysis must also bear in mind the vicissitudes of networks within which organizations operate. A regulatory/policing body requires a number of functional prerequisites if it is to work within an inter-organizational field (Clarke 1989). This includes competing successfully for scarce resources, producing the 'output', holding a 'marketing niche'[5] and managing the relevant technologies. The organization must develop 'sense-making' modalities that selectively identify, amplify and classify matters of interest in the environment (Weick 2001). The flux and flow of events, the range of stimuli, has no intrinsic meaning; it must be conferred by organizational processes. This process of sense-making is a part of the cultural study of risk or 'bias' – the tacit assumptions about the nature, location and character of risk in society (Douglas 1986). The leading edge of the organization is its communicational system and the modes of access to, and penetration of, the external world through organizational boundaries (Bordua and Reiss 1967). This implies a coding system by which facts are processed and converted into useful information. In a most radical sense, organizations do not 'see' that for which they are not looking (MacKay 1981). In addition, organizations exist in an inter-organizational environment of constraints, exchanges and patterned transactions (Clarke 1989; Vaughan 1996). The connections between organizations sustain a broader network that responds to and processes similar kinds of risks, e.g. crime, disease, poverty and death.

Within an organization, sense must be made; segments exist within the organization with different political interests and values; these may be based on rank, age, skill, or gender amongst others. Mini-ideologies that value work differ, as do aspirations and skills (Jackall 1988). Clusters of organizational interests are bases for power and often ideologically driven. When they are clothed in rhetoric and a known vocabulary, they become part of forces espousing often competing rationalities (Espeland 1998). All organizations are thus arenas for the negotiation of differences. It follows then that a key question in the study of the regulation of risk is how the contingency at issue becomes the basis for enstructuration of

---

[5] I use the term 'marketing niche' loosely. Public policing is not in competition in an economic market but in a market of symbolic capital – seeking prestige, respect, deference and compliance and extending trustworthiness.

the organization (Heimer 1985). This is best revealed by a close study of practices because these dramatize and make overt the focus of the organization.[6] The second theme of this chapter, the shaping of temporary organizations via co-operation in a single instance, is not well studied.

Having advanced this general outline of themes, it is important to tie it to matters arising in the course of organizational practice. Clearly, an institution such as the police dramatizing a variable contingency and associated risks must both account for that contingency and display convincingly its efforts to manage it (Carruthers and Espeland 1991). These two streams of identifying/symbolizing and affecting or shaping have been termed respectively *presentational strategies*, those which dramatize the uncertainty, and *resource allocation strategies* which set out deployment of personnel, budgeting, depth of people in given roles, and pattern practice or tactics (Manning 2003: 249). The two streams, presentation and allocation, are easily confused as symbolization (reassurance, confirmation, validation, values expressed in decisions, competence of the deciders) and instrumental action (effective in consequence) are always intertwined (Feldman and March 1981:177–8). The organizational infrastructure for tracking such matters in policing is provided by official data on reported crime and other output indicators such as clearances, warrants served, seizures and internal process monitors, such as overtime expenditures. Internal data in the annual report of a police department or agency fix in institutional memory the overt consequences of resource allocation. Thus, one function of what might be called internal coding is that of 'soaking up' uncertainty that remains about the organization's mandate (March and Simon 1958: 165). In this way, the flow of events is broken into manageable strips of coherent events, problems, and incidents in the environment. Externally, presentational strategies, accounts for organizational action, serve to legitimate not only the actions taken but also the fundamental grounding for these in a given, named, located uncertainty, seen now firmly within managerial grasp. None the less, areas of ambiguity in the organization and in the organizational networks (here, competing organizations in the security provision industry) remain.[7] The ways in which the organizational network must grapple in practice with

---

[6] There is very little literature on temporary responsive organizations; most has emerged in the study of disasters, and concerns semi-structured arrangements for disaster relief, nationally and internationally, that have emerged through repeated use. However, consider the work of the International Red Cross, Médecins Sans Frontières, FEMA and the United Nations' relief efforts.

[7] One might distinguish security as a public collective sense, something like the collective consciousness, and the security industry which is engaged in producing, marketing, dramatizing and profiting from security concerns.

the division of labour and its moral meanings is the third theme of this chapter.

Anglo-American policing

Let us turn to Anglo-American public police as an ideal type. There are at least three types of policing present in everyday life in these societies: local policing, specialized policing by federal agents and high, or political, policing. Consider these three types.

There are 21,113 agencies in the United States: 14,628 local, 49 state (Hawaii provides law enforcement through the Department of Public Safety), 3,156 sheriff-headed and 3,280 special agencies. There are approximately 600,000 officers in these agencies (Maguire et al. 1998: 109–10). These agencies are primarily small, highly structured and reactive; rely heavily on local funding, political guidance, accountability and traditions of law enforcement; use violence (lethal and non-lethal) and criminal and civil sanctions; and are briefly and poorly trained in local academies with wide standards of recruitment and acceptance. Because of its local grounding, public policing serves the executive indirectly with the law as a mediating and constraining force, separate from courts and the legislature. Policing powers are quite wide and are shared with individuals, private investigators, citizen self-help groups, private policing agencies and, occasionally, the military (National Guard, reserves and regular forces). Territorial limits or jurisdictional boundaries, once binding in Anglo-American policing, are now largely irrelevant at the federal level since American law is extended and applied within foreign nations with startling impunity. Global and task-force-based transnational policing is growing (Sheptycki 2000).

Let us further characterize Anglo American public police forces.

• They are reactive and bottom-heavy (over 70 per cent of resources are allocated to random patrolling and answering emergency calls).
• They include some 4 per cent in administration and 5–8 per cent in detective work and other specialized units. The remainder are in staff positions.
• They include some 25 per cent civilian employees.
• They are divided into staff and line, with patrols carrying out 'line' while internal affairs, detectives and the service division carry out staff functions.
• They generally work alone, in partnerships or small groups. In most cities they patrol, ecologically separated in time and space but linked via communications networks, and are rarely directly supervised.

- They have a clear consistent image. The image and practice of the Anglo-American police is shaped by information technologies, screens of various kinds, visual displays of the police as both subject and object, and mass media depictions.

Federal agencies in the United States, for example, act as specialized arms of the government, carrying out various functions such as tax regulation, gun control, customs and immigration, the border patrol, domestic violations of other federal laws, drug control, external operations in connection with national security (NSA, CIA) and so forth. Maguire et al. (1998) estimated there are some thirty federal enforcement agencies and number federal and related special agencies officials at 58,689. Two modes of case-working exist. While the traditional mode of case-working is reactive and focused on violations of federal law, there are also border areas, such as domestic espionage and national security, in which a more proactive case-creation mode is used. The result is competition and conflict between the CIA, FBI and other agencies within the Department of Justice (Kessler 2003).[8]

All nation states have developed security police for the protection of sacred persons, places and buildings and carry out high policing which connotes questions of national security (Brodeur 1983; 2003). High policing includes (summarized from Brodeur): striving to maintain domination and legitimacy, or the hegemony of the present government; monitoring political dissent and terrorism; making extensive use of undercover agents and *agents provocateurs*; invoking preventive detention; mounting

---

[8] This distinction deserves some elaboration, but it does not figure directly in the analysis below except indirectly. The first is a sanctioning case-based model of reacting to known events with the aim of eradicating or radically reducing delicts. It thrives on punishment, demonizing of particular targets and criminals known for their past activity, and closing cases as a sign of activity. Information is property, kept secret, seen as a symbolic good representing the skills and competence of the individual agent, and rarely shared with colleagues. It is reactive, case-based and responsive to known crimes. It is ill-suited to respond to anticipated crime, conspiracies, and domestic and international terrorism. It begins with a crime and works backwards to find the perpetrator. Fears for security of data and the commodification of information make the introduction of effective electronic infrastructure difficult and unwelcome (Kessler 2003; 9/11 Commission 2004).

The second is a negotiating model which rests on compromise, reducing risk, managing the negative consequences of risk and in part preventing or anticipating future deviance. Going to law is the last resort of these agencies (Hawkins 2003). Their contingency is the irregular aspects of human conduct that lie just outside the criminal and immediate, where present trends and issues are used to predict the future (see Manning 1992). Information is negotiated between the regulators and the regulated. Compliance is the aim and restorative justice a desired outcome. Spies and informants may be required. Court is avoided in general. Rather than pursuing those who have broken a law, this model seeks advance identification of risks and risk management tactics that will reduce future threats rather than pin down past offenders.

secret raids and clandestine surveillance; preferring secret and preventative interventions to known and named 'police operations'; and mounting anticipatory actions rather than awaiting incidents, crimes or delicts. Such approaches to order appear and disappear from the public view, but nevertheless remain in place, flourishing secretly until such time as they are again needed. It is, in theory, lurking and invisible, often illegal, whilst claiming to produce reassurance. High policing is flexible, semi-visible and thus rediscovered and reconfigured as befits the times. Most revealing of the constant presence of high policing functions is the planning and execution of the policing of brief public events which are perceived to be threatened.[9]

The unknown enemy and iconic demonization

The 9/11 Commission Report (2004) reveals that the attacks on the World Trade Center (WTC) were not the first successfully mounted against American targets in the United States or abroad, and are part of an ongoing pattern of retaliation against American global power. The sources of these attacks remain somewhat obscure.[10] The 2001 targeting of domestic sites in the United States has made a distant, spectral reality a closer and more threatening idea to which Americans are unaccustomed. The imagery of terror is media-created, since few actually saw people leaping to their deaths or the collapse of the Towers. Yet it seems real, and is part of a political spectacle. The unknown, terrorism, is only *simulated* or cued indirectly by what we have seen. It should be recognized that the meaning of the events since September 2001 is anything but clear. While the powerful and immediate imagery of the Twin Towers being hit, the people fleeing, others jumping to certain death from buildings, the

---

[9] In the past, the odd scandal revealed the extent of these quasi-legal secret operations. In the Anglo-American world, these include the activities of the RUC against (primarily) the IRA in collusion with the Protestant Loyalists; the RCMP in connection with the Partie Quebecois and posing as environmental activists in Alberta; the FBI surveillance, called COINTELPRO (Blackstock 1976), of civil rights activists and anti-war protesters in the late 1960s and early 1970s; and rumours about the federal agents' use of the Patriot Act of 2001. These eruptions of public knowledge and concern are but the tip of a major and ongoing set of processes sanctioned and funded by the state against its citizens.

[10] The sources of this mayhem are probably small groups, linked in networks that are cell-like, united primarily by communication channels and in the international sources of their funds. In other ways, the terrorists appear to have violated cardinal rules of cell-like work: meeting together for joint flights to test their plan for the World Trade Center; meeting in small groups in Hamburg and the United States and using videos (such as those by bin Laden himself) as a way to announce threats without directly specifying named targets. In late October 2004, a new video from bin Laden was released in which he took credit for the World Trade Center bombings. The named sponsoring groups are shifting and changing (and have been for more than twenty-five years) which is confusing to Indo-European language speakers.

exhausted firefighters, and the Twin Lights monument opened in New York in March 2002 all suggest that what we saw was a reality, a palpable natural event, it was not. What we saw was edited, cut, repeated, focused, presented in various contexts (news, drama, docudramas, sport, entertainment of various kinds, politics) – memorable icons. These are not equivalent to witnessing the natural event. They substitute and confound it. Nor do they clarify the causes, the history of the 'attack', its significance to audiences around the world, or the economic, ideological, political and consequences of the event. In many ways, the imagery overshadows the not-yet-understood event – the image an illusory curtain that suggests the event was understood and has meaningful dimensions, a familiar shape, and knowable consequences. These matters are not known; they are imagined.

The label 'terrorism', iconically rendered, suggests the elusive flavour of the natural event: a bombing, a crashed airliner, an attack of anthrax via mail, or the bombing of a federal building or embassy. The media imagery 'rubs off' and shapes our memories of the natural event – connotation, association and metaphor drive policy (see Hersh 2004; Woodward 2004).

The ambiguity in naming the enemy, and the target, it is clear, elevates and dramatizes a few to-be-hated celebrities – iconic symbols (pictures that also symbolize 'terror', 'danger' and 'evil'). A panoply of iconic evils – Saddam Hussein, Osama bin Laden, the twelve 11 September terrorists and the Taliban – exist. Their faces arouse emotional response. In this sense, the elevation of a handful of people, known widely, featured in decks of playing cards issued in Iraq of leading figures of Saddam Hussein's government and on the covers of weekly news magazines and the front pages of newspapers, demonized, turned into dark, foreboding, thoroughly evil figures, stands for a subtle, complex set of ideas, networks of people, clandestine finance, historical conflicts and rebellions stretching throughout Arabic peoples and nations. This 'celebrity turn', labelling a single person or group, converting complexity into simplicity, and resonating with surface appearances, is complemented by the thin historical context of American life and memory.

Terrorism

Terrorism is not a thing. It is a violent, secretive, surprise-based tactic used by a non-national group (which may indeed have state sponsorship, support, funding, protection and the like), usually against vulnerable symbolic or personal targets in a nation state. It drains morale and increases the risks associated with everyday life. Its social geometry, in Black's (2002) terms, is known. It is a form of social control, a form of self-help directed up (revenge by the powerless against the powerful who are socially or economically superior), enacted, played out and displayed, dramatically, on a national or international scale (Black 2002). It aims to render immense resources impotent. These tactics mean that the conventional distinctions between civilian and military installations and personnel have no relevance to controlling or carrying out terrorism or anti-terrorism. Terrorism may be included in war, as a part of war, but is not itself a war and cannot be warred upon literally. War must be declared, can only be carried out by nation states against each other through alliances or agreements, or against a nation state by rebels in a state of revolution. War is governed in theory by conventions about the treatment of prisoners, the wounded and the dead, the avoidance, or at least the minimization, of civilian deaths, and has a specified, agreed upon beginning and ending. Violations of war conventions produce crimes; the position of the United States since 2001 has been that terrorism and terrorists cannot be given the protection of international law or of the Geneva Convention concerning torture, nor the right to counsel (Hersh 2004).

Terrorism is always elusive and shadowy, suggesting imminent danger from strange forces, sources or persons, and takes the shape of what might be called an iconic, culturally defined and shaped, other. Even in the midst of a 'war on terror' as it is currently defined, the enemy or source of the threat is unclear even in Iraq where US forces occupy the country. The rhetoric which began by being targeted in some vague way has eclipsed any specific agents, targets, or causes, which have now vanished into pointing and posturing about the enemies of America.[11] Even while the Bush administration obscures the targets, causes, dynamics and rationale for the 'war on terror', new forms of warfare are emerging.[12]

---

[11] The past three years show startling semantic shifts in the political and media naming of the enemy, who or what is to be conquered, or what is the cause or source of the outrage. Mentioned as enemies are miscellaneous people from Pakistan, Malaysia or other Islamic countries, the Taliban, ethnic warlords, rebel remnants of the former Northern Alliance, Tajiks, clans, 'insurgents', al-Qaeda, the al-Qaeda related to Osama bin Laden, the al-Qaeda that is Shi'a-Islam-based and the combined, almost hyphenated, al-Qaeda and Taliban forces. The enemy as icon is of course a contrast conception without a clear referent. The unfolding intelligence has shown the mistaken and superficial rhetoric of the Bush administration (9/11 Commission 2004; Bamford 2004; Hersh 2004), and at the same time its power in establishing this vague threat as real, ominous and continuing.

[12] For example, in Bosnia, Kosovo, Iraq and Somalia, war and peace are intertwined, not binary; civilians, combatants, women and children are considered threats and targets; there is no boundary between a war zone and elsewhere (as in guerilla warfare generally); culture, politics and society are targets as well as the 'military' opponents, and obvious facilities may soon be destroyed e.g. airfields, waterworks, electrical plants and barracks. It seems clear in this context that success is not defined by a beginning or ending point or 'surrender', and the enemy is less a solider and more an ideology.

Absent North American experience

Americans have fought few wars, and none on their soil save the Civil War, or wars between the states; and those they fought, they claimed to have won (save Vietnam). Historians do not count the slaughter of Native Americans as a war, although it certainly relied on systematic raids and terrorism. The few international wars were fought on distant shores, in Europe and Asia, and only two truly bloody, albeit brief, battles are recalled and memorialized: Iwo Jima and Guadalcanal. The Americans have no parallels that either resemble or conjure up dreadful, powerful images such as those associated with the slaughter of six million Jews by the Nazis in World War II; the incineration and radiation of 800,000 people in Hiroshima and Nagasaki, and the repeated fire bombing of 131 German cities, rendering 3.5 million homes destroyed, 7.5 million homeless and 600,000 dead (Sebald 2003: 3–4). Americans lack a rich historical texture within which to view wars when compared to the British and the French – consider the three bloody battles of Agincourt, Waterloo and the somme over 700 years (Keegan 2004). Americans have few grounding points for comparing and contrasting the complexities of a given distant war, and have not witnessed war waged close at hand, with its cries of terror, blood, rotting corpses, and smoke rising from still twitching dead bodies (Bowden 2000). Their dead are not shown on Fox News. They are returned in anonymous black plastic body-bags without media coverage and honoured in a thousand local funerals. Television's heavily edited and focused positive views of the 1991 Gulf War and the invasion and occupation of Iraq in 2003–4, unlike pictures of the Vietnam conflict, were mollifying rather than disturbing (Kellner 1990; 1992). The revolutionary aftermath of the March 2003 drive to Baghdad, a revolutionary conflict, resides as a mere footnote.

It is not surprising, given this inexperience, distance, and naïve and disingenuous view of war and its consequences, as well as Bush-fuelled chauvinism, that efforts to the present (January 2005) of the United States to combat terrorism are not based on systematic inquiry or previous antiterrorist efforts by its police forces; nor have they produced visible results in court or in world opinion.

Responses to terrorism at the local level

Consider some of the visible developments in North America, matters shaping local policing and security post-9/11, and their connection to what are considered known risks. Recall that organizational responses to these rare events are not those for which routines are available and known.

These developments include the positioning of troops, police and US marshals in, and at access points to airports and dispatching air marshals in civilian dress on flights; requiring airlines to install locked cabin doors and enhanced security in the pilots' cabins, as well as permitting pilots to carry arms; creation of the Transport Security Agency (TSA) with a half-life of two years, which hired over 6,000 people; and reorganization of border maintenance under the newly established Department of Homeland Security as well as information gathering and distribution. Finally, federal agencies were given new directions, funding and personnel.[13]

Most dramatic, perhaps, was the augmentation of visual electronic modes of surveillance at local points of entry and movement. In addition, a number of measures were implemented, including:

- Adding video surveillance to harbours and financial districts of cities. Boston, for example, has installed 128 cameras in the financial district, covering around 80 per cent of the area's buildings. O'Donnell (2003: 62) estimated there were 396 cameras per square mile in Manhattan, but also reported 25 million video cameras and 30 million cell phones, able to film, record and send images anywhere in the world. The Massachusetts Bay Transport Authority (MBTA) has cameras monitoring all of its platforms and stations 24/7.
- Increasing the number and range of means for systematically watching and recording the movements of people, especially travellers and their baggage. These include virtual (by a number of electronic means including magnetometer, video surveillance, computerized record checks of passports) as well as actual screening, and wand-based searches of passengers prior to boarding aircraft. These means, including the requirement that all baggage be screened, are complemented and accompanied by the usual profiling of passengers by Border Patrol and Customs and Immigration personnel at international points of entry.
- Installing computerized reading and storage of passports and travellers' data, and fingerprinting and photographing all foreign visitors (with or without visas).
- Using random searches to broaden coverage of the passengers who are least likely to arouse suspicion, who might in theory be used as dupes or covers for terrorism.

---

[13] Federal agencies, in addition to the Homeland Security Office itself, were augmented in budget and personnel. The budget allocations of the Drug Enforcement Administration (DEA) and the FBI provided more agents and additional money and foreign stations (DEA 2002). In a related idea, narcotics and terrorism were connected with a neologism, 'narco-terrorism' (DEA 2002).

- Considering the introduction of elaborate smart cards for individual travellers and electronic equipment that would identify people by their unique aspects – voice, pupil refraction, hand- and fingerprints etc.[14]
- Developing integrated data-bases from INS (Immigration and Naturalization Service), FEMA (Federal Emergency Management Agency), and local police, and developing and putting in place in public agencies detailed floor plans for major targets and schools, lists of buildings by location with explosives and firearms, staging areas for assembling police and troops in the event of an attack, and modes of controlling traffic access and egress to and from potential targets (interview with head of R&D, Boston Police, 2004). These maps and plans were not compatible before 9/11, but have been shaped by the Office of Homeland Security.

All of these political moves dramatized terrorism as it is known as a new form of contingency and negative risk, emphasizing technological innovations with little respect for the training, quality of experience, education or skill of the screeners and responders. Furthermore, at this point, it would appear that inter-agency conflicts, inefficient technology, lack of intelligence and analytical capacity makes these moves ritualistic and symbolic rather than instrumental and preventative. That is not to say that they are ineffective, as they alter everyday experiences. These primarily technological innovations are primitive adaptations to the last known successful terrorist acts. They are tangentially based on anticipating new forms of attack on new targets, involve little intelligence-gathering, and are focused on the here and now of travellers' movements.

Social control on the ground

Security as a collective public matter has traditionally been assumed to be the responsibility of local police in North America, and this assumption in part is rooted in a colonial and revolutionary past and an acute sensitivity to individual rights. Control of domestic terrorism is high policing. It requires a shift in emphasis from reactive, case-oriented work to a preventative focus involving the use of secret agents, *agents provocateurs*,

---

[14] The *Boston Globe* reports intra-agency conflict on the development of a universal fingerprint data-base (Anderson 2004). The conflict resides in practices: Homeland Security and the Department of State urge a two-fingerprint approach, and the Department of Justice urges the ten-fingerprint approach. The taking of ten fingerprints adds some one minute to processing time and would add to the workload of processing '7 million visa applications annually' (Anderson 2004). The FBI has more than 47 million fingerprint records. It is reported that only an estimated 1 per cent of the 118,000 daily US visitors are actually run through FBI files.

human intelligence and undercover and double agents as well as surveillance, monitoring and assessment. It rests on intelligence, facts known in advance, not known delicts. Yet the idea of such a risk had not, until 9/11, altered the concerns of local police. Their preparation lay in the form of responses to disasters, hurricanes, large ongoing fires, spills of hazardous materials and major accidents in the air or on the ground. For these, there are plans in place, federal agencies such as FEMA to supervise and a clear notion of the aims of the action – to reduce damage to property and people and to restore order.[15] Let us move from the question of national mobilization against terrorism to that of local co-ordination of policing.

Two cases

The problems of combating terrorism at the local level are revealed in the policing of two major events in the United States: the Winter Olympics in February 2002 in the Salt Lake City county area (SLCO), and the Democratic National Convention (DNC) in July 2004 in Boston. In this section, I first outline the similarities of the two events, then the differences, and finally draw some analytic inferences.

Similarities

There are a number of characteristics which are shared by the two (I spare the reader repetition of 'in both cases' – an implicit prefix). At the heart of the governance of security was the anticipated co-operation of networked agencies drawing on both regional and federal components. Both events were characterized by detailed long-range planning by a wide variety of public and private groups over periods ranging from eighteen months to seven years. The entire apparatus was designed to function for a designated short time under intense public and media scrutiny, under pressure to do well given the terrorist threat, and as part of a semi-visible network of social control. The higher levels of decision and management remain invisible, with the exception of the book by the head of the Salt Lake City Winter Games, Mitt Romney (2004). The military, the Air Force, the Army and the Coastguard, were present, but kept out of sight. It was a special sort of ensemble, a temporary network designed to function actively for a brief period of time and then decompose into constituent

---

[15] The World Trade Center scene, as richly described by the Commissioner of the NYPD at the time, Bernard Kerik (2002), is indicative of the chaos produced by such a disaster and of the inefficacy of the response to it. The importance of the WTC scenario, as frightening and appalling as it is from a human point of view, is as a microcosm of North American modes of response to disasters when local state and county, provincial and/or national forces are mobilized.

parts, some local organizations with continuing obligations remaining and others leaving the area permanently to return to their regular assignments. Further, the diversity of interests including the pay, overtime, uniforms and perks of volunteers, fire and emergency personnel, and state and local police had to be negotiated (Flynn 2004). Because both events were underwritten by both public and private sources – state, county and city governments, private corporations, and *ad hoc* co-ordinating agencies such as the Democratic National Committee and the Salt Lake City Olympic Committee (SLOC) – there were continuing market pressures to use money well, not to exceed budgets, to write off debts and to make a profit (Romney 2004).[16] Lurking behind these aims was the fear of a disastrous incident. From the outset, questions of budget overruns, abuse of overtime (for police in Boston, Salt Lake City and surrounding cities) and fears about unexpected demands on assets, resources and turnover in personnel were paramount. The tasks of co-ordination, transportation, feeding and housing of federal, state, local and volunteer workers, as well as the delegates to the convention and the athletes competing in the Olympics, were continuing and demanding.

Although nominally held in one city, the events encompassed multiple sites. The multiple sites were both symbolic and instrumental, i.e. in Boston, Boston Common, City Hall, and the state Capitol building, as well as nearby historical sites (Lexington and Concord where the American Revolution began), and in Salt Lake City, the Mormon Tabernacle, the state Capitol building and City Hall. While access to and egress from the areas surrounding the symbolic centres (the venues and the Convention Center in Boston) was impossible to control (they were part of the attractions of the city that made its bid a success), at both sites efforts were made to control entry to the symbolic centres themselves. A *cordon sanitaire* was maintained by plain-clothes police, civilian monitors, magnetometers, patrolling uniformed officers, walls, temporary fences and concrete bulwarks. Movement across the boundaries was filtered by credential checks. Furthermore, huge numbers of volunteers, servers and maintenance people, as well as the public, moved in and out of the site(s) and the cities in the course of the day. Parking, traffic and foot travel

---

[16] Romney (2004) undertook an organizational audit immediately upon discovering an almost $300 million debt when he took over leadership of SLOC. The arrangements for funding the Olympics are Byzantine and include corporate sponsorships (divided between protected and privileged corporations and others), outright gifts, governmental (state and local) funding, individual sponsors and donors, a division of profits with the international and national Olympic committees, speculative finance in the form of potential ticket sales, and contingency funding for such matters as overtime, emergency maintenance, policing the use of the Olympic logos, buses and transport for members of the International Olympic Committee.

required a large number of people to 'police' the streets, doors and access points. These were controlled at both the DNC and the Salt Lake City Olympics by close security checks of documents on the participants, and bag and electronic body searches for weapons on audiences and others. In effect, the security network spanned several locales from the symbolic centres to the periphery (in the SLCO, this was some thirty-five miles away). Officers of many agencies, dressed in bright identifiable uniforms, had dubious or unclear legitimate authority. While command centres existed, several in Salt Lake City and one in Boston, the co-ordination of multiple agencies across space and time was demanding and complex. In fact, the events were held both inside and outside with various degrees and kinds of access and control points. In both cases the area was inter-sected by two major north–south six-lane Interstate highways, and several major east–west routes. Diverse agencies were assigned different responsi-bilities e.g. SWAT (Special Weapons and Tactics) teams from LAPD (Los Angeles Police Department), traffic to the state police, internal control of the venues by the federal secret service and other federal agents.

The visual capacity for surveillance was massive: from the highways and roads, from the venues where the events were staged (via fixed cameras and helicopters with direct feeds), from patrols (on foot and on skis in Park City, Utah) and from observers outside and on the periphery of the venues and the Convention Center. The visuals were to be fed into each of the main command centers, but the helicopter-based feeds never worked in Salt Lake.

The federal presence was strong in each case, although, as discussed below, the secret service had ongoing duties with the candidates at the DNC, and only an evening to guard President Bush. In each case the federal agents, especially the Treasury agents (secret service and others) and the FBI, were seen to be in charge owing to their traditional respect and resources. Nothing happened in Boston or in the Salt Lake region, so the direct power and authority of the 'feds' was not tested. An effort was made to keep the federal armed military presence out of sight, con-cealed in former army barracks and other nearby facilities, well out of public view. The exception to this was the armed National Guard troops positioned outside the athletes' accommodation in the centre of Salt Lake City.

There was believed to be a risk of damage to trucks carrying haz-ardous materials and of some sort of attack with biological or biochemical weapons, and medical facilities (cots, blankets and temporary field hospi-tals) were available near the main sites. The communications channels in and out of the main centres were many and included cell phones, land-line phones and computers (via the Internet and e-mail connections), television cameras (fixed and moving), mobile digital terminals (MDTs) in county, state and city units and Nextel direct-connect phones in the command centres. In both cases, an inter-agency software network was created to communicate issues and concerns. This could be accessed by anyone in the command centers or units. It was not on-line. The incidents were not screened at any point unless someone chose to investigate a matter or if it was also noted in a call to one of the local command centres or police departments. The software network was largely ignored in both sites.

The driving notions here were long-term planning, rehearsals of responses to key events and a layered, ratcheted pattern of response and augmentation of resources. Personnel found boredom a more significant issue than action and response to an untoward incident. The working rule was to rely first on local, city and county assets before the federal assets were called in, but it was clear that the federal agents would seize control of any incident that they felt had imminent potential to escalate into a serious threat. Co-ordination tended to be tacit rather than being based on a written 'battle plan' although written plans existed; 'after action' meetings were held, and reports were filed. There was a semi-visible hierarchy of control rather than a strict hierarchy, but this was more complex in action in Salt Lake City. Inevitably, because of the ecology of both events, the distribution of the key players, athletes and politicians, there was much confusion, redundancy and anxiety in the air. The most troubling aspect organizationally was the anticipated floating debt incurred by the local agencies such as the Boston Police Department (BPD) and the several county police agencies (in the two-week period of the Games, the Salt Lake City police exceeded their budget by $500,000). Secondary to that was the potential conflict between the public appearance of a celebratory political convention and a sporting spectacle and the need for security and control, including violent coercive intervention. In many respects, *ad hoc* arrangements, individual leadership and willingness to adapt to conditions were seen in several venues at the Olympics and in co-operation among local police agencies in Boston.[17] Finally, the tension between and among local agencies and with the federal officers was a constant theme.

---

[17] For example, in one of the distant ski venues the local forest rangers, employees of the Department of Interior, took leadership because the region was policed by a small country force, the federal agents refused to appear and remain on duty, and the isolation of the area meant few police had knowledge of the mountainous terrain. In Boston, regional agreements between the state police organizations facilitated memorandums of understanding (MOU) and tacit agreements. The Boston police later protested that overtime due to them was being given to out-of-state officers.

Differences

The DNC, the Commonwealth and the City of Boston   It is useful to consider the local policing and formal social control in the Commonwealth of Massachusetts in 2003–4.[18] This is part of the first and third themes. It is a fiercely colonial, local, parochial and fragmented state whose politics remain rooted in these characteristics. The tradition of local government is glamourized and large-scale co-ordination is avoided. In the Commonwealth of Massachusetts, there are fourteen counties each with a politically weak county sheriff who does little but transport prisoners and keep a jail. There are some 351 towns and cities, each with a police and fire agency. There are two formal groups of chiefs, the Western Massachusetts Chiefs and the Massachusetts Chiefs, both with websites, and an informal group of chiefs representing the ten or so largest cities in the Commonwealth. The chiefs, given their locations, are organized around small-town politics and issues. The nature of Boston, its size, its position as the state capital and its national stature, makes the concerns and security obligations of the city's police fundamentally of a different order and more aligned with those of the larger cities than those of the formal associations of chiefs. Outside Boston, the police and fire chiefs are part of the local political scene, and lack the power that county sheriffs have in the Midwest or elsewhere where they are elected officials with a large payroll and a jail to staff and operate. Officers in local city police departments in Massachusetts have no statewide arrest powers; they cannot easily share personnel, for the visitors must shadow a local officer and observe obsequious manners and deference to the local officers and chief. The state police, called 'troopers', dressed often in wide-brimmed Stetson hats and high boots, and quite visible at main roads and airports in the Commonwealth, patrol the highways and investigate serious crimes outside the larger cities. Police agencies communicate largely in person or by phone or fax with other departments. Smaller departments still use teletypes. They have few scientific capacities (labs, crime analysis, etc.) and rely on the state or Boston police for forensics, ballistics and scientific

---

[18] I draw on background gathered at round-table meetings with groups of Massachusetts chiefs who met at Northeastern University, Boston, in August 2003 (I attended as an observer), and at the panel discussion on 30 September 2004 at Northeastern University involving Boston's Commissioner of Police Kathleen O'Toole, State Police Colonel Tom Robbins, Secretary of Public Safety in Massachusetts Ed Flynn, and US Attorney Michael Sullivan. Additional materials came from my interviews with Amy Farrell and Jack McDevitt who carried out systematic observations on the streets at the DNC, in the command centre and in the Fleet Convention Center (McDevitt and Farrell 2004).

support for evidence analysis. They variously relate to the local schools, fire chiefs, emergency medical people and state agencies in their local communities. They do not share data-bases, information, problems or personnel except in the rare case of a school-based officer.[19] Their radio frequencies do not permit cross-town or regional communications and their radios are on different frequencies to those of the federal governmental agencies. Often, even within a town or in a large city such as Boston, there are several channels that can be used to communicate so that missed messages and confusion result. Small cities that abut each other cannot communicate by radio even in emergency situations. Police have little or no communication with private security organizations, nor do they share radio or other communications facilities. They have local plans for evaluation and handling of hazardous materials. Every incident is newly negotiated, for example between the fire department and the police at disasters or large accidents where criminal charges may be involved. In large-scale disasters negotiation takes place that is largely based on personalities, the hierarchy of status among law enforcement agencies and local traditions of deference. Relationships between schools, fire departments and emergency services are *ad hoc*, negotiated from incident to incident and not guided by any formal legal hierarchy. Federal agencies have only periodic case-based operations in Massachusetts cities, and the US Attorney's Office has a presence only in Boston and in the western part of the Commonwealth.

Boston is the dominant city in New England and in the Commonwealth. It sits on a peninsula of land that has been extended into Boston Harbour and is intersected by several rivers. It has no townships; county sheriffs are weak, while the state police and the Boston Police Department are quite powerful political forces. Boston is one of the oldest cities in America, and arguably has one of the oldest police departments in the country. It is a centre of federal, regional and state agencies. The city has a population of 589,141 (1990) and covers 378.9 square miles. The police wear a shoulder patch dating to the beginning of the city in 1630, and the same patch is displayed on the seal above the door to Police Headquarters. The city is adjacent to a harbour at the mouth of the Charles River; it is surrounded by islands and, to the south, by the Cape, and, to the north, by Cambridge and other old affluent suburbs such as Brookline, Newton, Lexington and Concord. The city has a long and complicated

---

[19] Consistent with local traditions, local school officers have to build a role and a network of colleagues inside and outside the schools and the content of these roles differs widely (McDevitt 2001).

history that conjoins its early role as the centre of the Revolution with its later role as a cultural and educational centre. It has had one consistent theme over the last century – it is an immigrant city, some 30 per cent of the city being recent immigrants, about the same as after World War I. In some ways, race is an 'unmentionable' in the city; it is the axis of crime, of law enforcement and of the conflicts within the city between rising and falling social groups but the city defines itself as democratic, civilized and non-racist.

The city is governed by a historically strong Democratic machine, based on deep roots in the Italian and Irish section of the city and the highly educated population of the city itself. The links between City Hall and the Police Department are historic, powerful and continuing. The Mayor unofficially approves all hires, firings, promotions and appointments to top command, although this previously was official. The Mayor still appoints the Police Commissioner, who serves at his pleasure. Boston is also a strong union city, and this influence is felt on the Police Department.[20]

Boston is a crowded urban area bordered by the sea and river on one side and has very high housing prices as there is very little expansion to the suburbs. Boston is a historic city with some very narrow streets and areas which have been preserved. This is important for the very rich visual texture of the city and its moral topography, but for policing it is a reality – time and space cannot be collapsed and it is impossible to skirt above or around the city easily on freeways, even north to south. Response time means little in general in this city, although responsiveness to all calls for service is a policy of the Department.

The police in the region planned for about eighteen months to contain the threats to the DNC from demonstrators, terrorists and imagined dangers. A command centre was established under the control of the Boston Commissioner and staffed by the Boston Police Department (BPD). An electronic bulletin board (WEBEOC) was established to permit input of information by agencies involved in the event (small cities outside Boston were neither included in this network nor in planning and operations). Facilities for jailing and holding prisoners were made available at the Suffolk County Jail in Boston near the Convention Center, and a huge razor-wired enclosure built near the Center for temporary holding of those retained. There was one acknowledged centre of attention, the Convention Center, but many party and gathering venues at hotels, the

---

[20] The Boston Police Department is old-fashioned, with its strong influences from unions, ethnic groups (especially Irish and Italian), the party politics of the Democratic Party, and the state Civil Service Commission which reviews firings.

harbour, and in high-status residential areas such as Beacon Hill. Security was provided at the delegates' hotels. Aside from the candidates, delegates travelling by vans, buses and cabs were not accompanied by secret service agents. Major demonstrations were anticipated, but did not occur. Arrests of between 1,500 and 2,000 people were anticipated and the county jail made ready, but only six arrests around the Center were made and just four of those were DNC-related. The precise role of the Department of Homeland Security was unclear, although Mr Ridge, the Secretary, visited the site and praised the close co-operative arrangements among the many agencies; his office also supplied a considerable part of the funding for the DNC. A traffic plan was conceived and executed to close off, for periods during the Convention (four nights), the two Interstate highways, the tramlines across the Charles River and the tunnels under the river that virtually adjoin and run under the Fleet Center. The centre of Boston, the North End and the financial district were virtually deserted during the Convention, and businesses complained of lack of business. The huge Boston commuting population and that of the region was essentially staved off and the city was surprisingly quiet. On the other hand, the nearby coastal vacation area was packed with people avoiding and/or having left Boston.

Personnel involved included the Boston police and their specialized units such as harbour, special operations and mounted police, riot police (concealed nearby but not visible to the conventioneers) and undercover officers; officers from nearby cities and states; federal agents; the state police (1,700 were assigned of the total of 2,300 troopers), whose duties were primarily traffic control. The full Boston force, as well as officers from twenty other federal and state agencies, was in theory available. Training was to include 'suspicious package detection, bomb threats, hazardous materials response and evacuation procedures' (Smith 2004). According to Ed Flynn, Secretary of Public Safety of the Commonwealth, the budget for the security of the Convention was approximately $1 billion (it was first reported that $25 million was to be supplied by the federal government (Smith 2004)). Ironically, according to the *Boston Globe* (Slack 2004), although the overtime for police (not all of whom were Boston officers) was estimated as at least $6.6 million, a profit of over $8 million accrued to the city of Boston after this and other costs were recovered (Ebert 2005).

The strategy of control had four components, according to Commissioner O'Toole (personal communication, 30 September 2004). The first was advanced planning over eighteen months, with a captain fully detailed to this duty. The second was to emphasize intelligence (undercover officers posed as 'anarchists') and advance knowledge of risks. The third was to 'change the paradigm' of policing public order.[21] This entailed, according to the Commissioner, positioning uniformed officers on the site and around the Center in normal uniforms, soft hats and with the usual equipment, on foot and on mountain bikes. A second level of mobile field forces and federal assets were both held in reserve and out of sight but were dressed and ready if and when called. The experiences in Northern Ireland were used as a model (the Commissioner served on the (Patten) Commission on Policing in Northern Ireland) and she argued that 'if you are dressed for battle, you will do battle'. Finally, she argued that the fourth component was co-operation between federal and local forces and within local forces. O''Toole did not explain why or how, although a written agreement for co-operation between regional state police agencies, NESPAC, was signed in the 1970s. She also noted that command officers from the various forces (the large local and state forces) learned from the Super Bowl Model of gathering top command in a single command post.

Some examples of tension in practice are revealing.

• The area surrounding the Convention Center was secure but the airways, the sea and the waterways, in addition to the underground areas adjoining the Center, were not secure. The area under City Hall is honeycombed with tunnels and station routes left over from the razing, closing and sealing of the former Sculley Square.[22] This is also true of the area under the Fleet Center which is built on an elevated position adjoining a circle of rotaries, bridge approaches, and an Interstate highway. Although patrols were assigned to the harbour it is not difficult to imagine access via a boat to the area.

• The traffic plans, the communication system and the command centre were not co-ordinated with the surrounding communities. This was particularly awkward when the closure of the I-93 diverted commuters onto the ring road around Boston and other local roads leading into and, particularly, out of Boston.

• The symbolic and actual dominance of the Boston police in the area, respect given informally and past agreements meant that overt rank status and control were roughly equated in everyday activity. If, however,

---

[21] This proved a fateful remark. After Boston won the American League baseball title, fans rioted and one woman was shot and killed by police using a 'non-lethal' pepper ballistic. Three others were shot in the face in rioting involving some 8,000 people near Fenway Park. After the World Series victory (in baseball) riot police were trained and deployed, the areas around the stadium closed off and pepper spray rather than ballistic pepper balls was used to subdue demonstrators. Eighteen arrests were made that night (27 October 2004).
[22] Interview with former member of the BPD administrative staff, 26 October 2004.

a question required immediate action by an officer, his or her rank and command status would be problematic.

- The Secret Service controlled the symbolic venues and Boston police provided backup, but the federal agents had control of the order of the use of assets, not the BPD.
- A last-minute strike by Boston police officers who had been working without a contract was avoided in late July 2004 through concerted efforts by the Governor, the Mayor, negotiators for the unions and the city and, in the end, arbitrators. The police picketed pre-Convention events, held street demonstrations in Back Bay and, just before the Convention, forced Mr Kerry, the Democratic nominee and Boston resident, to declare that he would not cross the picket lines to give a planned speech. The potential chaos generated by such decisions was avoided but was always lurking in a strongly Democratic city with (still) strong municipal unions.
- US attorneys in the Civil Division were denied access to security-related documents as they lacked high (enough) security clearance (Sullivan personal communication, 30 September 2004).
- When protesters appeared at the rear entrance to the Fleet Center it was closed and one of the few incidents of the Convention occurred when two people tried to cut through a fence. Secret Service agents closed off the entrance magnetometer and Boston police took over.

The Salt Lake City Olympics   The Salt Lake City area is orga-nized into counties, cities and unincorporated areas. While similar to other national media events with worldwide implications, the Salt Lake City event was unique in that it was the first to be declared a National Security Event (Decker et al. 2002); it had extraordinary federal involve-ment because of the recent 9/11 terrorist attacks (the Games took place in February 2002); it required regional co-ordination and action late in the day when the entire planning committee was found to be corrupt and was replaced by Mitt Romney, now governor of Massachusetts. It was the largest co-ordinated domestic security event in US history (Decker et al. 2002: 3). Even more than the Boston assemblage, this was a regional effort, stretching up and down the Wasatch Valley to the adjoining sites of Logan, Park City and West Valley, with sixteen venues for competitions, three city police departments, three county departments, the state police and federal agents. It has been estimated that some 12,000 officers and agents were mobilized in the course of the two-week event. Located in the Wasatch Valley in north-central Utah, Salt Lake City has a population of 184,723. Because of the mountainous nature of the terrain surrounding Davis, Salt Lake and Weber counties the region is geographically isolated from other population centers (Decker et al. 2002: 14). Decker et al. state that:

> The security planning for the Utah Games spanned seven years . . . In addition, more than $310 million was spent on security for the games. Fully 88% of the dollars spent on security ($273 million) were direct federal expenditures, and the federal government provided an additional $15 million of the balance to UOPSC [Utah Olympic Public Safety Command]. Personnel comprised the single largest category of expenses (57%) with Housing (17%) the next single largest category. Interestingly, training comprised only one percent of total expenditures. In total, nearly twelve thousand individuals worked in security for the games (11,848). Of this total, 6,553 were sworn police officers, including 2,225 Utah state and local sworn officers and 2,100 federal sworn officers. The military contributed 3,500 individuals to the security effort, with 695 Law Enforcement Volunteers (LeVols), and 1,100 Fire and Emergency Management Services personnel. (2002: 13–14)

Within the Valley, the various law enforcement agencies had overlapping jurisdictions, territorial and political interests. This was further complicated by the involvement of the federal government's agents and soldiers, the local emergency response capacity, and the fire brigades or units. Private security had no role in the planning or actual policing of the Games. A list of some 200 private police agencies was assembled but these were not contacted in the course of events. Decker et al. summarize the organizational structure that emerged for this temporary network of control:

> One of the important issues to occur in the evolution of safety and security for the Salt Lake City Olympic Games was the passage of legislation in the Utah State Legislature. The Utah Olympic Public Safety Command (UOPSC) was created in 1998 under bill UCA 53–12. UOPSC was given responsibility for both the planning and operational phases of law enforcement and public safety for the 2002 Winter Olympic Games. UOPSC was made part of the State of Utah, Department of Public Safety, and was chaired by the Commissioner of Public Safety for the State of Utah. There were twenty named members of the committee including local, state and federal law enforcement, EMS, fire, emergency management, public works, public health and the National Guard. (2002: 15–16)

In addition to the UOPSC, which was a law enforcement network, the entire financial control was in the hands of the Salt Lake Olympic Committee headed by Mr Romney. Shared technology and communication platforms included an online bulletin board for entering incidents and a system for feeding images from fixed cameras and helicopters. The network had the following components.
- A hub created in the Salt Lake Police Department called the Olympic Coordination Center (OCC) in the Salt Lake City Police building. This contained forty TV screens with police and city attorneys present.

- In an adjoining room was the Crowd Management Center (CMC) staffed by members of the Los Angeles Police Department and shaped into teams trained in riot control, or POUs (public order units; this term replaces SWAT teams in the latest rhetoric).
- The sixteen venues in which competitions were held, protected by both local and federal officers as well as LeVols.
- The six command centres and substations as well as the police departments in which they were generally housed.
- Barracks near Salt Lake City in which the military were housed and fed.
- The various sites where the athletes were housed when not being transported to competitions or competing (they travelled in sealed buses, checked by magnetometers and visual inspections before the passengers boarded).
- Miscellaneous symbolic sites such as the Mayor's party tent, the Mormon Tabernacle, headquarters buildings, the Mormon Museum and the City County Building.

In theory, the security network was based on the idea of a cascading hierarchy controlled by the business-led coalition that brought the Olympics to Salt Lake City and the UOPSC that controlled the resources, or 'assets'. In effect, the commercial and political interests of the Salt Lake Olympic Comittee (SLOC), headed by Romney, trumped all the other interests – this was particularly true in the line of command with the SLOC on top, UOPSC as a secondary and responsive unit, and the local police and other assets, in effect, under both. The only notable incidents, covered in the Decker report (Decker et al. 2002) were matters involving commercial interests – the Mayor's beer tent, ticket scalping, and Mitt Romney's yelling at a security guard when a bus full of major sponsors was held up because they had no security clearance (Romney 2004: 364–5). While the security issues were highlighted by the media, the driving forces throughout the event-planning were accounting, money and budgets, the wind and weather (it was beautiful!) and dramatizing the 'spirit' of the Olympics.

Some examples of the tension in practice can be provided.[23]

- Communications were flawed in basic ways. The bulletin board did not serve to communicate useful information because it was not trusted,

[23] The only incident (there were several uneventful demonstrations that did not require remedial action) marking the Salt Lake City events was an ironic one in a Mormon town where drinking is closely monitored and against the principles of the religion. A protest on the last evening of the Games by patrons of the Budweiser beer tent in the centre of the Olympic area in Salt Lake City erupted. People who had left the tent sought to return and were refused, facing long lines. The LAPD-based POUs were ordered in.

was not on-line and not fact-checked to establish the veracity of the information. Instead, informal associations developed in and around the command centres and the venues that were channels of information from the centre to the periphery and back. The telephones provided by Nextel did not work in the mountainous Northern Utah ACC (Area Command Center); the federal phones were on 800 megahertz and the local officers' on the lower local frequency; personal cell phones were most often used but, of course, were not secure. The satellite phone system trucked in by the federal government was not used but would only have served the federal agents in any case. The local and the ACC systems were not linked, so that operators in each ACC had to communicate calls relevant to the Olympics to another computer for forwarding to the bulletin board data-base. The networking of phones that was supposed to use backtracking of emergency calls in the Summit County ACC never worked (this was software that would have notified everyone in the area in the case of an emergency).

- The planning orientations of the various organizations involved were fundamentally different. Fire brigade officials have national standards for approaches to disasters of various types and origins, are trained for these and have an emergency approach of gradual increases in the use of assets until control is obtained, with the originator of the response in command. Police are reactive, have limited intelligence capacity and eschew long-term planning. This was dramatized by the elaborate emergency planning of the West Valley ACC, headed by the fire chief, which contrasted with the rather loosely organized plans at other venues, their absence (Summit County ACC had none) and the quasi-independent status of the POUs.

- In the flow of events, negotiations ensued which revealed the power of the federal government to finesse or co-opt virtually any duties other than the day-to-day co-ordination of the ACCs. On the other hand, should a major incident have taken place, informants told us, the FBI would doubtless have taken command with their satellite system and federal lines of communication that would literally and metaphorically have gone over the heads of the local police, fire and political organizations.

- There was a constant tension between the SLPD, which wanted to control all the venues in the city and manage the POUs, and the Mayor's Office, which wanted control over the Mayor's party venue. Both of these were in tension with the wishes of the SLOC to maintain the appearance of a happy, amused crowd of international tourists that were patronizing official events and locations (the Mayor's beer tent was not an official Olympic location).

Some inferences

It is clear on the basis of these case studies that quite different uncertainties lie at the heart of the several organizations involved in the governance of security at these two events. Firstly, whilst the police are primarily reactive, as are the fire departments, they operate with quite different long-term planning approaches which are quite different from those of the federal agencies. The focus on cases, crimes, arrests and the criminal sanction mitigates against intelligence-based future-oriented work. The planning, training and skills of local police are attuned to respond to relatively rare events that appear routinely. They hold back resources for the imagined contingency. The essential practices that define the job are reactive to emergent events rather than preventive, anticipatory or intelligence-based activities.

Secondly, it is difficult to assess the actual capacity for co-ordination between the organizations involved in this type of operation. The training, planning and skills needed for the Salt Lake City Olympic Games required advance planning of the allocation of assets, personnel, and equipment as well as everyday comforts such as food, toilets and shelter. Negotiation and planning took seven-plus years in the case of the Olympic Games and eighteen months in the case of the DNC. To facilitate co-operation a number of *ad hoc* MOUs (memoranda of understanding) were drawn up in advance concerning funding of overtime, costumes and equipment to be used, practical matters of food, toilets and shelter, and the long- and short-term division of labour among local agencies and between local agencies and federal agents.

Thirdly, the idea that a network of social control, a patchwork quilt sustained by mutual regulatory concerns, is functioning to govern security is present here. Nothing sufficiently tested the sketch of responsibilities that was the plan. The idea of a coherent field or network of security is not helpful in understanding inter-organizational relationships at the Olympic Games. While the federal and local police and the National Guard undertook a single operation, private security had no role in providing security at the Games. Indeed, private security was not consulted nor brought into the work at hand at either event.

While networked information systems are growing and linked databases more likely to emerge as a result of the 9/11 disaster, my observations suggest that the complexity of information technology in policing has not been met by an increased capacity of the police and other agencies to use such devices to their own benefit (Abt Associates 2000; Dunworth 2000; Manning 2003). It is known that data-bases do not connect, federal data is not shared with local agencies and local police equipment has insufficient memory capacity to download big data-sets and does not have the memory capacity to store large data-bases. Many have antiquated software or hardware. Technically skilled people – computer engineers, repair people and crime analysts – are lured away by private business and the turnover is high in research and development departments. The frequent generational changes mean that new software must be updated periodically and city budgets are not designed to accommodate growing maintenance costs or retraining. Furthermore, the web of control across policing organizations is weak because databases are not wedded or linked; the software is incompatible; the management information system is a hodgepodge of *ad hoc* arrangements assembled over the last thirty years, and the introduction of new technologies such as geo-coded data, enhanced emergency and non-emergency call systems and cell phone processing has created new complexities and incomplete linkages within and across agencies. Police in urban areas have to switch channels to communicate with nearby agencies or cannot communicate directly with adjoining agencies. Incompatibility of the electronic infrastructure is compounded by the inadequacy of the support, maintenance and updating of systems themselves. The investment in the present expensive *mélange* of systems makes full-scale revamping too expensive. Police, fire and emergency services must communicate, if at all, via standard landlines. Some services, such as ambulance emergency services, are private; others are public and co-ordinated from a central communications centre. The most common form of communication between agencies is phone calls. Local police radio channels are incompatible or on lower frequencies than the federal agencies. The current phone systems cannot bridge the 154 megahertz and 800 megahertz (now used by federal agencies and in some large cities) radio channels.

While there is a regulatory network with internal ranking based on power and authority, the orientation of local state and county police is to the here and now of routine events, reactive scanning and collation of information. Federal agents, on the whole, are more inclined to the preventive view, although this is relative, not absolute. This means that the profound and 'grounding' contingency is more distal than proximal, and the mode of risk analysis and risk management more consistent with their thinking than sanctioning an outbreak of deviance or an incident. Each defends its independence and tries to reduce contingencies in inter-organizational negotiations.

One continuing phenomenon was the power of the federal agents to reserve the right to intervene, much like the technical engineers in Crozier's study (1964). In the case of the Games, federal agents were in control of the venues, had implicit authority in other events and at times did not bother to staff positions or participate in routine policing. They had the power to define the exception, and in this sense to control the distribution of control. In many subtle and not-so-subtle respects the federal agents (primarily Secret Service but also including others employed by the Treasury, IRS agents, US Mint Police and ATF) held themselves ready, but were not concerned with local matters and local policing:

- Federal agents chose not to appear at some venues and command centres and renegotiated their involvement in one case.
- They had no direct connection to issues of budget, local politics or local post-case obligations.
- They implicitly reserved the right to define the event as an exception or not – to redefine and intervene or not as they chose.
- They chose to stay close to three of the six symbolic centres of action – the Fleet Center, the candidates and the Salt Lake City venues.
- They maintained separate communications capacity via satellites, which was not shared with the other agencies present. In Salt Lake, they used phones provided by the Department of Defense which failed to work well in cold weather and in mountainous regions.
- They used a vast array of acronyms unfamiliar to local officers. This mystified their communication and created social distance between agencies.
- They did not wear visible uniforms or jackets, nor did they act as undercover agents *per se*. The most visible jackets were worn by volunteers (in yellow) and city police and firefighters who wore the official Olympic jacket.
- They held traditional latent respect from local police and politicians, and were assumed soon to be in charge in any major incident other than a mere street disorder.

In effect, the federal agents revealed their power to hold back or act – each of which serves to soak up ambiguity, or, as Crozier (1964) notes, reduces uncertainty. They fill in when needed, arrogate spaces and obligations, refuse other responsibilities and use their superior resources and flexibility (as well as not having a local audience and local funding). This was true even though many of the federal agents, e.g. those from the US Mint Police or Treasury, had no personal experience in actual security policing. They could reduce uncertainty by acting, shoring up a situation or providing unanticipated resources ('assets' in federal parlance). Furthermore, of course, the FBI maintained its position at the top of the hierarchy by sustaining uncertainty in its relations with other federal agents and agencies.

In summary thus far, recall that agencies see what they are designed to see, and what past practices have revealed to them are dangers and potential dangers. The definition of terrorism was local and included the consequences of the act – HAZMAT, biological attack, assassinations etc. – rather than intelligence, counter-intelligence or general monitoring (Decker et al. 2002). The objects of concern, what is seen, are sustained by the practices that have developed over time to detect them. For example, because random patrol is the assumed strategy of the police, they continued to do this around both cities in spite of the fact that calls for service were virtually non-existent (according to data we gathered in Salt Lake City and reports from the BPD). The training was reactive in every respect rather than intelligence-based or proactive. Moreover, the planning was shaped by practices and anticipation of the strengths of the agency in a crisis. The participating agencies in the two cases imagined the risks that they were to prevent and control quite differently. Reactive policing, the work of local county and state police, requires no theory of crime causation, threat or latent risk; what is needed is the ability to respond flexibly to a known incident with potential to worsen. Reactive policing rests on local territorial knowledge, a matter only imagined when a temporary organization is assembled. Federal policing was focused on the security of a few selected targets and persons and the agents' training alerted them to the role of intelligence. The logic of the event, in these schemata, determines the cascading of resources. None of this planning orientation is true for local agencies. Finally, the assumption of the paramilitary units was that they would act in a paramilitary fashion if ordered. In any event, given the skill of these highly trained riot police, rank and control would have been problematic given the mix of ranks and uniforms based on agencies and volunteers. There would have been no joint paramilitary action possible except from the planned, co-ordinated POUs, or the military if called. The scope of imagined events was that of those events to which the groups had in the past successfully reacted and controlled.

Conclusion

The chapter began with an overview of the relationships between contingencies, negative risks, organizational structure and practice. The *reflexive interdependence* of these matters is difficult to disentangle from the network of control agencies itself. The evidence of organizational research is that organizations refine and process the environment in a stylized fashion, almost using a tacit code. Facts are processed – extracted, edited, abstracted, chunked into useful bits, partial and stylistic, and recycled through the organization (Carruthers and Espeland 1991: 57–8) as evidence of the relevance of just those identified risks. In many ways, it is a recursive and tautological cycle.

In the two cases studied, the vision of control promoted publicly was that 'security' was to be provided but that the event was an international sporting event, an exercise in democracy and a celebration. Security was defined by the practices in which the officers engaged. State police patrolled and directed traffic; city police maintained the command centre (adjoined to their emergency call centre); county police patrolled the venues; fire personnel waited for fires or disasters, as did emergency personnel; the military stayed out of sight, patiently. Those who staffed the command centres watched traffic on large screens, movies or sports on TV, and gazed idly at the computer screens in front of them and gossiped among themselves. The LA-based public order units sat in a room and wrote possible incidents on the whiteboard as they heard of them until the last night when they were launched to control, with great panache, the beer riot. 'Security' remained defined situationally and contextually and this in turn was negotiated amongst the key groups. For some organizations in the network the concern was a profitable business enterprise that broached no interference from police; for some (those involved in UOPSC) it was a political opportunity to become a visible police executive; for other groups, it was providing hands-on security for the athletes, controlling access to venues and protecting the audience, while still other groups, such as the Mormon Church, wanted to keep a low profile on security matters but supplied a large number of officers from its private security organization (Romney 2004). No denotative or precise definition was used or was necessary. 'Order' and 'ordering' are open-ended political terms made more elastic by new threats and risks such as terrorism.

The first theme, differential perspectives on contingencies, is certainly revealed here in the two cases. The several agencies had quite different readings of what their 'risk concern' might be. The state police in both cases assumed it was managing traffic flow and control; with the Secret Service, it was protecting the boundaries of the most important symbolic venues; with the fire service, it was anticipating fires and hazards. Local police patrolled and stood at posts around the venues. There were concerns in both cases with 'protesters', 'demonstrators', 'anarchists' and miscellaneous others, but few appeared and all were well mannered. The full attention of these agencies was not given to the advance anticipation or planning, although some was done. The planning exercises were round-table simulations based on hypothetical situations. These were not viewed as valuable by those interviewed at the SLOC. As one police officer said, 'we are not very good at planning, but we know how to handle things'. The meaning of providing security was revealed in the practices of the agents. This meant reacting to the known, visible and traceable rather than the imagined, the future or the anticipated future-appearing other. In effect, terrorism was seen as something one dealt with if it arose, appeared and made its face known. Even that of course was a matter of interpretation. One officer, exaggerating (and laughing) in the Summit County ACC, said he had just received 'the ninety-sixth bomb threat of the day'.

Another way of expressing the conservative nature of such organizations is that they focus strongly on preventing *another of the last type of terrorist attack*. Thus they focus on passengers in airports, not shipping, the seaports, nuclear reactors and drinking water and make little mention of the violent, invisible anthrax attack that occurred in the fall of 2001. It is surprise, not the repetition of the last type of attack that gives terrorism its dreaded power. Hence the problem of imagining and preparing for the next event (9/11 Commission 2004: 399–428).

The second theme, of a temporary organization in action, was highlighted by the different mobilization of networks in both cases. This had to do in large part with the addition and viability of federal assets. This was in part a product of the 9/11 attacks, but also of the earlier tragedy at the Munich Olympics in 1972. The authority, in the event, arose directly from the 'reading of the code', making sense of what the traces mean, point to or indicate. Since there were no known features of 'terrorists' or terrorist groups active in either case, no intelligence was referred to. Threats, such as bomb threats during the events, were reported and investigated. One plastic carrier bag containing coated baby nappies was disposed of by explosive experts in Park City.

What of the networks of interactive dependencies? Power was latent in the networks. In effect, as argued above, the federal agents, many of whom had no competence in policing events, had the capacity to redefine an event ('up' as more dangerous, or 'down' as less dangerous, than it first appeared); to enter any venue, since they had sanctioned credentials (very few did work across the venues); vast resources including the military as assets; and the capacity to define an exception to the working rules that had been adopted at the sites (largely by face-to-face and informal communication on site). There were significant differences in bases in power, uncertainties and political aims, as indicated by these case materials. The cases show that whilst there was overt agreement on such matters as the safety and security of the Convention/Olympics, the underlying tensions indicated that there was a set of overlapping, anticipated and unanticipated, risks that structured the concerns of the several organizations in the network. Quite different definitions of 'security' were seen in perspectives on the events, depending on what was the reference:

- Controlling a venue, the athletes, their practices, locales or their transportation.
- Policing the event *per se* or maintaining local everyday policing of the cities and counties involved.
- Sustaining the 'atmosphere of public entertainment', ease of access and leisure or increasing control via checks, 'wanding' (running wands to detect metal over people entering the venues), magnetometers ('mags and bags') and searches.
- Symbolizing tight control or maintaining a profitable and efficient processing of fans, athletes and delegates.
- Increasing the flow of traffic around the events or reducing accidents.

There was a clear hierarchy of resort and resources, controlled by UOPSC and the Boston PD, but this was subject to redefinition by the federal presence in case of an incident. In a temporary arrangement such as these two cases represent, the configuration of interests increases the number of contingencies involved and 'on the table' rather than reduces them. Moreover, there was no systematic evidence of any kind of a terrorist threat or action in the two cases. Whether this was a deterrent effect of the well-organized assemblage, luck or a reflection of the lack of interest of terrorists in striking such events, no one knows. This collage of groups with a nominal linear command structure moved towards risk analysis rather than local knowledge and reaction. Because neither of the events saw a politically volatile incident, unlike the Atlanta Games, there was no media-based call for a public accounting of actions, planning or finances of the Boston Convention or the Salt Lake City Games. Rationality is only required if an account is demanded. The most continuing irony was that the more visible the personnel, the less their power and authority.

It would appear on the basis of these case studies that the new symbolization of terror does not reconfigure thinking or practices in providing massive security in locales and widespread events. It increases the costs and the rhetoric of fear about possible risks yet does not alter the everyday tasks of policing.

4   Power struggles in the field of security: implications for democratic transformation

Benoît Dupont

Introduction

There can be little doubt that the governance of security – both in its authorization and provision modes – has undergone profound changes over the past thirty years. Academic interpretations of those changes generally focus on two phenomena that are closely linked to the erosion of a previously undisputed state monopoly: the commodification of security, and the pluralization of policing. The concept of pluralization refers to the fact that public police agencies have lost their monopoly to a myriad of private and hybrid providers, although they clearly retain unparalleled coercive and regulatory powers. Bayley and Shearing (2001) have used the term 'multilateralization' to describe the same phenomenon. If some of those new players or nodes[1] remain peripheral in terms of size and power, others, such as large private security conglomerates employ thousands of agents (Johnston 2000a) and aggressively pursue new market shares alongside or in competition with public agencies. As shown in the previous example, the commodification of security goes hand in hand with its pluralization. They are two complementary concepts that allow us to understand the reconfiguration of security in terms not only of structure and functions, but also of the ties that bind all the authorizers and providers of security together. The constellation of actors that occupy the field of security rely to a large extent on open-market mechanisms to trade security goods and services in order to cater to specific – and solvent – constituencies (Loader 1999).

The author is grateful to Jennifer Wood and Lucia Zedner for their very helpful comments and suggestions, and the Australian Institute of Criminology for making the data available to him.
[1] In graph theory, a node represents an actor, and lines represent ties between actors (Wasserman and Faust 1994: 94). Hence, in the governance context, a node is an institutional actor whose structure, legal status, resources, mentality and technologies are highly variable.

The discrete concepts of pluralization and commodification are more relevant when describing the recent changes in the field of security than the term 'privatization', which restricts the transformation of the security field to a dichotomous and simplistic analytical framework impervious to the infinite number of combinations possible. For example, hybrid structures that are neither public nor private have emerged (Johnston 1992; Dupont et al. 2003) and public organizations have embraced private management practices and implemented cost-recovery programmes, or even marketed their own services and competed with the private security industry in certain cases (Crawford and Lister 2004: 21), just to cite a few examples of the limits of the privatization discourse. Hence, the continuum approach, with the 'public' and the 'private' at each end, and various unpredictable combinations of pluralization and commodification in the middle, seems more appropriate to depicting the current situation.

One of the dimensions of the governance of security that has not attracted the same amount of interest is the nature of the power struggles engaged in by various institutions involved in the authorization and delivery of security within a bounded organizational field. Following DiMaggio and Powell's definition (1983: 148), an organizational field is an aggregate of organizations that constitute a recognized area of institutional life. It is constituted of key suppliers, resource and product consumers, regulatory agencies and all other organizations with a stake in the production of similar services or products. Obviously, the notion of organizational field transcends the public–private distinction. Hence, if the outcomes described above are to a large extent the manifestations of deeper globalizing forces, it is essential also to acknowledge strategic and contingent initiatives that account for local variations and particular configurations. For example, in the expanding organizational field of security, the multiplication of institutional actors and corporatist interests that seek to maintain or enhance their position has created many sources of frictions and opportunities for power struggles, overt or covert (Johnston 2003). The *ad hoc* negotiated adjustments and arrangements that emerge from the resolution or stabilization of those struggles determine in part the pace and nature of changes in this particular field. Thus, a study of the nodal governance of security must not be limited to a simple mapping of the nodes and their architecture. It ought also to consider the more subjective relational sphere of each node, that is the perception of its own position in a larger organizational field, of the other nodes' roles, strengths and weaknesses, and of the resources that it can mobilize to achieve certain objectives derived from this reflective assessment.

Such an approach poses a number of methodological challenges, in the sense that it requires the collection of fine-grained and highly subjective data. As the strategic locus of control is generally situated at the top of an organization, it also requires access to its highest-ranking executives, a condition rarely granted to academics (Reiner 1991). None the less, thanks to the availability of oral history data collected by the Australian Institute of Criminology, this chapter will seek to overcome those hurdles and explore the transformations that have affected a field of security located in Australia as perceived by ten police commissioners[2] – both active and retired.[3] In due course, it would be important to study the other layers of police organizations in order to highlight probable internal dissonances, and also to mobilize additional methods such as police or private security ethnographies. Choosing the police as the focal node of study might seem counter-intuitive in a highly pluralizing environment, but the erosion of the public police monopoly has not prevented it from retaining a central status in the governance of security. Police services continue to command and co-ordinate extensive resources – both internal and external – and also remain unavoidable partners for other actors of the security assemblage through regulatory practices, memorandums of understanding, and more informal partnerships. To illustrate this point, the business plan of the Victoria Police for 2003–4 sets a target of no fewer than 920 partnerships in areas such as youth issues, family violence, substance abuse, road safety, public transport and community safety (Victoria Police 2003: 28). Furthermore, the police commissioners' perspective is particularly relevant for a number of reasons. Firstly, their strategic role in steering complex organizations has been insufficiently studied, despite clear evidence of their influence over security governance policies. Also, the research conducted by Reiner (1991), Loader and Mulcahy (2001), Biro et al. (2000) and Pitman (1998) in the UK, Canada and Australia clearly demonstrates the reflective multi-level analysis in which police managers constantly engage, and the impact of this process on policing.

---

[2] In Australia a police commissioner is the highest ranking officer of a police organization. Hence, there are only eight active police commissioners at any given time.

[3] The material was collected in Australia in 1999 for an oral history project sponsored by the Australian Institute of Criminology. The project collected a wealth of data on the career paths of commissioners who had led their organizations through the 1980s and 1990s, their perspectives on internal and external organizational changes, and policing strategies (Dupont 2003a). For the purpose of this chapter though, only relational data referring to the nature and quality of relationships with other policing stakeholders has been extracted and coded. It must also be noted that the interviews were conducted by a retired police commissioner, who greatly facilitated access to the respondents and probably elicited more open answers, but rarely pushed forward with questions additional to the list provided to him.

Furthermore, the role of private or hybrid security CEOs has also been totally ignored (Rigakos 2002; Singer 2003), despite their growing role in the governance of security, so the findings of this chapter should provide new insights that can partially apply to them. Before introducing the arguments of this chapter, it must be stated that the opinions expressed by police commissioners reflect their rationality and may be loaded with subtexts, implicit statements and disingenuous commentaries that are impossible to decode for the uninitiated. What is sought here is not an assessment of their truthfulness (which would warrant a separate chapter), but instead a glimpse of the sense-making they use to justify their decisions.

This chapter argues that in a rapidly changing environment, most of the external stakeholders are perceived as sources of undue constraints that curtail the ability of police organizations to make necessary adjustments. In the first part, the relationships with those stakeholders are described in ambivalent terms, with mixed tales of co-operation and conflict. Obviously, the actors discussed here are those that police commissioners see as the most germane to their power struggles in the field. This perspective would be different, and involve power struggles with a different set of actors, for other players in the field. The commissioners' understanding of the existence of a security field and the power struggles that structure it goes hand in hand with the belief that their organizations are equipped with different forms of resources to face them. In the second part, I use the metaphor of capital to categorize the different kinds of resources mobilized by police commissioners in the course of these power struggles. Finally, a third part outlines the implications of these findings for the democratic governance of security and suggests a few possible normative options.

The set and the cast: contextualizing changes in Australian policing

As in many other modern societies, Australian policing institutions have experienced deep structural, cultural and technological transformations. It would be arduous to review them all here, as others have provided extensive and in-depth studies (Chan 1997; Dixon 1997; Dixon 1999; Lewis 1999; Finnane 2002). The role of commissioners, however, has not received the attention it deserves, mainly because of the politicization of their appointment, which has precluded access for academics. In the past decades, commissioners have seen their role evolve from caretakers to innovators and change implementers. In the face of numerous public inquiries (Mark 1978; Lusher 1981; Fitzgerald 1989; Wood

1997), declining levels of public confidence, and pressed by governments to achieve more with less in times of fiscal frugality, commissioners have been exhorted to produce spectacular outcomes in the delivery of policing services. Depending on local contexts, some respondents were appointed with explicit reform mandates, while others had less urgent agendas. Nevertheless, all of them concurred in their analysis of the new expectations placed on police commissioners by governments and the media:

I can remember the time when I was a staff officer to a commissioner of police who was able to go home for lunch each day. He would arrive exactly at nine o'clock and he would go home for lunch for an hour and he would walk out at exactly five o'clock. Not that he was not doing his job, but he just did not have the role to play then. For instance, as I said, there was not the national policing responsibility, there was not the focus on policing that there is today, the accountability of policing that there is today and so the role of the commissioner has changed dramatically to become a very high profile. The commissioner before me had an interview with the media on the day that he was appointed and never spoke to the media again for the four years he was commissioner. You just have to visualize that that could occur in this day and age. (Respondent 10)

The role of commissioner has become much more public, much more political. I think what is underestimated is the public nature of the commissioner's role, the fact that it is a whole-of-life commitment. You are likely to be scrutinized twenty-four hours a day. You've got to be aware of the fact that no matter what you do, where you go, it is likely to be reportable material. (Respondent 4)

The main thread that can be identified in the various spheres of change is the relational dimension that characterizes modern policing, in contrast to the isolation of the previous era. At the structural level, partnerships and networking provided new templates for the organization and delivery of policing services. Community policing and the myriad of crime prevention initiatives sought to engage citizens, other state agencies and NGOs in the local governance of crime (Crawford 1997; Sutton and Cherney 2002). These new partnerships imply linkages and co-ordination mechanisms between security nodes, some public, some private and some hybrid. On the national stage, common police services were designed to allow fragmented state police organizations to pool their resources and establish institutional networks (Dupont 2004) that could respond to the challenges of national and international organized crime. The cultural change imperative prescribed by royal commissions and public inquiries gave rise to more intensive forms of accountability and oversight, which created a new set of external regulatory stakeholders closely linked to police organizations (Lewis 1999; Chan 1999a; Goldsmith and Lewis 2000). The expansion of managerialism simultaneously permeated the organizational culture and introduced performance evaluation mechanisms driven by outside agencies such as the Productivity Commission. Finally, information technologies promised to deliver more effective policing by transforming police officers into 'knowledge workers' who could instantaneously feed information to, and retrieve information from, numerous internally and externally connected data-bases (Ericson and Haggerty 1997; Chan 2001).

All those changes and reforms, whether they were genuine or simply presentational, whether they produced measurable outcomes or failed miserably, did not take place without their fair share of tensions, frustrations and frictions with other players in the field of security, as the interviewees made it abundantly clear. The unions and the media are omnipresent in the accounts of these power struggles. They are labelled by commissioners as systematic adversaries unresponsive to reform initiatives. Relations with governments and community groups appear more pacific, although not devoid of skirmishes, with governments in a position of authority and the elusive community cast in a support role. Finally, private security, interestingly enough, does not rate a single mention by the ten commissioners. This issue was not explicitly tackled in the interviews, but many open-ended questions provided an opportunity to reflect about it. I will come back to it later.

Political actors

Governments, ministers and parliaments represent the main authorizers of public security, passing laws, appropriating budgets and expecting responsiveness from police agencies in return. Over the past twenty years, Australian governments have placed law-and-order politics at the top of their agendas (Hogg and Brown 1998), which has compelled them to be more assertive in making police commissioners accountable for results. This has resulted in direct and indirect attempts to control operational policing in an effort to please the media and the public, tightening the screws around the historical doctrine of the independence of the constable.

There is no doubt that policing has become more political. The arm's length distance between politics and commissioners has shortened, particularly in state arenas. (Respondent 4)

I believe the relationships between the commissioners and governments have changed over the years; commissioners of police today find themselves whether they like it or not very much thrown in the political debate. We find ourselves on the public stage more than we necessarily would like and some of us even more so because of the demand and nature of [the] way the media portrays the law-and-order issue. And so the relationship with government is extremely important... Running a police service today is big business, particularly in the largest jurisdictions. From billion dollar businesses to million dollar businesses, governments are right to have an expectation of accountability. And so the leadership and accountability changes that have occurred have been quite dramatic and they will continue to occur and it is something police forces and police commissioners will have to focus on even more and more. (Respondent 6)

It seems to have been a significant increase in the political involvement with factors affecting the police management. (Respondent 7)

A new facet of the relationship between commissioners and government rests on contractual arrangements. At the organizational level, one government (the Australian Capital Territory) has, for example, negotiated a purchase agreement with the Australian Federal Police, tying the budget allocation process to the delivery of quantifiable outputs and outcomes. Individual employment contracts that include performance evaluation targets are also becoming more frequent for commissioners (General Purpose Standing Committee 2000).

The official Opposition to the government of the day represents another political stakeholder likely to manipulate policing and security issues for its own electoral purposes and to confront commissioners about their leadership:

I was not at all assisted by the Opposition – [of] whom the two leaders would eventually say 'Hey, fear of crime and crime is a huge issue in this state; it's bigger than in other states, and our surveys tell us that. This government has been elected on law and order; the next election is going to be fought for law and order; you're dreaming if you think we're going to give you a fair game.' (Respondent 1)

Unions: an ambiguous relationship

As the employers of large and heavily unionized workforces,[4] police commissioners recalled being constantly confronted by the resistance of union representatives, when they sought to implement new initiatives. The commissioners did not question the legitimacy of representatives, who were entitled to defend their members' interests, but instead the tactics being used. The uncommitted approach of the unions on most matters was commonly experienced as a source of uncertainty and frustration by commissioners who felt they had made every effort possible to develop good

---

[4] As of June 2001, the eight Australian police forces employed 43,501 sworn officers and 11,627 unsworn personnel for a total budget of AUSD 3.3 billion (Prenzler and Sarre 2002: 53). The current estimates place union membership levels at over 97 per cent (Fleming and Marks 2004).

relationships with them, and realized that very little could happen without a green light from the unions.

When we encouraged him [the new union president] to become involved in things, he said: 'No no, we can't do that because if we get involved and then the troops don't like it, then how can we bag it?' (Respondent 1)

At a strategic level, there is a reluctance on the part of the representative group to commit, rather adopting a wait-and-see attitude and the right to object when the time seems appropriate. (Respondent 5)

much of what I achieved, including merit-based promotion was done after considerable consultation with the union and in most cases actually with their concurrence. Not that they concurred openly, but they said 'we will not oppose it', which was fine. They said 'we'll sit on the fence', so that at least you did not get opposition unless there was a groundswell from the troops, and they jumped off the fence to take up the position of the troops generally. (Respondent 10)

At the strategic level, this wait-and-see attitude was equated by some police commissioners to a lack of courage and vision, which allowed them to take a moral stance on industrial relations matters.[5] An alternative – and complementary – explanation that transpired from the interviews is that police unions, through the creation in 1997 of the Police Federation of Australia have engaged in a co-ordinated and aggressive national strategy to improve working conditions. Police commissioners, who are answerable to state governments and face different local priorities and constraints, felt ill-equipped to face this challenge. Some of them did not hide their irritation with this approach, while others were reluctantly admiring of the unions' national strategy and even suggested that police commissioners, as a group, could learn some lessons from the approach.

The ambivalences at the origin of this difficult relationship are linked to the internal power struggles between the hierarchical tiers of police organizations and the respective subcultures and interests they develop (Reuss-Ianni 1983; Monjardet 1996; Manning 1997). Reciprocally, external power struggles can also reverberate inside the organization and lead to adjustments that are resisted or even rejected.

The media as catalyst

The role of the media in the governance of security and their capacity to influence the policy cycle by resorting to sensationalist headlines is well

---

[5] It is interesting to note the similar claims made by union leaders about police commissioners (Fleming and Marks 2004).

documented (Hall et al. 1978; Ericson, Baranek and Chan 1991: 263). Police commissioners have to continuously 'feed' information to the news media, despite the fact that they believe their efforts are not reported in a balanced manner and that the media contribute to the creation of unrealistic demands on the part of the public and political stakeholders.

I told the media that there wasn't enough news. Any crime, every crime gets celebrated from dawn until dusk, it gets celebrated . . . the whole day, early morning radio, talk back, the four TV channels, so the over-emphasis and advertisement almost, of crime has had a tremendous negative impact. (Respondent 1)

The other thing that has struck me to be a major impediment to progress and achieving the goals that needed to be achieved was the unfortunate, sensationalist and negative approach that the media has adopted in Australian news, and [the] sort of message that they delivered to the community and which was very difficult to balance from time to time. And I see the way that some of these things are presumed [to be] a real significant barrier. (Respondent 2)

Behind the excessive and unbalanced coverage, it seems that most of the resentment stemmed from the fact that it had become an impossible task for the police to control the power of the media. This situation and the unpredictable repercussions it could have in the context of relationships with governments and the public was perceived as an unpleasant but unavoidable distraction.

Community: master or servant?

The more assertive demands of the community regarding the level and quality of policing services is clearly acknowledged by police commissioners as a major determinant of the governance of security. These demands are of course fuelled by the media and their reporting of crime affairs, but also by higher direct accountability standards that cannot be ignored and that do not necessarily align with the police working ethos.

The other side of the coin has been the expectations of the community and the demands put by the community on the governments around Australia. And with these demands policing, law and order has become a very high-profile situation and frankly it's my view that some governments have lost track . . . (Respondent 6)

We are actually changing the way we're delivering service to the community, . . . and it is all about having our people go through a cultural change so that they actually understand that the only reason they exist is [to be] there to serve the community and work with the community to achieve some mutually agreed outcomes. (Respondent 2)

I think the big thing in policing culture was trying to convince the police, mostly good people, mostly hard workers, mostly competent people, that we had to be more openly accountable, that we had to win the populace to come with us – and to do that, you had to be much more open and proactive than in the past. (Respondent 1)

However, this realization did not imply a drastic re-engineering of the police–public relationship. Behind the presentational discourse, patronizing attitudes remained strong and the expected level of community involvement did not extend beyond participation in Neighbourhood Watch schemes and other forms of partnerships designed and controlled by the police. The ties with the community were mainly unidirectional, the community being there to provide information and assistance to the police, with the police imparting some of its expert knowledge and educating the people.

Neighbourhood Watch is a great awareness programme in terms of giving people . . . an understanding of the way they can best assist police. (Respondent 4)

Police officers must interpret the policy of the organization and explain why they do things the way they do and explain that to the community when they have been misguided about why we are putting so much interest in certain activities. (Respondent 8)

I believe we have not educated decent people, all people, the community as to their key role. In other words, it's always been a partnership . . . and we have not really sold that. People do not understand that. They accept it finally. (Respondent 1)

To end this review of the main partners and stakeholders identified by police commissioners, the absence of a single mention of the private security sector must be noted. No question dealt with this issue directly, but in an era when security guards and consultants outnumber police officers by a ratio of 2.2 to 1 (Prenzler and Sarre 1998: 2), and a growing chunk of police functions are outsourced to the private sector (Davids and Hancock 1998; Prenzler and Sarre 2002), such an omission seems peculiar. In contrast, a former New South Wales police commissioner openly discussed in a preliminary version of his service's 2001–5 strategic plan the possibility of delegating some core responsibilities such as fraud investigations to the private sector (Ryan 2000), while in the UK and Canada, other police executives have explored the regulatory options that could be applied by police organizations to the private security sector or the feasibility of competing with private businesses by providing 'lower-cost quasi police services' (Blair 1998; Richardson 2000; Crawford, this volume). Obviously, the devolution and containment strategies actively pursued by police all over the world seek to slow down, or in some cases reverse, the erosion of their symbolic monopoly over the provision of security. One interpretation of our commissioners' lack of interest for the private security sector and the challenges it poses to the traditional idea of the police could be that they did not know where to fit it in their traditional view of the field and therefore blocked it out. As meteorologists know, the eye of the storm is always calm! Alternatively, it could be attributed to the fact that, at this stage, they genuinely felt unthreatened and therefore unconcerned by the position of the private sector. To reinforce this hypothesis, other state agencies with overlapping responsibilities in the security field – and therefore more directly in competition with the police for scarce resources and programme leadership – were cited on a few occasions in disparaging terms.

This... concept is the way to go, but then, what's been the missing element in my view... is the tendency for the almost absence [of], or just lip service [to], co-operation from many other key government agencies. Now, we are running the score card for that, the local chairpersons are going to be canvassed about who attends and who doesn't, who participates and who doesn't, who can you get to come and co-operate and who can you not... and say [to these CEOs]: 'Hey Fred! The feedback from our forty-two committees around the state is, you've only got a 30 per cent appearance and participation rate, and we'll tell you where your people are not playing and you better fix it or the next stop will be the deputy premier's office to say "Agency X is not playing the... game."'... We had some good committees, but all we had was, the police, the good community people and local government and most of the others were each staying away in their droves. (Respondent 1)

In this statement, the implicit message is that other agencies are not embarking on police partnership initiatives in order to maintain their autonomy and launch their own initiatives. It goes without saying that police organizations, notwithstanding their virtuous discourse, embrace the exact same stratagem (Cherney 2005).

Public security entrepreneurs and the metaphor of capital

The first section of this chapter dealt with the actors or nodes that police commissioners consistently considered to be key stakeholders in the security field, and how their field of possible actions was shaped or constrained by these actors. However, even when they complained bitterly about the constraints placed on their decisions and actions by other players, such as governments, unions, the media and community groups, police commissioners did not feel disempowered, as the following statement shows.

The more I became involved in policing and the more I became aware of attempts to undermine the status of policing, the more I was determined to do something to ensure that the police in this country was protected from unnecessary changes to the detriment of policing, and any changes brought in were first dependent on policing in the country. (Respondent 9)

This second section examines how police commissioners exercised their agency and manoeuvred through this field of possible actions. The dominant strategy to emerge from the interviews consists of the mobilization of a palette of resources that are seen as strategic organizational assets of the police. The resources alluded to are heterogeneous: beyond financial assets, they also include more intangible holdings such as processes (new selection criteria or training requirements), organizational structures that make the organization more efficient, privileged relational ties with decision-makers and community groups, or even public legitimacy. Although they could be considered as desirable ends in themselves, those resources were often described by commissioners as the means to achieve a broader tacit outcome: the organizational autonomy of public policing grounded on a vague notion of professionalism and located above a subservient security field. At this point, the capital metaphor seems helpful to illustrate the complex processes by which different categories of resources are accumulated, invested and traded, either defensively or offensively (Crozier and Friedberg 1980). Social capital has become a very popular concept in the social sciences (Portes 1998), but extending the metaphor to other forms of non-economic capitals such as cultural capital, political capital and symbolic capital can also yield some heuristic value.

Economic capital

Like other public services, police organizations depend on governmental and parliamentary arbitrations during the budgeting process. Although this constraint can be an impediment in times of fiscal frugality, when the interests of political stakeholders and a commissioner are aligned, economic capital will facilitate the accumulation of other forms of capitals.

The external budgetary environment is always a difficulty and an impediment. We were doing this reform process at a time of budgetary restriction and negative growth so that created an additional problem. (Respondent 4)

The government totally supported me in my aims and that is reflected in the fact that in my five years as commissioner, the financial budget...has increased by just 100 per cent of what it was when I arrived. (Respondent 6)

...we have had a long term strategy which is really well articulated and we've been able to sell that to the government, and as a consequence to that, they've been prepared to invest in the organization. (Respondent 2)

Securing sufficient levels of economic capital could be achieved by using a number of strategies:

It is useful to note in recording of this that prior to the Graduate School, police agencies by and large paid for all of their own education and professional development programmes. By creating the Australian Graduate School of Police Management, and by negotiating special arrangements with the Commonwealth, we estimate than an additional twelve to fourteen million dollars has been invested into police education which otherwise would have had to come from police budgets. (Respondent 3)

The impact of these reviews is that they have an influence, a persuasive capacity that doesn't allow you to easily walk away from the results and puts a pressure on police organizations and police practitioners and governments to implement things even at a cost that otherwise you might have thought a bit too difficult or controversial to do. (Respondent 4)

Some of the organizational reviews mentioned in the previous quotations were intentionally arranged by police commissioners to strengthen subsequent requests for budget increases:

Another objective from the outset was to convince government that they needed to commit to a review of the police organization, because without that review, I wouldn't have the chance to move forward to convince government that there was a need for a major injection into the . . . police service. And having that review completed and having it accepted by government, I then set about reforming the organization, particularly from the overall financial base, to rebuild and to ensure that what the community expected of the police service was returned and given to them, because certainly I found in arriving that it just was not the case. (Respondent 6)

Contrary to private security firms that amass economic capital through market mechanisms, police organizations' levels of economic capital are heavily dependent on their access to political capital.

Political capital

Political capital is tied to constant interactions with other 'cogs' in the complex machinery of government and will define a commissioner's ability to influence policy in a way that fits with the police organization's interests. While governments and other political actors have been busy strengthening their grip over public policing, commissioners have developed subtle ways to strategically invest their reserves of political capital, sometimes by adopting a conciliatory approach, sometimes by mobilizing legal arguments and at other times by using the media as a relay.

A commissioner has no chance of being effective unless he has credibility with the government and the key stakeholders with whom he or she works. And political awareness and political acumen is absolutely critical to the effective performance of commissioner responsibilities . . . Having said that, there is a nervousness some-times in people's minds about the use of those words, because there is quite a distinct difference between having well-developed political acumen and being politicized or compromised as a commissioner. You need to be aware, you need to develop an understanding of what is likely to be the political agenda, to have a real appreciation of how you can properly service that agenda. How you can do that without in any sense compromising your oath of office or the legality of what you do. (Respondent 4)

I said: 'Should not the police commissioner be looked upon as a community leader? Isn't he more than just another CEO? Just another person who is beholden to, and subservient to the minister, and the minister's minders?' I feel very strongly about that and I've got to say, [in regard to the] Premier . . . and his various min-isters and other cabinet members, [when] my honest opinion is given publicly on issues such as prostitution, abortion – these are things that arose when I was there – and a number of other things, . . . they wouldn't have been . . . But I was never chastised, I was never threatened, no one really attempted to intervene or to muzzle me, although, on occasions, another point of view is expressed to me. But you know, when you realize this is a very sensitive public political issue, and I did, . . . I still really believe that police commissioners and [the] separation of powers and their leadership role can't be overstated. (Respondent 1)

Of course, this use of political capital is not the preserve of commissioners, and police unions, for example, have been acutely aware of its benefits. Hence, police executives have also turned their attention to an additional form of capital they can more easily harness.

Cultural capital

Cultural capital can be defined as the explanatory and actionable knowl-edge that an organization can mobilize, at the individual and collective lev-els. The explicit component of cultural capital is developed, accumulated and passed on through constantly updated training programmes, R&D efforts and the incessant adoption of more powerful knowledge manage-ment technologies. Cultural capital also incorporates the tacit knowledge developed by police officers – sometimes in contradiction to the 'official' organizational knowledge – known as the police culture (Shearing and Ericson 1991; Chan 1997). The emphasis placed on 'authorized' cul-tural capital by police services can be found in the constant references to police professionalism and, more importantly, the partnerships estab-lished with tertiary education institutions. By the end of the 1990s, each police organization in Australia had forged links to one of its local higher education institutions:

> Another highlight was to create the first graduate school with Charles Sturt University, which became known as the Australian Graduate School of Police Management. This would never have occurred had it not been for the original intentions of the commissioners, which I referred to earlier, in the late 1980s to create a plan to transform policing from occupational to professional status. (Respondent 3)

> On the top of my pole was also the academy: this purpose-built, co-located police academy, co-located with a tertiary institution [is] the enshrinement in the organization of training and development as key elements for the organization and what it is, and what it does and how it does it. It's all about training and development. (Respondent 1)

> I've also introduced the executive management course which is linked with [our partner university] and can be taken right through to a Master's degree if one would choose to do so. We've also tertiary-linked all our major training and promotional courses. (Respondent 2)

These linkages are potentially fraught with ambiguities and tensions, as Lee and Punch have shown in a different context (2004). Internally, the injection of cultural capital can significantly alter the rules that determine promotions and, as a result, encounter significant resistance. Besides, one of the common features found in police cultures all over the world is the tendency to devalue organizational cultural capital (Van Maanen 1973; Chan 2003). Nevertheless, it is seen by police executives as an essential asset in order to reclaim partial control over the knowledge created about policing, which influences to some degree the position of police services in the security field.

> Also, this group of commissioners recognized that up until this stage much of the history of policing was actually recorded in Royal Commissions, documents of inquiries and official reports. And in a sense, this meant that other people were constantly making commentary about policing and the way it was done. (Respondent 3)

> I see also the ownership by police of its own body of research, certainly the ownership by policing of its own educational development facility, as a symbol of policing's commitment to the development of its own people, and certainly as a mark of its credibility. (Respondent 4)

In a sense, cultural capital was an asset that could impact positively on social capital, as well as on symbolic capital.

Social capital

Many definitions of social capital can be found in the literature, some focusing on the individual character of social capital (Bourdieu 1986; Coleman 1988; Burt 1997; Lin 2001), others insisting on the collective efficacy conferred by social capital at the community level (Fukuyama 1999; Putnam 2000). Despite this ongoing debate, most authors generally agree on the multi-faceted benefits that derive from the capacity to initiate and maintain social relations with other groups or individuals. One of the main criticisms directed at the police at the end of the twentieth century was precisely the social capital deficit created by an over-reliance on car patrolling and reactive policing, as well as by anti-corruption strategies that discouraged close ties with the community, a far cry from the Peelian ideal of policing. Community policing and inter-agency partnerships were seen as the most promising paths towards the restoration of depleted stocks of social capital, despite the resistance that was encountered.

The message from that level downward was to all the other key government agencies, family and children services, housing, health, education, etc., [to] all be a part of this solution . . . The trouble is that the other government agencies had key roles to play, but didn't see that in their chart or in anywhere – they . . . were not participating or collaborating, or sometimes not even co-operating. (Respondent 1)

There is always a need to continually develop the relationship with the community through community programmes through working with the community. Partnerships come in so many different ways . . . I talk about our ability to work with the community, our ability to relate, our ability to talk and to interact with the community. Policing must be seen as part of the community and not separate to it. (Respondent 6)

And it was a major change of direction from this reactive policing to a blend of proactive policing and it took a lot of convincing; a lot of convincing of government, of community itself, and in particular of the police force. [There was] a lot of suspicion; [the] general attitude of the community was: 'What's wrong? Have you lost control? You're asking us, the community, to be involved.' Their immediate reaction was that I was asking them to be involved in the reactive side, because they had never heard of a proactive side of policing. But gradually we were able to convince people. (Respondent 10)

Social capital was also seen by some commissioners as being an asset in improving the relationship with the unions.

For the relationship to be valuable and constructive, I think there is mileage in involving union executives in the problem-solving process, and if you involve people in that process, they have a better understanding of what the issues are and they have ownership of the solutions and outcomes. (Respondent 9)

Economic, political, cultural and social capitals represent resources only
to the extent allowed by symbolic capital, an intangible asset that could
be associated with institutional legitimacy.

Symbolic capital

The distribution of symbolic capital results from the complementary outcomes produced by the four other forms of capital, as well as from external
factors. Hence, the cycles that govern its accumulation are much longer
and harder to control. Symbolic capital allows the police to maintain its
strategic position in the field of security as the central node and to speak
with authority on a range of issues (Loader and Mulcahy 2001), as well as
to justify how other forms of capital are invested. The symbolic dimension is clearly acknowledged by commissioners, but only to the extent
that it does not jeopardize the governability and operational effectiveness
of the organization. Low levels of symbolic capital were directly associated with the public inquiries that uncovered patterns of corruption and
recommended stronger external oversight. As a result, compromises were
made to avoid further erosions.

We're also conscious of the outcome of the Fitzgerald commission in Queensland,
the Wood Royal Commission of New South Wales, and the Mollen commission
in New York. Well, they sent some fairly clear message about the requirements
for an organization to be committed to the issues of ethics and integrity. As a
result of that, we ... set up an ethical standards department with a very proactive
role in the organization as well as in the investigative arms [and] investigative
complaints. That has really led to a substantial drop in public complaints and I
think a concurrent increase for the public's respect for the organization ... We've
done that and it's worked very well for us. As a result, I think we're probably one
of the most independent police forces operating in Australia. The only oversight
mechanism we have is the Ombudsman who reviews police investigations. We
don't have any other watchdogs, criminal justice commissions, crime commissions, all of those other types of bodies, and there's really no need for them in
this jurisdiction because I believe that we have committed ourselves publicly – as
a result, we have government and public support. And the big warning flag for
others is that if you don't commit yourself and you don't apply the resources, at
some point in time, you'll pay a price for it. (Respondent 2)

I think the role of an Ombudsman or an external accountability process such as
the PIC in NSW, are important features in the process, and clearly there needs to
be an external oversight of many investigations. It is not enough for justice to be
done; there has to be a clear demonstration of the fact that it is. I think there are
two issues: one that it is not so much that malpractice occurs in an organization,
as what the organization is prepared to make or to do about it. And secondly, that
internal inquiries are never going to be sufficient to satisfy the public or the critics,

with the result that external oversight will become more important, regardless of the capacity of the organization.(Respondent 4)

Less dramatically, another strategy that was mentioned by one of the respondents involved a simple but significant name change.

Over time the position of the Institute has changed. It's changed first of all by its name. It was [initially] called the Australian Police College. By 1986, it had changed its name to the Australian Police Staff College, which is part of the symbolism commissioners were keen to achieve in the move toward greater professionalism. In the early parts of the 1990s, it changed its name once again to the Australian Institute of Police Management. And this was another symbolic attempt to move away from things connected with the military. (Respondent 3)

The sequential presentation of the five forms of capital must not obscure the fact that they are highly interdependent. For example, cultural capital can be expensive to acquire and insufficient resources will limit its availability; the erosion of symbolic capital will have repercussions on political, social and economic capitals; social capital will be instrumental in enhancing cultural capital, by facilitating the transfer of knowledge and the diffusion of innovation (Jones and Newburn 2002a).

The capital categories described in this chapter are also porous and the proposed typology does not preclude empirical overlaps. What are described in this chapter as political and symbolic capitals could indeed be labelled social capital. This unorthodox 'arbitrary' approach results from the desire to reflect the diversity of resources mentioned by the respondents, and how these resources appear to be influenced by as much as they influence, the context of policing. The concept of capital should not be seen as rigid. Instead, it is applied and used as a metaphorical lens that helps understand the rationalization and representation processes that police executives constantly deploy in highly complex environments, in order to give meaning to their decisions and to communicate this meaning to their membership. It is also a way for them to assign meaning to external constraints and pressures according to their own professional and personal references (Manning 1997: 137). In this respect, it is essential – but empirically extremely difficult – to distinguish the organizational from the personal dimension: charismatic leaders will create and harness economic, political, cultural, social and symbolic capitals much more effectively than less gifted ones, with dramatic consequences. The repeated successes of Bill Bratton in Boston and New York against many odds offer a compelling example (Kim and Mauborgne 2003).

Of course, the rationality that results from this process is partial, one-sided and shifting to accommodate new conditions, interests and strategies. As others within and outside the organization experience the same process, contested rationalities (Espeland 1998; Manning 2003a) are bound to collide in the organizational field. Hence, the reconfiguration of the security field is to a large extent an incremental and messy process that owes less to neat causal relations than to contextual, short-term and often implicit factors. As this contest to dominate the security field through the accumulation of different kinds of resource or capital unfolds, a number of implications for the governance of security ensue.

Governing security beyond corporatist interests

The governance of security is not only influenced by trends such as the pluralization of actors or the commodification of service provision, but also by power struggles that result from those trends. As the number and capacities of alternative security providers expand, police organizations are inclined to contest the legitimacy of resources deployed by the newcomers and adjust their own capital allocation strategies accordingly in order to maintain their status and position at the centre of the field. This does not imply that they seek total control of the field and that new entrants cannot carve a niche for themselves or even appropriate a significant share of certain activities – in fact, police organizations also purchase services from private security providers (Ericson and Haggerty 1997; Grabosky 2001). But this seems possible only so long as those new entrants limit their ambitions or do not openly challenge the dominant role of the police. Meanwhile, other actors such as governments, the media, unions and the public will intervene in those struggles, and use their own specific resources to further their interests. Hence, the data presented above seek to complement other theoretical approaches to the governance of security by emphasizing that this governance also results from strategic contests and 'shifting alliances rather than as the product of (state-led) "steering and rowing" strategies' (Johnston and Shearing 2003: 145).

The power struggles and corporatist interests that fuel them contribute little to the optimization of security as a public or common good (Shearing and Wood 2003a; Loader and Walker, this volume). In this context, justice, equity and accountability are sometimes used as instrumental issues that are played in the public discourse to maintain symbolic capital and eventually discredit competing organizations. In turn, those groups that are more apt at amassing and investing economic, social, political, cultural and symbolic capitals will take advantage of the opportunities created by the power struggles that structure the field and be able to claim 'security' as a club good (Hope 2000; Crawford, this volume), or impose their agenda on the rest of the community (Becker 1973).

The final part of this chapter will therefore offer some normative considerations seeking to minimize the occurrence and impact of those power struggles and enhance the democratization of security governance. If capitals are used competitively to gain a positional advantage over other actors, the incentive to act in this manner can be neutralized by facilitating widespread and equal access to the five forms of resource. This can occur naturally through the process of institutional isomorphism, when the social actors of an organizational field adopt similar structures, cultures, technologies and practices. The convergence that characterizes this particular state creates the condition for a better diffusion of norms and more effective sharing of information, resources and practices. However, the competition dimension is not absent from isomorphic environments, since dominant actors are in a position to dictate the standards to which others will have to adhere. But other factors can also trigger the mimetic process, such as the existence of a common legal environment or the normative pressures stemming from professionalization (DiMaggio and Powell 1983). These factors can obviously be stimulated by the appropriate policies. Of course, the need to shape the security field so that all organizations that are part of it share the same institutional features is problematic; it involves further blurring of already disintegrating boundaries between public, private and hybrid institutions, a process whose unforeseen effects can hardly be predicted, let alone controlled.

A more promising avenue seems to focus isomorphic change policies on regulatory mechanisms. The uncertainty and the strategic contests generated by the pluralization of providers and differentiated access to resources in the field of security may well be offset by a more intensive use of nodal regulation tools. One of the most common complaints voiced by police organizations and unions in the face of aggressive private competition is the differential in the accountability burden experienced by both groups. They highlight the contrast between the many – often uncoordinated – layers of accountability that are imposed on them and the lack of equivalent controls on the private and hybrid sectors. A broader exposure of the whole security field to an integrated and responsive regulation system has the potential to guarantee universal compliance to democratic principles, while the benefits that derive from the field's diversity are preserved. The complexity of the field would make hierarchical integration impossible. Instead, it would rely on a meta-regulatory framework, that is, a framework making possible the regulation of regulation (Grabosky 1995b; Parker 2002).

In an organizational field such as the one dedicated to the authorization and provision of security,[6] where various forms of resources are mobilized as a result of external stakeholders' actions or mere existence, all the problems that arise from the strategic motivation of certain decisions cannot be solved through sole compliance to a set of formal rules. Resistance or avoidance behaviours can always be expected and formal rules become just another constraint that can be overcome with the help of the appropriate form of capital. At this stage, the research carried out on inter-organizational networks within the sociology of organizations provides some stimulating insights. Although organizational fields are more loosely coupled (or, in other words, less connected and co-ordinated) than networks, some of the properties used to study the latter can be easily 'transferred' to the former. Density and centrality are two network-specific properties that can prove particularly relevant to conceptualizing the power struggles witnessed in the present chapter. The density of a field refers to the ratio of existing to possible connections between organizations and stakeholders belonging to it (Wasserman and Faust 1994). In theory, the maximum density level of a field is reached when all its components have established all possible connections with others in the field. These linkages or partnerships are polymorphous (Grabosky 2002): they can be formal – memorandums of understanding – or informal – personal contacts between members of different organizations. A lot of them involve the exchange of information, but others take the form of regulatory mechanisms such as external oversight, or contracts for the provision of services. The majority of those ties are voluntary but some can be coercive or even parasitic.

Centrality is a second property that helps an understanding of an organization's position in the field, as measured by the number and pattern of its connections. The more connections are maintained by an organization and its members relative to the field's average, and the more diversified and redundant these connections, the more central this organization will be; it will be able to activate more contacts (and hence leverage more resources) than competing organizations, to influence the direction of the field and to rely on more alternatives to further its interests. Different forms of centrality can be measured (Wasserman and Faust 1994), but all the measures produced around this concept seek to assay the status and influence of organizations over their field of activity, an essential asset in the context of power struggles. In the security field, police organizations score the highest on centrality, mainly because of their legal mandate and

---

[6] Or in any other organizational field for that matter.

the size of their membership, but other players such as professional associations and multi-national security providers are also characterized by high levels of centrality.

The impact of those two features on a field's regulation is quite significant: more densely connected fields enhance the circulation of information and knowledge between members and facilitate the emergence of shared norms, while the presence of a strong central player will discourage the formation of compromises and consensus (Rowley 1997). Dense fields that allow constant communications between all of their members and promote transparency lessen, by definition, the strategic advantages conveyed by centrality in a more loosely coupled environment. Collective bargaining and monitoring, the mutualization of the different forms of capital and the voluntary diffusion of norms and values become a more frequent – if not expected – behaviour, while the incentives for pursuing supremacy over the field – and the deployment of related strategies – decrease. By designing policies that facilitate or compel the development of various forms of linkages between all members of the security field, a more reflexive and nodal form of regulation relying on 'soft structures' (Considine 2002) could crystallize the common good and help ensure that the most optimal standards are applied in the delivery of security, whatever the nature of the providers.

This ambitious project must be preceded by a field mapping exercise that identifies all the stakeholders of the security field, their attributes (public/private/hybrid; authorizer/provider; size; organizational structure; mandates; access to the different forms of capitals, etc.), but most importantly their ties to the other stakeholders, whether they are part of the field in question or peripheral to it. Security networks (Dupont 2004), as subsets of the organizational field are likely to be discovered in the process. Systematically collecting attribute and relational data will help unravel the interests, constraints and contested rationalities that guide the decisions and actions of field members. The ability to understand and monitor the security field's structural embeddedness (Jones et al. 1997) is the first step toward the design of nodal regulation mechanisms that place the common good and democratic values such as justice, equality, accountability and efficiency at the heart of the governance of security (Law Commission of Canada 2002).

The recommendation made by the Patten Commission to establish a policing board (rather than a police board) in Northern Ireland is probably the closest attempt to date to design such a regulatory framework (Independent Commission on Policing for Northern Ireland 1999). The role of the board as envisaged by the Commission was to hold the chief constable and the public police institution accountable by setting objectives and performance targets, controlling the police budget and appointing upper managers (the chief executive included). The term 'policing' was chosen on purpose, as the Commission recommended that the board's responsibilities be extended to the co-ordination of public, private and hybrid organizations in the field of public safety, as well as to the regulation of the private security sector (Independent Commission on Policing for Northern Ireland 1999: 29). However, the selective implementation of the policing board recommendations, which abandoned the broader security mandate in favour of a more traditional form of police supervision, makes clear the normative challenges posed by nodal regulation. In the absence of an existing working model, old patterns represent a force of attraction which is hard to resist.

The idea of an overarching independent security authority with responsibility over public, private and hybrid actors within the same organizational field should nevertheless be pursued. This authority would not seek to control the activities of each member of the field, as external oversight and audit systems already exist. Instead, its mandate would be to identify the security field's democratic deficits, created by the sort of power struggles described above or by other factors, and to invent collective solutions to fix them. Its budget would be used to map the structure and transformations of the field, to identify incentives for co-operation or positive competition as well as disincentives for the pursuit of corporatist interests and to use them in order to increase the density and transparency of the field. This could take the form of initiatives that facilitate the flow of expertise between organizations, the adoption of minimum training or service delivery standards, the organization of public debates on security issues, the development of egalitarian partnerships or many other forms of capital exchange. As can be expected, persuasion alone is likely to result in disappointing outcomes, and robust regulatory powers should be made available as an option of last resort. To guarantee this authority's sustained focus on the common good, its membership would consist of community representatives appointed by the different stakeholders. It is expected its resources and mandate would come from the state. Its emphasis on openness and incentives rather than coercion would indubitably place it at the bottom of the responsive regulation pyramid imagined by Ayres and Braithwaite (1992). This pyramid's basic principle is that regulation should always start with persuasive means, and only escalate to more coercive tactics when defiance is encountered (Braithwaite 2002a). However, this low position would create the knowledge base to make the overall pyramid more effective: by knowing which types of capital are most useful or coveted by an organization, the upper stages of the pyramid could tailor penalties that are sure to elicit compliance.

Considering the power struggles highlighted in this chapter, intense resistance from the most powerful actors in the field, which have a lot to lose in such an experiment, can reasonably be anticipated. But conversely, they can also find benefits in it, for example in terms of social and symbolic capital. The challenge will be to make the benefits outweigh the losses. As Loader (2000: 340) so appositely stated, these are just starting points for – hopefully heated – conversations about new ways of thinking about and acting on the governance of security.

Conclusion

Although the normative implications briefly outlined above extend far beyond the empirical data presented in the first part of the chapter, the governance of security and the paradoxes that form an intrinsic part of it (Zedner 2003) are vital issues that demand our full attention. Through the testimonies of former Australian police commissioners active in the 1980s and 1990s, I have sketched the field of security as it was rationalized at the top of police organizations. This representation is of course incomplete and probably already outdated, as new players have entered the field, the interviewees represent a fraction of all the players, and alliances have been forged or rescinded in the specific environment studied here. What is much more constant is the process by which resources of different kinds were acquired and mobilized in order to negotiate the uncertainty that characterizes any organizational field and maintain or improve one's position within that field – implicitly in a contest with other members of the field. The capital metaphor was used as an analytical tool and five forms of capital were identified among the respondents: economic capital, political capital, cultural capital, social capital and symbolic capital. In the case of Australian police services, cultural capital was developed throughout the 1980s in order to compensate for some perceived or real decline in legitimacy among the public – symbolic capital. More emphasis was also placed on social capital, and community groups were engaged by the police more systematically under the auspices of 'community policing'. The respondents signalled a slight erosion of their political capital under the pressure of governments, which tied the allocation of economic capital to increased external oversight and audit. This typology of resources seems versatile enough to be transferred to other organizations in the field, private or hybrid. For example, one can envisage that a parallel exploration of private or hybrid security leaders' experiences would have stressed the importance of economic capital, which is acquired more efficiently by non-governmental actors. By contrast, political capital would not be assigned the same high value, unless the overall stability of the field was threatened. The power struggles uncovered here and the exchange strategies that security nodes deploy to resolve them determine to a much higher degree than expected the reconfiguration of the security field and its governance. Nodes tend to put their interests and survival ahead of other considerations, and will continue to do so unless this dimension is incorporated into regulatory mechanisms. In a context where everyone agrees that the field of security and the ties that bind its members together are plural, the relevance of regulation will also be judged by its capacity to reflect this complexity. In this respect, meta-regulation offers a promising normative framework (Parker 2002; Braithwaite 2003a; Shearing 2004). However, it will not be successful unless it tackles the nodal dimension of the field and takes into account the discrete resources, linkages and exchanges of the regulated organizations. The case presented here illustrates the difficulty of collecting the data needed to chart the 'nodal', and its situated nature. Nested within the tacit and fragmented knowledge of practitioners, it is nevertheless a strong determinant that theoreticians should not discard in their search for elegant models. As the traditional mental schemata governing security are challenged by the reconfiguration of the field, the fusion of actionable and theoretical knowledge becomes more needed than ever to ensure its sustainable democratic governance.

5   Policing and security as 'club goods': the new enclosures?

Adam Crawford

It has become generally accepted that governments alone no longer determine (if they ever fully did) what sort of security is needed by, nor are they the sole providers of policing on behalf of, the populations they govern. Groups other than governments or police, including businesses, landlords, housing providers and citizens, increasingly take control of their own policing needs and select their security providers. As Bayley and Shearing (2001) note, both the authorization and provision of policing are increasingly multi-tiered, fragmented and dispersed. In this context, policing and security have become *additional* to residual state policing. As individual and collective goods they have become commodified (Spitzer 1987). In a consumerist culture, policing has become encircled in a regime of choice. More so than ever, security is forged through the choices made on the basis of visits to the marketplace. This is not to suggest that policing and security have fundamentally changed nor that they were not previously the subject of a mixed economy (Jones and Newburn 2002c). Social historians forcefully remind us otherwise (McMullen 1996; Beattie 2001). Rather, this is to suggest that recent developments, notably in England and Wales (the focus of my concern in this chapter), but also elsewhere, have brought this mixed economy into sharper relief.

As a result, a second tier of policing and security has mushroomed, sometimes blind to, at other times in conflict or competition with, and at yet other times hand in hand with or steered by, state policing. It is the ambivalent and ambiguous interplay between these different tiers of policing that provokes considerable contemporary debate. It is my contention that these plural auspices and providers of policing cannot be conceptualized as a public/private dichotomy nor merely as existing along a continuum between public and private with state policing standing at one end, as one set of 'nodes' amongst many (Johnston and Shearing 2003). Rather, what we are witnessing is the fluid interpenetration of additional and residual security in which forms of state, municipal, private and voluntary policing coalesce in a mixed economy. Additional security has become a 'club good' either collectively attained and managed or

111

captured from erstwhile public auspices. Nevertheless, under current conditions, state policing occupies a residual position, one which is both symbolically and normatively different from other forms of security provision (Loader 1997a). The state is always 'in the background', allowing, licensing, regulating, facilitating or trying to contain, additional forms of security. Furthermore, what is different between residual state policing and other modes of security provision is that the former is always (in some way) affected by front-stage developments in security authorization and provision. As I intend to show, at an empirical level, we are witnessing the further residualization of policing as a public good through processes of capture, as well as the enclosure and collectivization of security as a 'club good'.

In this chapter, I want to offer a descriptive account of policing and security as 'club goods' in order to highlight: firstly, the contemporary enclosure of public goods by private and parochial interests; secondly, the manner in which private interests club together to provide collective local goods; and thirdly, the various processes and themes of exclusion (and inclusion) that underlie such contemporary policing developments. In this, unlike some commentators (Shearing and Wood 2003a), I am not advocating a normative conception of policing and security as 'common goods' nor am I seeking to reconstitute the connections between policing and the state (Loader and Walker 2001). Rather, I aim to explore the empirical and normative issues raised by contemporary processes of clubbing and residualization, ones that any robust normative conception of policing as either a public good or club/common good must contend with and address.

The marketization of policing

In some senses, the UK government and police have been left behind by the demand for security. The incapacity of the modern police to provide locally tied visible patrols has fostered an increasingly vibrant, and as yet unregulated,[1] market for visible patrols to which private security firms and other municipal policing initiatives[2] have responded. Estimates of

---

[1] The Private Security Industry Act 2001 seeks to regulate the industry by introducing a licensing scheme for private security officers and their managers. Licences will be granted only after a full criminal record check has been issued and suitable training undertaken. The legislation established the Security Industry Authority to implement the new regulatory regime. However, licensing of the security guarding sector is not expected to begin until 2005.

[2] Most notable has been the establishment of local authority policing personnel and the introduction of neighbourhood and street wardens funded by the Office of the Deputy Prime Minister (ODPM) and Home Office (see Crawford 2003a).

the size of the private security industry are notoriously difficult to make. According to Peter Hermitage, the chair of the newly established Security Industry Authority in the UK there are anything between 300,000 and 500,000 people employed in the private security industry.[3] Not all of these, however, are visible security guards. According to the British Security Industry Association (BSIA 2005) there are an estimated 2,000 security guarding companies and over 125,000 dedicated security officers. Jones and Newburn (2002c: 141) have used Census figures to show that the number of private security guards across the UK rose from 66,950 in 1951 to 159,704 in 1991. What is clear from these figures is that private security guards are no longer peripheral but key providers of policing. In many industrial estates, retail centres and residential areas, the market is driving the provision of visible reassurance.

As such, security has become a commodity to be bought and sold (Loader 1999; Rigakos 2002). However, as an additional good, it is available not only through commercial and municipal providers but also from the public police themselves, who have latterly become drawn into this marketplace. Recent changes in legislation have enabled the police to generate income by selling aspects of their services. Section 9 of the Police and Magistrates' Courts Act 1994 provides the statutory basis for the police to charge more widely for goods and services that they were previously obliged to provide freely, as part of normal duties, including the patrolling function. The potential of this new-found commercial freedom is being realized by an increasing number of UK forces, many of whom have appointed 'business development managers' to exploit private finance initiatives. Many forces have set up charitable trusts to further their income-generating and sponsorship potential. Some recent well-publicized examples include:

- Local councils and housing associations, sometimes in partnership, purchasing residential patrols, such as the Joseph Rowntree Housing Trust initiative in New Earswick, York (Crawford et al. 2003).
- Local authorities purchasing officers for city centre patrolling duties, such as the Liverpool Goldzone initiative.
- Leisure outlets and licensed premises purchasing officers to patrol parts of the night-time economy around pubs and clubs (Hobbs et al. 2003).
- Retail outlets and shopping malls purchasing officers to police within and around their premises, such as the MetroCentre in Gateshead, the Meadowhall complex in South Yorkshire and the Bluewater Centre in Kent.

---

[3] Personal communication, 16 June 2004.

Through such contracts police officers remain under the control of the Chief Constable and can be abstracted from their specified role if needed, but are otherwise drawn into the policing interests of the contractor.

Nevertheless, there remain considerable variations in the expansion of income-generation developments among different police forces in England and Wales. Policies at both local and national levels have been uneven. This is in part because some forces have a much lower potential sponsorship base than do others, but is also a result of different cultural attitudes towards income generation on the part of senior police officers including those at chief constable level (Bunt et al. 1997). There have also been concerns raised about the impact of income generation from both within and outside the police (Her Majesty's Inspector of Constabulary 1996; Loader 2000; Crawford and Lister 2004). Nevertheless, it has become an increasingly powerful dynamic in contemporary British policing, promoted by central governments keen to engender public sector reform through marketization (O'Dowd 2002).

However, it has been the introduction of Community Support Officers (CSOs) under the Police Reform Act 2002 that has significantly transformed the commercial involvement of the police in selling additional patrol services. Without the full powers or training of a sworn police constable, the CSO's role is to provide public reassurance through high-visibility patrolling (Crawford et al. 2004). CSOs have powers to issue fixed penalty notices and to detain a suspect for up to thirty minutes pending the arrival of a sworn police officer. They were initially introduced in late 2002 and now all but four of the forty-three police forces in England and Wales employ CSOs, some 4,000 in total. CSOs have afforded the police a commodity with which to compete with private and municipal policing. Moreover, the short-term nature of the initial Home Office funding programme for CSOs will necessitate that forces look to external income generation to fill the financial hole left once central funding dries up.

In the contemporary market, CSOs appear more attractive than a sworn officer. Firstly, they cost less given their limited training, lower pay and the fact that they do not have the same pension and sickness entitlements as sworn police constables. Conspicuously, the advent of CSOs has come at a time when the price of private security is set to rise with the introduction of the new licensing regime.[4] This is crucial in a marketplace where the

---

[4] It has been estimated by senior officials within the BSIA that this may amount to a one-off rise of about 7-8 per cent (David Dickinson, BSIA Chief Executive, personal communication, 7 July 2003). This is significant and will add to the extra costs arising from implementation of the European Working Time Directive.

BSIA estimates that 60 per cent of security contracts are awarded on price alone.

Secondly, as dedicated patrol officers with restricted powers, CSOs are freed from most of the pressures that serve to abstract constables from dedicated contractual arrangements and which often stymie the commercial marketing of police (Crawford et al. 2003). CSOs are also able to retain a competitive advantage over their non-police rivals on the basis of the sacred and symbolic value of the police uniform and the emotional investment by the British public in their 'bobbies' (Loader and Mulcahy 2003), as well as the logistical and organizational support that the police are able to afford CSOs.

Whether the provider is the public police, private security or municipal authority, the commodification of security engenders new relations between policing agents and the policed. It heralds different, largely elevated, consumer-based expectations on the part of the policed concerning the nature and quality of services provided. Commodification generates increased demands for greater 'ownership' through sensitivity to local sensibilities and values, and for responsiveness to incidents, calls for service, reports on activities and results (Crawford and Lister 2004). Furthermore, it fosters new forms of market-based accountability through contracts, audits and other instruments, providing members and beneficiaries (i.e. visitors) a greater investment in their own policing and security endeavours. As such, it allows for a potential re-engagement on the part of communities with locally based security processes and may enable a greater alignment between the security demands of the policed and those policing.

Conceptualizing public and private goods and interests

Policing is often described as a 'public good' evoking the sense both that it is a universal good, equally available to all, and that all consumers consume the same good; they are treated equally. In other words, there is equity in distribution, provision and service. At least, this is the policing ideal. This is contrasted with security as a private good that is competitively consumed such that one person's consumption prevents its consumption by any other. It is exclusive to the owner, as with the purchase and installation of a burglar alarm, for instance. However, it is between these extremes that the public/private dichotomy becomes problematic.

Researchers have increasingly come to recognize a variety of 'grey' or 'hybrid' policing bodies some with complex public or private status (Johnston 2000b). It is no longer appropriate to assume that the security of public places is the essential responsibility of public authorities whilst the role of private security is restricted to the protection of private property in the interests of its owners. Numerous policing commentators have shown how the role of the public police has increasingly penetrated private spaces, enhanced by technology and legislation (Marx 1987). Others, by contrast have demonstrated the manner in which privately owned spaces have taken on a decidedly public character (Shearing and Stenning 1981; Kempa et al. 1999).

Some commentators have preferred to advocate a continuum-based understanding of the public/private divide in contrast to a starkly dichotomous view which is increasingly difficult to sustain under contemporary conditions (Benn and Gaus 1983: 25). However, the degrees of publicness and privateness in policing are not a smooth continuum, nor a series of finely graded steps. Those perceived to be at the polar ends of the policing continuum, the central state-controlled police, at one end, and market-provided private security guards, at the other (Jones and Newburn 1998: 203), have themselves developed a more complex status. In England, this has been particularly arisen from two recent growing trends.

Firstly, as we have seen, there has been a significant expansion in the contracting out of state-controlled police officers and staff to various municipal and private interests. Within these arrangements, the public police have mutated into a largely 'private' resource. Secondly, an increasing amount of the funding for private security is now derived from public sources. Government grants, local authority spending streams and community development budgets of social landlords increasingly provide additional security and patrolling via the market. Consequently, commercial security guards are being drawn into public functions. The interests that they serve are much more broadly drawn. The consumers or beneficiaries of the service are not merely the purchasers but the wider public who have access to, or use, the areas policed. Added to this, in England and Wales, private security and municipal policing personnel under the Police Reform Act 2002 now may be granted legal powers over and above those accorded to the private citizen. The Act makes provision for Community Safety Accreditation Schemes,[5] whereby accredited persons

---

[5] Before establishing a Community Safety Accreditation Scheme the Chief Police Officer must consult with the Police Authority of that force and all the local authorities that lie within the police area. The legislation requires that employers of accredited persons make suitable arrangements to supervise the use of their conferred powers when carrying out community safety functions. Individual accredited officers will need to be vetted as 'suitable persons' and should be adequately trained before they can take on the accreditation powers.

may be empowered to issue fixed penalty notices for minor offences of disorder and anti-social behaviour.[6]

Where private security guards are duly accredited,[7] this will facilitate a form of 'responsibilization' by encouraging private organizations to take greater account of, and responsibility for, the policing and security consequences of their commercial activities. Subsequently, accreditation will bestow a certain 'public' status upon private security guards and their employers. Not only will accredited officers be granted limited 'public' powers over and above those exercisable by ordinary citizens, but also the manner in which they exercise their powers will be caught up in public interest requirements.[8] Moreover, accreditation further confuses public/private relations by placing the police in the ambiguous position of both accreditor and competitor within the mixed economy, raising certain conflicts of interest (Crawford and Lister 2004: 61).[9]

In contemporary policing debates, the dominant conceptual framework has tended to focus upon who does what and where. Less attention has been given to the question, 'In whose interests?' In other words, who are the beneficiaries of the good of policing? In focusing upon the interests served by different forms of policing we need to be mindful of at least two observations. Firstly, there is often a dissonance (unintended or otherwise) between declared intentions and routine practices. Much policing that claims a 'public interest', by professional police or others, may actually serve private interests or ends. Additionally, the implementation of policing norms, given the important role of discretion, means that there is considerable scope for 'street-level bureaucrats' (Lipsky 1980) to inject discriminatory practices.

Secondly, peoples' security interests are neither homogeneous nor static. Interests and the goods that seek to secure them may be contradictory and ill thought through or poorly articulated. Security operates at both subjective and objective levels; it is both symbolic and material (Zedner 2000). As the demand for security has grown it has also become more differentiated. Questions about the interests served by specific policing and security arrangements need to be determined empirically within

---

[6] Originally, it had been proposed that accredited persons would have detention powers analogous to those of CSOs; however, this was rejected at the Third Reading in the House of Lords (25 April 2002, *Hansard*, H. L. vol. 634, cols. 416–21).

[7] Accreditation powers came into effect in April 2003. To date, there has been an uneven and limited development of private security accreditation.

[8] Despite the fact that the Act does not specify that accredited people are caught by s.6 of the Human Rights Act 1998, it seems clear that private employers and their accredited employees will be treated as 'public authorities' for the purpose of the human rights legislation.

[9] As a further commercial twist, police forces are able to charge for the cost of accreditation.

given contexts. This suggests an approach that forces an empirical consideration of how inclusive norms of policing are and whose interests these norms represent.

An economic theory of public goods

The economic concept of public goods focuses upon the qualities of commodities that render them 'unmarketable' or not efficiently marketable. Samuelson (1954) offers a 'pure public good – pure private good' dichotomy. A pure public good is defined as 'non-excludable', 'indivisible' and 'non-rival'. These are features that render commodities non-marketable and hence better provided by a collective political authority, namely the state. Here, market norms of commodification and efficiency are taken for granted. Goods that cannot fit into this model have to be accounted for as 'public'. From a market perspective, they are residual; what is left over after commodification is assured.

Non-excludable goods are those that cannot be provided for some and yet excluded from others. Here, denying anyone the benefits associated with a good is either not possible or prohibitively expensive. The classic example often given to illustrate the non-excludability of some goods is the lighthouse. All ships, regardless of where they come from or the nature of their business, benefit from the presence of the lighthouse to guide them into harbour and away from rocks. *Indivisibility* means that the good cannot be consumed in part, whereas *non-rivalry* implies that one person's consumption of the good does not prevent someone else from using it. The quantity consumed by one does not limit its consumption by others. Pure public goods are capacious, in that the domain has an unlimited capacity for the entry of extra individuals, such that there would be no depletion (of quality or quantity), even in the case of unlimited public consumption. In the case of non-rivalrous consumption, one individual's consumption does not detract from another's.

As there are few goods that possess all these qualities at once, there are few examples of 'pure public goods'. With the development of technology even the contemporary equivalent of the lighthouse can be rendered excludable. Many other public goods suffer congestion. This has led some commentators to differentiate between 'pure public goods' and 'crowded public goods' (Samuelson 1954). Crowded public goods are those goods that are limited or in scarce supply and, hence, subject to rivalry. They may become congested and crowded and, hence, depletable. As a consequence, they demand some form of managing congestion through limited access or rationing, as such they are 'quasi-' or 'semi-' public goods.

An economic concept of public goods takes the notion of an unregulated market for granted and with it the legitimacy of the institutional framework of private property. However, ideal markets do not exist in any pure form. They depend upon political decisions, social organizations and infrastructures, as well as non-market-based social institutions. The most obvious of these are families, which develop and inculcate 'practical ethics of care and support', very different from instrumental and self-maximizing market mentalities (Williams 2004). The economic conception of public goods reminds us that the commodification of certain things may necessitate that other things remain uncommodified.

Furthermore, as Foldvary notes, much of the literature on public goods ignores the fact that 'most civic goods are provided within some bounded area and affect the demand for the use of that space' (1994: 25). Territorial collective goods are those where the significant impact or use is confined within some geographic territory. Most civic goods supplied by government are territorially based, including policing. The organization and substantial impact of much police work is territorialized to force areas and, within them, to Basic Command Units. Territorial goods are capitalized within their area of impact. Such goods constitute a limited and precious resource that needs to be rationed to avoid congestion.

As a consequence, the distribution of safety as a 'public good' is rarely just or even. Policing is a good example of a 'quasi-public' good for which additional users increase the cost of provision. The contemporary congestion of policing means that police protection and response do not exist to a degree that they can absorb an increased demand. Quite the contrary, it is the insatiability of demand that has stimulated a market in additional policing and security. Over recent years, demands upon police time have grown significantly. The most immediate indicator of this is the greater numbers of emergency and non-emergency calls to the police. Police telephone control rooms in England and Wales now handle about forty million calls each year, including at least twelve million emergency calls. Driven by greater access to telephones, particularly with the expansion in mobile phone ownership, much public demand requires from the police some form of response. As demand for policing has grown, so too the effectiveness of the police response has diminished due to the congested demands upon it.

Consequently, police forces around the country are routinely required to ration response by screening out what might be regarded by many members of the public as serious crimes. The level and speed of response by the police may be dependent upon police – not individual or public – assessments of seriousness, available evidence or potential for prosecution. This is a form of exclusion from the public good of a police response, whether it is by the decision of a call-handler on the basis of information given against criteria set or through the exercise of discretion by a police officer. Like many forms of exclusion it can be self-perpetuating. The experience of a lack of, or an inadequate, response by the police to a call or request by a member of the public may mean that the individual concerned might not call upon the police on a future occasion. This self-exclusion may not merely stem from direct personal experience but also may be influenced by vicarious experiences of others and folkloric stories of inadequate or slow response by police to people living within an area.

An economic theory of club goods

An economic theory of clubs was first advanced by Buchanan (1965). His concern was for cases of non-pure public goods, where sharing arrangements and congestion problems arise. He used the example of the swimming pool, jointly supplied by members of a club for each other but surrounded by a fence to exclude non-members. This renders the pool's use non-rivalrous among a limited number who all contribute to the cost of maintenance and avoids the disadvantages of congestion by others (nonmembers). He suggested not only that is it possible to identify an optimal size of the good to be shared and an optimal number of members to share the good, but also that these two factors are interdependent. For an ideal club to exist both the membership size must be optimal relative to the provision rate of the good and the size of the good must be optimal relative to the size of the membership. Club goods, therefore, are those 'quasi-public' goods that are available to members of a club but restricted in some form or other to non-members. The forms of restriction may entail access control or entry charge, but also may relate to inaccessibility or inconvenience due to travel time or spatial separation.

Buchanan's idea of clubs, as sharing arrangements to address congestion problems, prompts a number of issues. Firstly, it fails to differentiate between club members' preferences. Members cannot be assumed all to hold the same view about the value of the shared good (its optimal quantity) or the size of the club. Clubs need to develop norms, structures and processes that restrain or inhibit members from mutually unproductive internal competition and foster successful competition with non-members. Secondly, it tells us little about how the good is to be financed or provided – how contributions are to be assured – and what organizational form this is to take. A third and related issue concerns the nature of the bonds of interdependence or common interests among group members; in other words, the relative intimacy and social meaning of club membership. This can range from the highly impersonal, where membership has little social meaning or implies minimal interaction, to the very intimate, where membership is an aspect of social identity and forges social interaction. In the former, membership may be more a reflection of 'connections of convenience' or 'bonds without consequences' that may easily be swapped as circumstances dictate (Bauman 2001). These are contemporary 'contractual communities' rather than 'communities of fate'. In more intimate clubs, membership may have greater permanence and encompass the ties that bind humans together through shared values. This axis of differentiation alerts us to the fluid and changing social dynamics of club formation and development.

A theory of club goods is intrinsically bound up with issues of inclusion and exclusion, and hence, how members are selected and non-members excluded. This implies some notion of discrimination. Club formation also has impacts in terms of negative externalities for non-members. As Jordan notes, club theory 'offers a crucial theoretical tool for the analysis of processes of collectivization and fragmentation in welfare states' (1996: 65). He goes on to suggest: 'There is increasing evidence of an overall tendency within welfare states towards the formation of new and smaller clubs with more homogeneous memberships . . . The exclusion of bad risks and the grouping together of narrower risk pools in such systems reinforces the residential segregation of rich and poor achieved through "voting with the feet"' (1996: 68). This does not occur only in residential segregation, but also in retail and commercial segmentation. Such processes of collectivization and fragmentation are increasingly structured around fear of crime and concerns for security. Accordingly, policing and security are more frequently provided by and through collective 'club' arrangements, often with implications for the experience of public policing, which is left to manage the consequential negative externalities, notably in the form of crime and disorder displacement, and to police the bad risks excluded from club membership.

Whilst individual crime prevention technology and security devices are available for individual or household purchase, the high cost of policing performed by human agents is likely to be prohibitive – except for the very wealthy who may be able to afford a bodyguard. Additional human security will usually require the clubbing together of those seeking to benefit from the collective good. In such clubbing endeavours, the problem of the 'free-rider' enters the fray. Individuals may prefer to benefit from a service without paying for it. As the 'prisoner's dilemma' reminds us, each person, household or business has an incentive not to co-operate even though all would gain more if all co-operated rather than all not co-operating.[10] However, this ignores the various incentives to co-operation (or disincentives not to co-operate) that may exist, rooted more in social, rather than economic, capital. Where collectivities are bound together by other interdependencies – social networks, mutual exchange, shared values, social identity and belonging – these may be put at risk by free-riding. Individuals may find that their 'rational' economic decision not to co-operate will put in jeopardy their standing in relation to other matters in which they are required to engage or interact with other individual users. Again this will be dependent upon the level of intimacy and interaction within a given club. In this way, private communities can, and do, finance collective goods outside of the state, in the face of and belying traditional economic theories of market failure with regard to public goods (Foldvary 1994).

The process of clubbing may entail using diverse levers to encourage 'consensual' co-operation, where a narrow economic interpretation of self-interest might suggest otherwise. Individual users are induced to pay for a portion of the good such that the total amount of the good is paid for. Size, as Buchanan reminds us, may be a relevant factor in clubbing together. Too many individual units may dissipate the powers of inducement and social standing, and make collective agreement difficult. Too few individual units may mean that the transaction costs are too high to make collective co-operation worthwhile.

Using data from the British Crime Survey, Tim Hope has demonstrated how even 'private' activities, such as the introduction of security devices as forms of crime prevention against the risk of burglary may have a 'clubbing effect'. He shows how '"affluent" suburbs offer property-owners a *club good* of security' (2000: 97). This is due to the fact that the externality benefits of private security goods – the individual crime prevention actions by owners to protect their property – are retained, whereas in poorer and inner-city areas there is no equivalent externality benefit. Risks of burglary are reduced the more that higher-value property is surrounded by similar property.

In such a context, a collective good of security is shared among residents. The principal mechanism inhibiting congestion, by others seeking to benefit from this club good and internalize the externality, has been the private housing market, which has kept prices high, affordable only

---

[10] The prisoner's dilemma derives from game theory and serves to illustrate collective action problems that arise where, if one person co-operates, it will always be in the interest of the other to defect, such that each player's best strategy is not to co-operate, despite the fact that if both co-operate they would derive the greatest overall benefit.

to the most affluent. Moreover, the housing market has itself internalized the value of security and perceptions of risk as important in house prices, both directly and indirectly through insurance premiums. Consequently, contemporary British cities are marked by the highly segregated nature of housing markets.

The suburb's capacity to exclude others, primarily via the price mechanism, also guarantees that its positional advantage – that is, its capacity also to retain private security externalities (club goods) – is not diluted by the demands from those excluded from the suburb's security ... The more 'exclusive' the suburb, the more it can exclude unwarranted risks by maximising avoidance of risk through spatial and cultural distancing from 'criminogenic' places and people. (Hope 2000: 102)

Hope provides a good example of contemporary clubbing of a more-or-less intentional form, in which security benefits are captured for members with subsequent implications for non-members and where membership is conditioned by the fee of elevated house price. The good, in this instance, is in part internally produced – the collective benefits of household crime prevention installation – but clubbing can also take the form of the capture of existing public goods. Here, as elsewhere, the possibility of capture of a good is often conditioned by wealth, power and access.

This process is well illustrated by the case of education in England and the manner in which those who can afford property prices in school catchments are able to capture the good of publicly provided education. The 1988 Education Act further facilitated the process of clubbing by devolving school budgets to headteachers and governors (many of whom are elected parents) and by allowing schools to leave the orbit of their local authority,[11] thus achieving greater autonomy over the school ethos and selectivity of prospective pupils. The education example is useful as it reminds us that the strategies of one school can and do have impacts on other (notably surrounding) schools. As Jordan notes: 'As opted-out schools have sought to cream off high-yield/low-cost children, they have forced other schools to adopt similar strategies, and made it far harder for those with no such strategic option to achieve success, either in terms of examination results or in establishing a satisfactory mix of pupils' (1996: 138).

These examples reinforce the spatial dimension to 'clubbing'. Hence, club formation can be facilitated (and undermined) by spatial landscape, architecture and environmental design. However, clubbing will often be stymied by the prisoner's dilemma related costs of co-operation. Let me

---

[11] Subject to appropriate voting procedures.

illustrate this with the example of Trafford Park, Europe's largest industrial park, in Greater Manchester. As a result of high crime within the park in the late 1990s, concerns were raised about businesses relocating away from the park to potentially safer locations (thus exercising their power of exit). To counteract the threat of theft and other crime, most individual businesses employed private security firms, cost often being the overriding factor. As a consequence, the park was policed by a plethora of security firms with little collective co-ordination. This in turn introduced new security concerns over the extent to which some security provision within the park was either exposed to organized criminality or seen as insufficiently robust. Whilst it was in the interests of all businesses to render the site more secure, high transaction costs were associated with this. A variety of initiatives were introduced which illustrate some of the difficulties of clubbing (Crawford et al. 2005). Firstly, the industrial park's large size did not help. Assisted by the council, road closures and environmental planning changes were implemented to encourage smaller subunits that might club together. The ambition was to help clusters of businesses in implementing greater situational crime controls, as well as in purchasing security from fewer (if not a single) suppliers. Secondly, a Guardsafe scheme was introduced with the support of the local police to try to standardize the quality of private security through limited training and to introduce a form of regulation.[12] Thirdly, Business Watch, the collective voice of businesses within the park, worked with the local police to co-ordinate security provision and sought to provide additional policing through a variety of funding sources. Finally, the police encouraged businesses to form Crime Risk Management Groups in an attempt to familiarize themselves with their 'shared' risks or experiences of victimization and, hence, to seek collective solutions.

None of the above strategies fully addressed all the problems of clubbing in the area. Trafford Park remains policed by a fragmented private security presence and many businesses prefer not to participate in Business Watch activities. The absence of a sufficiently powerful collective authority has been a stumbling block to the provision of security as a club good. Interestingly, in many of these endeavours the police acted as 'honest brokers', helping to facilitate club formation.

As this example illustrates, the problems of group action will usually mean that clubbing will be facilitated by the existence of some collective authority that can encourage, induce or coerce co-operation. In the field

---

[12] This pre-dates the introduction of the Private Security Industry Act 2001, the implementation of which is introducing the first forms of national licensing to the private security industry in England and Wales.

of policing and security this collective authority is likely to be a land-lord or property owner – be it housing association, housing authority or corporation – a management body, tenants' association or a political authority, such as a neighbourhood forum or a devolved local authority organization. Funding may arise through rent, fees, service charges or government sources (ultimately through taxation).

Enclosure

Anton argues that a conception of public good as a commonstock is both logically and temporally prior to economic notions of public good (2000: 12). Historically, private property is a product of laws, most notably the Acts of Enclosure. Metaphorically, he suggests, 'enclosures can be thought of as applying to all that is held in common that is now being converted to private ownership' (2000: 8). Whilst this presents an overly stark understanding of contemporary common ownership versus private ownership, the idea of *enclosure* is a useful one in understanding the processes by which public goods are captured by private or parochial interests and clubs. Enclosure, thus understood, is not merely a product of legislation and state activity. Although it incorporates this, it is also the product of human agency and collective action whereby individuals, groups and institutions capture 'public goods' for their own interests (Olson 1965), as illustrated by the example of state schools highlighted earlier.

The two most symbolic forms of contemporary enclosure are 'gated communities' and privately owned shopping centres. Nevertheless, the development of such 'mass private property' also includes industrial estates, business parks, leisure venues and sports stadia where the provision of additional security has also been a central feature of clubbing. In most instances, the development of these forms of enclosure have been facilitated, aided or licensed by modern states. This is particularly the case where previously public spaces are sold into private ownership.

Gated communities

Gated communities are succinctly defined as 'walled or fenced housing developments to which public access is restricted, often guarded using CCTV and/or security personnel, and usually characterised by legal agreements (tenancy or leasehold) which tie the residents to a common code of conduct' (Blandy et al. 2003: 2). Compared to the USA, the number of secure private residential estates and gated communities in the UK is relatively small. Nevertheless, many urban planning commentators suggest that we are likely to see a significant growth of gated communities in future years. A report published by the Royal Institute of Chartered Surveyors concluded that the popularity of gated enclaves is on the increase, often fuelled by concerns over education and crime (Minton 2002). Interviews with innovative developers spearheading market development in city-centre living in the UK indicate the extent to which the privatization and gating of communal space within schemes has become an accepted design and selling feature (Webster 2001). Areas most likely to see this growth are smart city-centre condominium-style residences and small suburban developments. The expansion of gated communities, most likely, will be facilitated by current weaknesses in planning policy with regard to social mixing and the protection of greenbelt sites.

A recent survey of planning authorities identified around 1,000 gated communities in England (Atkinson et al. 2004). These developments are generally small (mostly less than fifty units) but are spread across the country, albeit particularly clustered in the south-east of England. As yet, many gated communities in the UK do not have additional security personnel and rely rather on restricted access and technology as security features. It is clear, however, that urban developers and local authorities seeking to lure affluent people back to city centres will increasingly look to security systems, gating and visible guarding as means of achieving this.

Shopping centres

Shopping malls, as privately owned spaces to which the public has easy access, embody a particularly open form of club. They embody an interesting tension between the liberality of their inclusive invitation to the general public and their commercial desire to keep out 'undesirables'. Their enticement to 'good customers' is mirrored by their interdiction of 'failed consumers'. As citadels of consumption, their *raison d'être* is to encourage public access and foster commerce and consumerism. Furthermore, they embody both the development of commercial clubs and the capture of erstwhile public spaces. Shopping malls represent a conspicuously symbolic test to the limits of private ownership and the legitimacy of exclusion.

Exclusion from quasi-public spaces

Understanding policing as a club good highlights the centrality of dynamics of exclusion (as well as conditions of inclusion) in contemporary social and spatial interactions. Exclusion is one of the principal tools vested in the power of private property. Hence, security and police operating in shopping malls such as the MetroCentre in Gateshead deploy a variety of informal and formal modes of exclusion and expulsion (Crawford et al. 2005).[13] The most routine form of exclusion is ejection of perceived 'undesirables' from the premise on the basis of private property rights asserting a civil trespass order. Those who are 'not good for the image' of the centre are 'asked to leave' as a type of pre-emptive exclusion of those who have no commercial value or who are not seen to 'belong'. At a second tier, more formal 'exclusion notices' are sent by centre management and categorized either for 'crime' or 'disorder' purposes. Records and images are kept and policed through the extensive CCTV system and the large number of security guards and contracted police officers operating throughout the shopping malls. Banning orders usually last for twelve months. If a person breaks an exclusion notice they are warned that they are liable to be sued for trespass. In addition to these forms of 'private justice', shopping malls can and do resort to the courts for exclusions either in the form of an exclusion order or an Anti-Social Behaviour Order (ASBO, to which I return below).[14] Exclusion orders are obtained through the magistrates' courts, where management have also sought to attach exclusions to bail conditions. Given that this can take some considerable time and orders can only be extended via the courts, private security services often prefer the informality and discretion of their own exclusion notices. They tend only to rely on formal exclusion orders and ASBOs when informal means have been unsuccessful and/or an offence has been committed. Hence, recourse to the public courts is reserved for individuals who do not comply with 'private' methods of exclusion or where these have somehow failed.

Two recent British legal cases illustrate the interplay between forms of exclusion and suggest that, in relation to the UK, private property vests an almost unqualified common law privilege to exclude or eject strangers

[13] MetroCentre, Gateshead, is one of Europe's largest out-of-town shopping and leisure centres, attracting 25 million visitors a year, and employing more than 6,000 people. It was one of the first major shopping centres in Britain to enter into an agreement with its local police authority to finance a team of nine Community Beat Managers. These police officers adopt the role of 'village bobby' within the communal areas of the centre. Each officer has his or her own beat, with the aim of establishing a regular rapport with retailers and shoppers.

[14] The ASBO is available to the police, local authorities, registered social landlords and British Transport Police and can be issued against any person (at least ten years old) who has acted in an anti-social manner 'that caused or was likely to cause harassment, alarm or distress to one or more persons not of the same household' as that person. It is a 'hybrid' order which combines civil prohibitions with criminal sanctions for breach, up to a maximum of five years' imprisonment. ASBOs last for a minimum of two years and can prohibit individuals from doing and saying certain things, meeting with named others or being in certain places.

arbitrarily, without good reason or objective rational justification. The first case, *CIN Properties Ltd* v. *Rawlins*,[15] involved a shopping mall in the centre of the market town of Wellingborough. The owners of the mall imposed a lifetime ban on entry to the mall precincts on a group of local unemployed youths. After a failed criminal trial, CIN Properties obtained injunctive relief to reinforce the privately imposed ban on entry, resulting in a lifelong civil sanction against the youths. The Court of Appeal unanimously overturned a county court ruling that members of the public, subject only to a requirement of 'reasonable conduct', had an 'equitable' or 'irrevocable' right to enter and use the shopping mall during its normal opening hours. The court declared CIN Properties to have been perfectly entitled to withdraw the implied invitation enjoyed by the youths to enter the shopping centre.[16]

The second case takes this exclusionary logic even further as it involved exclusion from previously public land that had been transferred into private ownership. In 1987 Postel Properties purchased most of the town centre of Washington, Co. Durham, known as The Galleries, from the Washington Development Corporation. As was required, a government minister had approved the sale. Postel Properties subsequently banned a group of campaigners from protesting within the town centre against the closure of a local playing-field site. The protestors petitioned the European Court of Human Rights on the grounds of breach of Articles 10 and 11; interference with their freedom of expression and assembly. In the resulting judgement, *Appleby and Others* v. *The United Kingdom*,[17] the court held that the relevant articles do not bestow any 'freedom of forum' for the exercise of that right and that so long as 'alternative means' for the expression of the right exists there was no obligation on the British government to interfere with the applicants' exercise of their rights. According to the court, the applicants were not 'effectively prevented from communicating their views to their fellow citizens'. The court seems to have agreed with the British government's contention that it was not 'for the Court to prescribe the necessary content of domestic law by imposing some ill-defined concept of "quasi-public" land to which a test of reasonable access could be applied'.

Interestingly, in his dissenting judgement, Judge Maruste argued: 'The old traditional rule that the private owner has an unfettered right to eject

---

[15] [1995] 2EGLR 130.
[16] The House of Lords denied leave to appeal and the European Court of Human Rights declined to intervene, not least because the UK had never ratified the guarantee of liberty of movement contained in Protocol No. 4, Article 2 of the European Convention.
[17] Application No. 44306/98, ECHR.

people from his land and premises without giving any justification and without any test of reasonableness being applied is no longer fully adapted to contemporary conditions of society.' According to him, public authorities continue to bear responsibility for deciding how the forum created by them is to be used and for ensuring that public interests and individuals' rights are respected. This view would appear to be more in line with developments in other parts of the common-law world, where courts have begun to demarcate certain kinds of location as 'quasi-public' spaces to which citizens must be allowed access on a non-discriminatory basis and from which they can be evicted only for good cause.[18]

Nevertheless, these two judgements imply that in a British context private property remains tantamount to raw exclusive power. In many senses, the legal power of exclusion from private property in other spheres such as gated communities and industrial parks is likely to be stronger as the invitation to open access is more discriminating than in a shopping centre. This raises pivotal questions about the effectiveness of constitutional protection of individual liberties on privately owned but publicly accessible land. Given the private enclosure of urban space, exclusion has become a dominant and powerful dynamic in urban relations. As Gray and Gray note: 'the theme of exclusion will bulk large in the social history of the next 25 or 30 years ... [and] fairly huge outcomes will turn on whether we attribute continued vitality to the unqualified exclusory function of "property" or choose instead to fashion our property thinking to accord with more inclusive, more integrative visions of social relationship' (Gray and Gray 1999: 15). Yet this theme of exclusion is not restricted to privately owned land.

Exclusion from public spaces

Analogous modes of exclusion have also been introduced in recent years in relation to public places. The most notable of these is the ASBO, first established by section 1 of the Crime and Disorder Act 1998. After a degree of reluctance on the part of local police and councils to use the new orders, and on the back of chastisement from government, ASBOs have now become a significant and increasingly used tool in the policing of public spaces (Home Office 2004: 50). Across England and Wales, more than 2,400 ASBOs have been issued since they were introduced

---

[18] In US case law the terminology of 'quasi-public' property has become more commonplace in relation to shopping malls and retail outlets. Such locations must be accessible to all citizens on a non-discriminatory basis, from which they cannot be evicted except for good cause. Such grounds must be objectively and communicably reasonable.

in April 1999, with 1,323 taken out in the year to March 2004.[19] In a well-publicized operation known as Cape, ASBOs were issued against sixty-six young people in a small residential area (Little London) of Leeds on the same day in September 2003. One teenager was banned from setting foot in the area for ten years except to visit his mum, doctor or dentist!

For local councils and the police, sometimes in consultation with private authorities, ASBOs represent a novel way of managing low-level disorder as well as reasonably persistent criminality. The lower evidentiary burdens that accompany a civil order, supported by criminal sanctions (if breached) and the much broader range of restrictions that ASBOs afford in relation to behaviour, activities, places and people, make ASBOs attractive to public and private authorities as a means of governing conduct. In addition, the absence of press reporting restrictions enables the use of local media to promote deterrence through the public shaming of individuals and as a means of encouraging ordinary citizens and businesses to police any exclusions and restrictions granted under an order. Local newspapers often assist these endeavours by publishing names and photographs in prominent places.[20]

More recently, Part 4 of the Anti-Social Behaviour Act 2003 creates a power to disperse groups of two or more people (s. 30). With local authority agreement, a senior police officer can designate an area where there is believed to be persistent anti-social behaviour and a problem with groups causing intimidation. Once a senior police officer and the local authority have agreed to designate an area, they must publish that fact in a local newspaper or through notices in the area, and it can then be designated for up to six months. In these areas, police and CSOs will have a power to disperse groups where their presence or behaviour has resulted, or is likely to result, in a member of the public being harassed, intimidated, alarmed or distressed. The individuals can then be excluded from a specified area for up to twenty-four hours.[21]

---

[19] For example, the use of ASBOs in three cities in the north of England demonstrates this growth: 422 issued in Greater Manchester since 1999, up 232% since 31 March 2003; 59 issued in Liverpool, up 139%; and 122 issued in Leeds, up 430%.

[20] For example, Manchester City Council produced 200,000 leaflets which were delivered through neighbours' doors listing an ASBO's prohibitions and urging residents to report any transgressions. 'Not Wanted' posters have been put up on some streets and the *Manchester Evening News* has assisted by publishing names and photographs on its front page (Aitkenhead 2004). In addition, the *Sun* newspaper has run a national campaign, supported by a number of chief constables.

[21] The group does not commit an offence because an officer has chosen to use this power. However, if individuals refuse to follow the officer's directions to disperse they will be committing an offence.

Whilst ASBOs require some evidence of past individual conduct upon which the exclusion is based, the dispersal order only requires that anti-social behaviour has been a 'significant and persistent problem' in the area and the individuals' behaviour or *presence* is likely to offend a member of the public. Unlike the ASBO the length of the exclusion is much shorter. The dispersal power is likely to be used against young people and may be broad enough to prevent youths from gathering simply because some youths have behaved in a persistently anti-social manner and some members of the community find the mere presence of even a small group of youths makes them fearful. In both developments, people are being, and will be, denied access to public (and quasi-public) places on the grounds of potential risk of future offending. In so doing, the powers bypass the agency of the individuals concerned (Von Hirsch and Shearing 2000). These forms of preventative exclusion may restrict some people's access to publicly available resources and services and significantly curtail freedoms of movement, assembly and access to public space.

Parochial policing as a club good

Commentators tend to define 'public spaces' as open to all citizens, in contrast to 'private spaces' where citizens can, by virtue of their ownership and control, place limits on who can use the space (Shearing and Wood 2003b). What is absent is a less legal and more sociological understanding of the diverse forms of *de facto* exclusion that operate in so-called public spaces and conversely the various processes of inclusion that exist in so called private spaces.

By contrast, Webster suggests that 'most public realms serve *particular* publics and are better conceived of as *club* realms' (2002: 398). Few urban spaces and the facilities and services that they provide convey the same benefits to all residents. They are likely to give greatest benefit to those who live nearby. Whilst spatial proximity structures the differential access to the resource, what differentiates *local public goods* – where local people derive greater benefit because of proximity (otherwise referred to as 'distance-attenuated benefits') – and *club goods* is the question of excludability. Whether a good can be made excludable will depend on more than mere legal issues; it will also depend on technical, financial and cultural factors (Webster 2002: 399). If a shared good can be rendered *de facto* or *de jure* excludable it may be better described as a 'club good'. 'Proprietary communities' are the most obvious form of such 'collective consumption clubs' (Webster 2001).

However, club goods may be located within public space as well as on private property. This means that processes of exclusion can be found in operation within the public realm. As Webster notes, the more the facility or service is prone to congestion or overuse the greater the likelihood of exclusion. Public-realm facilities such as schools and health services exclude by rationing, by cost (the time and money associated with travel) or by congestion (too many people trying to use or access the same service at the same time). Webster makes the important observation that 'very little urban space is truly public realm . . . in a very real sense cities comprise multiple consumption-sharing clubs, many of which have very clear spatial definition' (2002: 410).

Like other clubs they provide goods and services that are 'public' for those included. Membership, whether on the payment of a fee or not, affords club members access to goods and services that are shared freely to all members. Club membership may set out conditions of behaviour and the means of monitoring conduct therein. These are the rules of inclusion, whether to a school, a housing estate, a residential community, a library or a swimming pool. Here, contracts are supported by potent powers of removal, dismissal, exclusion or termination of membership that constitute compelling incentives to conformity. These are the administrative instruments of control engendered by 'contractual governance' (Crawford 2003b). In the private security context, the contract of membership becomes a fundamental means of accessing privately controlled public spaces. Accepting membership or entry is to accept the forms, terms and conditions of existing regulations. Here, social obligations are recast in a 'private' form of inward-looking parochial control.

As privately supplied public realms, they have a parochial public character. A security club is set within a larger environment, and as such constitutes a 'semi-autonomous social field', in that '[i]t has rule-making capacities, and the means to induce or coerce compliance; but it is simultaneously set in a larger social matrix which can, and does, affect and invade it, sometimes at the invitation of persons inside it, sometimes at its own insistence' (Moore 1973: 720). In these clubs, reliance upon the state for risk management and social control constitutes a backup of last resort. Here, the state is regarded as a tactical resource to be drawn upon at particular moments in support of club governance.

Where a quasi-public good is rivalrous to the degree that demands are placed upon contemporary public police, it is liable to 'capture' by private interests. As public policing is largely demand-led, the creation of new demands by private or parochial interests can significantly skew scarce resources.

Let me illustrate this with two different examples. First is the manner in which the expansion in the night-time economy in urban centres has generated new security demands to which the public police have been required to respond (Hobbs et al. 2003).[22] These demands have drawn police resources into policing the crime and disorder consequences of the commercial operations of the licensed trade and alcohol-based leisure industries. Consequently, residual public policing has been displaced from other times and places. The new security demands of the night-time economy have also generated a massive proliferation of additional security provided by 'door supervisors' or 'bouncers', whether internally employed or contracted to security firms. For revellers wanting access to nightclubs, these private security personnel constitute the dominant form of policing. Nevertheless, this level of additional policing has itself generated further burdens *vis-à-vis* the regulation and policing of commercial security staff (Lister et al. 2003). Whilst it is clear that much of the policing of the night-time economy rests in private hands, it would be wrong to suggest that it has occurred regardless of or despite the state's (in)activity. This 'progression of a commercial frontier' has been actively facilitated – or licensed – by the local state's deregulatory stance and its encouragement of 'municipal entrepreneurship'.

A second example is the manner in which organized communities are better able to respond to police-led community crime prevention initiatives and hence may draw upon police resources. The classic example here is Neighbourhood Watch. The evidence shows that in order to establish and sustain Neighbourhood Watch schemes police assistance and support are vital (Hussain 1988). Yet, research from the UK and America confirms that Neighbourhood Watch is easiest to establish in more affluent, suburban areas with low crime rates, rather than in inner-city, crime-prone public sector housing estates with heterogeneous populations (Skogan 1990). Hence, community-based crime prevention developments, such as Neighbourhood Watch, may actually skew police resources – to set up and service the demands generated by them – towards those places which may least need them and those people most capable of protecting themselves. There is also evidence to suggest that additional policing initiatives, whether provided by the police, municipal authorities or private security, by their very presence, can generate new demands upon residual public policing: to respond to calls for support and assistance; to process information and community intelligence generated; and to co-ordinate and regulate the services provided. As one

---

[22] For example, between 1998 and 2001 there was a 240 per cent increase in the capacity of Manchester city centre's licensed premises. During almost the same period there was a 225 per cent increase in the number of city centre assaults (Home Office 2001).

chief constable, in interview, noted wryly to me of the growth of private security patrols in residential areas in his area:

it was proved conclusively that all that having private guarding services in residential suburbs did was divert the police resources out of the areas of greatest need in the inner city to answer peripheral and largely meaningless 999 calls from security guards wandering around in leafy suburbs, jumping at the sight of their own shadows.

Allied to this are wider policy developments around fear of crime and re-assurance policing which may reflect the political capture of local policing.

Reassurance policing

Recently, *reassurance policing* has become a surrogate term in government and policing circles for responding to public demands for visible uniformed patrols. In 2004, the Home Secretary announced £5 million to fund the reassurance policing programme, to strengthen community involvement in policing, and to identify and tackle crimes that fuel fear in local neighbourhoods. This extends ongoing trials in eight police force areas aimed at delivering dedicated high-visibility police, making officers more accessible to local residents and increasing the quality and quantity of community intelligence. The British government's commitment, announced in the spending review in July 2004, dramatically to expand the number of CSOs is the primary vehicle through which public reassurance is to be delivered. In addition to the estimated 4,000 CSOs currently patrolling the streets of England and Wales the government is now committed to financing a further 20,000 by 2008.[23]

These recent developments reflect the political commitment from within government and senior police managers to respond to concerns over fear of crime and anti-social behaviour and tackle the 'reassurance gap'. Whilst overall crime levels have declined since 1995,[24] the public have increasingly lost confidence in the capacity of the professional police, notably to deliver locally based visible patrols (Mirrlees-Black 2001). For the government, increasing police visibility is a key means of realizing tangible public sector reform that impacts upon front-line service delivery, something that critics say it has been slow (or unable) to achieve. It also appears as a relatively simply and cost-effective way for the government to demonstrate that it is taking crime and the fear of crime seriously and

[23] In addition, it is also committed to expanding the number of neighbourhood and street wardens (Home Office 2004).
[24] There was a 35.8 per cent fall in the overall crime rate between 1995 and 2003 (Simmons and Dodd 2003).

responding to the ubiquitous public demand for more uniformed police on the streets. As such, it acknowledges that public perceptions of safety are crucial to winning hearts and minds in the presentational battle over crime control. To paraphrase David Blunkett (the then Home Secretary) at the launch of the reassurance programme, 'if the public don't feel it, they won't believe it'. CSOs have become the linchpin in convincing the public that they can feel the difference (Crawford, in press).

Given the different spatial and social distribution of crime risk compared to the fear of crime, the reassurance agenda may foster the capture of a new policing resource (officers dedicated to high-visibility patrols, notably CSOs) by those anxious and fearful middle classes with the loudest voices, the largest political influence and the deepest pockets. The idea that policing should be demand-led, as the reassurance agenda presupposes, raises problematic distributional questions, as the capacity to demand is not tantamount to need. By contrast, the capacity to demand often skews distribution away from need. Capture is likely also to occur through the market, as the future funding of CSOs will become increasingly linked to income generation through subcontracting and matched funding arrangements. Maybe it is not coincidental that 'reassurance policing' has been strongly associated with, and promoted by, the former chief constable of Surrey – Dennis O'Connor – the commuter belt home of 'middle England'. The key normative question therefore is to what extent, in the name of reassurance, should public policing as a residual public resource, be drawn into low-level incivilities in areas where fear of crime may be high but the incidence of crime low, and hence away from areas with more serious crime problems.[25] This is not to say that policing should not be responsive to public sentiments and values, but that should deployment of a rivalrous resource be driven by perceptions of fear, it is likely to be captured by certain parochial interests.

In responding to public demands, the 'eyes and ears' function of visible patrol officers can also serve to increase demand on the police organization as a whole, by lowering the threshold of tolerance to antisocial behaviour and low-level disorders. This is what Moynihan (1993) referred to as 'defining deviancy down', whereby the previously 'acceptable' is declared deviant and the deviant is unmasked residing within the normal. Yet, at the same time, many police forces are routinely screening out relatively serious crimes. This contradictory strategy of 'defining

---

[25] Interestingly, this is occurring at the same time as the public police are being subjected to pressures of technocratic rationalization through the introduction of the National Intelligence Model, which seeks to direct policing resources to intelligence-led understandings of prospective crime risks.

deviancy up' (Krauthammer 1993) sees the normalization of 'crime as everyday life' as a 'rationalistic' means of limiting the level of demand placed upon the police and criminal justice system (Garland 2001).

Conclusions

'Post-Keynesian policing' (O'Malley and Palmer 1996) may entail not only the replacement of risk management by social institutions with that by private insurance, but also risk management by, and through, exclusive clubs. Here we see a narrowing of the community of risk-sharers through processes of exclusion and inclusion. This narrowing produces forms of parochial policing, delimited to the interests served and the goods provided. While clubs enmesh individuals within 'circuits of inclusion' their central dynamic is that of exclusion. The conditions of inclusion will be bound up with norms of governance, as will the powers of exclusion and expulsion, all of which may amount to the denial of access to fundamental goods and services. Club governance supported by contractual arrangements may be the bedrock of what Young (1999) refers to as the 'exclusive society'. This raises fundamental questions about the nature of citizenship, social solidarity and justice. To what extent do parochial forms of club governance contribute to a broader notion of *public good?* Do they enhance social cohesion between 'collective consumption clubs', or further promote social segmentation?

In contrast to a nodal concept of security, in which 'no set of nodes is given conceptual priority' (Johnston and Shearing 2003: 147), this chapter has sought to illustrate two arguments. Firstly, security clubs are both normatively and empirically different from state policing. Ultimately, they rely upon and deploy state resources either as threat or opportunity. They can use state policing as a background asset, sometimes drawing it into the foreground for symbolic or instrumental purposes. In so doing, they can exploit its general, all-encompassing and sacred mandate.

Secondly, there is a dark side to the notion of 'governing security for common goods' presented by Shearing and Wood (2003a; 2003b). Security clubs can, and often do, have deleterious implications for state policing as a public good, as well as for the experience of public spaces. This occurs both through residualization of policing as a congested resource and the segmentation of security risks, as good risks are increasingly policed through additional auspices and bad risks policed by a residual public service. Powerful and exclusive clubs can capture and exploit scarce publicly provided resources.

In their discussion of 'collective capital', Shearing and Wood (2003b: 408) fail to differentiate between 'bridging capital' and 'bonding capital'

(Putnam 2000: 22). Security clubs may provide 'bonding capital' in that they unite and bind together all of those (members) who have access to the security provided. Bonding capital is inward-looking and tends to reinforce exclusive identities and homogeneous groups. However, security clubs do not necessarily provide 'bridging capital', which is outward-looking and encompasses people from across different social groups in ways that foster reciprocity and mobilize solidarity. Furthermore, bonding capital, 'by creating strong in-group loyalty, may also create strong out-group antagonism' (2000: 23).[26] To reiterate, parochial policing – with its narrow particularistic focus – is not the same as 'public policing'.

In understanding the interrelationships between the emerging forms of policing we need to develop finer and more appropriate analytical tools. In so doing, we would be foolish to throw out the state with the conceptual bath water. As Bayley rightly warns, we should not get carried away with 'a giddy sense at the moment among many intellectuals that the state is passé' (2001: 212). The role that the state – and professional police in particular – occupies within the field of security governance is pivotal and of a qualitatively different order to other forms of policing, in its symbolic power, regulatory role and residual position with regard to other forms of plural policing. The role of state policing may be being reduced, encircled and transformed, but it constitutes more than 'one node among many'. We need to be able to conceptualize the publicness of private forms of policing and the privateness of the public police, without discarding the distinctiveness of state action. The notion of 'policing as a club good' allows us to focus upon the degrees of exclusivity that forms of modern policing herald, as well as the complex relations between state and non-state governance. This is not to deny, but to reaffirm, that much policing is now conducted beyond the state, and it forces us to explore the nature of alliances and network co-ordination within and between plural actors. Relations between the state and private governance are changing such that there is a borrowing of policing and security strategies and, consequently, a blurring of their distinctiveness. The state is increasingly regarded as a tactical resource for non-state governance. Reliance upon the state for risk management becomes a 'backup of last resort'. The extent to which private and club governance contribute to the state's capacity to manage its populations is less evident.

---

[26] More generally, in their use of the term 'collective capital', there is a failure to recognize that 'the social' and the 'community' or 'collectivity' are not necessarily complementary aspects of the same broad rationality of rule, but constitute different and potentially 'competing problematics of government' (O'Malley and Palmer 1996: 140).

As well as a more rigorous conceptual armoury, we need to explore the empirical make-up of policing practices and security networks as well as their normative implications. For too long the debate within Britain has been long on conceptual musings and short on these being grounded in empirically based research findings (cf. Jones and Newburn 1998). The impact of policing as a club good remains an empirical question that needs further analysis. Here I have simply sought to outline the contours of such an analysis. However, it is important to note that in the preceding discussion I have not been seeking to advocate a normative conception of policing and security as 'club goods'. In their chapter in this volume, Loader and Walker provide a convincing normative argument for policing as a 'public good'. My purpose has been to highlight the existence of powerful counter-tendencies that are increasingly serving to pull policing in different, more parochial, directions. The contentions offered in this chapter, therefore, stand not as a direct critique of Loader and Walker's arguments but rather highlight a set of countervailing dynamics with which a resilient normative conception of policing as a public good must contend.

6   The state, the people and democratic policing: the case of South Africa

Monique Marks and Andrew Goldsmith

This chapter is concerned with the state of public policing in the 'new' South Africa and how policing can be democratized in years to come. We argue, in agreement with Loader and Walker (this volume), that while policing in South Africa, as elsewhere, is carried out by a multiplicity of social agencies, the state should assert itself as the 'anchor of collective security provision'. The need for such state anchorage in South Africa is particularly important given the country's status as an emerging democracy, a term we feel is appropriate given South Africa's dramatic shift to democratic governance just ten years ago. This is because, more than is the case in established democracies, effective and collectively accepted ordering devices need to be instituted which enable all citizens to participate publicly in a secure social environment and which facilitate the forging of a collective identity based on shared 'sense of trust and confidence and of rootedness in the social world' (Loader and Walker 2004a: 25). At present in South Africa such rights and freedoms are limited. A national identity is only just beginning to be constructed but is constantly under threat given socially constructed images of dangerous and endangered groupings. Fears of insecurity and of becoming a crime victim pervade the society at all levels whereas, as we know, the capacity to mitigate or minimize these risks is unequally distributed (Brogden and Shearing 1993).

Our argument for strengthening the state and reaffirming its primacy in the provision of security (as dealt with in the third section of the chapter) is based upon the particular need to improve security for, and reassure, those citizens who are socio-economically disadvantaged and who reside in communities in which informal social control is either weak or occurs in an arbitrary and discriminatory fashion. For these people, while the state may be distant, the alternatives too often are unaffordable and/or unpalatable (Goldsmith 2003). The 'dark side' of communitarian justice that we will outline shortly makes a strong state essential for these communities. In our view (and building on the work of Loader and Walker) the state is best placed in terms of capacity, legitimacy and effectiveness to provide equitable policing services. Where this is, in fact, not occurring because state institutions remain weak, these institutions need to be bolstered for democratic governance to take hold (Fukuyama 2004).

Democratic rights and practices are yet to be fully instituted in South Africa, particularly within historically disadvantaged and disenfranchised communities. For democracy to be enduring, strong institutions – both government and civil society – are required. This is because, as Karstedt (2004: 5) argues, strong democratic institutions produce strong democratic practices which in turn promote democratic values and the creation of new democratic institutional frameworks. As we argue below, the state police in South Africa are a key state institution required to bear primary responsibility for enforcement activities, to minimize the harm caused by crime (Leggett 2004), to demonstrate that a rule of law exists (Bayley 1994) and to regulate the provision of effective security services that are in line with citizen needs and expectations. 'Good governance' is a precondition for overall social and political progress and a sound government without a reliable, effective and just policing agency is highly unlikely (van der Spuy, in press).

Admittedly, it is a tall order for the state police in South Africa to take the lead in promoting fair rules and generating widespread collective security. This is because state policing in this country has been (and in many ways still is) characterized by excessive 'meddling, favouritism, stupidity and monoculturalism' (Loader and Walker, this volume) as well as by historically constructed subcultures of brutality, chauvinism and unaccountability. What we contend in this chapter, therefore, is that for the public police in South Africa to navigate the path to democratic policing, they need to undergo a process of radical reform. While this process is under way, it is far from complete. We begin this chapter by examining the extent of change that has take place within the South African Police Service (SAPS) and try to make sense of the transformation deficit that clearly exists. We do this by addressing the issue of 'police culture' and conclude the chapter by exploring ways in which the police can generate democratic cultural change within their own organizations.

Whatever other developments are occurring in terms of reconceptualizing and reorganizing the institutions of criminal justice ('multilateralization of security', 'nodal governance', 'restorative justice'), reform of key state criminal justice institutions remains essential. Such reform should be the primary focus of those concerned with the democratic governance of policing. As we will show, for reasons of social inclusion, cross-group equity, legality and practicality, criminal justice reform needs to focus on the state's role and especially on finding ways of strengthening its capacity to meet the security needs of its most isolated and weakest members (Goldsmith 2003).

This chapter thus examines four central sets of questions: why is it appropriate to argue for the principal role of the state in achieving democratic governance of policing? What are the limits of public police transformation in South Africa and how can we explain this? How can cultural change be brought about within the police so as to effect more democratic policing? And, what can the public police do within their own organization to deepen the prospects of democratic policing?

Transforming the state police in South Africa

With the shift to democratic governance in South Africa in April 1994, a major overhaul of the criminal justice system became central to the new governance project (Shaw 1994). Consequently,

the new government of South Africa devoted much attention and resources to transforming the police force of the apartheid regime that focused on order maintenance into a democratic police service that is working to be more integrated with the community and respectful of all citizens' rights. (Shearing and Kempa 2000: 206)

But have the South African police democratized? Have they become more oriented to human rights and the community? Are they responsive to local needs and are they operating in ways that are both accountable and transparent? Do they demonstrate a concern with equity and fairness in their conduct? Are they effective in their key roles of crime control and prevention, maintaining public order and securing recently bestowed democratic rights?

Like all other questions about policing in South Africa, answering the question 'Have the police really transformed and become more democratic?' yields a number of incongruous answers.

There are those policing scholars in South Africa who believe that significant changes have taken place and that the police are now operating more in line with democratic norms and principles. While van Zyl Smit and van der Spuy, for example, bemoan elements of the state-centred approach to policing, particularly the trend towards 'tough talk and muscular action' (2004: 192), they argue that a number of (positive) permanent changes have been achieved:

A new style associated with democratic policing has made serious inroads into the colonial-style policing that dominated under apartheid ... Principles of accountability, demographic proportionality and equity of access are firmly part of the criminal justice discourse. The structures created to institutionalise new rules and principles look very different from those that operated under apartheid. (2004: 202)

Leggett also recognizes the headway made by the public police, particularly in regard to their greater acceptability by the South African public. His crime survey of 1,100 households in Johannesburg (the most crime-ridden city in South Africa, and perhaps even the world)[1] found that 'the police get top marks for visibility, seem to be doing well in terms of community contact, and are not accused of brutality or racism' (2003: 5). Similarly, Altbecker states:

Policing has improved vastly in three areas. One of these is the approach to crime prevention. Even more important is the acceptance that all South Africans require policing services. Policing is no longer viewed as the protection of the white community from the dangers of the black masses. The degree to which there is consensus that policing must take place with the consent of, and in consultation with, the entire community has also improved dramatically. Thirdly, the management of crowds... [has] improved beyond all recognition. (1998: 28)

Research conducted by the first author focusing on the transformation of the Public Order Police unit confirms that major changes have taken place with regard to the management of crowds and public order events. Almost all events are policed without incident, and consultations with stakeholders are conducted throughout such policing operations. A survey conducted within the unit in 1999 revealed that members recognized the importance of newly awarded democratic rights to freedom of association and freedom of expression. They have almost without fault policed huge international events marked by ongoing protest and demonstration such as the World Aids Conference (July 2000) and the World Conference Against Racism (August 2001). This policing was so exemplary that, following these events, international organizations such as the United Nations publicly lauded the unit and suggested that other countries could learn from the Public Order police in South Africa (Marks 2003).

Others, however, remain more sceptical about the degree of change since 1994. Shaw, perhaps the most erudite scholar of crime and policing in South Africa, concludes that:

To be fair, it is too early to tell whether these new initiatives will work; some appear to hold promise, others do not. But, the institution of accountable and service-oriented policing, an absolute requirement for the implementation of new plans and laws, still seems some way off. (2002: 120)

---

[1] During the year 2000, some 2,575,617 crimes were recorded by the police. Of these, 1.9 million cases were either withdrawn or undetected. Approximately half a million were referred to court and just over half of these resulted in prosecutions (International Council on Human Rights Policy 2003).

The cautionary tone expressed by Shaw is echoed by other policing scholars in South Africa. Schärf, for example, in a recent paper about community justice and community policing in post-apartheid South Africa
claims that 'South Africa is in its sixth year of transforming its police
agency and there are VERY FEW signs of improvement for the better'
(2000: 22). Similarly, Malan (from the Institute for Security Studies)
reckons that despite huge donor funding for police democratization initiatives, the process of police reform based on the 'democratic policing
model' is ongoing and its outcomes are uncertain. In his view, 'the laws
of bureaucratic inertia still operate in the post-conflict environment and
nothing short of a total purge and rebirth will nullify this fact (1999: 9).
Such a 'rebirth' is, of course, highly unlikely. The International Council
on Human Rights Policy is also somewhat cynical in its review of public
policing in the 'new' South Africa. It argues that 'old police culture is well
entrenched and there are few incentives for adopting new ways' (2003:
83). It also expresses concern at the poor capacity of the SAPS to deal
effectively with rising crime.

Most worryingly, perhaps, the frustrations on the part of the SAPS
and the South African public as regards high levels of crime has led to
increasing calls (including on the part of public officials) for the police to
be 'tough on crime' (Leggett 2004: 9). The new rhetoric about policing
has promoted a backward turn towards militaristic policing and a new
discourse among both the police and the public that portrays human
rights as an impediment to crime prevention and combat (Neild 1999;
Leggett 2004). What seems to exist currently in South Africa, then, is a
contradictory process within the police where reform is geared towards
the democratization of policing but where operational 'imperatives' and
public discourses incline towards an authoritarian approach, suppos-
edly required for police effectiveness. Similar trends have been noted
in many other nations of the developing world where 'fear of crime
and perceptions of increasing social disorder are widespread' (Neild
1999: 1).

Concerns about the lack of transformation within the SAPS have also
been voiced in the popular media. Recently, the editor of a local South
African newspaper made the claim that 'the police remain the most
untransformed institution in South Africa' (*THISDAY*, 14 June 2004).
This followed the release of a report by the police oversight body, the
Internal Complaints Directorate, stating that there had been a notable
increase in the recorded number of deaths in police custody in the past
decade. The solution, it is suggested in the article, is to get rid of those
'recalcitrant police' who have not reoriented their behaviour or their value
systems in line with what is expected from police serving in a democracy.

Clearly then, whether or not the police in South Africa have transformed towards more democratic frameworks and practices is difficult to gauge and is dependent on the benchmarks of reform that assessors use. What is apparent, however, is that there are clear transformation deficits. The police in South Africa, at this point, have not adequately reoriented their practices and schemata in line with democratic policing frameworks. The slowness of change in state police organizations is, of course, not peculiar to the South African case. Similar observations have been made about police reform in both developing and established democracies (Gill 1994; Huggins 1998; Koci 1998).

The quagmire of policing in new democracies is a major concern for those who cherish ideals of democratic governance and policing in South Africa. The challenge, then, is to understand why police continue to act in ways that are undemocratic and to think about ways to promote speedier change within these organizations.

Reflecting on the contradictory outcomes of the police democratization

There are many possible explanations for the slowness and incompleteness of police reform. A significant literature exists on this topic, particularly as it pertains to police in emerging democracies and transitional societies. Explanations range from the lack of political will, to public pressure for harsher policing due to high crime rates and feelings of insecurity, to institutional underdevelopment, to poor police working conditions, and even to the inappropriateness and poor adaptability of international assistance programmes (Neild 1999; Leggett 2004; van der Spuy and van Zyl Smit 2004). We will not deal with any of these explanations in this chapter. Instead, drawing largely on the work of Chan (1996; 1997; 1999b), we have chosen to concentrate on the informal cultural level of police organizations in explaining the limitations of police reform programmes in South Africa and beyond.

Reforming police organizations is, without doubt, a daunting task. This is particularly the case when these organizations have long histories of authoritarian and partisan conduct. Over time, established practices and experiences of the police on the streets reinforce ways of acting towards the public, ways of thinking about their own organization and the world around them as well as ways of interpreting their own and others' actions. Occupational cultures and subcultures are fashioned within police organizations (as with any other work-based organization) enabling the police to make sense of their work and their environment and providing systems of legitimation for their behaviour. This cultural realm is, in general, inadequately addressed in thinking about ways of reforming police organizations. Greatest attention is given to structural reform and to the provision of new policy and training, all of which have proven inadequate mechanisms for effecting police organizational change (Shearing 1995; Marks 1999; Marenin 2004). Despite the widespread use of the term police culture in the policing literature, very little has been written as to how exactly change in police occupational culture is to be achieved.

Chan arguably provides the best account of police culture and police organizational change and her paradigm facilitates alternative thinking about effecting police cultural change. According to her, both the potential and the limits of police reform are to be found within the realm of deeply embedded police organizational culture. Drawing on the work of Sackman and Schein, Chan contends that police culture should be viewed as constituted of shared cultural knowledge containing 'basic assumptions about descriptions, operations, perceptions and explanations about the social and physical world' (1999b: 105). This cultural knowledge informs police rationales, understandings of actions and ways of seeing people with whom they interact, and also their use of strategies and tactics. Chan suggests that police negotiate their structural world according to 'systems of dispositions' or 'habitus' (2001: 119) which are shaped through the transmission of 'cultural knowledge'. In order for police organizational change to occur, 'deep level' cultural change needs to take place. This demands changes in the cultural knowledge of the police. Chan, however, also reminds us that 'members of a group operate in a particular social and political context that consists of certain structural arrangements of power, interest and authority' (1999b: 105) – the 'field' of policing. Changes in cultural knowledge therefore need to be supported by changes in the field if real behavioural change and changes in self-perception and perceptions of police work are to transpire.

The slowness and incompleteness of police reform programmes, we believe, lies largely with the fact that police members hold onto basic assumptions and values – their established cultural knowledge. But what leads police to 'hang onto' this cultural knowledge? Chan has argued that change efforts in the police are often unsuccessful given the 'ineffectiveness of cosmetic efforts such as policy statements and operational guidelines in challenging assumptions and changing attitudes' (1999b: 131). The preoccupation with these mechanisms for effecting police reform is customary with international advisors and donor organizations who are keen to direct and facilitate police reform in democratizing countries (Bayley 1999b; van Zyl Smit and van der Spuy 2004). Changes may have resulted but most agree that these changes are limited, having altered 'rhetoric rather than the reality of operational policing' (Dixon, cited in van Zyl Smit and van der Spuy 2004: 7). Converting international norms about democratic policing into locally effective and legitimate policing systems driven by police officers with reoriented value systems, 'has proven complex and difficult' (Marenin 2004: 108).

This is not to say that changes in policy and training are unimportant. New policies provide police with reformulated goals, principles and procedures to be adopted. However, policy on its own does not transform deep-seated assumptions about the police role and the police environment, nor does it lead automatically to a commitment to changed behaviour. The impact that policy has is in many ways dependent on the leadership provided by police managers and supervisors and the extent that police feel that new policy can be applied to their actual daily work. New policy is often adhered to mechanically and, if not accompanied by shifts in beliefs and values, can be overlooked in situations that are complex and difficult. In such situations, the tried and tested often take primacy.

Training too is an important mechanism for changing police organizations. It provides police with new skills and knowledge and the use of new methods. However, training on its own is but one socializing agency (Fielding 1988). There is a myriad of influences that shape and reinforce values, assumptions and knowledge about environments and the police role. What is taught in training is often altered dramatically when real police work begins. The way in which police see their own role and mission, their organizational milieu, as well as what methods of policing are most effective, will for the most part be determined by their daily policing experiences. For 'mind change' to take place and be sustained, police members have to be convinced that new philosophies and ways of acting actually work and are effective in achieving desired outcomes. Furthermore, police themselves have to be willing agents of change.

Change that results from new policy, training and operational guidelines is usually the consequence of police compliance with rule-tightening and top-down instruction. It cannot be equated with a reorientation of beliefs, values and assumptions. Important and enduring facets of police organizational life, such as memory, remain untouched by these mechanisms of change. Police hang onto their memories in times of change, often as a defence against the decimation of their own work histories. Memories are recalled in the stories that the police tell and these stories reflect deeply embedded knowledge of the roles of the police, appropriate and effective responses, and the nature of particular communities that are served (Mulcahy 2000: 69). Past experiences of policing may provide police members with 'skills' and 'expertise' that they are not keen to relinquish (Bayley 1999a; 1999b).

Another source of police reluctance to let go of established practices and assumptions is that they often lack the confidence to respond to old problems in new and unfamiliar ways. Changed behaviour requires directive supervision and role modelling from those who have authority and are familiar with new policing frameworks. This is often absent in police organizations characterized by high levels of discretion and low supervisory oversight. Police tend to learn 'on the streets' (Waddington 1999) as they carry out their daily work. So long as new methods and motives are not demonstrated as effective and valued by police supervisors, rank-and-file members will see little benefit in challenging the tried and tested.

Traditional hierarchical leadership style within police organizations also retard change programmes. Rank-and-file members, particularly those within organizations such as the South African Police that have had extremely authoritarian management systems, are most often excluded from decision-making and problem-solving processes. As a result, lower ranking members are not party to discussions as to why and how change is taking place and do not feel like partners in the change process (Goldsmith 1990). They are provided with few or no opportunities to deliberate on or contribute to new strategies, approaches and principles. This, compounded with the uncertainty generated by change itself, has the potential to lead to low levels of commitment within police organizations and to both formal and informal resistance (Washo 1984).

A final point on the slowness of democratic police reform in places like South Africa: as Chan insists, we need to take stock of the broad socio-economic environment in which police organizations operate. What can be witnessed in emerging democratic societies such as South Africa is that while significant changes may have taken place at the political and legislative levels, the social and economic conditions of police 'customers' usually do not change at the same rate. Historically marginalized and disadvantaged communities tend to remain in impoverished environments well after the shift to democratic governance. While processes, legislation and institutions are usually created to promote and safeguard a vast array of political and human rights, access to these is uneven. These people lack the confidence, knowledge and necessary access to networks of power to secure the basic rights that they have been awarded. The police, aware of this limited access, may act in unreconstructed ways when policing marginalized groupings, secure in the knowledge that those with limited access to important processes and institutions will most likely not challenge them. This point was clearly borne out when one of the authors joined a unit of the Public Order Police unit on a night patrol in one of the townships in Durban. Throughout the night, police behaved extremely violently towards poor township residents. When asked why they had done this and why they appeared unafraid of being admonished, members of the unit claimed that the harder they 'klap' (physically beat) these residents, the smaller is the chance of their conduct being reported. According to them, township residents are afraid that police would strike out even more forcefully if they laid a complaint against them, indicating their poor knowledge of legal process and their lack of faith in the authority of police oversight bodies in safeguarding the rights of disadvantaged citizens (Marks 2003).

Taking into account these explanations for the slowness of police cultural change, what can be done to expedite the democratization of policing in South Africa? There are a number of potential approaches that could be taken in answering this question. In the first instance, the slowness and the contradictory nature of public police reform may lead us to search for alternatives outside of the state to deal with democratic institutional deficits. These alternatives include looking towards the market as an effective provider of policing services and/or prioritizing the skills and capacities of localized communities in creating safe and secure environments. Both of these responses have become well entrenched in the past few decades given 'critiques of big government and the attempt to move activities from the state sector to private markets or to civil society' (Fukuyama 2004: ix).

A number of scholars have drawn attention in recent years to the proliferation of policing activities by non-state actors (Johnston 1992; Garland 1996; Grabosky 1996; Stenning 2000; Shearing and Johnston 2003). According to these authors, these actors have been located outside the state within community and private enterprise settings. Recognition of the varieties of informal and private social control is often accompanied by propositions about the inevitability of such phenomena and even their desirability. The argument from inevitability is frequently linked to shortcomings of state capacity and inclination to tackle the basic tasks of ensuring citizen safety (e.g. Dupont et al. 2003). It is also seen as a way of linking (or networking) resources together to provide a more effective system of public safety (Brogden and Shearing 1993). The argument from desirability often implies or asserts the importance of citizen participation and influence over policing policy, often against a background (as in South Africa) of longstanding alienation between the majority population and the state security apparatus, as well as of self-governance initiatives by disenfranchised South Africans throughout the apartheid era.

We accept that given the obvious democratic deficit of public policing in places like South Africa the active participation of private agencies and civil society is both inevitable and necessary. Indeed, involving active and engaged citizens in policing activities promotes a communitarian and democratic agenda (Hughes cited in Carson 2003: 29). The plurality of civic-life engagement also allows for a diversity of representation, the contestation of government and the ability of local community members to direct the daily governance of lives, all of which are crucial to democratic governance. Added to this, civic engagement allows for the diversification of the knowledge base and possible intervention strategies of the public police, potentially establishing new mindsets and cultures within these organizations (Wood 2004a).

However, as we argue in the next section of the chapter, turning to the market and to civil society as alternative providers of policing services often has highly problematic outcomes. Additionally, while in many instances the incorporation of non-state agencies in policing enterprises is necessary (given the inadequacies of the public police), their involvement is far from sufficient for meeting the governmental and security requirements of citizens. What is required for democratic governance to take hold and be enduring is an institutional capacity on the part of state agencies in order for them to implement and enforce policies, particularly in emerging democracies where new sets of rights need to be conferred and protected (Fukuyama 2004: 96). The absence of proper institutional frameworks in emerging democracies as a result of neo-liberal global agendas has tended to render these countries worse off after 'liberalization' than previously as new policies are difficult to bring into effect and apparatuses for the distribution of public goods are all but absent (Fukuyama 2004).

State institutions, particularly those concerned with law and public order do matter and are essential for the effective provision of other 'public goods' such as health and education. Safe and secure environments create the 'space' for other public goods to be provided since security offers 'freedom from care, anxiety, apprehension and alarm' (Loader and Walker 2004a: 11). But security as a public good itself is also important (particularly in countries struggling with new 'nationhood') in facilitating collective sentiments and identities. According to them, 'the aspiration for security against internal and external threat is prominent among the matters that help to found and give meaning to people's sense of 'we-feeling', a means by which stable communities register and articulate their identity as stable communities engaged together in a common project' (Loader and Walker 2004a: 12). This sense of 'we-feeling' is fundamental for democracy to have any real meaning. The question that needs to be asked is, given the plural structure of public goods provision, which agency or institution (or array of these) has the capacity, legitimacy and efficiency to provide security? We take our lead here from

150   *Monique Marks and Andrew Goldsmith*

Loader and Walker who argue that the state has 'remained the traditional community of democratic attachment and the principal . . . institutional locus of efforts to subject security practices to forms of public scrutiny, legal control and regimes of human rights projection' (2004a: 3). While other agencies both above and below the state are now inevitably involved in the provision of security, 'we must start with states in building the institutional and social framework' (Loader and Walker 2004a: 27) for achieving the type of security that promotes both objective safety as well as a more subjective 'we-feeling' of national and global citizenry. States in this view are the 'primary motors of common action and sources of institutional initiative' (Loader and Walker 2004a: 27) within an arrangement of anchored pluralism.

Having now outlined our theoretical premises for state primacy in the provision of policing/security, we now turn to a more normative discussion as to why the state is so crucial to any programme of police democratization, particularly within emerging democracies. Thereafter, we will consider some practical cultural change strategies for police organizations themselves aimed at speeding up public police democratization.

The state and democratic policing

More than a decade ago, Bayley highlighted the importance of government provision of policing within an increasingly pluralized policing environment. He argued that:

governments will inevitably remain central to crime prevention in modern societies – not because other institutions are not important but because the state cannot renounce the responsibility. The maintenance of domestic order is as crucial to the legitimacy of government as defence against external enemies. (1994: 144)

This need *by the state* to protect citizens from threats is, we believe, heightened in emerging democracies where insecurity and fear of crime are pervasive everyday experiences. South Africa, like the rest of Africa is beset with problems of major social conflict (Shaw 1994; Marks 1999) and high levels of crime (Shaw 2002; Leggett 2003; Leggett et al. 2003; Goldsmith 2003),[2] usually experienced most directly by poorer communities. These social problems fuel insecurity and restrict citizen participation in public life, resulting in limited prospects for personal and collective

---

[2] While recorded crime levels in South Africa appear to be beginning to stabilize, levels of recorded violent crime remain exceptionally high. 'For example, during the 12-month period of 2001/02 financial year, some 21,500 murders were recorded – an average of almost 60 a day or one murder every 25 minutes' (Leggett et al. 2003: 6). This murder rate is 25 per cent higher than the United States murder rate.

development. The African intellectual Sadiq, in writing about the inextricable link between security and development in Africa, implores
that

Serious efforts need to be made by African countries to put conflicts to an end,
and to achieve greater political stability, peace and social integration . . . A primary
human development goal in Africa ought to be the preservation of human lives
and limbs intact, which is right now a number one concern of a large section of
African people. (Sadiq 1995: 188)

But who has the capacity, not just the responsibility, to safeguard human
lives and create secure environments? There can be little doubt that government agencies may not 'own' the capacity or even the knowledge
needed to reduce the crime and conflict that threaten life and limb.
Such knowledge and capacity may be, as Shearing (1999) contends, harnessed within localized community groupings and this local knowledge
and capacity must be mobilized in developing solutions to problems of
insecurity. However, as Loader and Walker (2003) insist, security is a
public good which should be enjoyed by all, and public institutions (the
police in particular) are indispensable in co-ordinating the provision of
security, ensuring that the security is provided in a manner that is equitable and inclusive. What is required is strong state policing.

We should now make clearer what we mean by 'strong state policing'
before giving further reasons for its essential role in South African criminal justice. Firstly, by this we do not mean various forms of 'regime' policing characteristic of authoritarian states and some post-colonial regimes.
In such countries, the police tend to act to support the regime, often
repressively and brutally, at the expense of the everyday crime and insecurity needs of the general population. To use Marenin's distinction, in such
countries police focus upon the 'specific order' buttressing the regime at
the expense of the 'general order' that advantages the population at large
(Marenin 1990). This certainly describes state policing in South Africa
during the apartheid era. Such state police fail to protect society's most
vulnerable people and almost always lack public legitimacy.

Secondly, the 'strong state' concept applied to policing indicates a set
of constitutional arrangements under which the police are mandated to
uphold the rule of law and according to which they will be held accountable should they fail to do so. In part, this idea establishes the police
role as one responsible to a set of universal, public norms which in turn
governs their relationship to the people at large. Under this notion, the
criminal law becomes the pretext for interfering with peoples' rights as
well as a means for establishing persons' entitlements to personal security
from crime. But at the same time, having a strong state entails keeping

the police at bay by the restriction and monitoring of their activities by governmental and civic oversight and regulatory bodies.

Thirdly (and vitally), strong state policing implies a capacity as well as a willingness to put these various values and normative goals into practice *with or without local community support and assistance.* This, as in the South African example, has often proven to be an enormous practical challenge. However, it does not diminish the normative argument for its establishment, and a detailed presentation of this argument serves as a reality check on some of the more romantic claims made by advocates of alternative justice models, especially those that privilege informal, local systems. We sketch some of the grounds for arguing for state primary in security provision in the following paragraphs.

The state's international obligations and the domestic application of the rule of law

The contemporary state retains its key strategic function with respect to the monitoring and implementation of obligations under international law, including respect for human rights and ensuring that abuses are properly investigated and redressed. This is a key state responsibility which is not readily amenable to major delegation to substate or civil society actors. Sadly, many abuses that occur within weak states are in direct infringement of these fundamental rights. The reasons for infringement are related to weaknesses of state capacity or inclination in combination often with the arbitrary and unaccountable actions of civil society actors (Goldsmith 2003). The International Council on Human Rights Policy has argued that the role of state policing is crucial in transitional societies that are plagued by rising levels of crime and social conflict because 'states have human rights obligations to people under their jurisdiction – to protect their security and to provide services that prevent crime and violence against the person' (2003: 5). States, on this view, have an obligation to provide basic security to the people they govern including the protection of the 'right to life, physical integrity, freedom of movement and others' (International Council on Human Rights Policy 2003: 17).

Promoting individual freedom and restraining the actions of the majority or powerful groups within a society towards minorities are key functions of the rule of law. States have the task in liberal democracies of ensuring that the law is applied transparently and equitably to the population at large. There is a presumption against the law being applied to an individual without advance notice; there is also a set of procedural entitlements associated with the application of the law to any person that constrains the activities of state institutions. In other words, the accountability of the state for actions impinging upon personal liberty is provided for in the law in a direct, proximate way. Non-state policing agencies are not bound by these same international and domestic legal obligations.

This case is made strongly by Tshehla, a South African criminologist. Having extensively evaluated non-state policing initiatives within disadvantaged black communities in the Western Cape, he makes a plea for 'an opening up of the state justice system to accommodate all South Africans both in terms of substantive and procedural law. It is after all their right – and the state's duty' (2002: 66). In large part, Tshehla's entreaty is the result of his observation of the shortcomings in many communitarian alternatives, and he laments that:

Sadly all the forms of non-state ordering discussed [in South Africa] are aimed at the poor black township residents. And they all appear to be some form of second class justice. If so then the township resident is a second class citizen in South Africa, at least as far as justice is concerned. And what does that say for the country's democracy? (2002: 66)

Citizens of historically abusive or neglectful regimes require strong states committed to greater personal liberty through effective operation of the rule of law. They should not have to depend upon the locally generated self-policing initiatives, as has tended to have been the case. The rule of law's implementation demands an authority strong enough to ensure its operation across social divisions.

The need to address all categories of crime

The state has a key responsibility for addressing crime in the round, not just the localized concerns of particular communities. Some categories of crime are less visible than others. Some have few, if any, unhappy or significant victims. Some fraud and drug offences meet these criteria. There is often little interest or capacity within local communities in addressing crimes that are deemed insignificant or in dealing with complex crimes that reach beyond the local. In other words, local communities themselves do not view these crimes as priorities for action. As Brewer et al. observed in Northern Ireland:

The structures and mechanisms by which popular crime management is accomplished are incapable of managing the rise in crime in isolation from a socially acceptable and effective set of formal controls. Local crime management, for example, is ineffective in dealing with sophisticated, organized crime, which is not amenable to the local moral economy and community structures. (1998: 583)

In the absence of a clear authority responsible for crime management, they suggest, 'organized crime expands; rich criminals become richer at

154   *Monique Marks and Andrew Goldsmith*

the expense of petty criminals who are forced to prey increasingly on relatively poor victims from their own or neighbouring local ties' (Brewer et al. 1998: 583).

There are similar risks to be faced in South Africa without effective state policing. As van Zyl Smit has noted:

> The difficulties of a primarily communitarian approach are compounded when it comes to dealing with crime that cuts across communities or interest groups or, even more dramatically, the cross-border and transnational crime to which South Africa is now exposed. (1999: 212)

A comprehensive criminal justice system cannot, and should not, depend upon communitarian sentiment to dictate or drive its goals, laws and programmes. The state's obligation to protect the economy and the body politic demands a more broadly based set of criminal justice norms as well as a system capable of responding nationally and in often technically complex areas across a range of crimes that affect different and often all levels of society.

A counter-balance to populism

Throughout the 1980s and 1990s, township residents (particularly youths) came together in street committees and self-defence units in an effort to protect community members against threats. In broad terms, these groupings operated as one of many layers of the liberation movement and provided a form of 'popular justice' (Marks 2001). In many cases, these groupings were the sole providers of security services, given the lack of protection provided by government agencies (Sekhonyane and Louw 2002: 1) and they played an invaluable role in protecting local communities from threats of crime and the repression of state security agencies. However, even during the period of lauded popular justice, concerns were voiced about the convergence of political and criminal motivations within popular justice structures (Marks 2001).

In more recent years, concerns have been expressed about the use of extra-legal methods by some informal policing groups in response to what they perceive to be weak and irresolute policing, particularly in contexts of rising crime (Schärf 2000; Goldsmith 2003). Sekhonyane and Louw (2002), for example, write about a well-known grouping in the Northern Province called Mapogo-a-Mathamaga. This grouping has 70,000 paying members and has support across race and class lines in both rural and urban areas. This support is based on the belief that Mapogo will deliver swift and harsh punishment and thus deter crime. Today there are seventy-five branches of Mapogo throughout the country. Interested parties are required to join and pay a membership fee. In a way, they operate like a private security company. Initially, Mapogo worked within the parameters of the law. However, over the years, co-operation with the police collapsed and Mapogo increasingly operates in ways that are illegal and in defiance of human rights principles. Over twenty people have died at the hands of Mapogo and scores have been injured or incapacitated after being beaten with rods, shot, electrocuted or thrown into crocodile-infested rivers. Seknonyane and Louw have argued that Mapogo's methods, because they are viewed as 'effective' by localized community members under threat of crime, have 'undermined popular support for the rule of law' (2002: 8).

Similarly in Cape Town, a (largely Muslim-supported) grouping called People Against Gangsterism and Drugs (PAGAD) was formed in the mid 1990s. Their stated mission was to protect communities against the ravages of drugs and gangsterism that plagued certain (black) communities in Cape Town. While PAGAD had significant local support, it was also implicated, and its members charged with involvement, in acts of arson and murder (Schärf 1997).

The main problem with populism is its unprincipled hypersensitivity to public demand. The risk it poses is that unpopular groups or individuals run the risk of excessive and unfair attention. Populism pressures officials and others to take direct, often arbitrary action against persons without due weight being accorded to legal rights and evidential standards of proof (Carson 2004). In the South African context, as van Zyl Smit observes, '[t]here is a considerable danger that outsiders, be they illegal immigrants in a township made up mostly of black South Africans, or black robbers captured in a white suburb, will be treated particularly harshly' (1999: 212).

While public support may exist for popular community-generated policing in many poorer areas of South Africa (Vera Institute of Justice 2003), this support can falter and may in fact be hollow where paramilitary type groups are engaged in challenging the legitimacy of the state (Knox 2002). Too frequently, experience shows us, parallel and informal justice mechanisms have been engaged in enforcing their authority as much as (if not more than) in dealing with 'offences' against the people. At best, this situation is 'second-class justice'; at its worst, it is tyranny. We should not therefore romanticize localized initiatives for self-directed governance. As Habib appropriately counsels us:

Care must be taken not to fall into the trap of so much of the writings on the informal economy, and to celebrate these associations as representing the energies and vibrancy of South African society. Indeed they should be recognised for what they are, which is the survivalist response of poor and marginalised people who have no alternative in the face of a retreating state that refuses to meet its socio-economic obligations to its citizenry. (2003: 236)

As we have suggested, the universal reach of group-based justice cannot be reliably ensured. The very constituency category of *group*, or indeed of self-identified communities, logically implies an 'outsider' or 'other' who may often, therefore, be vulnerable and relatively unprotected.

A partner in and guarantor against failure, in alternative justice systems

The Vera Institute of Justice (2003: 76) suggests that we need to pose the following set of questions to non-state policing institutions: do they provide what is generally recognized as safety and justice? Do they have broad or narrow support in the communities that they serve? Do they protect people who are most vulnerable? While, in specific localities, the answer to the first two questions may be 'yes', there is less reason for optimism on the third criterion, as will be made clear below. There thus remains a clear role for the state as guarantor of minimal standards of respect for rights and the capacity to address substantial issues in ways that minimize further harm. The ability to tackle organized crime should not conflict with or be compromised by local justice experiments in restorative justice, for example. Both have a valuable role to play in improving justice. But where the effectiveness or general application of one is unproven, the need for some guarantees of firm, capable responses to problems is even more pressing and important.

The most researched and published of these are the peace committees in Zwelethemba (north of Cape Town) which resolve threats to security at the local level. These peace committees, Shearing and Kempa argue, allow for the effective resolution of security problems while giving 'participating communities democratic ownership over the ways in which they are policed' (2000: 212). While much is made by some of the Zwelethemba model of community peace committees operating in the Western Cape and elsewhere, as Dixon (2004) has recently noted, it remains largely unevaluated and unproven (cf. Roche 2002). Its pertinence to some disadvantaged communities in South Africa, especially those in larger urban environments, is at least questionable. A failure to account for profound differences between communities in terms of their capacity to organize informal social control and the disposition of such informal mechanisms to act in accordance with the law is one difficulty of this approach. Too much is assumed by its proponents in terms of community cohesiveness and a clear shared moral code, critics such as van Zyl Smit (1999) point out.

For example, in a massive township such as Khayelitsha, located on the outskirts of Cape Town (estimated population: 750,000), the conditions conducive to restorative type approaches are more problematic and elusive (Tshehla 2002; Dixon 2004). These are communities in flux, defined 'thinly' by shared poverty and sheer propinquity rather than in the 'thicker' sense of having shared histories and common traditions. In such settings, too much can be left to chance. Communitarian models also have to compete for public support with the various 'new entrants to already highly diversified and ruthlessly competitive security markets', particularly in larger metropolitan areas (Dixon 2004). Many such entrants, as Loader and Walker (2001) have observed, lack a conception of policing as a public good.

Greater legitimacy

States that are constituted to be democratic and to uphold the rule of law are by their nature inclusive and responsive to a broad array of community concerns about crime and public safety. An important source of state legitimacy is its capacity to protect its citizens from unprovoked violence and depredation; a state that will not or cannot make this a core responsibility has little claim on the allegiances of the people living under it (Bayley 1994; Goldsmith 2003). Effective state policing becomes therefore a *sine qua non* of democratic government. Thus, establishing a new democratic order in South Africa requires the establishment of a police agency that is deserving of broad public support through its commitment to, and effectiveness in, securing the conditions of basic public safety.

The provision of effective state policing in South Africa cannot be dismissed as an imposition of a reform priority by the North (developed countries) on the South (the developing world). In emerging democracies, as elsewhere, very often *the people expect and want* state police primacy: in developing as well as in mature states, 'ideas about policing and the public guarantee of security remain deeply sedimented within the "mundane culture" of everyday life' (Loader and Walker 2004a: 32; also Goldsmith 2003). A recent survey of residents in the inner city of Johannesburg indicated that 86 per cent of people believed the government to be responsible for changes in the crime rate. Leggett concludes that 'the public believe that the government possesses the ability to control the crime rate and that failure to do so represents a lack of service delivery' (Leggett 2003: 7). One reason for this public expectation, one of us has hypothesized elsewhere, is a combination of heightened awareness of the existence of effective, protective police forces in other countries and personal or family member negative experiences of alternatives 'justice' forms (Goldsmith 2003).

In present-day South Africa, the Government's commitment (enshrined in the Bill of Rights[3]) to creating an environment free of crime and violence is arguably one of the greatest tests of its legitimacy and efficacy. The safety of the person and the effectiveness of the rule of law in deterring crime are viewed by government as the backbone of sovereign stability (van Zyl Smit and van der Spuy 2004). Safety of the person is also no doubt viewed as a determining factor in quality of life, and quality-of-life indicators are a measure of the effectiveness of government. People who are victimized by crime may hold perceptions that government has failed them and this then could lead to a withdrawal from societal participation including the right to partake in civic duties or the right to vote. When experienced collectively, such a response to perceived government failure may seriously damage the democratization endeavour in South Africa and other democratizing countries.

Complementarity in security provision, even built-in redundancy, is set to continue in South Africa. Non-state policing initiatives will doubtless continue to operate in parallel and in conjunction with the public police (Schärf 2000; Shearing and Kempa 2000; Shaw 2002), at times resulting in overlap, competition, and conflict (Johnston and Shearing 2003). However, the extent to which these communities, commercial entities and individuals will willingly engage in self-policing or 'for hire' initiatives is likely to wax and wane as they adapt to changed personal and collective circumstances. And as the political, social, economic and global environment in which South Africa is embedded changes, so too will the configuration of pluralized policing. But, communities and individuals (particularly those previously disadvantaged) will continue to hope and expect that the state will protect them and make their environments more secure.

We have argued so far that the nature of alternative policing models in South Africa, for reasons of formal duties and obligations, the distribution of power, ethnic difference, location, resources, and competence inevitably leaves large lacunae of unpoliced space in which the most vulnerable individuals are likely to suffer inordinately and the rule of law

---

[3] The Bill of Rights forms Chapter 2 of the Constitution of the Republic of South Africa (Act 108 of 1996). According to the Constitution, the state must respect, protect and promote the rights in the Bill of Rights. According to the clause on Freedom and Security of the Person, everyone has the right to freedom and security of person which includes the right to be free from all forms of violence.

fails to operate equitably. Effective state policing, as many of these most vulnerable people know, still remains of vital importance and the best option irrespective of social location. But, there is still some way to go before one can conclude that the police in South Africa have undergone radical reform in line with democratic governance principles and practices. We turn now to some thoughts about practical ways in which the police can become key agents in bringing about democratic cultural change within their own organizations.

Accelerating and intensifying police reform

There are, we believe, a number of questions those interested in democratizing the public police should ask: how is it possible to hasten police cultural change so that they come consistently to view their role, the communities they serve and themselves through rights-based lenses? What incentive systems and changes of supervisory practice need to be instituted to get police to buy into change processes and to reconfigure their basic assumptions and values? In what ways can the police's experiences of social and labour rights reconfigure their assumptions about the rights of others? How is it possible to change fundamentally the culture of the police so that police come to view themselves as social agents with an important role in promoting and protecting democratic rights and freedoms?

In thinking about and effecting deeper-level cultural change within police organizations, greater recognition needs to be given to the fact that police themselves are change agents and that they have 'extraordinary experience, resources and knowledge' (Marx 2000: 2) to either block or encourage social change. It is therefore crucial, if change programmes are to be successful, that police officers 'buy' into and support these programmes and come to appreciate and even cherish the values, assumptions and techniques that underpin democratic policing. For this to occur, the very way in which the working lives of the police are structured needs to be reconstructed and police officers' own direct experiences of rights and freedoms need to be reconsidered and reconstituted. This involves, in the first instance, challenging established labour-management practices within police organizations.

Police supervisors and managers have a crucial role to play in facilitating police organizational change. Not only do they have a role-modelling function, but they are also primarily responsible for determining how work is structured and the types of relationships that exist between social groupings within the organization (Goldsmith 2001). Police leaders tend to fear change and they try to effect change within existing frameworks.

While police managers feel most comfortable with the 'tried and tested', they need to be more open to the uncomfortable aspects of organizational change (Kiel 1994).

One way of breaking with past practices and belief systems is to develop a new work structure that is more participatory and that is flatter than the traditional hierarchical structuring of police organizations. This restructuring would allow for an improved flow of information and communication. More participatory workplace structuring and ethos also make it possible for all members, regardless of rank and function, to have a say in how the organization really works and how change will be actualized. This is crucial if members of the organization are to feel motivated and committed to the change process (Goldsmith 1990). At the same time, mutual respect and support is built through partnerships, shared visions and joint problem-solving. The incorporation of participatory processes within the police organization also has the potential to change the way in which the police act within the communities they serve. Their direct experiences of the benefits of creating partnerships and joint problem-solving processes may help them to appreciate the need for community-oriented and participatory forms of policing. Internal organizational democracy spurs on external democratization (Berkley 1969; Marks 2004a).

Contrary to what some police leaders may believe, the practice of participatory management styles does not entail undermining the authority of police managers and supervisors (Cowper 2004). This brings us to our second point. While participatory management practices are crucial for long-lasting police organizational change, directive leadership is also required in times of transition. This directive leadership involves close and careful supervision and the provision of clear and understandable directives during policing operations. The development of appropriate and agreed performance indicators is also critical in the quest to develop new responses during policing interventions. Rank-and-file members should be encouraged to participate in formulating (group and individual) performance indicators. In so doing, a sense of ownership and responsibility is cultivated (Goldstein 1990; Birzer 1996).

Directive and responsible police leadership, particularly in the early stages of change processes, demands that supervisors accompany members as often as possible when they are deployed. This is important for three reasons: supervisors can provide continuous 'in the field' guidance and feedback; it allows for the close observation and monitoring of police conduct required for fair and informed performance evaluation; and supervisors can directly demonstrate what is meant by 'good' performance. Police leaders play an important role-modelling function particularly when members feel uncertain as to what changed behaviour is required of them. New on-the-street experiences are central to shifting assumptions about creditable performance and positive outcomes (Waddington 1999).

The basic assumptions and values that police members have about democratic rights and freedoms are shaped by their own personal and organizational experience of these rights. While the policing literature has concerned itself with the governance and democratization of policing, policing scholars have generally failed to recognize the interconnectedness of these matters to the rights of police officers. Police members at all levels are more likely to respond towards the public in democratic and fair ways if they themselves experience the benefits of such behaviour in their own organizational lives. Having realized the benefits of rights of freedom of association and speech in their own organizational and personal work experience, they are more likely to recognize and respect the integrity of such rights in the environment external to the police organization (Fitzpatrick cited in Finnane 1999:13). There is no guarantee that this will occur. However, there is a greater chance of police cultural change if the mechanisms for change touch the everyday organizational experiences and deeper-level assumptions and values of police officers than that which could be achieved through more conventional mechanisms of training and policy initiatives.

Rank-and-file members, therefore, should be permitted and encouraged to join employee representative organizations, be they unions or associations, or more loosely structured forums. This would provide members with alternative forums to engage in deliberate discussions about their own conditions of service, but also about policing policy and practice and the changes that policing is undergoing. In so doing, they actively produce new cultural knowledge and transform the organizational ethos by providing an alternative voice (to police managers) to the governance of security. The very existence of such collective representative bodies, and the challenges they pose, directly confront the traditional hierarchical nature of police organizations as well as the unspoken expectation of members' quiescent conduct. They may also provide a watchful eye over police managers should they digress from the goals of the organization's transformation process.

But there is another (perhaps more important) reason for encouraging representative police employee bodies that relates more directly to the democratic practice of police members. If the democratization of policing is to occur, public policing needs to become less oriented to state protectionism and more oriented towards community needs and equitable service delivery. For this to occur, members within public police agencies need to directly experience democratic practices and mentalities within their own organization. Police representative organizations can play a key role in redefining notions of citizenship, informed by their own quest for rights and freedoms within police organizations themselves and by their identification with members of communities that they serve (Marks and Fleming 2004).

Finally, it is important for the police to change the way in which they present and represent themselves in their daily discourse and in the stories that they tell. For police transformation to take place, new memories and stories have to be created that will transform the 'sensibilities' of the police (Shearing 1995). Selective memories of the 'good old days' and of past triumphs can block organizational change since they provide the police with 'ready-made schemas and scripts' (Chan 1997: 70) for justifying past actions and attitudes as well as for resisting the inculcation of new organizational values and approaches. The police tend to hold onto the past particularly when past epochs represent periods of apparent social control and police effectiveness (McLaughlin and Murji 1998). New stories need to be created that allow the police to let go of their defensive identities by producing new mirrors in which they can reflect on themselves and on their roles. Such mirrors need to reinforce what is functional, what really works, and what is valued in the work that they do. By so doing, they will be able to think of themselves as different from what they formerly were.

But how exactly is it possible for the police to create new stories and foster new memories that provide them with a sense of pride, accomplishment and collective identity? As simple as it may sound, we would like to suggest that one way of changing existing stories and replacing old memories is for policing organizations to collectively and actively celebrate successes and positive outcomes. Two examples will illustrate this point. Firstly, the police organization could acknowledge and reward the peaceful outcome of a political demonstration in which the police successfully deployed new 'soft' public order techniques. Secondly, the police leadership could publicly acknowledge and reinforce the contribution made to police standing and reputation by a whistleblower who had brought serious corruption or other malpractice within the ranks to the leadership's attention (Goldsmith 2001). These types of collective celebration also present learning opportunities for the police as they reflect on how positive results were achieved and what was done differently. In so doing, the knowledge of the police is transformed as they incorporate new ideas about what is valuable and what behaviour is most acceptable. These positively reinforcing and celebratory moments are likely to be remembered fondly and will be recalled time and again when the police speak about the 'good times'.

Conclusion

South Africa is now entering its second decade of democratic governance. High levels of crime and ongoing social and political violence continue to plague this new democracy. Both these social problems pose serious threats to the legitimacy of the 'new' democratic government as insecurity (both real and perceived) leads citizens to question government capacity and commitment to secure the life and property of all South Africans. High levels of crime and violence and the fear that results from this also limit civic participation generally.

Police primacy in public safety in South Africa is more, not less, important in the face of these legitimacy problems and ongoing feelings of insecurity among the South African public. State legitimacy is ultimately served by doing more rather than less in areas such as public safety and crime prevention. A state that fails to protect its citizens loses its *raison d'etre*. While 'networks' may have a role to play in security provision, citizens will need reassurance from a capable state that some 'nodes' do not degenerate into rent-seeking, self-interested and discriminatory behaviour at odds with the enhanced security of all and respect for constitutional and human rights obligations. One reason for the degree of public acceptance of private security in developed countries may well lie in its perceived supplementary role in 'adding' to state-provided security measures. Where state protective services have been unreliable or absent, community reliance upon the alternatives will almost always, we suggest, reflect necessity rather than unimpeded free choice or a freely chosen preference with a realistic possibility of *exit* or *voice* (Hirschman 1970).

Despite the traditions of civic engagement (and resistance) and the dominant government neo-liberal discourse, South Africans (particularly those previously disadvantaged) desire and anticipate that the new government will provide services that were previously denied them. Democracies in late modern societies must be characterized by participation. However, there are a number of other characteristics of these societies that we believe stand against continuous and dedicated locally generated policing. In the first instance, contrary to what those who advocate the mobilization of local knowledge and capacity in the governance of security would argue, ties that 'link individuals and groups to institutions, that build bridges between groups, and that provide generalised trust and tolerance between members' are usually weak (Hope and Karstedt 2003: 16). Secondly, people are more often than not aware of the 'costs' of their involvement in policing activities in terms of time, effort and potential conflict with others resulting from such activities (Karstedt 2004). Thirdly, for democracies in late modern societies to be effective, individuals and groups should be able to express their right to disagree and to dissent in all aspects of their lives. Democratic institutions are therefore required and desired to mediate disagreement, to help build ties and to facilitate participation, as well as to provide the space for the positive expression of individualism.

It is not surprising that South African citizens and the South African government have hugely invested, both emotionally and in terms of resources, in the reform and democratization of the South African Police Service in the quest for democratic governance outcomes. While attempts at democratizing the police in South Africa are well under way, the ability of the state police to behave and think in more democratic ways is constrained by historical legacies and memories, enduring cultural knowledge, organizational ineptitude and a socio-political environment characterized by high crime rates and social inequality. The time has come for policing scholars, international police advisors and police leaders themselves to think more creatively about new mechanisms for hastening police democratization processes. In particular, a lot more thought needs to be given to the vexing problem of deeper-level cultural change. We suggest that serious consideration be given to the way in which police work is structured and the social and labour rights of the police themselves in helping police to reorient their values, assumptions and entrenched practices.

7   Necessary virtues: the legitimate place of the state in the production of security

Ian Loader and Neil Walker

Thus far . . . we have no reason to suppose that there is any better general
solution to the problem of security, and little, if any, reason to regard
any other possible countervailing value as a serious rival to security as
the dominant continuing human need.   (Dunn 2000: 212)

In their recent book *Governing Security*, Johnston and Shearing pinpoint
what they see as a significant shift in criminological writing about 'the
problem of the state' (2003: 33–4). Three decades ago, they contend,
'cutting-edge criminological theory' posited the state as the 'problem' –
structurally tied to class interests, systemically and unjustly directed
towards coercing the poor and weak, incapable of defending public interests against narrowly drawn private ones. It was, as such, a force to be
struggled against and, ultimately, transcended. Today, by contrast, such
theory has come to invest in the state as 'solution' – a means of articulating
and defending the 'public interest' in a market society whose neo-liberal
champions triumphantly proclaim that no such thing exists. Johnston and
Shearing describe this situation as a 'strange paradox' (2003: 34).

But perhaps this is not so very paradoxical. In an age of 'solid modernity' (Bauman 2000) it could indeed be claimed that the task of defending
dispossessed individuals and groups from the overweening and intrusive reach of the coercive, bureaucratic state pressed itself with particular
urgency upon the forces of progressive politics, whether liberal or social-
ist. But we no longer inhabit such a world. To be sure, states around the
world continue today to adorn their 'shiny uniforms' and abuse 'people's bodies and souls' (Castells 1997: 303). The problem of state power
has scarcely withered away and nor, with it, has the practical work of
subjecting its deployment to public scrutiny and legal control. But the
state today cannot simply be assumed to be pre-eminent as a means of

We wish to thank the volume editors, Benoît Dupont and Jennifer Wood, together with
Lucia Zedner, for providing constructive written comments on an earlier version of this
chapter. The usual disclaimer applies.

either authorizing or delivering policing and security, as Johnston and Shearing, among others, have so persuasively shown. The 'governance of security' is now conducted by a multiplicity of institutions. These encompass not only public police forces, but, in addition, other security-oriented agencies of local and national government; a plethora of large and small commercial security interests; residents' associations, community groups and other institutions of civil society; not to mention the complex institutional networks engaged in policing and security practices in the transnational arena (see Loader 2000; Crawford 2003a; Walker 2003). In this pluralized – often market-driven – environment, the problem has become not so much (or at least only) the arbitrary, discriminatory exercise of sovereign force, as the absence of political institutions with the resources and legitimacy required to prevent those with 'the loudest voices and the largest pockets' (Johnston and Shearing 2003: 144) from organizing their own 'security' in ways that impose unjustifiable burdens of insecurity upon others. Or, to put the same point more widely:

These days, the main obstacle to social justice is not the invasive intentions or proclivities of the state, but its growing impotence, aided and abetted daily by the officially adopted 'there is no alternative' creed. I suppose that the danger we will have to fight back in the coming century won't be totalitarian coercion, the main preoccupation of the century just ended, but the falling apart of 'totalities' capable of securing the autonomy of human society. (Bauman and Tester 2001: 139)

This, at any rate, is the argument we want to pursue in this chapter – one oriented to the dual task of, first, developing a sociologically plausible and normatively robust conception of the human good of security and, second, indicating the legitimate place that the state occupies in the production of security thus conceived.[1]

Proceeding thus requires us to enter into a dialogue with what remains a pervasive, if often implicit, scepticism towards the state within policing and security studies, one that generates among (especially Anglo-American) policing scholars a tendency to think about security in ways that 'either downplay the importance of the state form or denounce it altogether' (Ferret 2004: 50). In the first part of the chapter, we therefore

---

[1] In what follows, we consciously avoid positing an essentialist answer to that simple but most basic of questions in political theory: what is the state? Rather, our claim is that the state is known through, and best conceptualized in terms of, the diverse *effects* associated with a very broadly conceived institutional and cultural matrix within which public authority is imagined, asserted and pursued as a unitary whole. We examine the multidimensional nature of these effects – both negative and (potentially) positive – at some length as the argument unfolds. For a consideration of this question, and a resolution along these lines, see Runciman (2003).

offer a hermeneutic excavation of this sceptical disposition. We consider, in particular, four variants of it that depict the state, in turn, as a *meddler*, a *partisan*, an *idiot* and a *cultural monolith*. In respect of each, we outline a 'best case' version of the strand of scepticism under discussion, indicate its strengths and highlight the particular challenges it poses for the position we wish to defend. But we will also, in each case, pinpoint certain blindspots that our positive argument strives to make good. In part two, we develop this more positive case – one that is alive to the dangers that each variant of state-scepticism alerts us to, while none the less maintaining that the state's place in producing the public good of security is both necessary and virtuous.

Forms of state-scepticism in policing and security studies

To be a friend of the state has been made to seem an index either of stupidity or of corrupt purpose. To be a dependant or client of the state has been made to seem odious and degrading. By contrast, the state's enemies have vindicated their enmity as a direct expression of their own practical insight and purity of intention. (Dunn 2000: 246)

Scratch below the surface of many a text in policing and security studies and one tends to encounter the signs of a more or less powerfully felt scepticism towards the state. On occasions this scepticism is explicitly stated, sometimes passionately and loudly so. But more often it lies buried, unarticulated or defended, an implicit assumption that quietly guides inquiry and analysis. Generally what is being assumed is that sovereign state power is a baleful presence in social and political life (an evil), or at best a presence whose force is only to be prevailed upon at moments of last resort (a necessary evil). In either case, the state is postulated as a standing threat to the liberty and security of citizens, an entity that requires eternal vigilance, oversight and control. Much less is it assumed that the state may play a positive role in producing the forms of trust and abstract solidarity between strangers that are a prerequisite of secure, democratic political communities.

We lack the space here to make good these bold claims. Still less can we engage in the kind of 'sociology of the sociology of policing' (Ferret 2004: 50) that might tell us why the intellectual field is structured in these ways. But we do want to consider in some detail the concerns about the state that figure in different variants of state-scepticism, as well as the intersections that are posited between the state, security and liberty, and the alternatives that are projected to the alleged dangers of state-centric conceptions of security. With these matters in mind, we have assembled four 'ideal-typical' forms of state-scepticism that we believe can be located in the social analysis of policing and security (and in political studies more broadly). These overlap in significant respects, not least in the assumption that it is the state's monopoly of legitimate violence – its capacity, as it were, to act as a *bully* – that lies at the core of the 'problem of the state'. Each, however, coalesces around a specific elaboration of this problem and an attendant set of worries about the operation and effects of state power. They are thus worth considering in turn.

The state as meddler

This variant of scepticism towards the state has at its focus the capacity of the state to violate or undermine the liberty and security of individuals. Though this represents a widespread concern about the nature of state – and more especially police – power (one, it should be noted, that we share), it is pressed with particular clarity and force within neo-liberal and libertarian writings on the state. Here it takes two closely connected forms which in different ways highlight the propensity of states to meddle illegitimately with the entitlements and voluntary market exchanges of sovereign individuals.

The first of these takes as its axiomatic starting point the arresting proposition with which Nozick begins *Anarchy, State and Utopia*: 'Individuals have rights, and there are things no person or group may do to them (without violating their rights)' (Nozick 1974: ix). On this view, the only justification for the state and its monopoly of the authorization of legitimate coercion is as a necessary bulwark against the (greater) threats to individual liberty and security that would ensue in 'the state of nature'. The state is theoretically reconstructed as the outcome of a notional social contract in which individuals agree to trade a quotient of their liberty in exchange for the state's guardianship of their person and property, or else, as in Nozick's (1974: part 1) account, viewed as emerging via an 'invisible hand' from the contest between 'protective associations' that the state of nature is assumed to generate. The resultant entity is only, however, legitimate in its minimal form, enforcing criminal law, punishing transgressors and prohibiting acts of 'self-exemption' (Holmes 1995: 27), as well as providing the stable legal framework necessary for market exchange. Any further extension of the redistributive functions of the state involves immoral acts of coercion – the forcible removal of one individual's legitimate holdings in order to improve the lot of another (Nozick 1974: part II). But even in its minimal form the state remains a dangerous thing, a power whose capacity to monitor, arrest, detain, interrogate and inflict pain upon individuals has to be subject to eternal suspicion, vigilance and control. The state on this view provides the minimum necessary conditions of security for the exercise of individual freedom. But it is an evil none the less.

A second line of scepticism arises from the attempt to apply economic theory (and its axiomatic presumption that individuals are rational utility maximizers) to government known as 'public choice economics' (Buchanan 1978). Four charges are from this standpoint levelled at the state as a mechanism for producing and distributing social goods, including security. First, that as public bureaucracies (especially those of a monopoly kind such as the police) have no price signals to which they are required to respond, they have no incentive to be efficient and keep costs down. Second, that state provision tends to be colonized by vested bureaucratic interests, thereby subordinating consumer interests to those of producers. Third, that state forms privilege the interests of the articulate, active or merely noisy over and above those of people who do not wish to make political participation central to their conception of the good (Seldon 1990: 99). Fourth, that public bodies offer consumers only the 'cumbrous political channels' (Friedman 1962: 91) associated with what Hirschman (1970) calls 'voice', channels whose efficacy is hindered by the inability of consumers to 'exit'. This style of thought does, it should be noted, recognize a sphere of 'public goods' whose non-excludability (and the associated problem of free-riding) makes it necessary for such goods to be collectively financed and provided, and policing is generally held to be among these. But the necessary involvement of the state in security stands as but a pathological – and still dangerous and inefficient – exception to the liberty-respecting purity of the free market (Hayek 1979: 46).[2]

Both these forms of state-scepticism consequently tend to couple a grudging acceptance of the necessary, albeit constricted place of the state in the production of security with a disposition towards the extension of private security practices that is relaxed, if not positively welcoming (e.g. Forst 1999). In part, this amounts to the belief that state policing (or at least the non-coercive aspects of it) should be exposed to the full blast of competition from the private sector. But it also means that sovereign individuals should be able to break free from their undignified dependence on the state and pursue their own self-determined security interests. They should not, in other words, be prevented from clubbing

---

[2] There are some 'anarcho-capitalists' – such as Rothbard (1985) and Benson (1990) – who cut through the arguments about the necessary minimal role of the state offered by the likes of Nozick and public choice theorists, arguing that the state – and its law enforcement functions – can be dispensed with altogether and replaced by 'a fully privatized enterprise of law' (Benson 1990: 357). For a fuller discussion, see Loader (1997c).

together with others to realize their freely chosen security goals (by, for example, forming private residential associations or gated communities) or seeking through voluntary market exchanges to purchase the hardware and services they believe will make them secure, whether they be burglar alarms, gates, CCTV systems or commercial security patrols. Indeed, one of the fears neo-liberals and libertarians have about the state is that its actors may seek to discourage, control or even prohibit (in short, meddle in) these voluntary acts of security seeking (Hayek 1979: 47). Hence the efforts made by neo-liberal governments across the world in recent years to encourage their citizens to take more personal responsibility for the security of their person and property (e.g. Home Office 1994). Hence also the attempts of some neo-liberal economists to urge that governments act to stimulate security markets by, for instance, offering tax incentives to individuals who 'improve the security of their own property and purchase private policing services' (Pyle 1995: 54; see also Elliot 1989).

Several – if by no means all – of these claims and concerns about the state have a resonance beyond the parameters of neo-liberal/libertarian thought. This form of state-scepticism quite properly, in our view, emphasizes that security is a basic good that serves as a precondition for the meaningful exercise of liberty, even if it holds security to possess no non-instrumental value beyond that. And it rightly concedes the necessary place of the state in offering guarantees of security *to all*, even if it sees no legitimate security-enhancing place for the state beyond that. Indeed, many liberals worry that it may be injurious to liberty to expand the idea of security, and the state's place in its production, any further than this.

The neo-liberal/libertarian variant of state-scepticism is, moreover, quite properly alert to the paradoxes that arise from concentrating the capacity to exercise legitimate force within a given territory to a single entity – the paradox being that the very monopoly of violence that exists to guarantee the security and basic liberties of individuals stands as an ever-present threat to that security and liberty (Walker 2000: 4–6). It highlights, in other words, the inherently 'double-edged' character of police institutions (Walker 2000: 6), even in their capacity as upholders of what Marenin (1982) calls 'general order' – the maintenance of public tranquillity and safety that is the indispensable basis for social routines and the pursuit of individual purposes in which all sections of a society have a stake. In so doing, it pinpoints the propensity of state police forces to exceed or abuse their power in ways that directly impinge on the very individual rights and entitlements they are 'contracted' to protect – a tendency most glaringly apparent in weak, failed or authoritarian states (Goldsmith 2003), but which remains a feature of state policing even in more sustainably democratic settings. At the very least, this scepticism about state power – a scepticism apparent in the long-standing preoccupation of police studies with the (arbitrary, violent) operation of police powers and discretion (e.g. Westley 1970; Dixon 1997) – indicates the importance of forms of constitutional and political regulation within any schema that seeks to defend the proper place of the state in the just and democratic production of internal security.[3]

Yet the more expansive conception of the state–security nexus we want to defend in this chapter must also address certain shortcomings exhibited in neo-liberal/libertarian scepticism towards the state. Let us briefly highlight three. The first concerns the preconditions that are required to create and sustain limited, constitutional, rights-regarding states. There is, as Canovan (1996: 38) points out, a tendency in classical liberal theory to assume 'that any fool can establish a nightwatchman state' and a corresponding disregard for the forms of trust and abstract solidarity between strangers (of the kind supplied by secure membership of a political community) that provide the cultural conditions of possibility for the minimal, rule-governed state that libertarians find acceptable. But surely such states require citizens to care, and be prepared to do something about, abuses of police power or, more broadly, to identify with a polity in which the police are held to account and the rights of all equally guaranteed? This, of course, raises some thorny matters pertaining to the affective dimensions of social and political life (to which we return in the second part of this chapter), issues that neo-liberal/libertarian writers have tended to steer well clear of. They have remained too preoccupied with the (problem of the) state and the threat it poses to individual freedom, and insufficiently attentive to the trust-building functions of political community upon which the liberty and security of citizens depend.

A second issue concerns the forms of individual security-seeking that neo-liberalism is eager to promote (or at least prevent the state from preventing), and the conception of security upon which these rely. This conception is both atomistic and unrelational. It takes the form of individual security-seeking practices that are self-defeating and in a profound sense oxymoronic (Loader 1997b), an 'expression of the desire for sovereign agency' (Markell 2003: 22) that depends upon and projects a semblance of security produced by lifting oneself out of co-existence with others

---

[3] There is here – as one of us has pointed out elsewhere – a further paradox of police governance entailed in such regulatory efforts. This more specific paradox inheres in the fact that the national and local state is both the source of regulatory control over the police and, as one of the main beneficiaries of the police's ordering capacity, part of the problem that regulation seeks to address (Walker 2000: 4–6, 54–67).

in order to render one's own existence less contingently vulnerable and the future more predictable. These practices are often at the same time exercises of private power. They eschew democratic political life in order to achieve 'distributive outcomes according to one's assets, skills and preferences' (Offe 2003: 450) in a manner corrosive of the forms of trust and solidarity upon which any sustainable notion of the public good of security draws and, in its turn, replenishes. Neo-liberalism remains committed, in other words, to forms of security that 'organize the world in ways that make it possible for certain people to enjoy an imperfect simulation of the invulnerability they desire, leaving others to bear a disproportionate share of the costs and burdens involved in social life' (Markell 2003: 22).

The current proliferation of these private – anti-social – security practices raises the question, thirdly, of whether – as neo-liberals maintain – the state's always potentially intrusive and counter-productive attempts to 'insert some logic into the messy human predicament' (Bauman and Tester 2001: 137) is *the* source of misery in the world today. Might it not be suggested, instead, that the fragmentation and weakness of public political authority lies at the heart of the contemporary security constellation, whether in respect of weak states whose repression of their citizens serves so often to mask their lack of effective infrastructural power, or in liberal democracies faced with growing market-induced disparities in the security resources available to their citizens. Against this backdrop, neo-liberal/libertarian forms of state-scepticism seem simply to be 'barking up the wrong tree' (Bauman and Tester 2001: 137). As Bauman says: 'Too much of the state is a catastrophe, but so is too little' (Bauman and Tester 2001: 137).

The state as partisan

This form of state-scepticism is associated more with the political left than the neo-liberal/libertarian right. It shares with the latter a concern about state violence and the paradoxes inherent in concentrating the power of legitimate coercion in the container of the state. But it argues that this violence is not merely a necessary precondition for the maintenance of a consensual general order. The police are, rather, a vehicle for upholding what Marenin (1982) calls 'specific order', a means of fortifying the interests of those constituencies favoured by the present unjust pattern of economic and social relations. The state is, on this view, a partisan actor in social and political life, as are its agents the police. It is, as such, an evil, an unwanted and unwelcome force that needs to be monitored, exposed, struggled against and – depending on the particular variant of leftist politics – radically reformed or transcended.

We cannot in the space available here detail either the range of radical perspectives on the state, or their application to questions of policing and security.[4] Let us instead, using two now rather unfashionable categories borrowed from the Marxist philosopher Louis Althusser, indicate some of the ways in which it is claimed policing institutions act to sustain relations of domination. It can be said firstly that the police function as part – arguably, the sharpest part – of what Althusser (1971) calls the *repressive* state apparatus. Under this heading, one might pinpoint several salient dimensions of policing practice. First, the ways in which routine police deployments focus disproportionately on the economically and socially excluded so as to reproduce patterns of domination organized around class (Cohen 1979), race and ethnicity (Keith 1993), gender (Brown and Heidensohn 2000) and age (Loader 1996). This becomes most nakedly apparent in respect of those social groups (such as vagrants) whose disconnection from economic and social institutions renders their social control almost exclusively a matter of policing – groups evocatively referred to by Lee (1981) as 'police property'. Second, the manner in which police force is called upon at moments of socio-economic and political crisis to quell acts of violence and dissent and uphold the status quo. This itself is most glaringly apparent in authoritarian or colonial settings, where the police frequently operate as regime tools propping up discredited, unpopular governments through the surveillance and suppression of political opposition and protest (e.g. Ahire 1991; Huggins 1998). But this remains a feature of policing in 'democratic' political systems governed by the rule of law. Here policing has repeatedly in recent decades been mobilized to handle the presenting symptoms of economic and social divisions – whether in respect of urban unrest, industrial strife, or political protest – often in ways injurious to the liberty and security of already marginalized populations (e.g. Cowell et al. 1982; McCabe et al. 1988; della Porta and Reiter 1998).

But policing and security institutions also function as part of what Althusser calls the *ideological* state apparatus, as one of a range of bodies – the media, churches, the family, education systems – whose practices seek to manufacture and sustain the consent of the ruled by masking the unjust or oppressive 'realities' of prevailing economic and social arrangements. Part of this involves finessing the coercive character of the

---

[4] A useful overview of Marxist state theory can be found in Jessop (1990); applications of it to policing include Spitzer (1981), Brogden (1982) and Grimshaw and Jefferson (1987). On feminism and the state, see MacKinnon (1989); on 'race' and the state, see Goldberg (2001). Scraton (1987) offers a representative set of critical essays on the intersections between these axes of social division and the operation of policing and criminal justice.

state itself. Radical critiques have, in this vein, sought to expose how the formal protections associated with the rule of law are undone by the practical application of substantive categories of inequality (McConville et al. 1991). Such critiques have similarly contended that various 'soft' policing strategies – notably community policing – aim principally to win the consent of routinely policed populations by obscuring the 'hard' realities of the 'coercive state' – the velvet glove covering and cushioning the iron fist (Bernstein et al. 1982; Gordon 1984). But policing institutions also serve as an ideological unifier in a more general sense. Through their socially authorized power of 'legitimate naming', they are able to diagnose, classify and represent the world in ways that apply forms of social glue at moments of political crisis; articulating the crisis as one of 'law and order' and highlighting and censuring assorted 'folk devils' as the cause of moral breakdown and social malaise (Hall et al. 1978; Loader and Mulcahy 2003: chap. 7). As this dimension of state rule segues closely with its capacity to act as a 'cultural monolith' we consider it further under that heading below.

This radical variant of state-scepticism is valuable in highlighting the intersection between policing and security and various axes of social stratification; in pinpointing how in structurally divided societies the security of some groups is maintained at the expense of others; and in its suggestion that the state is no mere neutral umpire holding the ring in conflicts between different societal interests. As such, it poses a number of distinct challenges to the position we want to defend in this chapter. When confronted with the suggestion that security can be conceptualized as a public good it asks: whose security? Which public? What good? It stands quizzically aghast at the idea that forms of trust and solidarity can (or indeed should) be fostered between constituencies with such structurally divergent interests. It asks what is the point of democratizing security if the rules of the political game are stacked in such a way that certain groups find themselves losing time and again. And it questions the value of a perspective that places such a partisan entity as the state at the heart of a project to produce more equitable distributions of policing and security resources.

These are far from trivial objections. But they arise from a standpoint that is not itself without shortcomings, as we hope to show in meeting them. This radical variant of state-scepticism tends, first of all, towards a structural fatalism that overlooks the overlap between the production of specific and general order such that disadvantaged groups and communities have a considerable stake not only in controlling state power, but also in using public resources (including policing resources) as a means of generating more secure forms of economic and social existence. In a cognate vein, it remains insufficiently attentive to how the mix between general and specific order (the extent, in other words, to which policing is shaped by public as well as sectional interests) is conditioned by political struggle and the varieties of institutional settlement this gives rise to, thus varying over time and between polities. This disposition tends, secondly, towards a politics that privileges the monitoring, exposure and critique of the operation and effects of state power (as, for instance, in the inde-fatigable efforts of the British-based NGO Statewatch), while radically under-specifying the feasible or desirable alternatives to current insti-tutional configurations and practices.[5] Finally, one might suggest that this radical anti-statist sensibility rests (in ways that curiously parallel neo-liberalism) on a one-sided appraisal of the sources of inequality and insecurity in the world today, forms of social injustice that are much more the outcome of state impotence and neglect than they are of its malign coercions. These, we shall argue, demand not the wholesale critique and transcendence of state forms, but more robust regulatory interventions by democratized state institutions.

The state as idiot

Let us take as the exemplar of this form of state-scepticism the recent work of Clifford Shearing, Les Johnston, Jennifer Wood and their collaborators in the Security 21 project based at the Australian National University (e.g. Johnston and Shearing 2003; Shearing and Wood 2003a; 2003b; Shearing, this volume). Unlike many of those who view the state as par-tisan, Shearing et al. take security seriously as a valued human good (Johnston and Shearing 2003: chap. 1). They refuse, however, to privilege the state – in either their explanatory framework or normative register – among the multiplicity of bodies that may contribute to its realization, whether as sponsor/regulator or provider. Foremost among the reasons for this is the Hayekian claim that the state lacks the knowledge and capac-ity to deliver security to diverse local communities and, moreover, that its attempts to acquire such knowledge and capacity evince a strong tendency towards authoritarian outcomes. The state is in this as in other domains of public policy an idiot, an entity whose bureaucratic remoteness ren-ders it at best unable to make good on its well-intentioned promises, at worst a clumsy, homogenizing force riding roughshod over the possibili-ties created by more locally responsive, 'bottom-up' security institutions.

---

[5] Often this entails a kind of gestural anticipation of – or longing for – non-state forms of communal ordering, as in Rigakos' (2002: 150) claim that 'the only real alternatives to current policing practices are pre-capitalist, non-commodified security arrangements'.

According to Johnston and Shearing (2003) the state has become but one 'node' among several now engaged in the 'governance of security'. Whether as 'auspices' (sponsor) or 'provider' (Bayley and Shearing 2001), the state co-exists with, competes against, or supports a range of security actors from the private sector or civil society. This, it is contended, has contributed to the chronic security inequalities – or 'governance deficits' – one encounters across the globe today, with poor communities being unable to tap the kinds of policing and security resources to which more economically advantaged groups have ready access. But Shearing and his collaborators refuse, in seeking remedies for this, to resort to what they term the 'nostalgic, hopeful' path of 'turn[ing] our back on this trend and seek[ing] to reinstate strong state governance' (Shearing and Wood 2003a: 217), not least because the legacies of oppressive state violence form part of the security problem across many of the sites – notably South Africa and Argentina – in which the Security 21 team have intervened. Thus, instead of depending on 'familiar and comfortable' 'mental schemata' associated with the state (Dupont et al. 2003: 16), and the blanket dismissals of neo-liberalism that such thinking tends to invoke, Shearing et al. urge that we recognize the force of the Hayekian critique of state forms and seek to harness local knowledge and capacity in ways that expand and enhance 'community governance' (Shearing and Wood 2003a: 217).

'Bottom-up', non-state-based security programmes are, on this basis, promulgated as alternative solutions to problems that the state is institutionally incapable of tackling successfully. Remedying 'governance deficits' means creating security markets in which poor communities can effectively participate such that security is identified, promoted and regulated as a 'common' – rather than 'public' or 'private' – good. In their most recent theorization of this strategy, Shearing and Wood (2003a) argue that this entails effort along the following three lines. Firstly, to enhance 'community self-direction'. This means communities defining and pursuing their common interests in respect of security, thereby functioning as autonomous security auspices and 'not simply providers in the game plan of other nodes' (Shearing and Wood 2003a: 213). Secondly, to create and sustain different forms of 'community capital', not only the social capital (or strong social networks) with which Shearing and Wood argue poor communities are replete, but also the economic capital that reinforces it, as well as knowledge and capacities (cultural capital) and recognition (symbolic capital) (see also Dupont 2004). Thirdly, to pursue strategies aimed at improving 'community regulation' or 'accountability' (Shearing and Wood 2003a: 218), whereby local people – in determining, for instance, how to allocate security budgets – regulate the provision of their own security.

What Shearing and Wood offer here is a theoretical elaboration of the community peacemaking and peacebuilding programmes that Security 21 has helped to develop in South Africa and Argentina, and are currently promoting elsewhere – notably the 'Zwelethemba model' of local capacity governance (Johnston and Shearing 2003: 151–60; Shearing and Wood 2003a: 218–21; cf. Roche 2002). As such, it is a conceptualization of security that actively seeks to relegate the state as a (potential) player in the production of local security. This move is Hayekian in that it rests upon the economist's claim that the state necessarily lacks the knowledge to respond effectively to – in this case – demands for order.[6] But it is 'left-Hayekian' in that in seeks to supplement or supplant the state, not in the name of the sovereign individual and untrammelled market forces, but through deliberative local capacity-building practices informed by the values of equity and human rights. It offers in this sense a provocative challenge to state-centric thinking about security issued in the name of experimental local democracy; one that that works through the 'window of security' (Shearing and Wood 2003b: 417) in an effort to forge common interests and collective problem-solving mechanisms within dispossessed communities. It offers, at the same time, a radically decentred account of belonging and political authority whose project is oriented more towards securing 'denizenship' for poor people across a range of communal spaces than with the – old statist – project of connecting people as citizens of national political communities (Shearing and Wood 2003b).[7]

Matters, however, are more complex than they at first appear. A close reading of Shearing et al.'s work reveals that the state, in fact, continues to assume a far from insignificant role in their preferred conception of security. At least three such roles can be discerned. Firstly, Shearing and

---

[6] We must, Shearing and Wood urge, 'recognize the soundness of many of the values that neo-liberalism and associated sensibilities of governance advocate. This involves looking afresh at many Hayekian arguments, particularly the view that governance is best exercised when it relies heavily on local knowledges and capacities along with the view that markets often provide the best means of mobilizing these knowledges and capacities' (2003b: 415).

[7] There are some striking parallels in these respects between the work of Clifford Shearing et al. on security and that of Sabel and his collaborators on 'directly deliberative polyarchy' (e.g. Cohen and Sabel 1997; Gerstenberg and Sabel 2002). Foremost among these are, firstly, a concern with democratic experiments in local collective problem-solving and learning that eschews the communitarian language of belonging and solidarity and, secondly, the strongly felt sense that certain emergent governance practices (whether they be South African peace committees, or new techniques of co-ordination and rule in the European Union) need to be understood and encouraged using a novel conceptual language not tied to outmoded political categories. These two perspectives also in our view share common shortcomings, not least a tendency to neglect the co-ordinating and solidarity-nourishing role of state entities in getting the political game started in the first place and sustaining it in democratic forms thereafter.

Wood concede that, as well as fostering community security institutions, one must continue to 'explore regulatory strategies designed to retain state control over non-state providers where their actions affect public interests' (2003a: 217). Secondly, Shearing et al. envisage a role for the state in generating and (re)distributing the collective resources that are needed to place local community capacity-building projects on a firmer footing (Johnston and Shearing 2003: 155). Thirdly, state police forces are clearly intended to remain as the site of 'last resort' coercive intervention, albeit as reformed entities acting in ways that are sensitive to the ordering mechanisms of local communities (Wood 2004a: 39–40).

This is hardly a trifling set of competences. Yet in each case we find in the work of Shearing and his collaborators a relatively undeveloped account – both sociologically and normatively – of how the state may be reconfigured in these ways, and of the relationships that can be expected (or ought) to obtain between the state and the local security programmes that Shearing et al. ultimately privilege. This gap invites a series of difficult but unavoidable questions. First, there is the question of what constitutes the 'public interest' and how the 'public interest' gets constituted. This remains deeply under-specified. So too does the related issue of what the purposes and limits of the state might be in acting as (meta) regulator of the security practices of both rich and poor. How are we to discover or construct the kinds of common regulatory norms (Hirst 2000) that may prevent community security practices becoming an (often) emotionally charged 'medium of injustice' (Markell 2003: 158), and on what basis and on what terms does the state, as opposed to any other putative holistic regulator, get to play such a central role in the refinement and monitoring of what is in the public (as opposed to private or communal) interest.[8]

Second, the far from trivial question of how the state can obtain for itself the authority and legitimacy required both to do this basic ordering

---

[8] There is an evident tension at this point between the somewhat passing references to the state as mediator of the public interest and Shearing et al.'s overarching concern with facilitating 'community self-direction'. Two related issues arise here. Firstly, faced with a situation of deep security inequities between rich and poor – or what Markell (2003: 181) calls 'a relation of privilege and subordination' – Shearing et al. prioritize a strategy that strives to 'include' poor communities by providing them with resources to enhance their own security, rather than seeking to 'dismantle or attenuate the privilege itself' (Markell 2003: 181) – in this case, by calling into question the anti-social security practices of the rich. This, secondly, tends to invoke a fantasy of security as sovereign mastery of one's own destiny, except that on Shearing et al.'s account such 'mastery' is to be exercised by communities rather than – as in neo-liberalism – by sovereign individuals. What is entailed in each case, however, is a downplaying of the *mutually constitutive relationship* that exists between the security of the privileged and the insecurity of the subordinated and, more broadly, of any recognition that the public good of security depends upon the *mutual acknowledgment* of our connections and obligations to others.

work and to raise and distribute funds to ensure the longer-term viability of 'bottom-up' local security programmes is glossed over, as is the wider matter of how levels of economic, cultural and symbolic capital inside communities can be enhanced without the resource-allocating and recognition-granting functions provided by the state.[9] At the very least this would appear to require the existence/cultivation of a sense of belonging to a wider political community sufficient to persuade, in this case, South Africans or Argentinians to identify with the plight of their co-citizens and support, for non-instrumental reasons, both a framework of common regulatory cause and acts of solidarity towards them. Shearing et al.'s locally oriented, state-sceptical politics – with its tendency to treat community, democracy and security as unmediated, face-to-face relationships – has little to say either about the necessary virtues of these mediated forms of political community, or about the institutional 'architecture of sympathy' (Sennett 2003: 200) that may give practical effect to them.

Third, in what is otherwise a potentially promising rearticulation of Kinsey et al.'s (1986) theory of 'minimal policing', relatively scant attention is given to the question of how – historically violent, deeply partisan – states are to be democratized, constrained and reoriented along the lines suggested, such that they come to respect local security practices and intervene only when called upon to do so.[10] In this context, we are led to pose again the question that neo-liberal advocates of the minimal state have not in our view adequately answered, and which contemporary theorists of nodal governance have scarcely begun to address – namely, how can one create the kind of rights-regarding constitutional state that is needed to encourage and facilitate local security practices that are consistent with democratic values such as 'equity and human rights' (Shearing and Wood 2003a: 212)?

In our judgement these various lacunae are the symptoms of a single underlying problematic. It is a problematic that at each of these turns gestures towards the positive ordering and cultural work that the state performs in the production of security. But it is also one where the will to promote non-state experiments in local security, and the cognate sense that the state – for all its indispensability – remains a problem, prevents

---

[9] It is noteworthy in this respect that the principal funding for these programmes has to date come from foreign governments, the Finnish and Swedish governments in the case of South Africa, and the Canadian International Development Agency with regard to the project in Rosario, Argentina.

[10] The only partial exception to this is Dupont et al's (2003: 345) claim that the involvement of non-state actors in security 'can "buy time" and relieve pressure in a manner that can allow legitimate state institutions to emerge or regenerate'.

a full appreciation and exploration of the crucial role of the state as a conduit for the realization of democratic and just forms of security. Ultimately, the state remains a necessary evil – wanted, but not welcome.

The state as cultural monolith

That part of Shearing et al.'s critique concerned with the state's propensity to trample over local diversity is broadened and deepened in a further strand of state-scepticism that explicitly addresses the relationship between the state, security and national culture. Several closely connected claims permeate this position, each of which speaks to some aspect of the state's capacity to act as a cultural monolith, creating and sustaining what Tully (1995: chap. 3) calls an 'empire of uniformity'.

This account of the state addresses its role as a mediator of belonging in ways that bring to the fore the affective dimensions of social and political life. It does so, however, in a critical spirit, pointing out that the state tends to foster forms of 'imagined community' (Anderson 1991) that are unitary and homogeneous, that rest on an unreflexive conception of political membership and that 'admit only one – although largely abstract – identity, in relation to which struggles among all other identities are expected to take their proper place' (Walker 1997: 73). This, it is argued, has two deleterious effects. First, an illiberal posture towards minority groups whose practices and values do not (or are deemed not to) accord with the dominant articulation of national culture. The consequent failures of cultural and political recognition, and the attendant calls for assimilation of those who do not share 'our way of life', foster multiple forms of symbolic – and on occasions physical – violence against the minority cultures concerned. Second, the elevation of national boundaries (and associated distinctions between inside/outside, us/them, here/there) in ways that, at best, limit or undermine forms of solidarity and moral concern towards others and efface or refuse the mutual interdependencies that obtain under conditions of globalization and, at worst, generate forms of xenophobic hostility towards those marked out by territorial frontiers as 'foreigners'. These two claims form the basis for a deep-seated scepticism towards the state as an appropriate mediator of political community issued in the name of cosmopolitanism – one profoundly suspicious of a nationalist politics that 'substitutes a colorful idol for the substantive universal values of justice and right' (Nussbaum 2002: 5).

The field of policing and security is a prime site for the articulation and reinforcement of these monolithic, anti-pluralist predilections, as recent work in 'critical security studies' has emphasized (e.g. Krause and Williams 1997). The tendency of security to 'saturate the language of modern politics' (Dillon 1996: 12), and set the limits of our political imagination, functions in this regard to do two things – both of which are fuelled by security being 'more within us as a yearning, than without us as a fact' (Ericson and Haggerty 1997: 85), a condition beyond our grasp that appears endlessly to require more 'security measures'. Firstly, it privileges and cements the state itself as the subject of security in ways that naturalize its 'tangible, all-pervasive, ghostly presence' in the life of modern societies and, with it, the institutional violence that underpins 'democratic' politics (Benjamin 1985 (1920): 141–2; see also Taussig 1997; Neocleous 2000). By invoking 'security', the state activates what Schmitt (1985 (1922): 5) called its sovereign right to 'decide on the exception'. Security thus operates as an anti-political political practice wherein state actors declare the problem at hand (be it terrorism, or drugs, or asylum, or . . .) to involve imperatives, not value trade-offs and political choices, to call for authoritative decision rather than democratic deliberation (or in Schmitt's view, indecision), and to warrant the restriction of basic liberties as the price to be paid for the maintenance of public security.

Secondly, 'securitizing' practices (Wæver 1995) serve in particular ways to rally and reify a 'unitary people' whose social existence is threatened and whom the state seeks to protect.[11] The generation of political community around the idea of danger tends to foster forms of solidarity that cohere around common enemies, such that national life is re/constituted through an antipathy towards those outsiders (whether within or beyond territorial borders) represented as hostile to 'our' freedom and 'our' security – something that has been discernible in Britain and the USA in the aftermath of 9/11. But it also generates an affectively charged, close to unconditional identification with those institutions (notably policing institutions) that come both to embody the 'way of life' under threat and be tasked with keeping the dangerous other at bay. The resulting investment in a policing solution to the security question (and often within that in particular repressive police strategies) can all too easily coexist with a tendency to overlook or condone abuses of power committed by 'our' police and turn a blind eye to practices that undermine the liberty and security of unpopular minority groups (see Loader

[11] The state can, of course, and this is a key insight of the cultural monolith critique, become a site in which individuals and groups practically and emotionally over-invest as a means of transcending their own vulnerabilities as individuals and groups. They see in the state and its sovereign force a vehicle for producing the fantasy of total security that they lack the resources to secure alone. The state on this view becomes an obstacle, in Markell's (2003) terms, to producing a conception of security based upon an acknowledgement of our mutual vulnerability to and dependence upon each other.

and Mulcahy 2003: chaps. 5 and 9; and, more generally, Cohen 2001). Security, accordingly, becomes not a precondition for the exercise of critical freedom, but a standing threat to it. And when it is coupled in these ways with a politics of belonging, the illiberal, anti-pluralist consequences are plain for all to see.

This variant of state – and security – scepticism teaches a number of salutary lessons. It is highly attentive to the emotive dimensions of security and community and possesses a razor-sharp sensitivity to their pathological consequences. In so doing, it warns those, such as ourselves, who wish to draw democratic virtues from the inescapable presence of political affect that they are 'playing with fire'. It supplies, further, a cogent account of the dangers of placing security at the ideological heart of government, of the capacity of security politics to colonize public policy and social life in ways that are injurious of democratic values, and of its propensity to foster and sustain fear-laden, other-disregarding forms of political subjectivity and collective identity. In all these ways, it reminds us that security 'cannot be dissociated from even more basic claims about who we think we are and how we might act together' (Walker 1997: 66; see also Dillon 1996: 34).

Yet 'critical security studies' remains, in our view, skewed in its account of these associations. It concludes too easily from the above that there can be no progressive democratic politics aimed at civilizing security, that security is so stained by its uncivil association with the (military and police) state that the only radical strategy left open is to deconstruct and move beyond it (e.g. Dillon 1996: chap. 1).[12] In so doing, this strand of state-scepticism commits two mistakes. It forgets, first of all, that while the affective connections between the security, state and nation are deeply entrenched and largely inescapable, they take no necessary or essential substantive form. They can, in other words, be remade and reimagined in ways that connect policing and security to other more inclusive, cosmopolitan forms of belonging – to political communities that 'do not necessarily equate difference with threat' (Dalby 1997: 9). It tends, secondly, to forget that the 'pursuit of security' not only grounds forms of technocratic, authoritarian government and impoverishes our sense of the political (Dillon 1996: 15). Security *is* also a valuable human good, one that is a key ingredient of the good *society* as well as being axiomatic to the production of other individual goods (most directly, liberty). It

---

[12] An alternative course has in recent years been tracked by those associated with the Centre for Peace and Conflict Research in Copenhagen. This seeks not to abandon, but to work centrally with, the concept of security while broadening its horizons beyond 'national security' (and its sole referent object, the state) to encompass the pursuit of freedom from threat along five inter-connected sectors – 'military, political, economic, societal and environmental' (Buzan 1991: 19–20 and *passim*; Buzan et al. 1998).

is our contention that security can be rethought along these lines, and that the state possesses a central place in the production of security thus conceived, that we develop in the next part of this chapter.

The state, political community and the public good of security

The cumulative critique of the role of the state in policing laid out in the first part cannot easily be gainsaid. The state *can* be and often has been a physical and psychological bully. It *is* prone to meddling, to interfering where it is not wanted. It *does* take sides, and in so doing packs the hardest punch. It *will* tend towards stupidity. Not only does it lack the means to answer all the key questions about individual and collective security, it often seems unable or unwilling to recognize this deficiency. Finally, it undoubtedly *does* seek, and in some measure is successful, to set the cultural climate, and to make life difficult or impossible for those who do not conform to the norms it encourages and defends.

Yet, as our scepticism about state-scepticism has sought to make clear, in concentrating on its dangers and limitations, the state-sceptics have tended to be inattentive towards the continuing positive contribution of the state. In particular, they have paid insufficient regard to the possibility that the state, or its functional equivalent, remains indispensable to any project concerned with optimizing the human good of security, or at least, to the full implications of that possibility. To remedy that defect, and indeed to move beyond mere scepticism about state-scepticism, demands a closer specification of the role of the state both in the generation of social meaning and in the ordering of social practice pertaining to security. It is with these two closely interrelated questions that this second part is concerned. For the most part, and for reasons of restricted space, we treat this inquiry at its most fundamental sociological level, through an argument about what the very fabric of social relations implies about the state's role in the generation of common security. But in conclusion we also begin to indicate the type of regulatory matrix which would be most conducive to the state's promotion of common security, while at the same time checking its bullying tendencies and retaining and releasing the potential of communities of practice or attachment other than the state to find their own security solutions.

Security as a 'thick' public good

The key to this revised conception of the role of the state lies in a more rounded exploration of what is meant by security conceived of as a valuable collective or common good or, for reasons which will become obvious, as what might still best be characterized as a *public good*, albeit in a different and deeper sense than applied by economists. This involves introducing two dimensions of the contribution of security to any conception of the good society which are often neglected, and arguing that these two 'thicker' social dimensions are inextricable from and necessary to the effective realization of a third dimension of security – one which *is* accepted as an irreducible component of a well-functioning society across the whole range of perspectives considered above. The dimension which is generally, indeed universally, accepted as necessary we may call the *instrumental* dimension. The other two dimensions which we argue to be symbiotically related to the instrumental dimension we call the *social* and the *constitutive* dimensions of security respectively. Only if we can appreciate the close clustering of these three dimensions of security, we argue, can we appreciate the full extent of the state's necessary implication in the production of security.

The *instrumental* dimension of security concerns the sense in which security is seen as prerequisite to the effective liberty of individuals, which in turn is seen as prerequisite to the 'good life', however conceived. As we have seen, it is axiomatic even to theories of the *minimal* state that without measures put in place to protect the person and property of individuals through some framework of coercive self-organization, those individuals will be unable to pursue their ends free from interference or the pervasive threat of interference. In turn, this basic liberty of the person and property may be seen as instrumental to all sorts of other collective goods that are necessary to a more expansive conception of human freedom, and, perhaps too, that are *predicated upon* a basic or expansive conception of human freedom. For example, it is impossible to envisage stable and reasonably inclusive and responsive democratic decision-making – an important collective good in itself and one that may also be conducive to other individual and collective goods – without the prior and continuing guarantee of private freedom.[13] Equally, the various infrastructural goods which we may associate with the production of a more positive conception of freedom, such as widespread distribution of education, health provision, and social security, cannot be conceived of without the baseline of security – of negative freedom – and the stability of democratic politics and public administration which flows from

---

[13] As Holmes (1995: 31) nicely puts it: 'Citizens will not throng voluntarily to the public square if their homes can be ravaged at will by the police'. That is to say, political autonomy always presupposes private autonomy (and vice versa). For a similar argument as to the symbiosis of private and public autonomy and the co-originality of basic rights and the democratic principle, see Habermas (2001).

this. Further, to the extent that we might want to treat some collective goods such as solidarity as valuable components of the good life in themselves quite apart from their contribution to a more active conception of individual freedom – a deeply complex and controversial issue between liberals and communitarians – the security baseline is again indispensable. In sum, however modest or expansive our conception of freedom, and irrespective of whether freedom and other individual-centred values are the only relevant entries in our index of the good life or whether other collective goods have an independent value – both matters of profound disagreement – security is a constant foundational presence as the most basic instrument in the realization of that particular conception of freedom.

The *social* dimension of security concerns the sense in which the value of security for human society cannot, in Waldron's words, 'be adequately characterizable in terms of its worth to any or all of the members of that society considered one by one' (Waldron 1993: 358). This social dimension, it must be emphasized from the outset, need *not* involve any kind of collective metaphysics – any idea that the *value* of security is anything other than reducible to its value to the aggregation of individuals who benefit from security. What it *does* imply is that the security of any individual depends in some significant fashion upon the security of others, and thus that the very idea of 'private security' is oxymoronic (Loader 1997b).

To begin to unpack this idea, we need to identify two separate but connected senses in which the security of any individual is dependent upon the action and attitudes of others. Firstly, and most obviously, there is what we might call the inter-subjective dimension. When we think of the objective or inter-subjective 'security situation' of any individual, we have in mind the relationship between the catalogue of person- and property-securing measures put in place to protect that individual on the one hand and the propensity of third parties to threaten the individual's security interests notwithstanding this catalogue of protection on the other. Both sides of the situational equation depend crucially upon the actions and attitudes of others. The positive side – the catalogue of protective measures – depends in large part upon the commitment and co-operation of official security providers as well as that of others – commercial security agents, neighbours, friends or concerned fellow-citizens – who are strategically located such that they are able to contribute to an individual's security measures. The negative side – the propensity of third parties to avoid or overcome the security measures in place and threaten or harm our security – is also of course dependent upon the actions and attitudes of others, in this case those putatively threatening others.

But the individual's sense of security does not just depend upon the person- and property-securing measures objectively – or, rather, inter-subjectively – put in place and sustained by others, but also upon a second factor; namely how these objectively or inter-subjectively constituted measures are subjectively interpreted and experienced by the individual. The individual, in order to *feel* confident in his or her ability to pursue his or her ends without interference, must feel reasonably secure that the conditions for the effective and ongoing realization of his or her objective security are themselves reasonably secure. In turn, this is a function both of that individual's *perception* of the attitudes and commitments of official security-providers and other individuals whose behaviour may be capable of having a bearing upon his or her security, and of how this impression fits in terms of the individual's personal threshold of manageable fear – of vulnerability to intimations of insecurity. In other words, the overall measure of an individual's sense of security is the extent to which that individual feels free of *anxiety* about the existence, extent and stable reproduction of the objective or inter-subjective conditions of his or her security. Clearly, the objective 'security situation' of the individual is an influential factor in his or her level of anxiety, but, just as clearly, it is not the only factor.[14]

Even if we accept the intrinsically socially dependent character of our security, the specification of the optimal conditions for the provision of a low-risk and anxiety-free security environment are contingent, complex and far from uncontroversial. There may be a temptation, having produced the social card and revealed something of the intensity of our reliance on others for our security, to start the bidding high by claiming that the optimal fulfilment of our sense of freedom from anxiety about security depends upon the equal fulfilment of the sense of freedom of anxiety about security of all others to whom we are socially 'connected' inasmuch as they can affect the objective conditions of our security. Or, at the very least, we may be tempted to offer this as a kind of ideal to which our understanding of the social dimension of security might reasonably approximate. Yet this temptation should be resisted, as such a proposition would have to rest on one of three assumptions, none of which can be convincingly sustained.

First, the proposition would hold if 'security' had the properties of those kinds of communal goods such as 'fraternity' or 'solidarity' where the production of the sentiment in each person is directly and reciprocally dependent upon its production in certain others (Waldron 1993: 358–9).

---

[14] As has been demonstrated by countless studies of the non-linear relationship between people's 'fear of crime' and their antecedent levels of objective risk (see Hale 1996).

But security is not a constitutively other-regarding sentiment in the sense of these other goods. It is meaningless to talk about enjoyment of a sense of fraternity or conviviality other than *with* some other person or persons. Security is not of that character. Its relationship of mutual dependence is not, unlike these others, one of mutual *constitution*. Second, the proposition would hold in conditions of precise equality of vulnerability and of strategic deployment of harm-capacity between all individuals in a community. Where each were as able and willing as each of his or her significant others to affect the security of each of his or her significant others (full symmetry of vulnerability), and if this were mutually acknowledged (full consciousness of that symmetry), we would be able to conceive of mutual security in terms of a self-reinforcing social equilibrium. But absent a Robinson Crusoe type scenario, this does not describe the conditions of any actual human society. Thirdly, short of these conditions of equality of harm-inflicting capacity, if we could nevertheless envisage conditions of full mutual empathy and altruism as regards the security concerns of significant others (however widely defined), then again we might be able to sustain the strong mutual dependence thesis. If our anxiety about security could not be assuaged unless and until we were sure of the security of others, *just because* we defined security as a good which was meaningless unless enjoyed by all and were thus unable or unprepared to take comfort in our own security unless and until it was equally guaranteed to these others, then our very moral orientation would be such as to guarantee security as a collective virtue. Again, however, beyond the scale and scope of extremely small 'immediate' social units such as families or otherwise tightly knit groups where the affective ties of friendship or loyalty are particularly strong, this is an implausible assumption to make about actual human societies.

The last two scenarios, those of strategic reciprocity and altruistic concern, do however offer a clue as to how we can cash out the social dimension of security. Our threshold of anxiety *is* affected by our appreciation of the capacity of others, officials and laypersons, to affect our security, and by our appreciation of how our capacity and propensity to affect their security influences their attitude towards our security. So in the day-to-day monitoring of our levels of anxiety about security and evaluation of the conditions of such anxiety, we do take account of the relationship between the threat posed to us by others and the threat posed to them by us, even if there is no equality of mutual influence and even if we understand others' propensity to affect our security as being of a different order than our propensity to affect theirs. Moreover, since, as noted, our security has an irreducibly subjective dimension – since anxiety about security is itself a form of insecurity – to the extent that our monitoring of our levels of anxiety preoccupies us and our evaluation of our conditions of security requires sustained vigilance, then this itself is an indication that our existential state of security is suboptimal, that we are too vulnerable to our perceptions of insecurity.[15] Thus we aspire to a situation where our monitoring of our security environment may be a highly tacit and routine affair, an activity which takes place largely at the level of 'practical' rather than 'discursive consciousness' (Giddens 1984); one where we rarely feel it necessary to peep round the veil of our security cover, and our checks when we do so need only be cursory. So, ideally, our level of trust in our security environment should be very high, the reminders of our vulnerability few and routine, neither palpable in our physical environment, intrusive in our daily routines, nor prominent in our discursive consciousness.

As well as reinforcing our appreciation of the importance of the strategic nexus connecting our security to others, this sense of the exacting condition of optimal security also helps to explain how more altruistic considerations enter the security equation. We need make no assumptions about altruism being a natural human condition to conclude that in our techniques for monitoring and reducing anxiety about security, concern for the security of others finds many prompts, many contexts in which it can come to appear to us as a necessary virtue. For our strategic monitoring of our own security concerns inevitably raises our awareness of the security concerns of others, and our desire to lower the anxiety 'transaction costs' of taking care of our own security anxiety may lead us to conclude that the best guarantee – the most transaction-free insurance policy – of our own security is the equal guarantee of the security of others to whom we are connected. And in this complex and iterative calculation, the security of others may come to be appreciated as a good in its own right. That is to say the very circumstances of security anxiety are such that we may become educated in the virtues of security altruism and come contingently to endorse the very proposition whose pretensions to innateness and universalizability were criticized earlier – namely, that the enjoyment of security by others *is* indeed a defining condition of our enjoyment of our own security, rather than simply a strategic prerequisite. And even if there are limits to that altruism, the practical coincidence between prudent self-interest and independent concern for the security

---

[15] One may, among many illustrative instances of this, cite the case of gated communities and other affluent middle-class enclaves, environments where conditions of objective or inter-subjective safety tend to coexist with a pervasive sense of subjective insecurity, especially in relation to the conditions and possibility of social life 'beyond the walls' (see Girling et al. 2000: chap. 5).

of others may often be so strong, sustained, and mutually reinforcing, that these limits are rarely put to the test.

Let us turn, finally, to the *constitutive* dimension of security. What we are concerned with here is how security as a social or collective good of the sort we have begun to describe is implicated in the very process of constituting the 'social' or the 'public'. Often, and not only in the economics literature on 'public goods' discussed earlier, the emphasis in discussion of goods which are in some sense collectively enjoyable is upon the social or public quality of the *process* of delivering the good or of the beneficial *consequences* of the good, or upon the nexus between process and consequences. Indeed, we can see just this emphasis on process and consequences in our discussion of the social dimension of security above. However, there are some goods, and arguably security is one of these, which are also deeply implicated in the constitution of the very sense of what the 'social' is and who the 'public' are.

On one view, the very distinction between the emergent and consequential dimensions of 'publicness' on the one hand and its constitutive dimension on the other may seem a dubious one. Is our sense of the 'social' or the 'public' not merely the fluid, context-dependent and diversely manifest outcome of the multifarious situations in which individuals put or find things in common? Clearly our understanding of who 'our' relevant public is and what is the nature of the social tie is constantly mediated through new experiences, new strategic and affective contexts of coming together. But this does not do justice to the independent and constitutive role of the public in the social imagination. Our most basic anthropological understanding of human sociability tells us that the institutional and symbolic organization of 'publics' and of the 'public domain' is more profound than that. Our sense of group organization and identity, rather, is deeply embedded and continuous across different situations and over long periods of time. This is not the place to investigate all the reasons for such a relative stability of group identity; suffice it to say that they concern the significance of stable group organization in meeting two sets of aspirations. First, there is their instrumental significance for resolving collective action problems, for allowing us to achieve under conditions of relatively stable agreement what we cannot do in the absence of these conditions. Second, there is their significance for consolidating a social sense of self – in providing an identity whose self-affirming traits, the way it speaks to positive conceptions of self generally such as personal dignity and a sense of personal authenticity (Smith 2001: 25–33) – recognizes and resonates with the irreducibly social character of our experience.

Now, it is clear that in any actual context of social development these two sets of factors – instrumental and affective – will often be closely linked, indeed mutually interdependent. For their part, as we suggested earlier, the instrumental reasons for getting or staying together to resolve collective action problems are often deemed insufficient in themselves for reasons of short-term self-interest, poor information and low trust. Something additional is needed that allows individuals to overcome their ambivalence about collective commitment. If that additional factor is not, should not and cannot be (or, at least cannot *only* be, certainly in the long-term) the persuasive force attendant upon the coercive potential and display of some already powerful group, then the glue must be supplied by some prior and continuing investment in a sense of social identity and aspiration. The affective factors, conversely, need to be grounded in the many particular lessons of social experience, in the varied contexts of practical reason from which the very idea of social identity derives meaning. They must, in other words, be predicated upon a set of actual or projected ends which vindicate the very value of conceiving and pursuing ends *as* common ends and which as such provide ongoing corroboration of our self-understanding as social animals. They demand, in short, a sense and an experience of collective projects that could be justified in instrumental terms.

In saying that for communities of purpose to stabilize and to enjoy sustained success they must also be affective communities, and that affectivity is itself generated through a commitment to common purpose, we are not pointing to some abstract ontological puzzle of first causes, but to countless self-reinforcing historical dynamics of mutual cause and effect. And in the operation of these dynamics, it is inevitable that the sense of social identity that is cultivated in the generation of stable communities is itself heavily infused with the content of the instrumental purposes that both ground and are abetted by that sense of social identity – as well as with the practical means and conditions conducive to the pursuit of such instrumental purposes, most notably common language and common territory. The wish for common security is one of these instrumental purposes – indeed, perhaps, for the very reasons we have already given in discussing security's foundational role in the group project that is the constitution of liberty – *the* most important such instrumental purpose. Accordingly, it is no surprise that the celebration of or yearning for common security against internal and external threats often looms so large in the materials – the mentalities, metaphors and iconography – through which stable communities register and articulate their identities as stable communities, as indeed do the sense of common language and common territory. This, then, is the sense in which we can talk of security, just as we can of language and territory, as a *constitutive* public good – one whose actualization or aspiration is so pivotal to the very purpose of community that at the level of self-identification it helps to construct and sustain our 'we feeling' – our very felt sense of 'common publicness'.

As a preliminary to the reintroduction of the state into our analysis, let us now say something about how our three dimensions of security – instrumental, social and constitutive – hang together. First, and most importantly, as already intimated, it is impossible to conceive of the effective realization of security as instrumental to individual liberty – the value of security on which all are agreed – without also attending to its social and its constitutive dimensions. As we saw, the social dimension of security is internal to our very conceptual understanding of what security is. If security has a subjective as well as an objective dimension, if it is as much about freedom from anxiety about safety as it is about the objective conditions of safety, then confidence in one's security environment becomes an indispensable feature of security. Further, in conceiving of security as a constitutive public good, we are making an even deeper claim about the social face of security. For what is being contended here is that in establishing the very frameworks of stable community which make the provision of *objective* security measures possible there must already be present and must continuously be sustained some common sense of social identity. Given the inextricability of collective purpose and social sense of self in this process of ongoing construction and reconstruction, the idea of common security becomes one of the central structures of meaning through which the development and sustenance of that sense of community is experienced and articulated.

In the second place, if we look more closely at the relationship between the social and constitutive dimensions of security, both of which are independently necessary to the provision of security as instrumental to individual liberty, we can discern an intimate and mutually supportive set of connections between them which further reinforces their role in the constitution of individual liberty. At least three such links can be traced. Firstly, the constitutive framework helps generate and sustain the sense of common purpose and instrumental commitment necessary to provide the stable material and regulatory wherewithal that a general scheme of security provision demands – something that theorists of the minimal state and nodal governance have both neglected. We cannot fund and we cannot order the mix of steering and rowing mechanisms required for collective security provision, whatever form that mix might take, in the absence of a constitutive commitment to put things in common.

Secondly, given that, as argued, the objective or inter-subjective security situation of the individual depends not only upon the commitment to public provision, but also upon the propensity of some to aid or co-operate in the provision of one's personal security cover and on the disinclination of others to threaten one's personal security, again the constitutive achievement of relatively stable political community becomes crucial – in two senses. On the one hand, and most directly, to the extent that the sense of common social identity presupposed by and nurtured within stable political community can encourage a sense of confident and committed membership of that community of attachment, this can lead to more active support for and co-operation with official and unofficial security arrangements, or at least to less intense threats towards these arrangements. On the other hand, more indirectly, and focusing on the instrumental capacity of collective political community, such a community can use the 'battery of power' (Canovan 1996: 72–5) it derives from its common affective commitment to put things in common to provide through distributive measures the spread of resources and associated forms of social status likely to minimize the mutual resentments, antipathies and indifferences which lead to non-co-operative or hostile behaviour. This combination of direct and indirect influences can, in short, help to trigger a 'virtuous circle of crime control' (Audit Commission 1993: 49) – the optimal use and effective supplementation of the scarce resources of security provision and minimization of the pressures on these resources, necessary for achieving effective levels of inter-subjective security.

Thirdly, and finally, we should note that the relationship between the constitution of political community and the social dimension of security is not just causal, in the complex ways suggested above, but also conceptual. Freedom of anxiety about security, as we have argued, is a function not just of one's objective or inter-subjective security situation, but also of one's perception of the adequacy of one's security coverage, which is also in some part derived from one's ongoing general threshold of psychic vulnerability, or manageable fear in the face of one's social environment. This, in turn, depends upon a more general sense of 'ontological security' – of 'confidence or trust that the natural and social worlds are as they appear to be, including the basic existential parameters of self and social identity' (Giddens 1984: 375). Where this sense of 'ontological security' comes from is of course a deeply complex and multi-levelled question, but as Giddens himself intimates, one crucial level is that of social identity. A sense of dignity and authenticity, of ease with one's social environment, are crucial to ontological security, and as we have seen, it is these very aspects of social identity which are implicated in the process of constitution of political community. In other words, to be a member of a stable political community and to feel oneself confident in that sense of membership is already to raise one's threshold of vulnerability – to possess crucial resources in the management of fear and avoidance of security anxiety.

The necessary virtue of the state

We have, thus far, made an argument for the indispensability of the social in the provision of individual security, and for the indispensability of some constitutive idea of 'publicness' and of political community to the full flowering of the social – conditions required even if we want the provision of individual security to be tailored to strictly liberal ends. But a further argument still has to be made before we can allocate the state a primary role in the constitution of security. In particular, we must face two further challenges and answer two further questions. First, why the state rather than some other idea of political community? Second, even if we can make a persuasive case for the centrality of the state, we still have to deal with its propensity towards meddling, favouritism, stupidity and monoculturalism.

As regards the first question, if it is the case that for the effective supply of security as a social good there must be some level of constitutive political community which is involved not only as a last resort of coercive authority, but also – since the two activities are inextricable – *both* in instrumental ordering work *and* in the work of cultural production of social identity, then we need to locate *some* species of political community which combines all of these functions. We need not call that entity the state, but, whatever our squeamishness about labels, we do need to accept the indispensability of a form of political community that is preponderant *to the extent that* it can perform all of these functions. In other words, if, as we have argued, necessary virtue in terms of security production inheres in the state or its functional equivalent, then we have no choice but to accept that necessity and ensure that it is as virtuous as possible.

In so doing, we must try to recover what is virtuous about the state tradition while seeking to eradicate or minimize its vices. We must recognize that states have indeed historically been involved as ordering devices, as sources of the rules, resources and administrative capacity necessary to the production of collective security. We must acknowledge that through the development of a sense of belonging, dignity and authenticity in the form of national identity, they have also been engaged in crafting social identities which provide the motivational force both for providing and maintaining the ordering infrastructure and for nurturing a social environment in which civility is relatively high, security risks are relatively low, and thus the ordering infrastructure is reasonably sufficient for its task. We must, finally, concede that the identity construction work of the state, quite apart from its complex instrumental benefits, is also importantly continuous with the very sense of social rootedness which makes the self-management of unease and anxiety a manageable task. And in accepting that the state can succeed, and in some cases and to varying degrees has succeeded, in performing these tasks, we must also accept that notions of security, just because of their deep inscription in the kind of purpose and practices for which political communities are formed and through which they are sustained, provide an important part of the vernacular of collective identity formation at the state level. In particular, in many well-documented cases, policing institutions have been active symbolic agents in the forging and mutual reinforcement of the nation-state nexus (Walden 1982; Emsley 2000; Loader and Mulcahy 2003) while in mature state forms, ideas about policing and the public guarantee of security remain deeply sedimented within the 'mundane culture' of everyday life (Loader and Mulcahy 2003: chap. 2).

Of course, the flipside of this historical record of instrumental and cultural work is another historical record which documents the propensity of the state to meddle, to reflect and enact the bias of the most powerful, to decide without sufficient knowledge or foresight, and to mobilize and celebrate an intolerant idea of cultural uniformity. Could not, then, the state-sceptics respond to our invocation of the necessity of the state with a necessity clause of their own? Namely, that the vices are the unavoidable downside of the virtues, and that any attempt to mobilize the virtues is fated, in the long run at least, to mobilize the vices? The only answer to that question, and the note on which we will finish, is to argue and legislate for, first, as much openness as possible and as many checks as can be incorporated against undue meddling, bias, uninformed decision-making and cultural imperialism in the ordering and cultural work of the state and, second, as much recognition as possible of the ordering and cultural work of other sites of collective security as is consistent with the elements of state preponderance set out above.

This argument clearly requires further elaboration. Suffice it for now, by way of conclusion, to say that it translates into what we would call an *anchored pluralism*. The state, in the sense set out above, should remain the anchor of collective security provision, but there should be as much pluralism as possible, both, internally, in terms of the constitutional inclusiveness, representativeness and minority protection mechanisms of the democratic and administrative processes through which the aspiration of collective security is reflected upon and pursued (Loader 2000), and, externally, in terms of the recognition of the appropriate place of other sites of regulatory and cultural production (Walker 2002). In this second and external dimension – the prospects of the flourishing of which are of course intimately associated with and dependent upon the openness of the first or internal dimension – the role of the state in the ordering field should be as a meta-regulator and in the cultural field as a wide boundary of social and security identity within which other sorts of social and security identities may be nested.[16] In both cases, the aim of the state is both positive and negative. Positively, it is to ensure the widest possible community consistent with the minimum affective ties necessary to deliver the regulatory and cultural infrastructure of a single security space, with all the risk-reducing and fear-abating benefits that such a common security environment can bring. Negatively, it is to ensure that other ordering and cultural sites, for all that they can contribute in more knowledgeable, responsive and intimate ways to the production of more localized or more practice-specific security spaces, do so in a way which does not frustrate the attainment of a more inclusive regulation of security and security of regulation, either through regulatory norms which contradict the wider regulatory field or through forms of parochial solidarity which may be inconsistent with membership of the wider security community, or indeed, with the equal security of their own members. The challenge remains one of finding the necessary commitment and institutional imagination to strike the optimal balance. It is a challenge, in our view, that can only be effectively addressed by remaining rigorously open-minded about the dynamics of transformation and by avoiding the temptation of assuming that the state is either any more or any less in need of justification for prominent inclusion within the matrix of security provision than any other institutional and cultural site.

[16] It remains an open question of course, in the light of the development of transnational forms of security practice, whether it can or should be the *widest* boundary of social and security identity. We have developed this point further elsewhere (Loader and Walker 2006).

8   From security to health

Scott Burris

Introduction

Security matters to health. Crime victimization causes death, injury and illness. Injury or death is an occupational hazard for police. The criminal justice system causes injury and illness in the course of attempting to punish and deter crime. Policing policies and practices can have a significant impact on the ability of other public and private agencies to implement health interventions successfully. Police themselves routinely deal with people who have serious health needs, and even on occasion are the primary agents implementing health interventions. The health consequences of law enforcement are far from trivial, making it important for health to be integrated as a matter of concern into criminological research and law enforcement practice. The link between health and policing, and the significance of health outcomes, should be more fully accepted in criminology. Likewise, the governance of security is an important matter for public health research and practice.

If health outcomes are seen as an important product of security arrangements, conventional policing can be reconfigured to reduce negative health consequences and promote positive ones. There are, however, limits to the extent that state-centred policing can be expected to change. The theory of nodal governance and the programmatic work of innovators in the governance of security movement offer useful insights into the co-ordination of health and security outside the state-centred policing framework. Experience with both health and security-based schemes shows the promise of 'microgovernance' strategies that promote health and security by mobilizing local knowledge and capacity among poor people with historically poor relations with conventional police systems. Serious practical and theoretical questions can be raised about the long-term prospects of these strategies, particularly the capacity of small groups of poor people to manage events flowing from more generalized and more powerful sources. While valid in some respects, however, such criticism misses the 'democratic experimentalism' at the heart of the governance of security approach.

Security's influence on health

There are obvious and well-recognized ways in which health is influenced by the practice of security and policing (Aral et al. 2002). Interpersonal violence is a significant source of mortality (Krug et al. 2002). The World Health Organization estimated that there were 569,000 deaths due to intentional violence (excluding war and suicide) in 2002, accounting for 1 per cent of global deaths. Because homicide tends to strike younger and otherwise healthier people, intentional violence accounted for 1.4 per cent of the disability-adjusted life years lost (Beaglehole et al. 2004). This level of incidence puts homicide squarely in the ranks of significant global health threats, on a par with measles and colo-rectal cancer, more serious than breast cancer and about four times more costly in human life than war (Beaglehole et al. 2004). Broken down by age and geography, the statistics tell an even more powerful story of concentrated health effects. For 2000, the WHO estimated a global age-adjusted homicide incidence rate of 8.8 per 100,000 population. For males aged 15–29 and 30–44, however, the rates were more than twice as great. The rate in the Americas was three times that of South-East Asia, and more than twice the European rate. The rate in Colombia was more than eleven times greater than the rate in Cuba, and four times the rate in Mexico (Krug et al. 2002: 11–12). Within the United States, the 2001 age-adjusted rate of homicide was 7.1 per 100,000 overall, but 4.9 for whites and 21.2 for African Americans (National Center for Health Statistics 2003).

Violence that does not result in death is an even more widespread phenomenon. Criminal justice data from the United Nations, while subject to various limitations, demonstrates a high level of criminal activity throughout the world. On average between 1998 and 2000, at least 713,000 people were prosecuted for a major assault, 1.63 million for an assault, 133,000 for rape and 1.1 million for robbery (United Nations Office on Drugs and Crime 2004). In the United States in 2002, a million and a half violent crimes against individuals were reported to police agencies (Federal Bureau of Investigation 2003a). Over 16,000 of those were murders; the remainder were rapes, robberies and aggravated assaults. That same year, the US crime victimization survey found over 5.3 million violent crime victimizations, with nearly a third of victims suffering physical injury (Bureau of Justice Statistics 2004, tables 38, 75). Surveys deploying a variety of methods in a range of countries have found significant rates of physical violence against women by their partners

198   *Scott Burris*

(Lo Vecchio et al. 1998; Grisso et al. 1999; Coker et al. 2000; Lejoyeux et al. 2002; Grande et al. 2003; Helweg-Larsen and Kruse 2003; Cox et al. 2004). More than 200,000 annual US violent crime victimizations are at the hands of a spouse or ex-spouse (Bureau of Justice Statistics 2004). As with other health stressors, crime victimization may be unevenly distributed within populations, striking the poor more severely than the rich (Thacher 2004).

The health consequences of such crimes are immediate and tangible, in the form of mortality and injury to victims; they are also deferred and intangible, in the form of long-term psychological stress on surviving victims, their families and their communities. Crime victims are at elevated risk of fear, depression, lowered self-esteem and post-traumatic stress disorder, effects that decrease over time but can be durable in some victims (Koss et al. 1991; Norris and Kaniasty 1994). Some studies have suggested that abuse increases women's risk of HIV infection (Cohen et al. 2000; Lichtenstein 2005). Children may suffer a variety of short- and long-term ill-effects from victimization or exposure to crime (Vostanis 2004), including lower educational performance and attainment and consequent harm to socio-economic status and overall wellbeing (Macmillan and Hagan 2004). Fear of crime may have an important impact on the health of people in neighbourhoods with more crime (Chandola 2001; Ross and Mirowsky 2001).

The means used to prevent and punish crime also have dramatic health consequences. Deaths and injuries caused by police in the pursuit, confrontation and arrest of criminal suspects are manifestations of this relationship (Cooper et al. 2004). In the United States, for example, police in the line of duty killed an average of 373 suspected felons per year between 1976 and 1998 (Bureau of Justice Statistics 2001). In 1996, an estimated half million of the individuals who had face-to-face encounters with US police were threatened with the use of force or had some degree of force used against them (Bureau of Justice Statistics 1997). In Thailand in 2003, more than 2,700 people were reportedly killed during a government anti-drug campaign (Wolfe and Malinowska-Sempruch 2004). The rate of police use of force (variously defined) in primarily US studies was found in one review to range from less than 1 per cent of encounters to nearly 60 per cent (Garner et al. 2002). Police work is also dangerous for police officers. In 2002 in the United States, fifty-six law enforcement officers were feloniously, and seventy-seven accidentally, killed in the line of duty. Nearly 10,000 were assaulted, over a quarter of whom suffered injury (Federal Bureau of Investigation 2003b). In addition to physical injury, workers in policing and corrections are reportedly exposed to unusually high levels of stress (Lennings 1997).

Imprisonment, even when accomplished without physical injury, can itself be dangerous to health (Burris 1992; Bollini 2001; Stern 2001; WHO Regional Office for Europe 2001; WHO Regional Office for Europe and Pompidou Group of the Council of Europe 2001). Prison populations exhibit an elevated prevalence of communicable disease (Hammett et al. 2002). Rape and violence are not uncommon features of prison life (Struckman-Johnson and Struckman-Johnson 2002; Robertson 2003). Consensual sex without condoms as well as drug injection and tattooing without sterile equipment are reported to occur at dangerous levels and to result in transmission of disease (Brewer et al. 1988; Mutter et al. 1994; Shewan et al. 1995; Taylor et al. 1995; Mahon 1996; WHO Regional Office for Europe and Pompidou Group of the Council of Europe 2001; Wolfe et al. 2001; Krebs and Simmons 2002; Zachariah et al. 2002; Centers for Disease Control and Prevention 2003; Beyrer et al. 2003; Gyarmathy et al. 2003; Levy et al. 2003). Serious outbreaks of tuberculosis (Greifinger et al. 1992; Trebucq 1999; Sretrirutchai et al. 2002; Mclaughlin et al. 2003) and elevated rates of suicide have been reported (New Zealand Department of Corrections 1999; Dyer 2003). A record of incarceration has been identified as a risk factor for drug abuse, HIV infection and sexually transmitted infections (Estebanez et al. 1990; Choopanya et al. 2002; Buavirat et al. 2003; Calzavara et al. 2003).

There are also some effects of policing and security practices that are not so well recognized or obvious. Policing practices can increase the risk of behaviours like illegal migration, prostitution and drug use. The health behaviours of injection drug users (such as attending a syringe exchange, using a sterile syringe, sharing syringes and calling for medical assistance in the case of overdose) have been found to be heavily influenced by laws and police practices (Burris 2002; Burris 2004; Davis et al. 2005). The same is true for sex workers (Aral et al. 2002; Blankenship and Koester 2002). Internal and cross-border migrants are influenced in a variety of ways by laws and law enforcement: they are often not able to bring their families to the area where they work, creating more demand for commercial sex; they may be unable or unwilling to seek health care or health information; they may be deported to their home countries or regions, contributing to the spread of disease (Anderson et al. 2003; Lagarde et al. 2003; WHO 2003).

Imprisonment of a spouse and parent may be stressful to spouses and children left behind. Where incarceration occurs at a high rate, large numbers of people are susceptible to the subtle but potentially significant effects of stigma, loss of emotional support, and reduced socio-economic status (Freudenberg 2001). In the United States, for example, more than 1.5 million children under eighteen have a parent in prison (Iguchi et al. 2002). Contemporary theory about the spread of sexually transmitted and blood-borne disease focuses on the role of sexual and drug-use networks. Networks without disease remain free of disease unless and until members of the network become infected through participation in other networks where disease is prevalent. Once one member is infected, disease can spread rapidly throughout the network (Hoffman et al. 1997; Potterat et al. 1999; Friedman and Aral 2001). If these theories are correct, high rates of imprisonment can increase community risk by promoting rapid change in sexual and drug-using networks, which increases exposure to prevalent sexually transmitted and blood-borne infections like HIV.

Being labelled as a criminal can have a significant impact on the future life course of an individual. Criminal status has tangible civil consequences for the individual who has completed a prison sentence, such as subsequent ineligibility for social benefits, education loans, occupational licences and so on (Iguchi et al. 2002). Criminal status may be stigmatized to some degree, with unknown long-term psychological consequences. Stigma is a powerful mode of social control, with extremely potent consequences for the individual. While we lack data on the specific effect of criminal stigma on the life course (Anon. 2003), the research on the operation of stigma would suggest a healthy respect for its potential negative consequences to individual well-being (Goffman 1963; Burris 2002). At the social level, criminalization may reflect deep social divisions of race or class, and contribute to the difficulty of winning support and funding for drug treatment and other health interventions. As Morone writes, making drug addiction a crime 'perpetuates the trusty impulse to rest social problems on individual shoulders' (Morone 1997: 1012).

Law enforcement personnel act as providers of public health and healthcare intervention. A few major public health programmes, most notably the effort to reduce drunken driving, are administered substantially by the law enforcement system.

Criminalization of drug use makes the criminal justice system, from the police officer through the court or drug court to the prison, a player in the provision of drug treatment (Ramsey 2003; Welsh and Zajac 2004). In some countries, the United States being one, the deinstitutionalization of the mentally ill combined with a lack of health service has left prisons to care for patients who would once have been in the psychiatric treatment system (Accordino et al. 2001).

These health effects of crime policing are not evenly distributed across the globe. Some places have very low rates of violent crime, reasonably salubrious prisons and police forces trained and equipped to minimize the use of injurious force. Security conditions and policing practices reflect a variety of factors in the social environment that may be beyond the control of security agents or reformers (Link and Phelan 1995; Kawachi 2000; Kawachi and Berkman 2000). Nevertheless, this account of health and its relation to policing supports the view that the governance of security is an important area to consider in the pursuit of population health. This chapter now turns to the question of whether security can be a fruitful as well as an important area.

Healthy change within the state-centred framework

The data surveyed above point to the continued value of good, honest policing along conventional lines. The agenda for action in that respect is easy to describe, if not to accomplish. Where the police are corrupt, reform. Where they are overburdened or under-performing, provide better resources of money, training and equipment (Stone and Ward 2000). In equally broad terms, the data point to the need to re-evaluate major criminal justice policies. The dogmatic prohibitionism of the war on drugs must sooner or later be fundamentally reconsidered (Bewley-Taylor 2003). In addition to the health consequences already described, the criminalization of drug use eats up security resources, raises the risk of corruption and is failing to meet its primary goals of reducing drug use and the availability of drugs (Maxwell 2003; Drug Enforcement Administration 2004). Current law is also a barrier to further innovation in public health, whether this takes the form of needle exchange (Bluthenthal 1997), heroin maintenance therapy (Fischer et al. 2002) or safe injection rooms (Broadhead et al. 2003). Much the same may be said of the criminalization of sex work (Albert et al. 1998; Law 2000). Beyond policy change, taking on a health role requires the sort of paradigm shift suggested in the concept of 'therapeutic jurisprudence', which began in the mental health area and has advanced the notion that laws and legal practices themselves have an effect on emotional well-being that can be harnessed for good but, without care, can be harmful (Wexler 1990). Within the more limited scope of this chapter, it may be useful to sketch three basic areas where more specific changes can be explored.

Three steps towards healthier policing

Putting fewer people in jail

The social costs of incarceration have not been sufficiently appreciated. It now appears reasonable to adopt a presumption that incarceration is bad for individual and community health, and so should be deployed as a tool of security only when it is reasonably clear that its benefits outweigh its costs. Improving systems for bail and pre-trial supervision, revisiting the war on drugs, and shortening sentences for non-dangerous offenders would be expected drastically to reduce the number of inmates around the world, potentially freeing resources for improvements in the conditions and services available in prisons. Prosecutors should have discretion to drop charges in cases where imprisonment would be counter-productive (by, for example, interrupting ongoing drug treatment or rehabilitation). Judges should not be required to impose custodial sentences where there is evidence that other sanctions will suffice to prevent reoffending. Even without changes in the criminalization of drugs, offenders can be diverted to treatment rather than prison (Reilly et al. 2002; Bull 2003; Bouffard and Taxman 2004; Evans and Longshore 2004). Incarceration may also be reduced through use of other means of sanctioning wrongdoers and satisfying the desire of victims for justice, such as through restorative justice (Strang and Braithwaite 2001).

Better health and social services can reduce prison populations through prevention of offending. Drug treatment, which can reduce crime, incarceration and the social cost of drug abuse, is first on the list (Sidwell et al. 1999; Freeman 2003; Godfrey et al. 2004). Despite the global drug pandemic, however, quality drug treatment, particularly substitution treatment, remains scarce (Friedmann et al. 2003; Auriacombe et al. 2004) and in some countries (notably Russia) illegal (International Harm Reduction Development Program 2003). The situation with mental health care is, if anything, even worse. Mental illness continues to be under-treated worldwide (Demyttenaere et al. 2004), and to the extent that seriously mentally ill patients are at higher relative risk of violent offending, better services in the health system are a sensible way to keep them out of the criminal justice system (Link et al. 1992; Accordino et al. 2001). Restorative justice programmes offer another mechanism for diversion from prison into employment or other welfare services (Braithwaite 2000).

*Reducing the harm and enhancing the benefits
of incarceration to health*

To the extent that incarceration is necessary, jails and prisons should be safe and hygienic. At a minimum, prisoners should receive care for prevalent diseases that is 'broadly equivalent' to what they would receive in the outside community (WHO Regional Office for Europe and Pompidou Group of the Council of Europe 2001: 5), including drug treatment (WHO Regional Office for Europe and Pompidou Group of the Council of Europe 2001; Sibbald 2002; Welsh and Zajac 2004). Research suggests that as many as one million inmates a year go through untreated alcohol or opiate withdrawal in US jails that provide no detox services (Fiscella et al. 2004). To the extent that drug use and sex cannot be prevented, harm reduction interventions like needle exchange and condom distribution are appropriate and, evidence suggests, can be carried on without harm to other prison goals (Bollini 2001; May and Williams 2002; Dolan et al. 2003). Mental healthcare is also important. Surveys in particular US jails and prisons have found rates of mental illness among inmates ranging from 7 to 14 per cent (Krieg 2001). From a positive point of view, prisons are places of public health opportunity, where a distillation of high-risk populations can be found and influenced (Burris 1992; Bollini 2001; WHO Regional Office for Europe and Pompidou Group of the Council of Europe 2001; Solomon et al. 2004). Risk-reduction counselling, diagnostic testing, partner notification, treatment and other basic disease control services can be effectively offered in prison given the resources and the willingness of prison authorities to create a conducive environment (Ehrmann 2002; May and Williams 2002). Such services may also be cost-effective (Varghese and Peterman 2001). Recidivism as well as health problems can potentially be reduced by holistic discharge planning that links released offenders to necessary health and social services (Richie et al. 2001; WHO Regional Office for Europe and Pompidou Group of the Council of Europe 2001; Von Zielbauer 2003).

Integrating and harmonizing police and health work

Police are routinely confronted with health and social problems that present no immediate criminal matter to be resolved. Such situations are frustrating to police officers and costly to taxpayers. It is likewise widely accepted that to some degree criminal justice systems must 'partner' or co-ordinate with other agencies and community institutions to do their job well (Johnston and Shearing 2003: 11). It is no great leap to the proposition that health-oriented actors may be able to do their jobs better through co-operation with police and that at least some of the responsibility for health may be efficiently placed on law enforcement shoulders (Wexler 1990; Grabosky 2000). A systematic effort to improve police functioning in relation to health would include elements of *surveillance, provision of services, referral* and *evaluation*.

Surveillance is used here in its epidemiological sense, as the systematic collection and analysis of information about the health issues police encounter, including their frequency, severity, causes and distribution. Criminal justice systems collect a great deal of information, and sophisticated data analysis is gaining currency under the rubric of 'intelligence-led policing'. Effective agencies analyse the data looking for recurring problems or other troubling phenomena and the effectiveness of the agency's response (Sanders 2000). Within criminology, the study of police use of force is a good example of such an epidemiological approach (Garner et al. 2002; White 2002). Working with health agencies, criminal justice agencies could identify data of health significance that is already or could be collected, share information from their separate surveillance systems and collaborate in analysis and response. The DUMA (Drug Use Monitoring in Australia) project samples police detainees at sites across the country for drug screening and interviews about drug use and behaviour (Milner et al. 2004).

In some instances, the law enforcement agency itself may be in a position to provide a health-necessary service. This may involve using a familiar policing tool in a way that is informed by health information – e.g. arresting the perpetrator of domestic violence (Fagan 1996) – or a medical service, like first aid. A broader view of the mission of the police, and reconsideration of other policies, may make it possible for police to use the opportunities for contact their work provides to distribute condoms or sterile syringes, for example, or to promote compliance with health and safety laws (Smith et al. 2001). Similarly, specialized courts (drug courts, domestic abuse courts) can be seen as examples of the adaptation of the criminal justice system to take on a more therapeutic role in which legal action is guided and calibrated by health concerns (Nolan 2002).

It will probably be more common for improved co-ordination to lead to better identification of referral needs and the creation of more user-friendly referral mechanisms. The police officer equipped with a computer and a cell phone is potentially a link between people in distress and the social and health service systems. This requires ensuring that officers are trained to spot substance abuse and mental health or other common health problems, and have the tools and knowledge to provide referrals. Placing outreach workers in police stations or allowing them ready access to arrested persons is another way to support a presumption of care over incarceration and to take advantage of the opportunity for intake that an arrest provides (WHO Regional Office for Europe and Pompidou Group of the Council of Europe 2001). Evaluation is important to establishing the efficacy of police interventions as well as serving as an accountability mechanism (Fagan 1996; Stone and Ward 2000).

Law enforcement agents and agencies can be expected to adopt health-promoting practices only if they are suitably equipped to do so. Equipment in a broad sense begins with a mentality – 'a framework that shapes the way we think about the world' – in which health issues are understood and placed within the responsibility of law enforcement (Johnston and Shearing 2003: 29). Training, policies, community consultation mechanisms and formal accountability for health outcomes are among the ways such a mentality can be inculcated (Midford et al. 2002; Chan et al. 2003; Burris et al. 2004). Change in practices also requires changes in the law enforcement toolkit (Johnston and Shearing 2003). If arrest remains the only way to get a mentally ill person in out of the cold, then jail will continue to substitute for inpatient mental health care or adequate supported housing. Hence the importance of programme and service integration, as well as the development of alternatives to incarceration and other forms of punishment at all stages of the system. Resources are essential for the development and use of new technologies of health/security. The more open-textured public management processes are one plausible route to aligning resources with needs and capacities. The notion of a 'policing budget' (Johnston and Shearing 2003) and the distinction between auspice and provider (Bayley and Shearing 2001) can be applied equally well to the health or drug treatment or mental health budgets.

Examples that demonstrate the possibilities for health-oriented security can be found throughout the world (Burris et al. 2004). Many have been referenced in the preceding discussion. Yet it is clear that promoting health by changing laws and the practices of state security agencies is a slow, difficult process. Many of the suggestions that arise from a focus on health seem to call for changes that hark back to the Peelian emphasis on prevention and run counter to an apparent trend in policing towards greater 'militarization' in equipment, strategies and outlook (Bayley and Shearing 2001). Political, cultural and economic factors will frustrate efforts for change, even assuming that the basic conditions for democratic control of policing exist (Stone and Ward 2000; Dupont et al. 2003). In any event, an exclusive focus on the state ignores a key insight of the governance of security literature, the extent to which security is governed or provided by private actors. Research in both health and criminology, and a number of active interventions, suggest that small, non-state local institutions can play an important role in improving health and security among the most vulnerable.

Beyond the state: health and the governance of security

The growing literature on the governance of security offers a set of insights to guide the search for new ways of providing security and health (Bayley and Shearing 1996; Bayley and Shearing 2001; Aral et al. 2002; Roche 2002; Dupont et al. 2003; Johnston and Shearing 2003;

Shearing and Wood 2003b; Dupont 2004; Wood 2004a). The standard state institutions of police, courts and prisons are necessary but not sufficient to the governance of security. They do not provide security to all people in all places where it is needed, in part because of resources, in part because of how resources are deployed by the people who control security institutions, and in part because these institutions are not suited for all the jobs that now need to be done. At the same time, these institutions cause unnecessary harm and fail to achieve feasible benefits. The big losers tend to be poor people. The task is to find ways to make security institutions more responsive to the least powerful, and where responsiveness, resources or ability to respond effectively are lacking, to redirect resources and power to new institutions that can do the job.

This new thinking about the governance of security has been influenced by Hayek's appreciation of governance mechanisms, like markets, that address the complexity of social phenomena by co-ordinating diffused knowledge and capacity, and which thereby avoid the limitations inherent in centralized planning and rule (Braithwaite 2000). Shearing and various colleagues have articulated the theory of nodal governance, describing governance as an ongoing social adaptation accomplished in significant part through the creation and operation of institutions called nodes (Shearing and Wood 2003b; Drahos 2004; Dupont 2004; Burris 2004; Burris et al. 2005). Governance, on this theory, is distributed in networks across social space, and is carried out by state and non-state actors. Thus corporations and the institutions of civil society govern, but so do illegal organizations and 'dark networks' like crime cartels and street gangs (Raab and Milward 2003). States have certain unique attributes for governance, but no monopoly. States themselves are governed. One implication is that the 'governance deficit' between rich and poor can be narrowed by creating institutions that mobilize the knowledge and capacity of poor people, and equip them with the means to project at least some influence into governance networks. The key elements of an institution that can serve this function are identified as ways of thinking (*mentalities*) about the matters that the node has emerged to govern; methods (*technologies*) for exerting influence over the course of events at issue; *resources* to support the operation of the node and the exertion of influence; and an *institutional structure*.

The insights of nodal governance are harmonious with ideas emerging from social epidemiology. In health outcomes, as in security, access to individual and social resources is the key to better outcomes, and so the poorer fare worse than the richer (Link and Phelan 1995; Marmot and Wilkinson 1999; Kawachi 2000; Kawachi and Berkman 2000; Krieger 2000; Krieger 2001; Maantay 2001; Siegrist and Marmot 2004). While improvement thus depends in part on macro-level policies and practices (Mackenbach and Bakker 2002; Hein 2003), there is also considerable interest in interventions at the local level. Communities 'remain essential as a site for the realization of public or social goods, such as public safety, clean environments and education for children' (Sampson 2002: 220–21). Figuring out at the community level how macro-inequality in status becomes health inequality in outcome – and what to do about it – has, however, proven difficult: the mechanisms are many and complicated (Lynch et al. 2004). Along with environmental stressors (like greater exposure to toxins), social stressors, social networks and local institutions have been identified as key influences (Ellen et al. 2001; Maantay 2001; Pettit et al. 2003). Much emphasis has been laid on rather general notions of supporting community institutions, increasing the capacity of non-governmental organizations, increasing volunteerism and generally improving social capital and social connectedness in poor urban areas (Israel et al. 1998; Geronimus 2000; Leviton et al. 2000).

To be sure, ' "[c]ommunity" now reigns as the modern elixir for much of what allegedly ails . . . society' (Sampson 2002: 213). Social capital has been an important explanatory device, but, in health as in criminology, the concept has been invoked in a way that does not always survive close analytic scrutiny or lead to productive, concrete interventions (Carson 2003). In a promising exception, health and criminology have come together in the work of the project on Human Development in Chicago Neighborhoods, led by Sampson, which has added the concept of collective efficacy to the social capital toolkit (Morenoff and Sampson 1997; Sampson and Raudenbush 1997; 1999; Sampson et al. 1999; Sampson and Morenoff 2000; Morenoff et al. 2001; Gibson et al. 2002). Collective efficacy is defined by Sampson and colleagues as 'the linkage of cohesion and mutual trust with shared expectations for intervening in support of neighborhood social control' (Sampson and Raudenbush 1999: 613). Collective efficacy refines the analysis of social capital at the neighbourhood level. Social capital is seen as a resource, while collective efficacy is the more specific capacity of the community actually to take collective action to deal with specific problems (Sampson and Morenoff 2000). While the ability to work together does depend in part on trust and solidarity among neighbours, it does not depend entirely on the strength and durability of social ties. People who are not close – 'lightly engaged strangers' (Carson 2003) – can, under the right circumstances, co-operate to achieve specific ends. Indeed, strong local ties may actually discourage certain kinds of collective management of the community (Sampson and Morenoff 2000: 375). To improve community conditions, it may be sufficient to find ways to enable people, regardless of the nature of their ties, to effectively co-operate on specific tasks. 'One of the keys to generating social goods...and...collective efficacy is institutions that are viewed as legitimate and are supported by strong government' (Sampson 2002: 221).

Both the new work in security and important strains in social epidemiology thus offer something of a common prescription: improve security and well-being by fostering local institutions that make it possible for people in particular communities to exercise effective control over more aspects of their communal lives, and to get better access to resources and decision-making outside the community. Nodal governance and ongoing innovations in the governance of security framework offer a useful guide to *how* to create such an institution of local capacity governance, and an ongoing project in South Africa provides a concrete instantiation.

The Zwelethemba model of local capacity governance was developed by Shearing and colleagues in South Africa beginning in 1997. The model, named after the community in the Western Cape in which it was first developed, creates a simple institution for the governance of security that uses minimal resources and user-friendly technologies to resolve small disputes and solve underlying community problems. It was created by a criminologist, but the aim goes beyond security. Security is thought of as a window that people in the community will want to look through but which will then afford them a wider view of the local situation. The model's two components, peacemaking (dispute resolution) and peacebuilding (community development), are conducted through peace committees made up of five to twenty people. Anyone in the community can join or start a peace committee. The single essential criterion for starting or joining a peace committee is acceptance of a Code of Good Practice (see Table 8.1). The values of the Code constitute the mentality that guides the work of the committee members.

Peacemaking is the core activity of a peace committee. When a dispute is brought to a member of the committee, members of the committee sponsor a 'Gathering' of people thought to be in a position to contribute to dispute resolution. The members facilitating the Gathering use a simple technology of community mediation. The people at the Gathering try to identify root causes of disputes, avoid blame, and look for solutions that let people move forward amicably in the future. Participation is voluntary and no coercion, punishment or violence is allowed. Although any dispute can give rise to a Gathering, the focus is on the small things that, if left unresolved, lead to big problems. Each time a Gathering is held, a payment is made to the committee. Half goes to the members conducting the gathering to compensate them for their time; half is paid into a fund used by the committee as a whole for community development projects.

Table 8.1. *The peace committee Code of Good Practice*

The activities of peace committees are carried out within an agreed framework of values and principles, the Code of Good Practice, which is read out at the beginning of every peace Gathering.

Code of Good Practice

Members of this peace committee use these guidelines in the course of their work as peacemakers:

* We help to create a safe and secure environment in our community
* We respect the South African Constitution
* We work within the law
* We do not use force or violence
* We do not take sides in disputes
* We work in the community as a co-operative team, not as inividuals
* We follow procedures which are open for the community to see
* We do not gossip about our work or about other people
* We are committed in what we do

Peacebuilding takes the knowledge about community problems and resources developed in peacemaking and puts them into practice in the cause of addressing underlying conditions that create disputes or otherwise reduce health and quality of life in the community. Projects to be supported out of the peacebuilding fund are selected in 'Needs Gatherings', in which community members work with the peace committee to identify problems, and 'Solutions Gatherings', in which peace committee members work with others in the community to identify individuals or groups that can be funded to alleviate needs. Peace committees have provided meals for sick people and AIDS orphans, organized the construction of play areas for children, provided jobs for youth and funded AIDS education. In Khayelitsha (Cape Town), the peace committee was funded by the United Nations Food and Agriculture Organization to apply peacebuilding methods to improving community nutrition.

The work of peace committees is supported by the Community Peace Programme (CPP), which raises funds, audits committee work and oversees contracts for development projects. The Programme is sustained by grant funding; the committees are succeeding in being funded from tax funds based on their demonstrated benefits to their communities. The CPP is also responsible for facilitating the development of new committees and for replicating and testing the model in other countries. Originally funded by foreign development funds, the peace committees were intended to be sustained in the long run by local public funding. The funding strategy was to demonstrate to local authorities that peace committees were in fact providing dispute resolution and crime prevention services, and so should be funded out of the 'policing' or 'dispute resolution' budgets.

As of March 2004, 22 working peace committees in 13 communities had facilitated 7,928 gatherings (Community Peace Programme 2004). Peace committees have secured some government funding, but the programme remains dependent on grant funding from international sources. In some places, peace committees are adopting new practices and building new relations with government agencies. In Nkqubela (Robertson), the committee and the police have developed a model of partnership in which the police station was converted into a 'Community Peace Centre' with a mixed staff of peace committee members and police officers. In this model, called Project iThemba, the police are responsible for law enforcement and emergency response, while the peace committee facilitates in the resolution of the many kinds of community problems and disputes in which the peaceful mobilization of local knowledge is the key to success. People bringing problems to the Centre can select whether they want to proceed through a police or a peace committee process with the possibility of later referral in both directions. The partnership gives peace committees a meeting place and access to cases, while allowing the police to redirect scare resources towards more serious crimes. Two more Community Peace Centres opened in early 2004, with at least seven more in the planning stages (Community Peace Programme 2004).

The Zwelethemba model has proven feasible. Its health effects have not been measured, and indeed would be difficult to measure directly, but broadly speaking may be of two types. In immediate terms, the solving of thousands of small disputes may prevent violence and police intervention, and thus their health consequences. From a perspective in social epidemiology, its potential impact in creating collective efficacy, and so addressing a basic determinant of community health, is as (or more) intriguing. The model, as it has worked so far, fits neatly into the niche suggested by Sampson's work, and appears to advance collective efficacy in several ways.

Firstly, *a peace committee is an institution that mobilizes local capacity and knowledge to solve local problems.* A lack of collective efficacy does not mean that there are not effective individuals in a place, but only that there is no mechanism through which that individual efficacy can be mobilized for collective action. Peace committees are a site where people in a community are able to work together on the specific task of resolving disputes and dealing with their root causes. In the typical site, thousands of people in the community will take part in committee gatherings in the course of a year.

The peace committee is a durable node for governance, an institution. As an institution, it provides both continuity and coherence to the joining of individual knowledge and capacity in collective tasks. Even loosely engaged strangers (perhaps especially loosely engaged strangers) need a way of identifying, analysing and acting in relation to problems if they are to work together effectively and with mutual satisfaction; this is what the institutional mentality provides. The institution is also a site where monetary and social capital can accumulate. The peace committee as a group accumulates a fund of money for local projects, and learning from its work, builds a fund of knowledge about how to get things done that can be drawn upon by new members (Dupont 2004).

The peace committee was designed for a particular kind of community, a poor South African township of formally illegal squatters. Its purpose was to fill a void left by the partial or complete absence of institutions of collective action. Thus the generic benefits of the institution are not particularly different from those conferred by other institutions like churches, sports clubs or civic improvement organizations. Nevertheless, the peace committee has some elements of design that make it particularly interesting from the point of view of seeding collective efficacy in places where poverty is the rule and existing institutions are insufficient. Peace committees are inexpensive to start and to run. The resources they bring to individuals and communities in the form of payments for dispute resolution and community projects are small compared to the costs of professionally run interventions. Professional oversight of committees is likewise minimal. Peace committees are non-exclusive: anyone can join one or form one; places may have multiple, competing committees. As a result, committees can fail without substantial loss of investment for members or for the funders.

Secondly, *a peace committee can reconfigure relations of governance within the community*. Places with low collective efficacy may have strong institutions and considerable social capital, but nevertheless have reached a state where the ability of people across the community to co-operate for at least certain kinds of ends may be limited. Powerful institutions supported by strong social capital may actually suppress collective efficacy. For example, a community with strong street gangs and strong churches has efficacy for some purposes, and high social capital, but may lack efficacy in key areas like crime control. In Zwelethemba, both the police and African National Congress street committees were present to control crime, but their methods were not useful for dealing with smaller disputes or reducing violence in the township. From a nodal governance perspective, the creation of a new node not only fills a gap in governance, but also has the potential to destabilize a stable but suboptimal community governance system in ways that lead to more efficacy (Post and Johnson 1998). Other nodes, like ANC street committees in the case of South African townships, react to the new node by competing (in the course of which they may also change), moving out of security, joining peace committees or starting peace committees of their own. These sorts of realignments are not inevitably for the good, but the experience of the South African project has been for the most part positive.

Thirdly, *peace committees can reconfigure relations of governance between the community and the larger systems it inhabits.* Collective efficacy is important for managing the events that happen within a neighbourhood, but in health, as in many other areas, local events are to a considerable extent the result of externally driven and governed processes. Likewise, the resources available to a poor community, though perhaps greater than is commonly credited, are rarely comparable to those available to the state or other powerful nodes of governance in the larger social system of which the poor neighbourhood is a part. An important form of efficacy must therefore be the ability of the community to influence the decisions and behaviours of governing nodes outside it. A governing node can accomplish this by creating connections with nodes in the larger surrounding network, and then using its resources to influence those nodes in ways that help the node do its business. The peace committee experience working with the police in Project iThemba is an example.

The Zwelethemba model is a hopeful instance of private governance of security for poor people, but these are early days. No matter how well it and other interventions like it work, there can be no question of the state disappearing in security or health. It is required as a funder, as a mediator among social disputants, as a provider of services, and as the ultimate guarantor of a basic democratic environment (Braithwaite 2000; Johnston and Shearing 2003; Loader and Walker, this volume). Given these important lasting roles of the state, and the related problem of expecting a small collection of weak people to make change beyond their immediate environment, some commentators have voiced doubts about how microgovernance is to coexist with traditional state governance as a practical and legitimate force for achieving social goods.

Reconciling microgovernance and state security: towards methods of democratic transformation

Perhaps the most basic question is how we can expect microgovernance institutions to change conditions shaped by so many forces beyond their control. As Carson puts it, 'the problem remains that if the basic lack of collective efficacy is rooted in extraneous structural factors like concentrated disadvantage, then the prospects for substantial success through intervention at the neighbourhood level seem limited indeed' (Carson 2003: 32). A bold effort to give poor people more control over their lives can easily evolve, as the overall system adapts, into a further instance of abandonment (Luhmann 1997). The state, happy to be relieved of the obligation of providing police, or health officers, offers best wishes and departs. Marginal, economically redundant communities are given a few insufficient resources of control and then blamed for their failure to overcome structural impediments. Thus, as Halpern has observed, 'those who have the least role in making and the largest role in bearing the brunt of society's economic and social choices [are left] to deal with the effects of those choices' (quoted in Geronimus 2000).

The premise of the question is undeniable: change from the bottom, by the weakest, faces long odds. Nevertheless, there are some answers. One is that even modest, marginal improvement in the immediate environment may have substantial value in reducing misery, which is not an inherent element of life in relative poverty (Burris 2004). An example of this may be found in the Sonagachi Project. Sonagachi was introduced as an HIV prevention intervention in Calcutta in the early 1990s. Organized as a workers' collective, it deployed a mentality of workers' rights and occupational safety among sex workers, using simple community organization techniques like peer education. It has grown to thousands of members, significantly improved sex workers' relations with madams, pimps and the police, and has been given substantial credit for the unusually low rates of HIV among Calcutta sex workers compared to other major Indian cities (Basu et al. 2004). Yet sex work remains marginalized in India as a whole, the underlying causes that bring women into sex work in India are unchanged or worsening, and the project has not been replicated with anything like the same degree of success elsewhere.

The Sonagachi experience suggests, by a certain kind of failure, another answer to the doubts about microgovernance: scale. The advantage of microgovernance is that it addresses big socio-economic problems like poverty and racism at the places they are instantiated in daily life – one community at a time. By the same token, such a bottom-up approach must happen in dozens or hundreds of communities if it is to be expected to have an effect on the social system at a regional or national level. The key to microgovernance as a source of serious change is replication on a large scale. Interventions must by design or otherwise have the capacity to spread, as Shearing has put it, like a 'cultural virus'. Design elements that could be expected to ease transmission include low cost, a simple technology that does not require extensive professional assistance, and a salient and attractive mentality. The spread of microgovernance also requires private and public funders willing to promote large ends by funding many small projects, which presents a serious cultural as well as practical challenge.

Syringe exchange programmes (SEPs) are an example of new nodes that directly address health by providing health services, and also of the way a new node can change a system. The first SEP was introduced in Amsterdam in 1984. Initiated by a drug user organization, it was soon adopted by the Municipal Health Department of Amsterdam, where it became a fundamental component of HIV prevention activities among intravenous drug users. In the late 1980s, SEPs were introduced in the United Kingdom, Australia, Canada and several other European countries, and have since expanded around the world (Burris et al. 2003). The SEP is an institution that deploys a simple public health technology – exchanging new sterile syringes for used ones, delivering basic health information and services – within a mentality of harm reduction. It is relatively inexpensive to operate, and can do so without public funding or even clear legal recognition. SEPs have spread throughout the world and influenced public health policy, legislation – and the spread of blood-borne disease (Drucker et al. 1998; Strathdee and Vlahov 2001; Coffin 2002).

The experience with syringe exchange also illuminates a set of questions having to do with the interrelationship of microgovernance institutions and the state. Loader and Walker suggest that Shearing and his colleagues fall back on an idealized view of face-to-face democratic decision-making, conveniently emphasizing the ways in which the relations between microgovernance entities and the state are complementary, without facing hard questions of potential conflict (Loader and Walker, this volume). Loader and Walker ask how the umpiring or meta-regulating state works to prevent local nodes from running amok. How does it legitimately define the public interest while at the same time leaving them the autonomy and control that are the main engines of good? If state recognition and funding are essential to the success of microgovernance, how do these entities escape reliance on the larger and more established forms of governance they are supposed to be challenging or replacing? And more broadly, how does one create the sort of rights-respecting state in which these entities could survive?

Schemes of local capacity governance could and probably will fail at some point in some place in each of these respects. It is difficult to imagine a small network of peace committees effectively operating to enhance democracy in a police state or a failed state – or in a neighbourhood controlled by violent gangs. It is not at all difficult to imagine a peace committee or some other institution of microgovernance achieving and abusing local dominance. We have seen with syringe exchange both community conflicts that had to be mediated by the state and the sometimes negative effect on the original mission of accepting state funds with the inevitable strings attached (Broadhead 1999; Bray et al. 2001).

As with the question of scale, however, it is important to see these as design considerations to be managed over time rather than problems that must be solved before taking action. The emerging theory of nodal governance underlying this work deals with issues of conflict, capture and legitimacy as questions of checks and balances – of competition mediated by design elements. As Braithwaite perceptively puts it, 'Shearing buys Hayek's explanatory theory of the limits of knowledge available to central planners, while rejecting the normative theory of the economy that he erects on this foundation' (Braithwaite 2000). In place of the capitalist market, Shearing and his colleagues posit an adaptive system of competing and co-operating nodes. Change in these systems does not depend upon a cross-sectional architecture of legitimacy satisfactory to the central planner, but on a longitudinal process of competition constrained within peaceful banks by culture and both private and public institutions. In this approach, basic democratic norms of non-violence, transparency and accountability are in no way discounted or set aside, but built as much as possible into the new institution. The important question is whether these values can be promoted through different institutional means (Cohen and Sabel 1997).

Practice in the governance of security framework can be understood as an exercise in grounded theory, in which experience and observation inform the development of theory, which is in turn tested and refined by further practice and observation (Glaser and Strauss 1967). In a narrow sense, it is 'a programme of empirical discovery of what is better provided publicly, by markets or by communities' (Braithwaite 2000: 223). More generally, it pursues what Unger has called democratic experimentalism. As Unger sees it, '[t]he theorist and the practical reformer share a stake in putting actual institutions in their place by understanding and judging them from the vantage point of suppressed and unrealized possibilities. We can keep this freedom-giving and superstition-subverting idea alive today only if we recast both legal analysis and political economy as institutional imagination' (Unger 1996). Unger observes that politicians, citizens and social and political theorists in the developed world have come to see our current institutional embodiment of democracy as the only viable model. This 'institutional fetishism' stifles the development of other ways of thinking about, practising and institutionalizing democracy (Unger 1996: 8–9). The effort to rethink the governance of security is an exercise of institutional imagination in the cause of finding contemporary forms of social organization that can deliver the good of security *and* other goods, like health.

Conclusion

Health and security are intertwined in fact, but not sufficiently in research and practice. This should change. The immediate and measurable effects of security on health can be addressed incrementally by efforts to better organize the governance of security and health. The criminal justice system currently causes more ill health than it should and prevents less than it could. Considering the relationship of security and health points to communities and to the fundamental question of how people in particular places live together in a peaceful, co-operative and healthy way. Efforts at the local, regional, national and global level to create more salubrious environments are essential, but so are complementary efforts that work from the bottom up. The experience of the Zwelethemba model of local capacity governance is an important sign that collective efficacy can be mobilized by intelligently designed nodes of governance. For the future, it will be necessary to bring together institutional innovation and social science research to creatively explore and rigorously evaluate new institutional forms that can deliver the benefits of self-determination and democratic participation to poor places on a large scale.

9 Research and innovation in the field of security: a nodal governance view

Jennifer Wood

Introduction

There is much talk in the field of security, as in other fields of governance, of the need to design and implement innovations and to diffuse them from one context or site to another. Broadly speaking, an innovation is 'an idea, practice, or object perceived as new by an individual or other unit of adoption' (Rogers 1995: 35 cited in Nutley and Davies 2000: 35). New organizational approaches within and across a variety of fields have become marketable commodities in our global era. In the area of security governance there has been an 'international trade in ways of understanding, and acting upon, more mundane, local, volume crimes' (Stenson and Edwards 2004: 211) as exemplified in the widespread diffusion of 'Compstat'-like programs across and beyond the United States (Weisburd et al. 2003). As well, models of 'community policing' are being marketed as service delivery 'packages' for improving crime prevention and enhancing public perceptions of safety (Wood and Font 2004).

The design and diffusion of innovations is, or should be, based on explanatory analyses of those sites wherein change or transformation is to take place combined with comprehensive assessments (instrumental and/or normative) of what exactly should be transformed and how. However, many scholars grapple with the question of whether, and to what extent, one can adequately describe and assess those sites that are to adopt innovations, particularly foreign locales characterized by unique social, political and cultural contexts (see Cohen 1982). Other observers focus on understanding the ways in which innovations are adapted and translated by local actors (see Dolowitz and Marsh 1996; 2000; Hassink 1996; Minogue 2002) as well as the role of complex variables that shape processes of diffusion (O'Neill et al. 1998; Nutley and Davies 2000; Wejnert 2002).

In the governance of security, scholars of 'plural policing' and 'nodal governance' have only just begun to explore the broad question of how to innovate in ways that are based on sound explanatory analyses of security authorization and provision combined with robust assessments of opportunities and conditions for change (Wood and Shearing 1999; Johnston 2000; Loader 2000). This work, however, remains very preliminary, with some scholars focused on developing better explanations of trends in security governance in order to know what normative interventions are possible and desirable (Shearing 1997; Jones 2003; Johnston, this volume). Others have conceptualized normative agendas which challenge the proposition that state-centred governance models are a necessary and sufficient pre-condition for democratic transformation (Bayley and Shearing 1996; Shearing and Johnston 2005; Burris, this volume). Taken together, this small and preliminary body of work supports the view that innovators need to be 'skilled tailors' (Nutley and Davies 2000: 35). This is based on the prior assumption that no single mentality, institution or technology of security governance is necessarily effective or desirable within a particular site, and as such, the opportunities or possibilities for instrumental or normative engagement are many and varied, as well as contingent within and across different contexts. Nodal governance theory in particular supports the proposition that tailor-made innovations are necessary because the process of 'translation' or 'adaptation' can involve forms of resistance and contestation during implementation, serving to alter or reconstitute the particular mentalities and technologies promoted by an innovation in the first place (see O'Malley 1996; Cherney 2005).

This chapter explores ways in which a nodal governance approach can inform an overall methodology for designing, implementing and diffusing innovations in the field of security. This methodology has three key components or stages. The first stage involves a comprehensive empirical 'mapping' of existing governance nodes and networks within specific sites. This empirical work can then inform the second component, which involves an assessment of gaps, limitations and ethical problems with the operation of existing nodes and networks. This instrumental and normative assessment would guide the third stage, involving the design and implementation of an innovation(s) aimed at transforming, or even inventing, new mentalities, institutions and practices of governance that serve to enhance the effectiveness and/or democratic character of security provision. The adaptation of the innovation within a specific site should consist of a continuous, flexible and iterative process of evaluation and reflection that adjusts to forms of resistance and contestation on the part of local actors.

What is proposed in this chapter is not based on a specific case study, but rather a set of reflections on the practical experiences that I and others have had throughout the course of research and innovation projects that we have been involved with, particularly within and across Argentine and Australian sites. While I pay particular attention to explanatory and normative issues across country contexts, the proposed methodology is intended to inform work across micro-level settings such as cities and regional areas within shared macro-level (country) contexts. In essence the proposed approach is one that aims to combine explanatory and normative work within a nodal paradigm. As such, the following section will review the key explanatory and normative assumptions of nodal governance theory as it has been developed to date.

Nodal governance

The concept of nodal governance has been described and critically appraised in this collection (see Shearing, Burris and Johnston and see Loader and Walker and Marks and Goldsmith, respectively). With that in mind, and at the risk of being repetitive, it is important to highlight some key tenets of this approach. I will focus in particular on the challenges it highlights for doing, and combining, explanatory and normative work.

Doing explanatory work

As the term suggests, the nodal governance approach centres on the notion of a 'node', described in terms of its *mentalities, institutional structures, technologies* (methods) and *resources* (Johnston and Shearing 2003; Burris 2004). Burris provides a useful elaboration:

> To be a governing node as this theory defines it, a node must have some institutional form. It need not be a formally constituted or legally recognized entity, but it must have sufficient stability and structure to enable the mobilization of resources, mentalities and technologies over time. A street gang can be a node, as can a police station or even a particular shift at a firehouse. A node like this may be primarily part of an integrated network, like a department in a firm; it may be linked to other nodes in multiple networks without having a primary network affiliation, like a small lobbying firm; or it may be what we call a 'superstructural node,' which brings together representatives of different nodal organizations . . . to concentrate the members' resources and technologies for a common purpose but without integrating the various networks – a trade association, for example. (2004: 341–2)

The nodal view thus assumes a certain level of plurality in the mentalities, institutions and practices that constitute governance processes within and across pre-determined geographical sites (e.g. particular neighbourhoods) or issue areas (e.g. terrorism or youth safety). Put simply, the nodal view assumes that governance is never fully actualized by a single node, even though some nodes may indeed be hegemonic. For researchers, this means that the explanatory work they carry out should not be driven by the assumption that particular nodes are more effective or, for that matter, more democratic than others.

A plurality of nodes and networks is assumed to be a common feature of security-producing *and* insecurity-producing activities across the globe, even though the precise nature of nodes and networks that carry out such activities are time- and space- specific and embedded in local cultures and politics. Although it could be said that nodal governance has been conceptualized primarily within the English-speaking world, empirical studies from other cultures and contexts have served to provide further support for the proposition that there exists a 'shared complex morphology that characterizes security assemblages in the present era' (Dupont 2004: 76). Such studies have covered areas including continental Europe (Ocqueteau 1993; Favarel-Garrigues and Le Huérou 2004; Ferret 2004), Brazil (Caldeira 2000; Wood and Cardia, in press), South Africa (Baker 2001; Nina 2001), the Philippines (Connell 1999), Hong Kong (Cuthbert 1995), China (Fu 1993), the Netherlands, (De Waard 1996), Germany (Nogalla and Sack 1998), India (Nalla 1998), Turkey (Aydin 1996) and Northern Ireland (Hillyard 1993).

In examining the unique character of nodes and networks across different sites or areas of security, scholars have begun to develop empirical 'maps', and have drawn from different intellectual traditions and empirical studies in doing so. For example, Johnston's analysis of commercial military service providers in this collection represents an important map-making project at the transnational level of security authorization and provision. Bayley and Shearing's report for the National Institute of Justice (2001) can be seen as the first major attempt to provide a typological understanding of the different mentalities, institutions and practices that constitute 'multilateral' policing, and Dupont's work (2004) provides a preliminary typology of security 'networks'. Manning's piece in this collection, whilst not advocating an explicit nodal governance approach, provides a much needed contribution to the map-making enterprise. Not only does his empirical focus on the governance of terrorism prove essential and timely, but he also provides new and important theoretical insights, including the point that networks are often constituted in contingent and temporary ways in response to particular time- and space-specific problems. Several studies of private or corporate security have also made important contributions to our understanding of the kinds of nodes and networks that comprise non-state or 'hybrid' governance activity; these include Jones and Newburn's English study of private security (1998), Rigakos' original research into 'para-policing' (2002) and Wakefield's analysis of policing on 'mass private property' (2003).

While the above is by no means an exhaustive sample of nodal mapping, it is undoubtedly the case that this kind of explanatory work remains in its infancy. Much more needs to be discovered about the nature of nodes themselves as well as the ways in which nodes come together in the form of networks. This general line of inquiry needs to be conceptualized, and subsequently undertaken, within a range of sites (e.g. micro, regional and global territories and virtual spaces) and according to different 'slices' of time. As will be discussed further below, until this explanatory work is more robust, opportunities to innovate in the form of sustainable instrumental and normative interventions will remain limited.

From a methodological perspective, a relatively small but significant body of scholarly work has undertaken research, particularly in the past fifteen years, in ways that are of direct relevance to the 'mapping' aspirations of those interested in the nodal governance approach. For instance, scholars – mainly within the Foucauldian 'governmentality' tradition (Foucault 1991) – have offered analyses of the governance 'mentalities' of (primarily state) organizations. Burris defines a 'mentality' as

the culture of the node, its way [of] thinking about itself and the world around it. A mentality operates to bring coherence and thus enable longevity and collective action within the node. Such a culture is not a blueprint for specific action, but a narrative of the world that guides the ongoing process of adaptive improvisation in a node (2004: 342).

Research during the 1990s on 'neo-liberal' mentalities (Rose and Miller 1992; Rose 1996) was popular and timely given the nature and degree of state restructuring around the globe, and provided an analytical focus for those interested in understanding the (primarily) organizational and managerial transformations taking place in security provider institutions like the police (O'Malley and Palmer 1996; O'Malley 1997) and corrections (Feeley and Simon 1992). Others have delved more deeply into the strategic mentalities of both state *and* corporate institutions of security governance, producing the overall finding that two seemingly distinct mentalities are in operation and circulation, one which is characterized by a past-oriented, punitive focus, while the other is centred on future-oriented, anticipatory risk-management (Johnston 2000b; Johnston and Shearing 2003).

While a 'punishment mentality' (Johnston and Shearing 2003) is often depicted as a key feature of security governance carried out by criminal justice institutions, and while a 'risk mentality' has been described as 'natural' to corporate security institutions (Johnston and Shearing 2003: 76), it has been recognized that these mentalities 'mix' and 'meld' within and across different nodes and networks in line with a range of instrumental and normative agendas. Of note is the work of Johnston who unpacks the ways in which 'broken windows' policing, and its 'zero tolerance' variant, effectively combines punitive and risk-oriented mental frames to produce a package of generally coherent programmes and practices that resonate with the penal populism of cultures in the United Kingdom and the United States (Johnston 1997; Johnston and Shearing 2003). Braithwaite similarly contrasts the ways in which corporate actors and state actors combine mentalities of punishment and risk (2003b).

From a comparative perspective, one can extrapolate from this finding that very different mixes of risk and punishment will occur in foreign cultural, political and economic settings. For example, O'Malley suggests that due to 'local political formations and social conditions' (O'Malley 2002) in Australia, the nature of risk-based governance in that national context diverges considerably from that which is found in the United States (the country seen as the 'exporter' of risk-based thinking). Because of a broader 'politics of inclusion' that exists in Australia, risk-based strategies of governance have tended to be more inclusive in orientation, a key example of which is its 'harm minimization' approach to drug use, in contrast to the more exclusionary politics found in the 'war on drugs' in the United States.

The challenge of undertaking comparative explanatory work is not a methodological problem that scholars of security governance have dealt with explicitly and comprehensively, probably because of the fact that the 'mapping' of nodes has privileged English-speaking contexts. In this way, governance scholars have much to learn from fields such as comparative criminology (Cain 2000), comparative criminal law and socio-legal studies (Nelken 1995; Zedner 1995; Nelken 2002). Taken together, this research cautions scholars against assuming a level of convergence among the mentalities, institutions, and practices of governance institutions within different sites, and in particular, across different cultures. For example, Zedner (1995: 518) highlights the challenges of 'reconciling sensitivity to local difference with the generalizing imperatives of the comparative'. As a means of developing an 'acute sensitivity to the peculiarities of the local' (1995: 519), Zedner suggests that scholars should pay more attention to the world-views of different cultures. While it is nearly impossible to understand world-views in any pre-discursive or natural sense, she argues that much can be learned at the discursive level – where natives/local actors construct their world in a variety of textual forms, including the media. As an empirical illustration, she contrasted 'law and order' discourse from Britain with that of Germany, and found that conceptions of 'security', 'fear' and 'disorder' varied significantly, with concrete implications for the nature and focus of criminal justice institutions and practices.

In line with Zedner, Melossi contends that while '[c]onversation between different cultures is possible, the process of "translation" is, strictly speaking, not possible. Any term, even the simplest, is embedded within a cultural context, or milieu, that gives it its meaning. If culture and even thought are inextricably linked with natural languages . . . neither language nor culture are hermetic entities' (2001: 404). In his comparative analysis of the cultural embeddedness of punitive orientations in North America and Italy, Melossi argues that punishment is conceived differently in these contexts on account of their different historical backgrounds (2001: 405–7). He focuses in particular on their 'foundational cultures' (Savelsberg 1999 cited in Melossi 2001: 415) of religion – Catholicism in Italy and Protestantism in North America. He observes that it is not so much a 'cultural determinism' shaping the punitive futures of such countries. Rather, it is the case that 'cultural toolboxes' provide a repertoire of motives within particular social, political and economic conditions. As well, cultural sensibilities can fluctuate, resulting in modulations in criminal justice mentalities over time.

Melossi's assertion that it is more realistic to 'converse' with, rather than 'translate' across, cultures was confirmed to a group of colleagues that I have been working with in a 'technology transfer' project involving Canada and Argentina.[1] In the course of designing and implementing normative interventions in the areas of community safety and conflict resolution (a topic to which I will turn later), we were concerned with understanding existing mentalities of security governance, the discourses that informed them, the language that was used, and the ways in which this language informed practice. In line with Melossi's analysis, there is a set of 'cultural toolboxes' that were originally produced during the establishment of Argentina's system of security governance. While Melossi examined the influence of religion, a notable influence in the Argentine context was the school of positivism that, melded with variants of a 'criminology of the other' (Garland 1996), exerted a profound influence on collective sensibilities surrounding criminal justice policy (Sozzo 2000; Wood and Font 2004).

How precisely this 'criminology of the other' manifests itself in different cultures is an empirical question in its own right, and one that we have only begun to explore in our comparison of Argentina with (exporter) countries like Canada and Australia. While Garland speaks of a 'criminology of the other' in places like the United Kingdom and the United States (Garland 1996; 2001), a 'conversation' with those who represent Argentine reality reveals a similar penological current at an abstract level,

[1] This project is funded by the Canadian International Development Agency and administered by the Centre for International Studies, University of Toronto.

but upon closer scrutiny of mundane criminological discourses, one finds forms of 'othering' that are embedded in unique sets of cultural references and meanings. For instance, Wood and Font (2003) examine how the 'dictionary knowledge' (Chan 1997: 4) of the police – expressed in categories they deploy to make sense of people and things – is informed by a determinism grounded in medicalized and pathologized conceptions of human agency. Because of the strong and continued influence of positivism, state agents have had a repertoire of motives and justifications at their disposal in undertaking forms of 'preventive' policing – often targeted at marginalized groupings – the likes of which have been generally unthinkable in established democracies, such as the detention and interrogation of individuals without any prior evidence of a criminal act (Sozzo 2000).

In our attempts to describe and explain the governance of security in Argentina, we thus quickly realized that comparative explanatory analyses can, at their best, identify forms of 'convergence and similarity' (Jones and Newburn 2002b: 176) at the level of broad mentalities. Indeed, in both Argentina and Brazil (and presumably in other Latin American contexts), the notion of a 'punishment mentality' – like the notion of a 'criminology of the other' – offers considerable explanatory power (Wood and Cardia, in press; Wood and Font 2004). Nevertheless, the ways in which this punishment mentality is expressed in concrete terms, from mundane criminological discourses to institutional arrangements, to technologies and resources, diverges considerably across these contexts.

This brings us to the issue of agency. Both individual and institutional actors deploy, mobilize and alter mentalities in accordance with a range of instrumental and normative agendas. This suggests that it is a difficult and partially misguided enterprise to provide an explanatory map of governance mentalities (expressed through 'official' texts and narratives) without moving beyond an understanding of 'ideal types'. In his critique of 'governmentality'-based research, Garland has the following to say:

[I]t would be a mistake to focus upon the structure of conceptual and technological assemblages at the expense of an analysis of the pragmatics of use. There is a need to study the way that these knowledges and techniques are put to use, and the meanings they acquire in context. We need to examine the extent to which they are implemented, their corruption in practice, the unforeseen consequences that they produce, and the relation they establish with the field that they seek to govern. (1997: 199)

Central to any understanding of the 'messy realm of practices and relations' (Garland 1997: 199) is an awareness of how practical actors contest, resist and reconstitute ways of thinking. Both Cherney (2005) and

Dupont (2003b; this volume) emphasize the importance of understanding how mentalities are realized in practical terms as well as how practices serve to manipulate mentalities. Cherney argues in particular that explanations of governance cannot rely solely on an analysis of structural transformations:

> [T]rends being witnessed in the governance of security are not simply the result of some inevitable sweep of history (i.e. globalisation trends or neo-liberalism), but are also the consequence of individuals and institutions acting as change agents. These actors exploit certain . . . mentalities . . . and employ strategies to support these mentalities and translate them into actual technologies and practices of governance. (2005)

Dupont's work illuminates ways in which the range of authorities and providers of security governance exercise considerable agency as they 'jockey for position' in the field (Dupont 2003b; this volume). Echoing Cherney's conclusion, Dupont suggests that whilst patterns can be distilled at the level of mentalities, institutions and practices, 'it is essential also to acknowledge strategic and contingent initiatives that account for local variations and particular configurations' (this volume: 87). In their discussion of the local-level implementation of central policies in the United Kingdom, Stenson and Edwards add that

> local actors can resist, contest and manipulate central commands to fit their own agendas . . . We need to develop, through empirical research, analytic tools that facilitate an understanding of local differences in the play of community governance, and the local forms of 'habitus' among political agents: the cultural, emotional and instrumental repertoires and dispositions for cognition and action. (Stenson and Edwards 2004: 217–18)

In a similar vein, O'Malley argues that one should not assume a coherent mentality of governance, but rather an 'imbrication of resistance and rule' (1996: 311). In his study of the implementation of 'self-determination' policy for Aboriginal groupings in Australia, he concluded that explanations of transformations in governance cannot be limited by a 'discourse determinism' that privileges analyses of official texts. Rather, there are forms of governance 'from below' that must be studied and captured, as they can serve to resist, destabilize and reconstitute formal governance agendas. He contends that 'politics is a far more open-ended process of contestation' (1996: 312) which calls for the incorporation of some sociological forms of analysis (1996: 312).

The above discussion implies that scholars of plural policing, and nodal governance in particular, must begin concerning themselves more centrally with the development of explanatory maps that move beyond ideal-typical descriptions of nodes and networks of security governance, even though ideal types remain vital for heuristic purposes. This has direct implications for how to think about designing, implementing and diffusing innovations because such innovations must first be based on sound understandings of the object or target of intervention. In the second part of this chapter I will argue that a more systematic approach to 'nodal governance mapping' projects is required and I will offer some preliminary suggestions, drawing from empirical examples, as to what the principles and parameters of this methodology should look like. Prior to this, however, I will highlight some challenges in doing normative work.

Doing normative work

From a nodal perspective, doing normative work – in the form of designing, implementing and diffusing innovations – is, or should be, based on a prior analysis of gaps, limitations and/or ethical problems with established mentalities, institutions, technologies and resources of governance in a particular site or area. Such an assessment is of course based on the kind of explanatory work discussed above. With that in mind, there are several challenges in carrying out the phases of design, implementation and diffusion which will be briefly considered here and which I will re-visit in the second part of this chapter.

At the design level, there are two kinds of challenge, both of which speak to the problematic nature of pursuing 'pre-packaged' innovations. The first challenge pertains to the forms of knowledge (tacit and expert) that are mobilized and brought to bear on the design process. It is a challenge to determine which forms of knowledge should be included, excluded or privileged (given more weight) in this process. Cain's reflections on the application of Western criminological knowledge in non-Western contexts are useful in explicating this point. Drawing on the work of Said (1978), she argues that much Western criminological discourse is grounded in an 'orientalism', involving 'the discursive constitution of an often romanticized but also wayward and unknowing "other" which ... requires the guidance and advice of "us" to find and/or accept its proper place in the world' (Cain : 239). 'Orientalism' is of particular concern when innovations are designed within one cultural context and 'exported' to another, such as from sites in 'developed' countries to sites in transitional societies. Blagg discusses the 'franchising' of restorative justice, and in particular the ways in which the Maori model of 'conferencing' was interpreted and subsequently 'appropriated' in the establishment of a conferencing model in Wagga Wagga, Australia. He argues that Australian advocates of 'reintegrative shaming' theory (Braithwaite 1989) 'read' the Maori justice reforms in New Zealand in terms of their alleged shaming dimensions, contributing to a 'westernized interpretation...denuding the process of its history, context and internal structures of meaning' (Blagg 1997: 484). Blagg explains:

> While gesturing in the direction of a specifically Maori 'tradition' in relation to the ceremony (Braithwaite and Mugford 1994) and acknowledging that Maori people have had a raw deal from the system; their reading...attaches little significance to what is historically conjunctural and political about this intervention as part of a broader power struggle between *Pakeha* [Western] and Maori cultures. The creation of the Family Group Conference system, in this political sense, represented a *counter-hegemonic* reform on a truly Gramscian scale: in that it has both created new structures and has shifted the balance of forces in a crucial region of Maori concern. This, of course, is not the only reading of the situation; it can be read as a reform of the juvenile justice system through reintegration conferences, a system of 'restorative justice', a means of involving victims and making offenders accountable, but – if we are to capture what is, in relation to Aboriginal peoples, its most innovative characteristic – it must also be read as an empowering and *de-colonizing* process which has led to the recovery of lost authorities, social relationships and ceremonies: while reducing the extent of welfare and penological colonialism. In this sense it constitutes a *reclamation* of the child from non-Maori institutions, rather than a *reintegration* ceremony. (Blagg 1997: 484)

Drawing from Said, Blagg goes on to provide a '"contrapuntal" reading', one centring on the fact that '[t]he system established in New Zealand following ground-breaking legislation, was part of a process of re-establishing Maori dominion and the mapping out of a distinctly Maori jurisdiction' (1997: 485). Blagg also examines the practical and often ironic consequences of the Western reading of Maori practice – while the Maori justice model was designed to reduce the degree to which the police intervened in the lives of Maori youth, the Australian model 'has led to the supplementation and extension of already significant police powers over young people' (482). Clearly, part of what Blagg depicts as the Orientalist discourse sounding the Australian model is the assumption that the institutions of criminal justice (right down to police officers themselves) are the most capable and legitimate institutions to advance informal justice processes (Shearing et al. 2004).

Assuming that an innovation (say, a justice model) addresses the potential for Orientalism, it must be implemented (involving a process of adaptation and translation) to the site in question. There are different ways of envisaging this process, one of which is to think about it as a 'technology transfer' exercise, which Snyder defines as 'the sharing of either human-produced things or the knowledge of how to do things between two or more people' (Snyder 1996: 184). The Canadian International Development Agency defines technology transfer as 'the sharing of specific Canadian approaches or models incorporating unique

Canadian knowledge, expertise or experience with strong and solid partner organizations . . . who are interested and capable of successfully adapting it to meet pressing local development challenges' (Canadian International Development Agency 2001: 5). The established way of thinking about the transfer of technology and know-how is to disseminate 'best practices' through imitation (Webster 1994). However, several observers warn that the potential for innovations to get 'lost in translation' is high. Karstedt suggests, for example, that 'even if the distance of travel is much shorter and the exporter and importing countries share at least some dominant characteristics of western culture, the distinct institutional and political cultures decisively shape the process of adoption and implementation' (2002: 113). This argument has been extended by scholars examining the transfer of policies from the United States to the United Kingdom, like Stenson and Edwards who are critical of 'naïve emulation' (Stenson and Edwards 2004). The 'naïveté' they refer to stems in large part from the growing 'technical' nature of academic advice and policy solutions. Pre-packaged solutions tend to stifle the innovation of local actors in debating 'the subtleties, variations in context, clashes of interest and culture that make up the local politics of crime control' (2004: 21).

'Naïve emulation' is compromised by the exercise of agency on the part of local actors during the implementation process, notwithstanding the existence of structural conditions that are conducive to change. According to Jones and Newburn, our understandings of how actors participate in, contest and reshape the implementation process would benefit from more 'nuanced policy histories' (Tonry 2001: 531 cited in Jones and Newburn 2002b: 180) '[allowing] us to explore the detailed ways in which . . . social and cultural forces . . . actually play themselves out within the perceived alternatives, priorities and actions of key policy actors and institutions. Such evidence is a necessary condition for a more detailed understanding of the respective roles of, and relationships between, agency and structure within penal policy making' (Jones and Newburn 2002b: 180).

The need for more 'nuance' pertaining to agency–structure dynamics, combined with the imperative to understand how local actors 'exploit certain mentalities' (Cherney 2005) is supported by the recent findings of Weisburd et al. who examined the diffusion of Compstat-like programmes across American jurisdictions (2003). This study demonstrated that local actors can 'translate' new ideas and practices in ways that 'cherry-pick' those features that resonate with established ways of thinking and acting, whilst stifling the most radical and challenging aspects of an innovation (see Wood and Font 2004).

Weisburd et al. identify several dimensions of the original strategic problem-solving model of Compstat as developed in New York. They then discuss the results of surveys they carried out with representatives of organizations that had allegedly adopted the model, as well as of those organizations that had not done so, in order to see whether there were any differences in the ways in which a strategic problem-solving orientation was embraced by those adopting the innovation versus those not adopting the innovation. Surprisingly (or perhaps unsurprisingly) the overall finding was that reforms in policing, like the implementation of a Compstat-type model, can be taken up in order to *preserve* existing ways of thinking and acting. For example, one dimension of the original Compstat model is a new system of internal accountability, where operational commanders are held responsible for demonstrating that they are aware of crime patterns and statistics in their area and that they have devised strategies to reduce particular problems (Weisburd et al. 2003: 428). This form of accountability thus seeks to devolve authority downwards, requiring commanders to think creatively about problems as well as to devise ways of addressing those problems more effectively. In their survey research, Weisburd et al. discovered that a significant proportion of organizations who had adopted a Compstat-like innovation took up this idea of internal accountability in a way that reinforced a militaristic command and control ethos. In fact, 'Compstat departments were twice as likely as non-Compstat departments to report that a district commander would be replaced simply if crime continued to rise in a district' (2003: 438). Furthermore, the authors did not find a significant difference between the Compstat and non-Compstat organizations with regard to their engagement in a wide array of crime prevention strategies. It was found that there was still a considerable reliance on traditional law enforcement tactics on the part of both sets of respondents, and, moreover, 'Compstat departments were significantly more likely to increase arrests for targeted offenders, and target repeat offenders, use checkpoints, increase gun seizures, or improve victim services' (2003: 444). The results of this research appear to confirm Johnston's claim that new 'innovations' in policing must be examined for the ways in which punitive mentalities are mixed and melded with mentalities of risk (1997). As Weisburd et al. conclude,

Compstat is appealing precisely because it holds out the promise of innovation in police organization, strategies and tactics but does not demand a revolution in the organizational structure of American policing. Rather, it preserves – indeed, claims to reinvigorate – the traditional hierarchical structure of the military model of policing, a structure that has been attacked by a powerful reform wave over the last two decades (2003: 446)

Having reviewed some challenges in doing both explanatory and normative work, I will now move to the second part of this chapter which sketches a preliminary proposal related to the future of research and innovation within a nodal governance framework.

Designing and diffusing innovations: a proposed methodology

In this part, and based on a nodal governance perspective, I propose a methodology for engaging in the design, implementation and diffusion of innovations that involves the following key phases.

(1) A comprehensive empirical 'mapping' of existing governance nodes and networks within specific sites.

(2) An assessment of gaps, limitations and ethical problems with the operation of existing nodes and networks.

(3) Design and tailoring of an innovation, involving the participation of actors with different forms of tacit and expert knowledge, aimed at transforming, or even inventing, new mentalities, institutions and practices of governance that serve to enhance the effectiveness and/or democratic character of security provision. The adaptation and translation of the innovation within a specific site should consist of a continuous, flexible and iterative process of evaluation and reflection that adjusts to forms of resistance and contestation on the part of local actors.

I will now examine each of these phases in turn.

Explanatory mapping

The explanatory mapping phase should be guided by a series of questions that are asked about the nature of the nodes and networks involved in the governance of security within particular sites or areas, with an emphasis on their mentalities, institutional structures, technologies and resources. In thinking about the kind of explanatory mapping required to inform the design and diffusion of security and justice models tailored to disadvantaged Argentine communities, Wood and Font (2004) propose the following (very) preliminary and general set of questions:

• Who are the actors (both formally organized and informal) who participate in the promotion of safety and security?

• What forms of knowledge, and what capabilities and resources, does each of these actors bring to bear in promoting security outcomes?

• What does this set of knowledge, capabilities and resources reveal about the world-view of such actors (e.g. how they imagine security as a state of being; their conception(s) of human agency underlying what they see as the causes of insecurity; their preferred strategies for influencing human behaviour based on their conception(s) of human agency)?

- What are their stated outcomes and how do they measure success?
- What are the ways in which these different actors relate to one another in the security field? For example, are nodal relationships co-operative, conflictive, competitive or non-existent? (On nodal relationships, see Bayley and Shearing 2001).
- Depending on the nature of each nodal relationship, how often does each node/actor 'interface' with another and in what situations?[2]

In seeking to answer these questions, a range of qualitative and quantitative methodologies would need to be devised and deployed. For example, in response to the first question, statistical data could be gathered on the nature and type of policing and security organizations, which is a rather straightforward process in some contexts (particularly in developed nations) but considerably less straightforward in transitional societies. In countries like Argentina and Brazil, for example, where clandestine security markets and forms of 'moonlighting' across the public and private sectors are the norm, data collected by journalists becomes very important (Wood and Cardia, in press). Collecting data on this first question also becomes complicated when it comes to measuring the activities of 'informal' actors or those who contribute to security production, but whose primary mandate is not that of security production (e.g. community workers). Research in this regard would require a qualitative component, such as participant observation or interviewing security agents to get a sense of with whom they interface, and how, in the course of their daily work.

The second and third questions are concerned with exploring the mentality(ies) or, as Burris puts it, 'the culture of the node, its way [of] thinking about itself and the world around it' (2004: 342). One means of discovering mentalities within nodes is to examine the type(s) of knowledge that nodal actors (individuals, organizational subgroupings) bring to bear on particular kinds of problems. Central to this is an understanding of the ways in which they 'problematize' (Foucault 1988) that which they are tasked with governing. For instance, Burris' chapter in this volume illuminates the different 'problematizations' expressed in 'security' discourses compared with 'public health' discourses. Such problematizations both reveal, and generate, the use of particular forms of professional and non-professional knowledge. They also reveal deeper conceptions of human agency, as when psychiatrists emphasize the psychological determinants of, say, sex offending while others advocate 'rational choice' models of behaviour. The collection of such data would obviously be multi-faceted, including the examination of a range of texts (written and oral) from

---

[2] I am grateful to Benoît Dupont who has been developing and testing a methodology pertaining to this last question.

individuals working in different organizational roles and utilizing different competencies. Based on previous discussions in this chapter, it should
be stressed that an analysis of 'official' and managerial narratives or texts
should not necessarily be privileged.

Answers to the fourth question should complement answers to the previous questions. Obviously, the desired outcomes (e.g. reduction in crime
rates) of organizations and organizational actors reveal a great deal about
world-views and organizational missions. However, there are also ways in
which organizational actors engage in 'creative compliance' (McBarnet
1997) with organizational objectives by producing outcomes in ways that
run counter to the original intent and spirit of organizational objectives.
Measurements of success are also indicative of governing mentalities. For
example, the achievement of particular quotas (e.g. numbers of arrests)
may trump more qualitative measurements that capture, for example,
victims' experiences of procedural justice, something which reflects different kinds and levels of commitment to democratic norms on the part
of governance authorities and providers.

The fifth and six questions are geared to mapping the ways in which
nodes relate to one another as well as the intensity of nodal relations.
Quantitative data will be important for illustrating patterns in types of
nodal relationships and the strengths and weaknesses of ties between
nodes. Qualitative data, through such techniques as interviews and focus
groups, would allow researchers to see how security actors themselves
understand and construct the relationships they develop with other nodes.

In answering questions like the ones above, ethnographic studies would
provide very rich and contextual data. Manning's chapter in this volume, which relies on ethnographic data, represents the kind of work that
can be done in mapping nodes and nodal relations in highly time- and
space-specific contexts. The use of ethnography in researching organizational transformation, such as change in public policing, is something
that Marks strongly advocates, adding that the use of this methodological tool should be reinvigorated. Its particular relevance to the study of
mentalities, including the iterative relationships between mentalities and
practices, is revealed here:

If culture is to mean 'deep level assumptions', then it cannot be read off structural
arrangements or quantifications of police attitudes. Instead, researchers need
to take on an ethnographic approach, whereby they prioritize the social actor
and his/her subjective orientation . . . and immerse themselves in a host society
in order to try, as far as possible, to see, feel and even act as members of that
'society' . . . This involves a process of 'indwelling' – of suspending one's own ways
of viewing the world in order to understand the world of others. (Marks 2004b:
870)

In the context of the sorts of general questions listed above, every map-making project will obviously be tailored to a specific empirical area. For example, a team of academics and practitioners with whom I work were tasked with informing the design of strategic and organizational innovations that would enhance an Australian police organization's ability to govern organized crime.[3] Locating ourselves within a nodal governance framework (which was supported by contemporary empirical research on the phenomenon), we first argued to police organizations and other governance institutions that they must devise an analytical capacity to 'map' nodes and networks of *insecurity* (in the form of organized crime) as well as nodes and networks of *security* (i.e. existing governance and regulatory responses to such nodes and networks). With regard to maps of insecurity, we argued that innovations in policing or in any other governance process must be based on a comprehensive understanding of the nodes and networks of people, as well as nodes and networks of activities, that constitute the phenomenon generically referred to as 'organized crime'. This requires an explanatory capacity and, more fundamentally, a knowledge collection capacity, one which is based on a set of questions about the mentalities, institutions, technologies and resources of such nodes and networks.

Based on established explanatory work that provides clear evidence of the market-based character of contemporary organized crime (Naylor 2000; Paoli 2002), we argued that the mapping process should be guided by a series of questions about the production, transportation and distribution processes of illegal markets. The questions that we devised, which remain very preliminary, centre specifically on enhancing our understanding of the institutional structures and resources that allow organized crime to flourish. In regards to the *production* of illicit commodities for example, we proposed questions such as:

• What are the goods or services being exchanged/traded?
• Where are they being produced?
• How are they being produced?
• What source or raw materials are required?
• What skills/technologies are required for production (hard technology and human expertise)?
• What physical resources are required for production?
• What infrastructure resources are required for production?

---

[3] The following discussion draws from a series of unpublished discussion papers as well as conference and workshop presentations (available from the author) prepared by members of the Organized Crime Project team (Watkins 2004a; 2004b; Watkins and Wood 2004; Wood 2004b).

- What material, financial and human resources are required for production?
- What knowledge management/information resources are required for production?
- How is payment made to the people involved in production?

We proposed similar kinds of questions of the *transportation* and *distribution* phases of illicit markets, such as:

- How are goods and services transported?
- How are they made transportable/packaged?
- What human skills/resources are required?
- What mode/vehicle is required for transport?
- Where are the goods and services distributed?
- To whom are they distributed?
- How are they distributed?
- What is the method of exchange/trading?

In examining such questions, and in seeking to answer them, governance institutions like the police would undoubtedly be required to assess their own knowledge-gathering methodologies. In other words, they may discover in the first instance that they do not have the existing capability, skills or resources to answer some of those questions. This assessment is, in our opinion, an important process in and of itself. Furthermore, answers to the above kinds of questions would require data that could be provided by a range of nodes including regulatory institutions (e.g. Tax Office, Transportation Authority), public sector service providers (e.g. educational institutions that provide specific kinds of training), organizations in the business sector (e.g. banks, transportation companies) and human informants generally. The data generated by other organizations would presumably come in a range of forms, from case files to statistical data-bases to oral testimonies, access to all of which may be circumscribed by ethical imperatives including various forms of data protection. As such, 'knowledge management' or data collection 'networks' would need to be developed in order to answer the above kinds of questions in the most efficient and democratic manner possible. Indeed, the problems of 'networked' knowledge management are no less of a challenge *within* police organizations, whose specific operational units collect different kinds of information for different purposes and according to different forms of data capture.

Following such a mapping of nodes of *insecurity*, we proposed that governance institutions should map their existing mentalities, technologies and resources in order to determine what nodes and networks of criminality – along the lines of production, transportation and

distribution – are currently being targeted and in what manner. At the production level, we proposed questions such as:
• How is the access to raw materials regulated?
• How is the use of raw materials in production regulated?
• How are processes of production regulated?
In regards to transportation, we suggested questions like:
• How is education, training and licensing regulated? By whom?
• How are transport modes/vehicles regulated?
• How are transport routes regulated?
And, in regards to distribution, we proposed questions such as:
• How are the spaces and places upon which distribution takes place regulated?
• How is the education, training and licensing of distributors regulated?
• How are the methods of distribution regulated?
Obviously, a breadth of knowledge-gathering techniques would need to be considered in answering the above types of questions, techniques which would involve the participation of other regulatory agencies, public sector service providers, and human informants, etc.

We proposed that this two-pronged mapping would provide an evidential base for assessing gaps and limitations in existing governance strategies and in devising innovations that would attempt to address such gaps and limitations. We will now turn to the issue of how to conduct assessments of explanatory maps.

Instrumental and normative assessment of maps

Burris (2004) provides a useful approach to conducting an assessment of existing governance nodes and networks. Whilst he expresses a public health focus, the following key steps are of general utility:
• [identify] opportunities for change in the internal characteristics of nodes whose governance behavior is important for health purposes but which are not currently addressing health issues;
• [Identify] weaknesses in the technologies, mentalities, or resources of existing health-promoting nodes that could be remedied to increase governing capacity;
• [Find] and [patch] 'missing links' – places in the network where new connections could be advantageously developed between nodes; and
• [Find] 'missing nodes' – clumps of local capacity and knowledge that are not currently mobilized to govern – and creat[e] nodes to fill the gap (2004: 347).

In order to conduct the kind of assessment that Burris recommends, one must carefully consider who should be involved in that assessment process and in what capacity. Burris suggests, for example, that there may be nodes that could contribute to the production of health outcomes but which do not currently do so. It could be, and has been, similarly suggested that there may be nodes that could contribute to the production of security outcomes but which do not currently do so. It will be important to solicit a range of views on this, given the fact that 'security' is 'problematized' very differently in accordance with different mentalities and world-views (see Wood and Dupont, this volume). For example, 'security' will only be seen as a 'social development' problem – hence requiring the involvement of social development workers – if people with a social development perspective participate in assessing existing security nodes and networks. A similar point can be made in regards to the second component of Burris' assessment process. The identification of weaknesses in existing mentalities, technologies and resources will be very much shaped by the knowledge and capabilities of individuals and groups involved in the assessment process. For example, a police manager may not identify a weakness in existing policing mentalities, whereas a social development worker might do so.

The identification of 'missing links' in existing networks can only occur in a comprehensive manner if robust explanatory data, of the kind discussed above, is available. This data would need to be able to 'paint a picture' of 'formal' networks as well as 'informal' ones, particularly those that are not captured in written texts and official narratives, but simply through forms of qualitative data collection, including interview-based and ethnographic approaches. Presumably, representatives of the existing nodes that constitute networks under study would participate, in some fashion, in identifying the ways in which existing links could be developed or improved. This leads to the last of Burris' steps, which is the identification of 'missing nodes'. In many cases this would refer to marginalized individuals and groups who, for reasons primarily of structural disadvantage and opportunity, are not currently participating in governance processes even though their knowledge, capacities and resources would be relevant to the achievement of particular governance outcomes. For example, in a 'youth safety' project recently initiated in a border town in Victoria, Australia, it was determined jointly by a range of representatives working with youths, along with academics, that youths themselves were often 'missing nodes' in the governance of their own safety. As such, it was decided to begin designing an innovation consisting in part of a new institutional structure that would allow youths to mobilize their own knowledge and capacities in acting on their own 'problematizations' of security. The next section considers the design phase.

Designing and diffusing an innovation

As stressed above, designing an innovation that is both instrumentally effective and normatively desirable for a pilot project involves more than simply copying an innovation from elsewhere. That being said, the design process can be guided by a set of principles that participants in that process can agree upon. This is the approach that a group of colleagues from Argentina, Canada and South Africa took in adapting the model of 'local capacity governance' (i.e. the Peace Committee model) that Burris describes in this volume (see Shearing 2001c).

At the core of this model rests a set of values which resonate partially, but not totally, with those of restorative justice, such as its emphasis on community self-direction, inclusion, and the future (rather than a past-oriented focus on retribution), all within a 'republican' framework of 'freedom as non-domination' (Braithwaite and Pettit 1990). Unlike restorative justice, however, the model does not see 'restoration' as a core value, but rather something that is 'nice if it happens' (Shearing et al. 2004).

While our intent was to 'diffuse' the Peace Committee model to Argentina we knew that there would still be 'design' work that would have to take place. This was based on an awareness of ways in which the Argentine context converged with, but also diverged from, the South African context along the lines of culture, politics and economics. At a broad level, there were some similarities with the South African contexts in which we were working. Like South Africa, we worked with poor and marginalized groupings primarily subsisting in shanty-towns. Also like South Africa, we were working in a country that had a history of authoritarian rule and that had been in a period of democratic transition. Also similarly to the South African context, we decided that given the history of state security governance (characterized by a range of human rights violations) conditions were not conducive to working with criminal justice institutions, at least in the first instance. Our focus was therefore to work with 'the grain of other institutional sensibilities' such as that found in the robust network of human rights organizations (Wood 2004a: 44).

At a general level, the local capacity model made intuitive sense to members of the network of organizations with whom we engaged, including not only human rights organizations, but municipal governments and a range of non-governmental organizations involved in local governance issues such as community development. That being said, differences

emerged early on in regard to the ways in which the 'mentality' underlying the model was being translated into micro-level institutions, technologies and resources. For instance, the language of 'Peace Committee'
did not resonate well in the Argentine context. Not only was the phrase
a difficult one in linguistic terms, the term 'peace' had connotations of
the state-sponsored impunity of those who violated human rights during
the dictatorship. In its place, the term 'Foro de Convivencia' – referring
roughly to 'peaceful collective living' – emerged rather organically as the
most appropriate language for capturing the model's mentality. Another
difference can be found in the 'cases' that were being brought to the
attention of 'Foros'. While the South African peace committees tended to
focus on individual-level conflicts, the Foros tended to focus their energies on addressing more generic issues of insecurity, particularly those
that emerged from a broader pattern of militaristic policing that disproportionately targeted the young members of shanty-towns.

There are undoubtedly a range of factors that have influenced the adaptation of the model to Argentina, including the particular cultures and
habits of the specific communities with whom we were working, as well
as the dispositions and agendas of the local implementation leaders that
included human rights activists and lawyers. Much more work needs to
be done on our part in describing and explaining the unique character
of the Argentine project, but suffice it to say that we allowed forms of
resistance and contestation – and subsequent reconstitution of elements
of the model – to occur at the local level in order to increase the chances
that the ultimate model design would be 'tailor-made' and sustainable.
Underlying this flexibility in the development of the institutional arrangements and managerial structures for realizing the values of the model
was the assumption that the implementation of the model itself was a
'discovery' process, a process of theory-building, and in the design and
redesign phases, local actors tasked with implementation functions were
considered theoreticians and innovators, rather than simply 'applicators'
of practices that they had no role in determining. Local knowledge and
capacity was seen to play a constitutive role in the design and diffusion
phases in the cases of both South Africa and Argentina. Indeed, in South
Africa, it took several years for all the design features of the local capacity
model to be developed, refined and crystallized.

Of course, it is not simply local innovators and 'end users' who play
a role in shaping the development of a model. An ongoing process of
assessment and evaluation must take place at the behest of the innovators which seeks to measure compliance with the outcomes and processes
of the model using a range of qualitative and quantitative data. While the
constitutive role that local actors play in the 'organic' development of the

model is important, the process of revising the model must be controlled by a structure and a set of processes. For example, in the case of the Argentine project, those of us in charge of 'diffusing' the innovation (a group of Canadians and South Africans) met and worked regularly with our local implementation team in order to assess their levels of comfort with the elements of the model. This involved discussions aimed at gleaning ways in which they had themselves taken up the mentality underlying the model as well as the ways in which they translated this mentality into concrete practices. Admittedly the ways in which we gauged resistance, contestation and local translation were rather *ad hoc* and lacked comprehensiveness, and this is something we wish to improve. For example, our field visits would have benefited from longer and more rigorously documented periods of participant observation or ethnographic research.

Within micro-level contexts of shared dominant cultures, there comes a time, as was the case with the South African Peace Committee model, when the design phase must stop and where increased rigidity must take over. This occurs when forms of resistance and contestation are minimal and when the mentalities, institutions, technologies and resources of the nodes that were transformed or newly established have been modified, tried and tested until they demonstrate stability, effectiveness and democratic outcomes. Indeed, diffusion is essential if an innovation is to move from the 'periphery' to the 'centre' of political discussion and debate (Karstedt 2002: 120). That being said, diffusion to an entirely new cultural context, or to contexts with distinctly different social and economic characteristics (even within a shared national culture) should begin with a robust explanatory mapping phase. Simply put, the cycle would need to start all over again.

Conclusion

As implied in the introductory chapter to this volume, there is much that we still do not know about what is happening in the governance of security and there is still much to think about in terms of what to do about those trends that concern us. For those preoccupied with the future of democratic security governance, this chapter suggests that explanatory work must be combined in a more systematic and robust fashion with normative work. This is essential if the design, implementation and diffusion of innovations is to be based on realistic and nuanced accounts of the opportunities for, as well as the complexities of, engaging in governmental transformation within time- and space-specific settings.

This chapter contends that a nodal governance perspective provides a useful framework within which to engage in new and interesting forms of research and innovation in the field of security. At present, however, established thinking on nodal governance – to which much of the work on plural policing contributes – must address its present theoretical and methodological limitations. Scholars within this emerging tradition must begin asking new kinds of questions surrounding the nature of nodes and nodal relations, and should engage more explicitly with the development of rich methodological approaches that combine quantitative and qualitative data-gathering techniques. The nodal governance perspective has to date been useful in its illumination of broad trends in the governance of security. As reflected in the efforts of scholars like Johnston, Manning and Dupont in this volume, the time has now come for our research and innovation projects to grapple more explicitly and systematically with the 'messy realm of practices and relations' (Garland 1997: 199).

Conclusion
The future of democracy

Benoît Dupont and Jennifer Wood

The diversity of contributions assembled in this book and their contrasted perspectives, as well as their implications for future research, highlight the stimulating challenges presented by our efforts to understand security: how it is experienced, produced, governed, and the price there is to pay for our insatiable need for it. This thriving area of inquiry is grounded, as Shearing reminds us, in an intellectual tradition which looks upon the state as the main provider of security. From Hobbes to Weber, the idea that a social contract binds citizens together and allows the state to devise, adjudicate and enforce rules in order to maintain good order and guarantee peace of mind has been prominent in post-feudal societies. The state is supposed to guarantee a universal coverage in exchange for a monopoly on the legitimate use of coercive force. But everyday reality tends to be impervious to such political or philosophical considerations, and this book has highlighted the intrinsically plural nature of security governance.

The domination of philosophical and legal thought over matters pertaining to social control and policing has for a long time sustained the fiction of the monopoly of the monolithic state over the legitimate provision of security. However, recent historical and sociological discoveries have uncovered a complex web of private and hybrid agencies that have always co-existed with the state, exploiting the flexibility of the market to cater for unfulfilled needs (Morn 1982; Johnston 1992; Nadelmann 1993). In this book, Les Johnston chronicles the rise on the international scene of global security conglomerates and private military companies that play a crucial role in the 'war against terror'. Grassroots initiatives are also becoming an option for communities that are denied access to satisfactory levels of public policing, as Marks and Goldsmith show. Far from being only relevant to the private sphere, Manning shows that a plurality of providers is intrinsic to the temporary assemblage of public agencies that provide security for large political or sports events. His case studies illustrate in a vivid manner the multiplicity of organizations that share the responsibility of producing security on behalf of the state as well as the difficulties such organizations have in operating in concert. Maybe the context is extreme, as such a high degree of fragmentation can seldom be found outside the United States, and perhaps the collapse of space and time around these events generates exceptional challenges.

The plurality of structures is echoed by a plurality of rationalities or mentalities whose collisions result in overt power struggles, such as the ones described by Australian police commissioners in Dupont's chapter, or unintentional but none the less damaging outcomes such as the negative impact of the governance of security on the governance of health outlined by Burris. As Manning indicates, these rationalities express organizational responses to contingencies. In that context, security becomes a volatile concept, being defined situationally and contextually.

The contributors to this volume seem to agree that by far the most problematic aspect of this pluralism is the fragmentation it entails, particularly in terms of inclusion and exclusion. Membership of 'security clubs' ensures access to higher levels of security while it ensures that 'bad risk' populations are kept at a safe distance. This exclusionary economy of security is the source of democratic deficits that erode both the capacity of state policing to offer a public good as well as the will of particular social groups to share a common destiny. In that respect, Loader and Walker stress the self-defeating nature of this approach, reminding us of the social and constitutive dimensions of security: security cannot be enjoyed by a few in isolation from the rest of society without creating the conditions of more insecurity. Democratic security embodies a common project that must extend to all members of society, irrespective of their economic, social and political capitals. The partial breakdown of these two dimensions is portrayed in the South African context by Marks and Goldsmith, where it is clear that the emergence of non-state forms of governance such as vigilante groups and local popular justice initiatives undermines the democratization process. Many weak and failing communities – and quite a few strong ones as well – face the same dilemma: endure the brunt of deficient public security mechanisms and wait patiently for hypothetical improvements to occur, or enlist alternative forms of security provision as a substitute or a complement, despite their potentially corrosive effects for democratic governance.

Johnston's effort to theorize 'optimal' security delivery offers one way out of this dilemma. To borrow his words, optimal systems of security would neither be 'quantitatively excessive' nor 'qualitatively invasive', while satisfying democratic values such as collective accountability, effectiveness and justice. This balanced model addresses the preoccupations articulated above concerning the potentially damaging impact of the governance of security on other spheres of social life such as health, education, housing or business. It also takes into account the unintended consequences of pursuing 'too much security' (Zedner 2003). Johnston's 'optimal' approach allows one to recognize those unbalanced governance models where the remedy offered up is more harmful to the patient than the illness it is supposed to cure. Optimal security governance clearly places collective values and outcomes above rigidly designed and unreflective institutional responses.

There is no monopoly on organizational idiocy and partisanship: private and hybrid structures share with their public counterparts a propensity to succumb to hegemonic postures, unless they are engaged in a democratic dialogue that results in common-interest governance. Microgovernance initiatives such as the ones delineated by Burris, that emphasize local knowledge and capacities to resolve conflicts and create better living conditions while eschewing arbitrary violence and coercion, represent one of the multiple forms this engagement might take. For some (probably most) observers, plurality is a good thing, at least in the abstract. The expansion of security above, across, and below current public policing calls for many other forms of governance, some of them entirely driven by local communities, while others will remain more closely integrated with corporate interests and (hopefully) many others will continue to be embedded in conceptions of the 'public' interest.

Under current shifting conditions, the empirical data needed to understand the architecture of these various forms of governance and their compliance to the values of optimal security mentioned above are rather thin. Wood argues that more systematic attempts at mapping transformations in governance and their interdependent manifestations need to be made. The typologies of various players (or nodes) based on organizational attributes such as their functional differentiation (authorization vs. provision), levels of public or private ownership, span of activity (local, national or transnational) and mandate are only the first stage of what ought to become a much more ambitious research programme. Another component of such a research programme would involve an analysis of the 'connections' formed between institutions of governance. The meaning of connection here needs to be distinguished from any notion of co-ordination. Instead, it refers to the dense web of relationships that link together 'nodes', including policing organizations, criminal justice agencies, parliamentary committees, security companies, regulatory agencies, media outlets, professional associations, residential communities and other interest groupings. These nodes are connected through tangible and intangible relationships (for example, exchanges of information, pooling of resources and joint projects), and indeed, the inclusion and exclusion processes described above can be related to the existence or absence of linkages between nodes or subgroups. The lack of co-ordination and, in some cases, the utter chaos that reigns in daily practices does not result from a lack of connections, but instead from a poor capacity displayed by each node to grasp the interdependent nature of its decisions.

Of course, the kinds of 'map' that Wood suggests be developed cannot be seen as anything more than representations of reality (in descriptive, conceptual and sometimes visual forms), and indeed 'network analysis' has repeatedly been criticized for providing little more than a methodology in search of a theory, obsessed by the meticulous description of complex structures. Nevertheless, robust explanatory mappings do provide the key to determining what knowledges and capabilities we want to establish, develop or strengthen for our normative agendas. This may involve the formation of new nodes, or it may involve the development of new nodal relationships in the form of networks. But unless we properly understand how the dynamics of these relationships operate, our efforts will prove ineffective or, worse, will unwillingly reproduce negative outcomes. Furthermore, we are acutely aware of the intrinsic complexity and unpredictability of human agency and local contingencies. We expect that this humbling empirical agenda will act as a constant reminder, motivating us to advance realistic normative designs that can accommodate this frustrating reality. Given the complexity of governance processes, combined with the chronic power struggles that structure the field of security, academics are uniquely equipped to engage other social actors in debates about how to shape regulatory mechanisms that combine robustness and versatility.

There is no doubt that future conceptualizations of democratic governance will centre on the delivery and distribution of security as a 'public good', whilst recognizing both the potentialities and dangers of 'common' (Shearing and Wood 2003a) or 'club goods' (Crawford, this volume). Drawing on Johnston's notion of 'optimal' security distribution, some contend that there is, in Zedner's terms (2003) 'too much security' for those able to participate in club governance and 'too little security' for those unable to articulate parochial interests and engage in the kinds of power play that both Dupont and Crawford describe. That being said, whether one believes in the ostensibly 'social' character of security (Loader and Walker, this volume) or in the fact that the state will always provide a 'residual' presence (Crawford, this volume; see also Marks and Goldsmith, this volume), an exclusively state-centred approach to the future of democratic security governance is not tenable, and this is something on which all contributors to this collection agree to varying degrees. Indeed, while the theoretical stances that underpin this book's chapters might diverge on the role of the state and its coercive institutions as guarantors of security, all converge on the need to keep the normative agenda of security governance on a realistic footing. For example, state dominance in the field of security will not prevent other forces from exploring alternative arrangements, and sometimes from achieving remarkable outcomes.

In this regard, there is perhaps a clearer normative consensus among the contributors than what might appear at first blush. There tends to be a convergence towards an approach that Loader and Walker describe in their chapter as an 'anchored pluralism', although some authors are more concerned with the 'anchor' than they are with 'pluralism' and vice versa. Some thinking has been done in regards to the development of innovative regulatory models that give concrete effect to this notion of 'anchored plurality', including the recommendation of the Patten Report for the establishment of 'Policing Boards' for the Police Service of Northern Ireland (Independent Commission on Policing for Northern Ireland 1999; Shearing 2001a) – that have the mandate and budgetary capacity to sponsor and oversee a range of security delivery arrangements – or Loader's notion of 'policing commissions' that would 'formulate policies and co-ordinate service delivery across the policing network, and to bring to democratic account the public, municipal, commercial and voluntary agencies that comprise it' (Loader 2000: 337).

These kinds of recommendations rest firmly within a paradigm of 'meta-regulation' (Parker 2002; Parker and Braithwaite 2003) which includes 'meta-monitoring' (Grabosky 1995b: 543) and auditing (Scott 2003) of the provision of security, including that which is provided through various contractual arrangements, such as those discussed by Johnston and Crawford in this volume. In ensuring that governance providers comply with normative standards of conduct, 'meta-regulators' deploy a range of tactics including, but not limited to, those reflecting a 'command and control' mentality (i.e. monitoring and enforcement of rules and the use of sanctions). This may include measures to enhance the 'self-regulation' of, say, private security companies, with the understanding that such activities can be monitored at any time (hence the notion of 'enforced self-regulation'). In ensuring that markets or quasi-markets operate in accordance with public interest objectives, a programme of meta-regulation may involve the establishment of service delivery standards across jurisdictions like municipalities (just as the Province of Ontario, Canada has done; see Wood 2000), regardless of the precise security arrangements these localities authorize and subsidize.

Presumably, 'anchoring' comes in many forms. In the first instance, one would imagine the plural governance of security becoming anchored in a set of universal norms of democracy and human rights. Compliance with such norms would then need to be measured using tools such as performance indicators and audits in addition to other forms of assessment that combine a range of quantitative and qualitative methodologies. Analyses of the various motivations governance institutions have for complying (or not) must also be examined. A solid body of work on the compliance of corporate actors can be found, for example, in the field of regulation studies. Here, just as in the governance of security, the limits of 'command and control' regulation have been acknowledged, and those working in traditions such as 'responsive regulation' (Ayres and Braithwaite 1992) have argued that corporate actors are, in some contexts, much more likely to respond to tactics of 'shaming' and 'persuasion', as well as the use of 'rewards' (Grabosky 1995a; Braithwaite 2002b), than to untempered law enforcement in meeting the requirements of regulators.

Others have challenged the view that state institutions are the most effective regulators, and look more broadly at the role of stakeholder-based institutions. This is illustrated in the work of Gunningham, Kagan and Thornton (Gunningham et al. 2003; 2004) which examines the reasons why some corporations 'over-comply' with legal regulatory standards of environmental protection. For them, motivations for corporate compliance are more complex than traditionally understood by theorists of 'command and control' regulation. Corporate actors do not simply weigh the costs and benefits of compliance in accordance with an economic rationality, or even in accordance with a sense of morality embodied in legal norms. They place a considerable amount of weight on social expectations expressed in the actions of community groups and non-governmental organizations that promote environmental protection and sustainability. In their study of the pulp and paper mills (big offenders in water pollution), the authors argue that such actors see their environmental responsibility as being shaped by a 'social licence' which they define as 'the demands on and expectations for a business enterprise that emerge from neighbourhoods, environmental groups, community members, and other elements of the surrounding civil society' (Gunningham et al. 2004). They add that '[i]n some instances the conditions demanded by "social licensors" may be tougher than those imposed by regulation, resulting in "beyond compliance" corporate environmental measures even in circumstances where these are unlikely to be profitable' (Gunningham et al. 2004: 308). Perhaps scholars of security have much to learn from areas like the environment that share common regulatory challenges.

In thinking about the future of regulating security provision, one must take into account the fact that the power struggles occurring in the domain of security are not taking place on a level playing field. Crawford highlights the fact that particular sets of interests dominate security authorization and provision, interests that inform the pursuit of specific instrumental and normative objectives, including fortification and enclosure. Because of such relations of power, the establishment of a universal normative anchor is perhaps a project that is possible in theory, but difficult to complete in practice. And obviously, any such project must be contextualized within particular time- and space-specific sites, whether such sites are in South Africa, Australia or the United Kingdom. What we do know is that power relations and power plays differ across such national contexts and as such, to return to Wood's claim, it is essential to continue our empirical inquiries into the range of actors or 'nodes' that participate in the authorization and provision of security, inquiries that 'map out' the sets of interests being articulated and pursued by those who have a stake in security production. This would inform an 'anchoring' project, one that is based on an understanding of where – in which institutional locations – one can locate the deepest threats to democracy. In some contexts, like Argentina, it is human rights non-governmental organizations, rather than state institutions, that are most concerned about normative anchoring and have made very notable progress in this regard (Wood and Font 2004). In such contexts, microgovernance projects of the kind Burris refers to may provide the most appropriate normative focus, at least for the time being, until reforms of the state – along the lines suggested by Marks and Goldsmith – are accomplished in an informed and sustainable manner. Such an attempt to bolster non-state governance may in turn serve to level the playing field in ways that allow those previously lacking the opportunities for 'exit and voice' to be included in the authorization and provision of security. This may serve to enhance the conditions that would support an 'affective commitment to put things in common' (Loader and Walker, this volume: 192).

For the time being, even if security is conceived, or ought to be conceived, as a 'public good' (Loader and Walker 2001), the reality of plural governance is such that inclusions and exclusions from particular goods will continue to occur. As Marks and Goldsmith remind us, '[t]he very constituency category of *group*, or indeed of self-identified communities, logically implies an "outsider" or "other" who may often, therefore, be vulnerable and relatively unprotected' (this volume: 156). Perhaps, however, a further conceptual move, one that we alluded to in the introductory chapter, would open up new explanatory and normative possibilities. How could we rethink the distribution of 'goods', like security, if *human beings*, rather than states or 'publics', became our central 'referent object'? Held's work on 'cosmopolitanism' provides us with a clue when he takes the normative position that 'human beings liv[e] in a world of human beings and only incidentally [as] members of polities' (Barry 1999: 35 cited in Held 2003: 469). Held explains that 'the ultimate units of moral concern are individual people, not states or other particular forms of human association. Humankind belongs to a single moral realm in which each person is equally worthy of respect and consideration... To think of people as having equal moral value is to make a general claim about the basic units of the world comprising persons as free and equal beings' (Held 2003: 470). If anything, this human-centric position prompts us to contemplate whether the future of democracy rests solely on the development of capable, effective and legitimate auspices and providers of security, or whether it rests more fundamentally on a renewed conception of that which should be our 'ultimate units of moral concern'.

References

9/11 Commission 2004. *The Final Report of the National Commission on Terrorist Attacks Upon the United States*. New York: W. W. Norton.

Abt Associates 2000. *Police Department Information Systems Technology Enhancement Project (ISTEP)*. Washington, D.C.: Department of Justice.

Accordino, M., Porter, D. and Morse, T. 2001. 'Deinstitutionalization of persons with severe mental illness: context and consequences', *Journal of Rehabilitation* 67: 16–21.

Ahire, P. 1991. *Imperial Policing: The Emergence and Role of the Police in Colonial Nigeria 1860–1960*. Milton Keynes: Open University Press.

Aitkenhead, D. 2004. 'When home's a prison', *Guardian* Magazine, 24 July.

Albert, A., Warner, D. and Hatcher, R. 1998. 'Facilitating condom use with clients during commercial sex in Nevada's legal brothels', *American Journal of Public Health* 88: 643–6.

Altbecker, A. 1998. *Solving Crime: The State of the SAPS Detective Service*. Monograph No. 31. Pretoria: Institute for Security Studies.

Althusser, L. 1971. 'Ideology and ideological state apparatus', in *Lenin and Philosophy and Other Essays*. London: New Left Books, pp. 127–86.

ANC 2004. Statement by the National Executive Committee of the ANC on the 92nd anniversary of the ANC, 8 January. http://www.anc.org.za/ (accessed 8 January 2004).

Anderson, A., Qingsi, Z., Hua, X. and Jianfeng, B. 2003. 'China's floating population and the potential for HIV transmission: a social-behavioural perspective', *AIDS Care* 15: 177–85.

Anderson, B. 1991. *Imagined Communities: Reflections on the Origins and Spread of Nationalism*. London: Verso.

Anderson, C. 2004. 'Agency fingerprint base delayed', *Boston Globe*, 30 December.

Anon. 2003. 'Shame, stigma, and crime: evaluating the efficacy of shaming sanctions in criminal law', *Harvard Law Review* 116: 2186–208.

Anton, A. 2000. 'Public goods as commonstock', in A. Anton, M. Fisk and N. Holmstrom (eds.), *Not for Sale: In Defense of Public Goods*. Boulder, Colo.: Westview Press, pp. 3–40.

Aral, S. O., Shearing, C. and Burris, S. 2002. 'Health and the governance of security: a tale of two systems', *Journal of Law, Medicine and Ethics* 30: 632–43.

Armah, A. 2005. 'African identity and our place in the world'. Presentation given at the Centre for African Studies, University of Cape Town, 1 March.

Atkinson, R., Blandy, S., Flint, J. and Lister, D. 2004. *Gated Communities in England* (New Horizons Research Series). London: ODPM.

Audit Commission 1993. *Helping with Enquiries: Tackling Crime Effectively*. London: Audit Commission.

Auriacombe, M., Fatseas, M., Dubernet, J., Daulouede, J.-P. and Tignol, J. 2004. 'French field experience with buprenorphine', *American Journal on Addictions* 13: S17–S28.

Avant, D. 2003. 'Beyond regulation: institutional lessons and the trade-offs of private security'. Paper presented at *In Search of Security: An International Conference on Policing and Security*, Montreal, 19–22 February.

Aydin, A. 1996. 'Private and voluntary policing service in Turkey', *Security Journal* 7: 129–33.

Ayres, I. and Braithwaite, J. 1992. *Responsive Regulation: Transcending the Deregulation Debate*. New York: Oxford University Press.

Baker, B. 2001. 'Taking the law into their own hands: fighting crime in South Africa'. 29th Joint Session of Workshops, ECPR, Grenoble.

Bamford, J. 2004. *Pretext for War*. New York: Doubleday.

Barry, B. 1999. 'Statism and nationalism: a cosmopolitan critique', in I. Shapiro and L. Brilmayer (eds.), *Global Justice*. New York: New York University Press, pp. 12–16.

Barstow, D., Glanz, J., Oppel, Jr., R. and Zernike, K. 2004. 'Security companies shadow soldiers in Iraq', *New York Times*, 19 April. http://www.globalpolicy.org/security/issues/iraq/occupation/2004/0419security.htm (accessed 20 November 2004).

Basu, I., Jana, S., Rotheram-Borus, M., Swendeman, D., Lee, S.-J., Newman, P. and Weiss, R. 2004. 'HIV prevention among sex workers in India', *Journal of Acquired Immune Deficiency Syndromes* 36: 845–52.

Bauman, Z. 2000. *Liquid Modernity*. Cambridge: Polity Press.
   2001. *Community: Seeking Safety in an Insecure World*. Cambridge: Polity Press.

Bauman, Z. and Tester, K. 2001. *Conversations with Zygmunt Bauman*. Cambridge: Polity Press.

Bayley, D. 1994. *Police for the Future*. Oxford: Oxford University Press.
   1999a. 'The most crucial and unresolved issue associated with community policing', in S. Einstein and M. Amir (eds.), *Policing, Security and Democracy: Special Aspects of Democratic Policing*. Huntsville, Tex.: Office of International Criminal Justice.
   1999b. *Democratising the Police Abroad: What To Do and How to Do It*. New York: National Institute of Justice.
   2001. 'Security and justice for all', in H. Strang and J. Braithwaite (eds.), *Restorative Justice and Civil Society*. Cambridge: Cambridge University Press, pp. 211–21.

Bayley, D. and Shearing, C. 1996. 'The future of policing', *Law and Society Review* 30: 585–606.
   2001. *The New Structure of Policing: Description, Conceptualization, and Research Agenda*. Washington, D.C.: National Institute of Justice.

Beaglehole, R., Irwin, A. and Prentice, T. 2004. *The World Health Report 2004: Changing History*. Geneva: World Health Organization.

Beattie, J. 2001. *Policing and Punishment in London 1660–1750*. Oxford: Oxford University Press.

Becker, H. 1973. *Outsiders: Studies in the Sociology of Deviance*. New York: Free Press.

Benjamin, W. 1985 (1920). 'Critique of violence' in *One-Way Street and Other Essays*. London: Verso.

Benn, S. and Gaus, G. 1983. 'The public and private: concepts and action', in S. Benn and G. Gaus (eds.), *Public and Private in Social Life*. London: Croom Helm.

Benson, B. 1990. *The Enterprise of Law: Justice Without the State*. San Francisco: Pacific Research Institute for Public Policy.

Berkley, G. 1969. *The Democratic Policeman*. Boston: Beacon.

Bernstein, S., Platt, T., Frappier, J., Ray, G., Shauffler, R., Trujillo, L., Cooper, L., Currie, E. and Harring, S. 1982. *The Iron Fist and the Velvet Glove: An Analysis of the US Police*, 3rd edn. Berkeley, Calif.: Center for Research on Criminal Justice.

Bewley-Taylor, D. R. 2003. 'Challenging the UN drug control conventions: problems and possibilities', *International Journal of Drug Policy* 14: 171–9.

Beyrer, C., Jittiwutikarn, J., Teokul, W., Razak, M. H., Suriyanon, V., Srirak, N., Vongchuk, T., Tovanabutra, S., Sripaipan, T. and Celentano, D. D. 2003. 'Drug use, increasing incarceration rates, and prison-associated HIV risks in Thailand', *AIDS and Behavior* 7: 153–61.

Biro, F., Campbell, P., McKenna, P. and Murray, T. 2000. *Police Executives Under Pressure: A Study and Discussion of the Issues*. Ottawa: Canadian Association of Chiefs of Police.

Birzer, M. 1996. 'Police supervisors in the 21st century', *FBI Law Enforcement Bulletin* 65: 5–11.

Black, D. 2002. *Terrorism as Self-Help*. AMICI Newsletter of the Law section of ASA.

Blackstock, N. (ed.) 1976. *Cointelpro*. New York: Vintage Books.

Blagg, H. 1997. 'A just measure of shame? Aboriginal youth conferencing in Australia', *British Journal of Criminology* 37: 481–501.

Blair, I. 1998. 'The governance of security: where do the police fit into policing?' Speech delivered at the annual conference of the Association of Chief Police Officers, 16 July.

Blandy, S., Lister, D., Atkinson, R. and Flint, J. 2003. *Gated Communities: A Systematic Review of the Research Evidence*. CNR Paper 12. Bristol: Centre for Neighbourhood Research.

Blankenship, K. and Koester, S. 2002. 'Criminal law, policing policy, and HIV risk in female street sex workers and injection drug users', *Journal of Law, Medicine and Ethics* 30: 548–59.

Bluthenthal, R. 1997. 'Impact of law enforcement on syringe exchange programs: a look at Oakland and San Francisco', *Medical Anthropology* 18: 61–83.

Bollini, P. (ed.) 2001. *HIV in Prisons: A Reader with Particular Relevance to the Newly Independent States*. Berne: World Health Organization (Regional Office for Europe).

Bordua, D. and Reiss, A., Jr. 1967. 'Law enforcement', in P. Lazarsfeld, W. Sewell and H. Wilensky, H. (eds.), *The Uses of Sociology*. New York: Basic Books, pp. 275–303.

Bott, E. 1971. *Family and Social Network*. New York: The Free Press.

Bouffard, J. and Taxman, F. 2004. 'Looking inside the "black box" of drug court treatment services using direct observations', *Journal of Drug Issues* 34: 195–218.

Bourdieu, P. 1986. 'The forms of capital', in J. Richardson (ed.), *Handbook of Theory and Research for the Sociology of Education*. New York: Greenwood Press, pp. 241–58.

Bowden, M. 2000. *Black Hawk Down*. New York: Penguin.

Brady, B. 2004. 'Hundreds of army officers resign to cash in on Iraqi security boom', *Scotland on Sunday*, 25 April.

Braithwaite, J. 1989. *Crime, Shame and Reintegration*. Cambridge: Cambridge University Press.

2000. 'The new regulatory state and the transformation of criminology', *British Journal of Criminology* 40: 222–38.

2002a. *Restorative Justice and Responsive Regulation*. Oxford: Oxford University Press.

2002b. 'Rewards and regulation', *Journal of Law and Society* 29: 12–26.

2003a. 'Meta risk management and responsive regulation for tax system integrity', *Law and Policy* 25: 1–16.

2003b. 'What's wrong with the sociology of punishment?', *Theoretical Criminology* 7: 5–28.

Braithwaite, J. and Drahos, P. 2000. *Global Business Regulation*. Cambridge: Cambridge University Press.

Braithwaite, J. and Mugford, S. 1994. 'Conditions of successful reintegration ceremonies', *British Journal of Criminology* 34: 139–71.

Braithwaite, J. and Pettit, P. 1990. *Not Just Deserts: A Republican Theory of Criminal Justice*. Oxford: Clarendon Press.

Bray, S., Lawson, J. and Heimer, R. 2001. 'Doffing the cap: increasing syringe availability by law but not in practice', *International Journal of Drug Policy* 12: 221–35.

Brearly, N. and King, M. 1996. *Public Order Policing: Contemporary Perspectives on Strategies and Tactics*. Leicester: Perpetuity Press.

Brewer, J., Lockhart, B. and Rodgers, P. 1998. 'Informal social control and crime management in Belfast', *British Journal of Sociology* 49: 570–85.

Brewer, T., Vlahov, D., Taylor, E., Hall, D., Munoz, A. and Polk, B. 1988. 'Transmission of HIV-1 within a statewide prison system', *AIDS* 2: 363–7.

Broadhead, R. 1999. 'The impact of a needle exchange's closure', *Public Health Reports* 114: 439–47.

Broadhead, R., Borch, C., Hulst, Y., Farrell, J., Villemez, W. and Altice, F. 2003. 'Safer injection sites in New York City: a utilization survey of injection drug users', *Journal of Drug Issues* 22: 733–50.

Brodeur, J. 1983. 'High policing and low policing', *Social Problems* 30: 507–20.

2003. *Les Visages de la Police*. Montreal: University of Montreal Press.

Brogden, M. 1982. *The Police: Autonomy and Consent.* London: Academic Press.

Brogden, M. and Shearing, C. 1993. *Policing for a New South Africa.* London: Routledge.

Brooks, D. 2004. 'Basic report analyzes contractors in Iraq', *IPOA Quarterly* Issue 1:4.

Brown, J. and Heidensohn, F. 2000. *Gender and Policing.* Basingstoke: Palgrave.

BSIA 2005. 'Interesting facts and figures in the UK security industry'. http://www.bsia.co.uk/industry.html (accessed 23 February 2005).

Buavirat, A., Page-Shafer, K., Griensven, G., Mandel, J., Evans, J., Chuaratanaphong, J., Chiamwongpat, S., Sacks, R. and Moss, A. 2003. 'Risk of prevalent HIV infection associated with incarceration among injecting drug users in Bangkok, Thailand: case-control study', *British Medical Journal* 326: 308.

Buchanan, J. 1965. 'An economic theory of clubs', *Economica* 32: 1–14.

1978. 'From private preferences to public philosophy: the development of public choice', in J. Buchanan (ed.), *The Economics of Politics.* London: Institute of Economic Affairs, pp. 1–20.

Bull, M. 2003. *Just Treatment: A Review of International Programs for the Diversion of Drug Related Offenders from the Criminal Justice System.* Brisbane, Qld: Department of the Premier and Cabinet.

Bunt, P., Boulting, A. and Price, S. 1997. *Selling Police Services.* Police Research Award Scheme 118. London: Home Office.

Bureau of Justice Statistics 1997. *Police Use of Force: Collection of National Data* (NCJ 165040). Washington, D.C.: Department of Justice.

2001. *Policing and Homicide 1976–1998: Justifiable Homicide of Felons by Police and Murder of Police by Felons* (NCJ 180987). Washington, D.C.: Department of Justice.

2004. 'Criminal victimization in the United States – statistical tables.' http://www.ojp.usdoj.gov/bjs/abstract/cvusst.htm (accessed 24 June 2004).

Burns, T. and Stalker, G. 1965. *The Management of Innovation.* London: Tavistock.

Burris, S. 1992. 'Prisons, law and public health: the case for a coordinated response to epidemic disease behind bars', *University of Miami Law Review* 47: 291–335.

2002. 'Disease stigma in US public health law', *Journal of Law, Medicine and Ethics* 30: 179–90.

2004. 'Governance, microgovernance and health', *Temple Law Review* 77: 335–62.

Burris, S., Drahos, P. and Shearing, C. 2005. 'Nodal governance', *Australian Journal of Legal Philosophy* 30: 30–58.

Burris, S., Strathdee, S. and Vernick, J. 2003. 'Lethal injections: the law, science and politics of syringe access for injection drug users', *University of San Francisco Law Review* 37: 813–83.

Burris, S., Blankenship, K., Donoghoe, M., Sherman, S., Vernick, J., Case, P., Lazzarini, Z. and Koester, S. 2004. 'Addressing the "risk environment" for injection drug users: the mysterious case of the missing cop', *Milbank Quarterly* 82: 125–56.

Burt, R. 1997. 'The contingent value of social capital', *Administrative Science Quarterly* 42: 339–65.

Button, M. 2002. *Private Policing.* Cullompton, Devon: Willan.

Buzan, B. 1991. *People, States and Fear*, 2nd edn. Brighton: Harvester.

Buzan, B., Wæver, O. and de Wilde, J. 1998. *Security: A New Framework for Analysis.* London: Lynne Reiner.

Cain, M. 2000. 'Orientalism, occidentalism and the sociology of crime', *British Journal of Criminology* 40: 239–60.

Caldeira, T. 2000. *City of Walls: Crime, Segregation, and Citizenship in São Paulo.* Berkeley: University of California Press.

Calzavara, L., Burchell, A., Schlossberg, J., Myers, T., Escobar, M., Wallace, E., Major, C., Strike, C. and Millson, M. 2003. 'Prior opiate injection and incarceration history predict injection drug use among inmates', *Addiction* 98: 1257–65.

Canadian International Development Agency (CIDA) 2001. *Canada–Southern Cone Technology Transfer Fund, Phase II: Information Guide.* Gatineau, Que.: Canadian International Development Agency.

Canovan, M. 1996. *Nationhood and Political Theory.* London: Edward Elgar.

Carruthers, N. and Espeland, W. 1991. 'Accounting for rationality', *American Journal of Sociology* 97: 31–69.

Carson, W. G. 2003. 'Communalism in crime prevention for Victoria', Crime Prevention Victoria, Melbourne. http://www.crimeprevention.vic.gov.au/ (accessed 7 February 2005).

2004. 'Is communalism dead? Reflections on the present and future practices of crime prevention', *Australian and New Zealand Journal of Criminology* 37: 192–211.

Castells, M. 1997. *The Information Age: Economy, Society and Culture*, vol. I: *The Rise of the Network Society.* Oxford: Basil Blackwell.

2000. *The Information Age: Economy, Society and Culture*, vol. III: *End of Millennium.* Oxford: Basil Blackwell.

Centers for Disease Control and Prevention 2003. 'Rapid assessment of tuberculosis in a large prison system – Botswana, 2002', *Morbidity and Mortality Weekly Report* 52: 250–2.

Chan, J. 1996. 'Changing police culture', *British Journal of Criminology* 36: 109–33.

1997. *Changing Police Culture: Policing a Multicultural Society.* Melbourne: Cambridge University Press.

1999a. 'Governing police practice: the limits of the new accountability', *British Journal of Sociology* 50: 251–70.

Chan, J. 1999b. 'Police culture', in D. Dixon (ed.), *A Culture of Corruption: Changing an Australian Police Force.* Sydney: Hawkins Press, pp. 98–137.

2001. 'The technological game: how information technology is transforming police practice', *Criminal Justice* 1: 139–59.

Chan, J., Devery, C. and Doran, S. 2003. *Fair Cop: Learning the Art of Policing.* Toronto: University of Toronto Press.

Chandola, T. 2001. 'The fear of crime and area differences in health', *Health and Place* 7: 105–16.

Cherney, A. 2005. 'Contingency and resistance: studying developments in the governance of security'. Unpublished paper, School of Social Science, University of Queensland.

Choopanya, K., Des Jarlais, D., Vanichseni, S., Kitayaporn, D., Mock, P., Raktham, S., Hireanras, K., Heyward, W., Sujarita, S. and Mastro, T. 2002. 'Incarceration and risk for HIV infection among injection drug users in Bangkok', *Journal of Acquired Immune Deficiency Syndromes* 29: 86–94.

Clarke, L. 1989. *Acceptable Risk. Making Decisions in a Toxic Environment*. Berkeley: University of California Press.

Clarke, M. and Stewart, J. 1997. *Handling the Wicked Issues: A Challenge for Government*. Birmingham: Institute of Local Government Studies, University of Birmingham.

Coffin, P. 2002. 'Marketing harm reduction: a historical narrative of the international harm reduction development program', *International Journal of Drug Policy* 13: 209–20.

Cohen, J. and Sabel, C. 1997. 'Directly-deliberative polyarchy', *European Law Journal* 3: 313–42.

Cohen, M., Deamant, C., Barkan, S., Richardson, J., Young, M., Holman, S., Anastos, K., Cohen, J. and Melnick, S. 2000. 'Domestic violence and childhood sexual abuse in HIV-infected women and women at risk for HIV', *American Journal of Public Health* 90: 560–5.

Cohen, P. 1979. 'Policing the working class city', in B. Fine, R. Kinsey, J. Lea, S. Picciotto and J. Young (eds.), *Capitalism and the Rule of Law*. London: Hutchinson, pp. 118–36.

Cohen, S. 1982. 'Western Crime Control Models in the Third World: Benign or Malignant?', *Research in Law, Deviance and Social Control* 4: 85–119.

1985. *Visions of Social Control*. Cambridge: Polity Press.

2001. *States of Denial: Knowing About Atrocities and Suffering*. Cambridge: Polity Press.

Coker, A., Smith, P., Mckeown, R. and King, M. 2000. 'Frequency and correlates of intimate partner violence by type: physical, sexual, and psychological battering', *American Journal of Public Health* 90: 553–9.

Coleman, J. 1988. 'Social capital in the creation of human capital', *American Journal of Sociology* 92: S95–S120.

Commission on Human Security 2003. *Final Report*. http://www.humansecurity-chs.org/finalreport/ (accessed 1 March 2005).

Community Peace Programme 2004. *Community Peace Programme Quarterly Report*. Cape Town: Community Peace Programme.

Connell, J. 1999. 'Beyond Manila: walls, malls, and private spaces', *Environment and Planning* 31: 417–39.

Considine, M. 2002. 'The end of the line? Accountable governance in the age of networks, partnerships, and joined-up services', *Governance* 15: 21–40.

Cooper, H., Moore, L., Gruskin, S. and Krieger, N. 2004. 'Characterizing perceived police violence: implications for public health', *American Journal of Public Health* 94: 1109–18.

Corpwatch 2004. *Iraq's Private Warriors*. http://www.corpwatch.org/article.php?id=11551 (accessed 20 November 2004).

Cowell, D., Jones, T. and Young, J. (eds.) 1982. *Policing the Riots*. London: Junction Books.

Cowper, J. 2004. 'The Myth of the "military model" of leadership in law enforcement', in Q. Thurman and Z. Jihong (eds.), *Contemporary Policing: Controversies, Challenges and Solutions*. Los Angeles: Roxbury Publishing Company, pp. 113–25.

Cox, J., Bota, G. W., Carter, M., Bretzlaff-Michaud, J. A., Sahai, V. and Rowe, B. H. 2004. 'Domestic violence: incidence and prevalence in a northern emergency department', *Canadian Family Physician* 50: 90–7.

Crawford, A. 1997. *The Local Governance of Crime: Appeals to Community and Partnerships*. Oxford: Clarendon Press.

2001. 'Joined-up but fragmented: contradiction, ambiguity and ambivalence at the heart of New Labour's Third Way', in R. Matthews and J. Pitts (eds.), *Crime, Disorder and Community Safety*. London: Routledge, pp. 54–80.

Crawford, A. 2003a. 'The pattern of policing in the UK: policing beyond the police', in T. Newburn (ed.), *Handbook of Policing*. Cullompton, Devon: Willan, pp. 136–68.

2003b. 'Contractual governance of deviant behaviour', *Journal of Law and Society* 30: 479–505.

Crawford, A. in press. 'Reassurance policing: feeling is believing', in D. Smith (ed.), *Police and People*. Aldershot: Ashgate.

Crawford, A. and Lister, S. 2004. *The Extended Policing Family: Visible Patrols in Residential Areas*. York: Joseph Rowntree Foundation.

Crawford, A., Lister, S. and Wall, D. 2003. *Great Expectations: Contracted Community Policing in New Earswick*. York: Joseph Rowntree Foundation.

Crawford, A., Blackburn, S., Lister, S. and Shepherd, P. 2004. *Patrolling with a Purpose: An Evaluation of Police Community Support Officers in Leeds and Bradford City Centres*. Leeds: CCJS Press.

Crawford, A., Lister, S., Blackburn, S. and Burnett, J. 2005. *Plural Policing: The Mixed Economy of Visible Security Patrols*. Bristol: Policy Press.

Critcher, C. and Waddington, D. (eds.) 1996. *Policing Public Order: Theoretical and Practical Issues*. Brookfield, Vt: Avebury Publications.

Crozier, M. 1964. *The Bureaucratic Phenomenon*. Chicago: University of Chicago Press.

1972. 'The relationship between micro and macrosociology', *Human Relations* 25: 239–251.

Crozier, M. and Friedberg, E. 1980. *Actors and Systems: The Politics of Collective Action*. Chicago: University of Chicago Press.

Cunningham, W., Strauchs, J. and Van Meter, C. 1990. *Private Security Trends 1970 to 2000: The Hallcrest Report II*. Boston: Butterworth–Heinemann.

Cuthbert, A. 1995. 'The right to the city: surveillance, private interest, and the public domain in Hong Kong', *Cities* 12: 293–310.

Dalby, S. 1997. 'Contesting an essential concept: reading the dilemmas in contemporary security discourse', in K. Krause and M. Williams (eds.), *Critical Security Studies*. London: University College London Press, pp. 3–31.

Daniel, J., Habib, A. and Southall, R. 2003. *State of the Nation: South Africa 2003–2004*. Pretoria: Human Science Research Council Press.

Davids, C. and Hancock, L. 1998. 'Policing, accountability and citizenship in the market state', *Australian and New Zealand Journal of Criminology* 31: 38–68.

Davis, C., Burris, S., Metzger, D., Kraut-Becher, J. and Lynch, K. 2005. 'Effects of an intensive street-level police intervention on syringe exchange program utilization: Philadelphia, Pennsylvania', *American Journal of Public Health* 95: 233.

Davis, R., Oritz, C., Dudush, S., Irish, J., Alvarado, A. and Davis, D. 2003. 'The public accountability of private police: lessons from New York, Johannesburg and Mexico City', *Policing and Society* 13: 197–210.

De Waard, J. 1996. 'The private security industry in the Netherlands: developments and future perspectives', *Security Journal* 7: 227–34.

Decker, S., Greene, J., McDevitt, J., Webb, V., Bynum, T., Manning, P., Rojek, J., Varano, S. and Terrill, W. 2002. 'Safety and security at the Olympic Games at Salt Lake City Utah.' Unpublished paper, Office of Emergency Preparedness, Department of Justice, Washington, D.C.

Deen, T. 2004. 'UN rejects private peacekeepers', *Inter Press News*, 27th August. http://www.globalpolicy.org/security/peacekpg/training/0827rejects.htm (accessed 28 August 2004).

della Porta, D. and Reiter, H. (eds.) 1998. *Policing Protest: The Control of Mass Demonstrations in Western Democracies*. Minneapolis: University of Minnesota Press.

Demyttenaere, K., Bruffaerts, R., Posada-Villa, J., Gasquet, I., Kovess, V., Lepine, J., Angermeyer, M., Bernert, S., De Girolamo, G., Morosini, P., Polidori, G., Kikkawa, T., Kawakami, N., Ono, Y., Takeshima, T., Uda, H., Karam, E., Fayyad, J., Karam, A., Mneimneh, Z., Medina-Mora, M., Borges, G., Lara, C., De Graaf, R., Ormel, J., Gureje, O., Shen, Y., Huang, Y., Zhang, M., Alonso, J., Haro, J., Vilagut, G., Bromet, E., Gluzman, S., Webb, C., Kessler, R., Merikangas, K., Anthony, J., Von Korff, M., Wang, P., Brugha, T., Aguilar-Gaxiola, S., Lee, S., Heeringa, S., Pennell, B., Zaslavsky, A., Ustun, T. and Chatterji, S. 2004. 'Prevalence, severity, and unmet need for treatment of mental disorders in the World Health Organization world mental health surveys', *Journal of the American Medical Association* 291: 2581–90.

Dillon, M. 1996. *Politics of Security: Towards a Political Philosophy of Continental Thought*. London: Routledge.

DiMaggio, P. and Powell, W. 1983. 'The iron cage revisited: institutional isomorphism and collective rationality in organizational fields', *American Sociological Review* 48: 147–60.

Dixon, B. 2004a. 'Cosmetic crime prevention', in B. Dixon and E. van der Spuy (eds.), *Justice Gained: Crime and Crime Control in South Africa's Transition*. Cape Town: University of Cape Town Press, pp. 163–92.

Dixon, B. 2004b. 'In search of interactive globalization: critical criminology in South Africa's transition', *Crime, Law and Social Change* 41: 359–84.

Dixon, D. 1997. *Law in Policing: Legal Regulation and Police Practices*. Oxford: Clarendon Press.

Dixon, D. (ed.) 1999. *A Culture of Corruption: Changing an Australian Police Service*. Leichhardt, NSW: Hawkins Press.

258   References

Dolan, K., Rutter, S. and Wodak, A. D. 2003. 'Prison-based syringe exchange programmes: a review of international research and development', *Addiction* 98: 153–8.

Dolowitz, D. and Marsh, D. 1996. 'Who learns what from whom? A review of the policy transfer literature', *Political Studies* 44: 343–57.

2000. 'Learning from abroad: the role of policy transfer in contemporary policy-making', *Governance: An International Journal of Policy and Administration* 13: 5–24.

Douglas, M. 1986. *How Institutions Think*. Syracuse: Syracuse University Press.

Drahos, P. 2002. 'Negotiating intellectual property rights: between coercion and dialogue', in P. Drahos and R. Mayne (eds.), *Global Intellectual Property Rights: Knowledge Access and Development*. New York: Palgrave Macmillan, pp. 161–81.

2004. 'Intellectual property and pharmaceutical markets: a nodal governance approach', *Temple Law Review* 77: 401–24.

Drahos, P. and Braithwaite, J. 2002. *Intellectual Feudalism*. London: Earth Scan.

Drucker, E., Lurie, P., Wodak, A. and Alcabes, P. 1998. 'Measuring harm reduction: the effects of needle and syringe exchange programs and methadone maintenance on the ecology of HIV', *AIDS* 12 (Suppl. A): S217–S230.

Drucker, P. 1995. *Managing in a Time of Great Change*. New York: Truman Talley Books/Plume.

Drug Enforcement Administration (DEA) 2002. *Senate Testimony 2002 on the 2003 Budget*. http://www.usdoj.gov/dea/ (accessed 18 February 2005).

2004. *Drug trafficking in the United States*. http://www.dea.gov/concern/drug_trafficking.html (accessed 5 October 2004).

Dunn, J. 2000. *The Cunning of Unreason: Making Sense of Politics*. London: Harper Collins.

Dunworth, T. 2000. 'Criminal justice and the information technology revolution', in J. Horney (ed.), *Criminal Justice*, vol. III. Washington D.C.: NIJ/Office of Justice Programs, pp. 371–426.

Dupont, B. 2003a. *Preserving Institutional Memory in Australian Police Services*, Trends and Issues in Crime and Criminal Justice No. 245. Canberra: Australian Institute of Criminology.

2003b. 'Public entrepreneurs in the field of security: an oral history of Australian police commissioners'. Paper presented at *In Search of Security: An International Conference on Policing and Security*, Montreal, 19–22 February.

2004. 'Security in the age of networks', *Policing and Society* 14: 76–91.

Dupont, B., Grabosky, P. and Shearing, C. 2003. 'The governance of security in weak and failing states', *Criminal Justice* 3: 331–49.

Dyer, O. 2003. 'Suicide among women prisoners at a record high, report says', *British Medical Journal* 327: 122.

Ebert, S. 2005. 'Boston panel reports surplus', *Boston Globe*, 8 January.

Eggers, W. and O'Leary, J. 1995. *Revolution at the Roots: Making our Government Smaller, Better and Closer to Home*. New York: The Free Press.

Ehrmann, T. 2002. 'Community-based organizations and HIV prevention for incarcerated populations: three HIV prevention program models', *AIDS Education and Prevention* 14: 75–84.

Einstein, S. and Amir, M. (eds.) 1999. *Policing, Security and Democracy: Special Aspects of Democratic Policing.* Huntsville, Tex.: Office of International Criminal Justice.

Elkins, D. 1995. *Beyond Sovereignty: Territory and Political Economy in the Twenty-first Century.* Toronto: University of Toronto Press.

Ellen, I., Mijanovich, T. and Dillman, K.-N. 2001. 'Neighborhood effects on health: exploring the links and assessing the evidence', *Journal of Urban Affairs* 23: 391–409.

Elliot, N. 1989. *Streets Ahead.* London: Adam Smith Institute.

Ellison, G. and Smyth, J. 2000. *The Crowned Harp.* London: Pluto Press.

Emsley, C. 2000. *Gendarmes and the State in Nineteenth Century Europe.* Oxford: Oxford University Press.

Ericson, R. 1994. 'The division of expert knowledge in policing and security', *British Journal of Sociology* 45: 149–75.

Ericson, R. and Haggerty, K. 1997. *Policing the Risk Society.* Oxford: Oxford University Press.

Ericson, R., Baranek, P. and Chan, J. 1991. *Representing Order: Crime, Law and Justice in the News Media.* Toronto: University of Toronto Press.

Espeland, W. 1998. *The Struggle for Water: Politics, Rationality and Identity in the American Southwest.* Chicago: University of Chicago Press.

Estebanez, P., Colomo, C., Zunzunegui, M., Rua-Figueroa, M., Perez, C., Ortiz, C., Heras, P. and Babin, F. 1990, 'Carceles y sida. Factores de riesgo de infeccion por el vih en las carceles de Madrid.' *Gaceta Sanitaria* 4: 100–5.

Evans, E. and Longshore, D. 2004. 'Evaluation of the Substance Abuse and Crime Prevention Act: treatment clients and program types during the first year of implementation', *Journal of Psychoactive Drugs* 36: 165–75.

Fagan, J. 1996. *The Criminalization of Domestic Violence: Promises and Limits.* Washington, D.C.: US Department of Justice, Office of Justice Programs, National Institute of Justice.

Favarel-Garrigues, G. and Le Huérou, A. 2004. 'State and the multilateralization of policing in post-Soviet Russia', *Policing and Society* 14: 13–30.

Federal Bureau of Investigation 2003a. *Crime in the United States.* Washington, D.C.: Federal Bureau of Investigation.

2003b. *Law Enforcement Officers Killed or Assaulted.* Washington, D.C.: Federal Bureau of Investigation.

Feeley, M. and Simon, J. 1992. 'The new penology: notes on the emerging strategy of corrections and its implications', *Criminology* 30: 449–74.

Feldman, M. and March, J. 1981. 'Information as signal and symbol', *Administrative Science Quarterly* 26: 171–86.

Ferret, J. 2004. 'The state, policing and "Old Continental Europe": managing the local/national tension', *Policing and Society* 14: 49–65.

Fielding, N. 1988. *Joining Forces: Police Training, Socialisation and Occupational Competence.* London: Routledge.

Finnane, M. 1999. 'Police unions in Australia: a history of the present'. Paper presented at the *History of Crime, Policing and Punishment Conference*, Canberra, 9–10 December.

2002. *When Police Unionise: The Politics of Law and Order in Australia.* Sydney: Institute of Criminology.

Fiscella, K., Pless, N., Meldrum, S. and Fiscella, P. 2004. 'Alcohol and opiate withdrawal in US jails', *American Journal of Public Health* 94: 1522–4.

Fischer, B., Rehm, J., Kirst, M., Casas, M., Hall, W., Krausz, M., Metrebian, N., Reggers, J., Uchtenhagen, A., Van Den Brink, W. and Van Ree, J. M. 2002. 'Heroin-assisted treatment as a response to the public health problem of opiate dependence', *European Journal of Public Health* 12: 228–34.

Fischer, D. 1994. *Paul Revere's Ride*. New York: Oxford University Press.

Fisk, R. and Carroll, S. 2004. 'Occupiers spend millions on private army of security men', *Independent*, 29 March.

Fitzgerald, T. 1989. *Report of Commission of Inquiry into Possible Illegal Activities and Associated Police Misconduct*. Brisbane: Government Printer.

Fleming, J. and Marks, M. 2004. 'The "conservative voice of reason"? Australian police unions in the 21st century', in P. Hyland and G. Stewart (eds.), *Regionalism and Globalisation: The Challenge for Employment Relations. Proceedings of the 12th Annual IERA Conference*. Rockhampton: Central Queensland University, pp. 130–7.

Fleming, J., Marks, M. and Wood, J. in press. 'Standing on the inside looking out: the significance of police unions in networks of security governance', *Australian and New Zealand Journal of Criminology*.

Foldvary, F. 1994. *Public Goods and Private Communities*. Aldershot: Edward Elgar.

Forst, B. 1999. 'Policing with legitimacy, equity and efficiency', in B. Forst and P. Manning (eds.), *The Privatisation of Policing: Two Views*. Washington, D.C.: Georgetown University Press, pp. 3–48.

Foucault, M. 1982. 'The subject and power', in H. L. Dreyfus and P. Rabinow (eds.), *Michel Foucault: Beyond Structuralism and Hermeneutics*. Chicago: University of Chicago Press, pp. 208–26.

1988. 'On problematization', *History of the Present*, Spring: 16–17.

1990 (1976). *The History of Sexuality*, vol. I: *An Introduction*. New York: Vintage Books.

1991. 'Governmentality', in G. Burchell, C. Gordon and P. Miller (eds.), *The Foucault Effect: Studies in Governmentality*. Chicago: University of Chicago Press, pp. 87–104.

Freeman, K. 2003. 'Health and well-being outcomes for drug-dependent offenders on the NSW drug court programme', *Drug and Alcohol Review* 22: 409–16.

French, M. 2004. 'Net-centric war needs security', *Federal Computer Week*, 11 March. http://www.fcw.com/fcw/articles/2004/0308/web-darpa-03-11-04. asp (accessed 20 November 2004).

Freudenberg, N. 2001. 'Jails, prisons, and the health of urban populations: a review of the impact of the correctional system on community health', *Journal of Urban Health* 78: 214–35.

Friedman, M. 1962. *Capitalism and Freedom*. Chicago: University of Chicago Press.

Friedman, S. R. and Aral, S. 2001. 'Social networks, risk-potential networks, health, and disease', *Journal of Urban Health* 78: 411–18.

Friedmann, P., Lemon, S., Stein, M. and D'Aunno, T. A. 2003, 'Accessibility of addiction treatment: results from a national survey of outpatient substance abuse treatment organizations', *Health Services Research* 38: 887–903.

Fu, H. 1993. 'The security service company in China', *Journal of Security Administration* 16: 35–44.

Fukuyama, F. 1999. *Social capital and civil society*. Washington, D.C.: International Monetary Fund.

2004. *State Building: Governance and World Order in the 21st Century*. New York: Cornell University Press.

Garland, D. 1996. 'The limits of the sovereign state: strategies of crime control in contemporary society', *British Journal of Criminology* 36: 445–71.

Garland, D. 1997. ' "Governmentality" and the problem of crime: Foucault, criminology, sociology', *Theoretical Criminology* 1: 173–214.

2001. *The Culture of Control*. Oxford: Oxford University Press.

Garner, J., Maxwell, C. and Heraux, C. 2002. 'Characteristics associated with the prevalence and severity of force used by the police', *Justice Quarterly* 19: 705–47.

General Purpose Standing Committee 2000. *Report on Inquiry into Contract of Employment of Commissioner of Police*. Sydney: Legislative Council.

Geronimus, A. T. 2000. 'To mitigate, resist, or undo: addressing structural influences on the health of urban populations', *American Journal of Public Health* 90: 867–72.

Gerstenberg, O. and Sabel, C. 2002. 'Directly deliberative polyarchy: an ideal for Europe', in C. Joerges and R. Dehousse (eds.), *Good Governance in Europe's Integrated Market*. Oxford: Oxford University Press, pp. 289–392.

Gibson, C., Zhao, J., Lovrich, N. and Gaffney, M. 2002. 'Social integration, individual perceptions of collective efficacy, and fear of crime in three cities', *Justice Quarterly* 19: 537–65.

Giddens, A. 1984. *The Consititution of Society*. Cambridge: Polity Press.

1998. *The Third Way*. Cambridge: Polity Press.

Gill, P. 1994. *Policing Politics: Security, Intelligence and the Liberal Democratic State*. London: Frank Cass.

Girling, E., Loader, I. and Sparks, R. 2000. *Crime and Social Change in Middle England: Questions of Order in an English Town*. London: Routledge.

Glaser, B. and Strauss, A. 1967. *The Discovery of Grounded Theory: Strategies for Qualitative Research*. Chicago: Aldine.

Godfrey, C., Stewart, D. and Gossop, M. 2004. 'Economic analysis of costs and consequences of the treatment of drug misuse: 2-year outcome data from the national treatment outcome research study (NTOS)', *Addiction* 99: 697–708.

Goffman, E. 1963. *Stigma: Notes on the Management of Spoiled Identity*. Englewood Cliffs, N.J.: Prentice-Hall.

Goldberg, D. 2001. *The Racial State*. Oxford: Basil Blackwell.

Goldsmith, A. 1990. 'Taking police culture seriously', *Policing and Society* 1: 91–114.

2001. 'The pursuit of police integrity: leadership and governance dimensions', *Current Issues in Criminal Justice* 13: 185–202.

2003. 'Policing weak states: citizen safety and state responsibility', *Policing and Society* 13: 3–21.

Goldsmith, A. and Lewis, C. (eds.) 2000. *Civilian Oversight of Policing: Governance, Democracy and Human Rights*. Oxford: Hart Publishing.

Goldstein, H. 1990. *Problem Oriented Policing*. New York: McGraw-Hill.

Goldstone, R. 1990. Report of the Commission on Inquiry into Incidents at Sebokeng, Boipathong, Lekoa, Sharpeville, and Evaton. Johannesburg: Commission of Inquiry regarding the prevention of Public Violence and Intimidation.

Gordon, C. 1991. 'Governmental rationality: an introduction', in G. Burchell, C. Gordon and P. Miller (eds.), *The Foucault Effect*. Chicago: University of Chicago Press, pp. 1–51.

Gordon, P. 1984. 'Community policing: towards the local police state', *Critical Social Policy* 10 (Summer): 39–58.

Grabosky, P. 1994. 'Beyond the regulatory state', *Australian and New Zealand Journal of Criminology* 27: 192–7.

1995a. 'Regulation by reward: on the use of incentives as regulatory instruments', *Law and Policy* 17: 257–82.

1995b. 'Using non-governmental resources to foster regulatory compliance', *Governance* 8: 527–50.

1996. *The Future of Crime Control*, Trends and Issues in Crime and Criminal Justice No. 63. Canberra: Australian Institute of Criminology.

2000. 'Managing violence and health: strategies, solutions, research and methodological issues', in WHO Center for Health Development (eds.), *Violence and Health: Proceedings of a WHO Global Symposium*. Kobe: WHO Center, pp. 415–28.

2001. 'Crime control in the 21st century', *Australian and New Zealand Journal of Criminology* 34: 221–34.

2002. 'Private sponsorship of public policing'. Unpublished manuscript, Australian National University, Canberra.

Grande, E., Hickling, J., Taylor, A. and Woollacott, T. 2003. 'Domestic violence in South Australia: a population survey of males and females', *Australian and New Zealand Journal of Public Health* 27: 543–50.

Gray, K. and Gray, S. 1999. 'Private property and public propriety', in J. McLean (ed.), *Property and the Constitution*. Oxford: Hart Publishing, pp. 11–39.

Greifinger, R., Keehfus, C., Grabau, J., Quinlan, A., Loeder, A., DiFerdinando, G. Jr. and Morse, D. 1992. 'Transmission of multidrug-resistant tuberculosis among immunocompromised persons, correctional system – New York, 1991', *Journal of the American Medical Association* 268: 855–6.

Grimshaw, R. and Jefferson, T. 1987. *Interpreting Policework*. London: Allen and Unwin.

Grisso, J., Schwarz, D., Hirschinger, N., Sammel, M., Brensinger, C., Santanna, J., Lowe, R., Anderson, E., Shaw, L., Bethel, C. and Teeple, L. 1999. 'Violent injuries among women in an urban area', *New England Journal of Medicine* 341: 1899–905.

Gunningham, N., Kagan, R. and Thornton, D. 2003. *Shades of Green: Business, Regulation and Environment*. Stanford: Stanford University Press.

2004. 'Social license and environmental protection: why businesses go beyond compliance', *Law and Social Inquiry* 29: 307–41.

Gurr, T. with Graham, H. 1969. *Violence in America: Historical and Comparative Perspectives*. New York: Bantam Books.

Gyarmathy, V., Neaigus, A. and Szamado, S. 2003. 'HIV risk behavior history of prison inmates in Hungary', *AIDS Education and Prevention* 15: 561–9.

Habermas, J. 2001. 'Constitutional democracy: a paradoxical union of contradictory principles?', *Political Theory* 29: 770–81.

Habib, A. 2003. 'State–civil society relations in post-apartheid South Africa', in J. Daniel, A. Habib and R. Southall (eds.), *State of the Nation: South Africa 2003–2004*. Pretoria: Human Science Research Council Press, pp. 227–41.

Habib, A. and Padayachee, V. 2000. 'Economic policy and power relations in South Africa's transition to democracy', *World Development* 28: 245–63.

Hale, C. 1996. 'Fear of crime: a review of the literature', *International Review of Victimology* 4: 79–150.

Hall, S., Critcher, C., Jefferson, T., Clarke, J. and Roberts, B. 1978. *Policing the Crisis: Mugging, the State and Law and Order*. London: Macmillan.

Hammett, T., Harmon, M. and Rhodes, W. 2002. 'The burden of infectious disease among inmates of and releasees from US correctional facilities, 1997', *American Journal of Public Health* 92: 1789–94.

Hardin, G. 1968. 'The tragedy of the commons', *Science* 162: 1243–8.

Hartung, W. 2004. 'Private military contractors in Iraq and beyond: a question of balance'. Prepared statement for the briefing on 'An incomplete transition: an assessment of the June 30th transition and its aftermath', American News Women's Club, Washington, D.C., 22 June. http://www.worldpolicy.org/projects/arms/updates/FPIFJune2004.html (accessed 21 November 2004).

Hassink, R. 1996. 'Technology transfer agencies and regional economic development', *European Planning Studies* 4: 167–85.

Hawkins, K. 2003. *Law as Last Resort*. Oxford: Oxford University Press.

Hayek, F. 1944. *The Road to Serfdom*. London: Routledge.

  1960. *The Constitution of Liberty*. London: Routledge.

  1979. *Law, Legislation and Liberty*, vol. III: *The Political Order of a Free People*. London: Routledge.

Heimer, C. 1985. 'Risk', *Annual Reviews of Sociology* (vol. XX). Palo Alto, Calif.: Annual Reviews Press.

  1987. *Reactive risk*. Chicago: University of Chicago Press.

Hein, W. 2003. 'Global health governance and national health policies in developing countries: conflicts and cooperation at the interfaces', in W. Hein and L. Kohlmorgan (eds.), *Globalization, Global Health Governance and National Health Policies in Developing Countries: An Exploration into the Dynamics of Interfaces*. Hamburg: Deutschen Übersee-Instituts, pp. 33–71.

Held, D. 2003. 'Cosmopolitanism: globalisation tamed?', *Review of International Studies* 29: 465–80.

Helweg-Larsen, K. and Kruse, M. 2003. 'Violence against women and consequent health problems: a register-based study', *Scandinavian Journal of Public Health* 31: 51–7.

Her Majesty's Inspector of Constabulary 1996. *What Price Policing?* London: Home Office.

Herbert, S. 1997. *Policing Space: Territoriality and the Los Angeles Police Department*. Minneapolis: University of Minneapolis Press.

Hersh, S. 2004. *Chain of Command*. New York: Harper Collins.

Heymann, P. 1992. *Towards Peaceful Protest in South Africa*. Pretoria: Human Science Research Council.

Hillyard, P. 1993. 'Paramilitary policing and popular justice in Northern Ireland', in M. Findlay and U. Zvekic (eds.), *Alternative Policing Styles: Cross Cultural Perspectives*. Boston: Kluwer Law and Taxation Publishers, pp. 131–8.

Hindess, B. 1988. *Choice, Rationality and Social Theory*. London: Unwin Hyman.

Hirschman, A. 1970. *Exit, Voice and Loyalty: Responses to Decline in Firms, Organizations and States*. Cambridge, Mass.: Harvard University Press.

Hirst, P. 2000. 'Statism, pluralism and social control', in D. Garland and R. Sparks (eds.), *Criminology and Social Theory*. Oxford: Oxford University Press, pp. 127–48.

Hobbes, T. 1985 (1651). *Leviathan*. London: Penguin Books.

Hobbs, D., Hadfield, P., Lister, S. and Winlow, S. 2003. *Bouncers: Violence and Governance in the Night-time Economy*. Oxford: Oxford University Press.

Hoffman, J., Su, S. and Pach, A. 1997. 'Changes in network characteristics and HIV risk behaviors among injection drug users', *Alcohol and Drug Dependence* 46: 41–51.

Hogg, R. and Brown, D. 1998. *Rethinking Law and Order*. Annandale, NSW: Pluto Press.

Holmes, S. 1995. *Passions and Constraint: On the Theory of Liberal Democracy*. Chicago: University of Chicago Press.

Home Office 1994. *Partners Against Crime*. London: Home Office.

2001. *Fighting Violent Crime Together: An Action Plan*. London: Home Office.

2004. *Confident Communities in a Secure Britain: The Home Office Strategic Plan 2004–08*, Cm 6287. London: Home Office.

Hope, T. 2000. 'Inequality and the clubbing of private security', in T. Hope, and R. Sparks (eds.), *Crime, risk and insecurity*. London: Routledge, pp. 83–106.

Hope, T. and Karstedt, S. 2003. 'Towards a new social crime prevention', in H. Kury and J. Obergfell-Fuchs (eds.), *Crime Prevention. New Approaches*. Mainz: Weisser Ring, pp. 461–89.

House of Commons 2002. *Private Military Companies*. Foreign Affairs Committee, Ninth Report of Session 2001–2, HC 922.

Huggins, M. 1998. 'Brazilian police violence: legacies of authoritarianism in police professionalism'. Paper presented at the *Legacies of Authoritarianism Conference*, Madison, Wis.

1998. *Political Policing: United States and South America*. Durham: Duke University Press.

Hughes, E. C. 1958. *Men and Their Work*. Glencoe: The Free Press.

Hurst, L. 2004 'The privatization of Abu Ghraib', *Toronto Star*, 16 May.

Hussain, S. 1988. *Neighbourhood Watch in England and Wales: A Locational Analysis*. London: Home Office.

Hyman, R. 1999. 'An emerging agenda for trade unions?' Discussion Paper No. 98, International Labour Organisation, Geneva.

Iguchi, M., London, J., Forge, N., Hickman, L., Fain, T. and Riehman, K. 2002. 'Elements of well-being affected by criminalizing the drug user', *Public Health Reports* 117: S146–S150.

Independent Commission on Policing for Northern Ireland 1999. *A New Beginning: Policing in Northern Ireland. The Report of the Independent Commission on Policing for Northern Ireland.* Norwich: HMSO.

International Council on Human Rights Policy 2003. 'Crime, public order and human rights', International Council on Human Rights Policy, Geneva.

International Harm Reduction Development Program 2003. *Unintended Consequences: Drug Policies Fuel the HIV Epidemic in Russia and Ukraine.* New York: Open Society Institute.

Irish, J. 1999. *Policing for Profit: The Future of South Africa's Private Security Industry.* Institute for Security Studies Monograph Series No. 39. Pretoria: Institute for Security Studies.

Isenberg, D. 2004. 'The case for pragmatic assessment of private military companies in Iraq'. Research Report. British American Security Information Council, September.

Israel, B., Schulz, A. J., Parker, E. A. and Becker, A. A. 1998. 'Review of community-based research: assessing partnership approaches to improve public health', *Annual Review of Public Health* 19: 173–202.

Jackall, R. 1988. *Moral Mazes.* New York: Oxford University Press.

Jessop, B. 1990. *State Theory: Putting the Capitalist State in its Place.* Cambridge: Polity Press.

Johnston, L. 1992. *The Rebirth of Private Policing.* London: Routledge.

1996. 'What is vigilantism?' *British Journal of Criminology* 36: 220–36.

1997. 'Policing communities of risk', in P. Francis, P. Davies and V. Jupp (eds.), *Policing Futures: The Police, Law Enforcement and the Twenty-first Century.* Basingstoke: Macmillan, pp. 186–207.

2000a. 'Transnational private policing: the impact of global commercial security', in J. Sheptycki (ed.), *Issues in Transnational Policing.* London: Routledge, pp. 21–42.

2000b. *Policing Britain: Risk Security and Governance.* Harlow: Longman.

2001a. 'Crime, fear and civil policing', *Urban Studies* 38: 959–76.

2001b. *Private Policing and its Links to Public Policing.* Unit 5, Course PS301, Open University of Hong Kong.

2002. *Policing Britain: Risk, Security and Governance.* Harlow: Pearson Education.

2003. 'From "pluralisation" to "the police extended family": discourses on the governance of community policing in Britain', *International Journal of the Sociology of Law* 31: 185–204.

Johnston, L. and Shearing C. 2003. *Governing Security: Explorations in Policing and Justice.* London: Routledge.

Jones, C., Hesterly, W. and Borgatti, S. 1997. 'A general theory of network governance: exchange conditions and social mechanisms', *Academy of Management Review* 22: 911–45.

Jones, T. 2003. 'Accountability in the era of pluralised policing'. Paper presented at *In Search of Security: An International Conference on Policing and Security,* Montreal, 19–22 February.

Jones, T. and Maguire, M. 2003. 'Community safety and the policing of marginalised populations: a review of research'. Paper published by the GRC

Exchange. http://www.grc-exchange.org/gthemes/ssaj_safety.htm (accessed 20 February 2005).

Jones, T. and Newburn, T. 1998. *Private Security and Public Policing*. Oxford: Clarendon Press.

2002a. 'Learning from Uncle Sam? Exploring US influences on British crime control policy', *Governance* 15: 97–119.

2002b. 'Policy convergence and crime control in the USA and the UK: streams of influence and levels of impact', *Criminal Justice* 2: 173–203.

2002c. 'The transformation of policing', *British Journal of Criminology* 42: 129–46.

Jordan, B. 1996. *A Theory of Poverty and Social Exclusion*. Cambridge: Polity Press.

Kaplan, J. E. 2004. 'Private armies seeking political advice in DC', *The Hill*, 14 April. http://www.hillnews.com/news/041404/blackwater.aspx (accessed 20 November 2004).

Karstedt, S. 2002. 'Durkheim, Tarde and beyond: the global travel of crime policies', *Criminal Justice* 2: 111–23.

2004. 'Democracy and violence'. Paper presented at the National Europe Centre seminar series, Australian National University, Canberra, 14 July.

Kawachi, I. 2000. 'Income inequality and health', in L. Berkman and I. Kawachi (eds.), *Social Epidemiology*. New York: Oxford University Press, pp. 76–94.

Kawachi, I. and Berkman, L. 2000. 'Social cohesion, social capital and health', in L. Berkman and I. Kawachi (eds.), *Social Epidemiology*. New York: Oxford University Press, pp. 174–90.

Keegan, J. 2004. *Intelligence in War*. New York: Knopf.

Keith, M. 1993. *Race, Riots and Policing: Lore and Disorder in a Multi-Racist Society*. London: University College of London Press.

Kellner, D. 1990. *Television and the Crisis of Democracy*. Boulder, Colo.: Westview Press.

1992. *The Persian Gulf TV War*. Boulder, Colo.: Westview Press.

Kempa, M., Carrier, R., Wood, J. and Shearing, C. 1999. 'Reflections on the evolving concept of "private policing"', *European Journal of Criminal Policy and Research* 7: 197–223.

Kerik, B. 2002. *The Lost Son*. New York: Harper Torch.

Kerr, P. 2003. 'The evolving dialectic between state-centric and human-centric security'. Working Paper, Australian National University, Canberra.

Kessler, R. 2003. *The Bureau*. New York: St Martin's Press.

Kiel, L. 1994. *Managing Chaos and Complexity in Government: A New Paradigm for Managing Change*. London: University College of London Press.

Kim, C. W. and Mauborgne, R. 2003. 'Tipping point leadership', *Harvard Business Review* 81 (April): 60–69.

Kinsey, R., Lea, J. and Young, J. 1986. *Losing the Fight Against Crime*. Oxford: Basil Blackwell.

Klandermans, B., Roefs, M. and Olivier, J. 2001. *The State of the People: Citizens, Civil Society and Governance in South Africa, 1994–2000*. Pretoria: Human Science Research Council.

Kleinig, J. 1999. 'The most critical and unresolved issue associated with community policing', in S. Einstein and M. Amir (eds.), *Policing, Security and*

Democracy: Special Aspects of Democratic Policing. Huntsville, Tex.: Office of International Criminal Justice, pp. 242–3.

Klinck, E. 2001. *Transformation and Social Security in South Africa.* Johannesburg: Friederich Ebert Stiftung, South Africa Office.

Knox, C. 2001. 'The "deserving" victims of political violence: "punishment" attacks in Northern Ireland', *Criminal Justice* 1: 181–99.

2002. 'See no evil, hear no evil: insidious paramilitary violence in Northern Ireland', *British Journal of Criminology* 42: 164–85.

Koci, A. 1998. 'Reform of the police in Hungary and Lithuania: empirical findings on the policing of public order', *European Journal of Social Sciences* 11: 307–15.

Koss, M. P., Koss, P. G. and Woodruff, W. J. 1991. 'Deleterious effects of criminal victimization on women's health and medical utilization', *Archives of Internal Medicine* 151: 342–7.

Krane, J. 2004. 'Private firms do US military's work', *Associated Press.* http://www.globalpolicy.org/security/peacekpg/training/1029private.htm (accessed 21 November 2004).

Kraska, P. B. 1999. 'Militarizing criminal justice', *Journal of Political and Military Sociology* 27: 205–15.

Kraska, P. B. and Kappeler, V. E. 1997. 'Militarizing American police: the rise and normalization of paramilitary units', *Social Problems* 44: 1–17.

Krause, K. and Williams, M. (eds.) 1997. *Critical Security Studies.* London: University College London Press.

Krauthammer, C. 1993. 'Defining deviancy up', *New Republic* 22 (November): 20–5.

Krebs, C. P. and Simmons, M. 2002. 'Intraprison HIV transmission: an assessment of whether it occurs, how it occurs, and who is at risk', *AIDS Education and Prevention* 14: 53–64.

Krieg, R. G. 2001. 'An interdisciplinary look at the deinstitutionalization of the mentally ill', *Social Science Journal* 38: 367–80.

Krieger, N. 2000. 'Discrimination and health', in L. Berkman and I. Kawachi (eds.), *Social Epidemiology.* New York: Oxford University Press, pp. 36–75.

2001. 'Theories for social epidemiology in the 21st century: an ecosocial perspective', *International Journal of Epidemiology* 30: 668–77.

Krug, E., Dahlberg, L., Mercy, J., Zwi, A. and Lozano, R. (eds.) 2002. *World Report on Violence and Health.* Geneva: World Health Organization.

Kuhn, T. 1967. *The Structure of Scientific Revolutions.* Chicago: University of Chicago Press.

Kurlantzick, J. 2003. 'Outsourcing the dirty work: the military and its reliance on private guns', *American Prospect*, 5 January. http://www.prospect.org/print/V14/5/kurlantzick-j.html (accessed 20 November 2004).

Lagarde, E., Schim Van Der Loeff, M., Enel, C., Holmgren, B., Dray-Spira, R., Pison, G., Piau, J., Delaunay, V., M'boup, S., Ndoye, I., Coeuret-Pellicer, M., Whittle, H. and Aaby, P. 2003. 'Mobility and the spread of human immunodeficiency virus into rural areas of West Africa', *International Journal of Epidemiology* 32: 744–52.

Law, S. A. 2000. 'Commercial sex: beyond decriminalization', *California Law Review* 73: 523–608.

Law Commission of Canada 2002. *In Search of Security: The Roles of Public Police and Private Agencies*. Ottawa: Law Commission of Canada.

Lee, J. 1981. 'Some structural aspects of police deviance in relation to minority groups', in C. Shearing (ed.), *Organizational Police Deviance*. Toronto: Butterworth, pp. 49–82.

Lee, M. and Punch, M. 2004. 'Policing by degrees: police officers' experience of university education', *Policing and Society* 14: 233–49.

Leggett, T. 2003. *Rainbow Tenement: Crime and Policing in Inner Johannesburg*. Published Monograph No. 78. Pretoria: Institute for Security Studies.
   2004. 'The state of crime and policing' in S. Buhlungu, J. Daniel, J. Lutchman and R. Southall (eds.), *The State of the Nation: South Africa 2004/2005*. Pretoria: Human Science Research Council Press, pp. 156–9.

Leggett, T., Louw, A., Schönteich, M., and Sekhonyane, M. 2003. *Criminal Justice in Review 2001/2002*. Published Monograph No. 88. Pretoria: Institute for Security Studies.

Lejoyeux, M., Zillhardt, P., Chieze, F., Fichelle, A., McLoughlin, M., Poujade, A. and Ades, J. 2002. 'Screening for domestic violence among patients admitted to a French emergency service', *European Psychiatry* 17: 479–83.

Lennings, C. J. 1997. 'Police and occupationally related violence: a review', *Policing* 29: 555–66.

Leviton, L. C., Snell, E. and Mcginnis, M. 2000. 'Urban issues in health promotion strategies', *American Journal of Public Health* 90: 863–6.

Levy, M., Quilty, S., Young, L., Hunt, W., Matthews, R. and Robertson, P. 2003. 'Pox in the docks: varicella outbreak in an Australian prison system', *Public Health* 117: 446–51.

Lewis, C. 1999. *Complaints against Police: The Politics of Reform*. Annandale, NSW: Hawkins Press.

Liang, H. H. 1993. *The Rise of the Modern Police and the European State System from Metternich to the Second World War*. New York: Cambridge University Press.

Lichtenstein, B. 2005. 'Domestic violence, sexual ownership, and HIV risk in women in the American deep south', *Social Science and Medicine* 60: 701–14.

Lilley, D. 2000. *The Privatisation of Security and Peacebuilding: A Framework for Action*. London: International Alert.

Lin, N. 2001. *Social Capital: A Theory of Social Structure and Action*. Cambridge: Cambridge University Press.

Link, B. and Phelan, J. 1995. 'Social conditions as fundamental causes of disease', *Journal of Health and Social Behavior* 36 (special number): 80–94.

Link, B., Andrews, H. and Cullen, F. 1992. 'The violent and illegal behavior of mental patients reconsidered', *American Sociological Review* 57: 275–92.

Lipsky, M. 1980. *Street-Level Bureaucracy*. New York: Russell Sage Foundation.

Lister, S., Hadfield, P., Hobbs, D. and Winlow, S. 2001. 'Accounting for bouncers: occupational licensing as a mechanism for regulation', *Criminal Justice* 1: 363–84.

Lo Vecchio, F., Bhatia, A. and Sciallo, D. 1998. 'Screening for domestic violence in the emergency department', *European Journal of Emergency Medicine* 5: 441–4.

Loader, I. 1996. *Youth, Policing and Democracy*. Basingstoke: Macmillan/Palgrave.

1997a. 'Policing and the social: questions of symbolic power', *British Journal of Sociology* 48: 1–18.

1997b. 'Private security and the demand for protection in contemporary Britain', *Policing and Society* 7: 143–62.

1997c. 'Thinking normatively about private security', *Journal of Law and Society* 24: 377–94.

1999. 'Consumer culture and the commodification of policing and security', *Sociology* 33: 373–92.

2000. 'Plural policing and democratic governance', *Social and Legal Studies* 9: 323–45.

2003. 'Governing European policing: some problems and prospects', *Policing and Society* 12: 291–305.

Loader, I. and Mulcahy, A. 2001. 'The power of legitimate naming. Part II – Making sense of the elite police voice', *British Journal of Criminology* 41: 252–65.

2003. *Policing and the Condition of England: Memory, Politics and Culture*. Oxford: Oxford University Press.

Loader, I. and Walker, N. 2001. 'Policing as a public good: reconstituting the connections between policing and the state', *Theoretical Criminology* 5: 9–35.

2004a. 'Locating the public interest in transnational policing'. Paper prepared for a workshop on *Constabulary Ethics and the Spirit of Transnational Policing*, Onati, Spain, 13–14 July.

2004b. 'State of denial? Rethinking the governance of security', *Punishment and Society* 6: 221–8.

2006. 'Locating the "public interest" in transnational policing', in A. Goldsmith and J. Sheptycki (eds.), *Crafting Global Policing*. Oxford: Hart Publishing.

Lovell, J. 2004. 'Boom times in Iraq for former dogs of war', *Reuters*, 22 September. CorpWatch: War Profiteers. http://www.warprofiteers.com/article.php?id=11536 (accessed 20 November 2004).

Luhmann, N. 1997. 'Globalization or world society: how to conceive of modern society', *International Review of Sociology* 7: 67–79.

Lusher, E. 1981. *Commission to Enquire into New South Wales Police Administration*. Sydney: Government Printer.

Lynch, J., Smith, G., Harper, S., Hillemeier, M., Ross, N., Kaplan, G. and Wolfson, M. 2004. 'Is income inequality a determinant of population health? Part 1. A systematic review', *Milbank Quarterly* 82: 5–99.

Maantay, J. 2001. 'Zoning, equity, and public health', *American Journal of Public Health* 91: 1033–41.

Macaulay, S. 1986. 'Private government', in L. Lipson and S. Wheeler (eds.), *Law and the Social Sciences*. New York: Russell Sage Foundation, pp. 445–518.

MacKay, D. 1981. *Information, Mechanism and Meaning*. Cambridge: MIT Press.

Mackenbach, J. and Bakker, M. (eds.) 2002. *Reducing Inequalities in Health: A European Perspective*. London and New York: Routledge.

MacKinnon, C. 1989. *Toward a Feminist Theory of the State*. Cambridge, Mass.: Harvard University Press.

Macmillan, R. and Hagan, J. 2004. 'Violence in the transition to adulthood: adolescent victimization, education, and socioeconomic attainment in later life', *Journal of Research on Adolescence* 14: 127–58.

Maguire, E. 2002. *Organizational Structure in American Police Agencies*. Albany: State University New York Press.

Maguire, E., Snipes, J., Uchida, C. and Townsend, M. 1998. 'Counting cops: estimating the number of police officers and police agencies in the United States', *Policing: An International Journal of Police Strategies and Management* 21: 97–120.

Mahon, N. 1996. 'New York inmates' HIV risk behaviors: the implications for prevention policy and programs', *American Journal of Public Health* 86: 1211–15.

Mail and Guardian Online 2004a. 'ANC kicks off bitter battle for third term'. http://www.mg.co.za/Content/13.asp?ao=29493&t=1 (accessed 13 January 2005).

2004b. 'Fears of South African poll violence'. http://www.mg.co.za/Content/13.asp?a=11&p=40754 (accessed 19 January 2004).

Maitland, F. 1972 (1885). *Justice and Police*. New York: Russell and Russell.

Malan, M. 1999. 'Police reform in South Africa: peacekeeping without peacekeepers', *African Security Review* 8: 9.

Manning, P. 1992. 'Big Bang decisions', in K. Hawkins (ed.), *The Uses of Discretion*. Oxford: Oxford University Press, pp. 249–85.

1997. *Police Work: The Social Organization of Policing*, 2nd edn. Prospect Heights, Ill.: Waveland Press.

2000. 'Policing the new social spaces', in J. Sheptycki (ed.), *Issues in Transnational Policing*. London: Routledge, pp. 177–200.

2003a. 'Crime analysis and situated rationalities'. Paper presented at a conference at the International Center for Comparative Criminology, University of Montreal.

2003b. *Policing Contingencies*. Chicago: University of Chicago Press.

March, J. and Simon, H. 1958. *Organizations*. New York: John Wiley and Sons.

Maré, G. 2003. 'The state of the state: Contestations and race re-assertion in a neoliberal terrain', in J. Daniel, A. Habib and R. Southall (eds.), *State of the Nation: South Africa 2003–2004*. Pretoria: Human Science Research Council Press, pp. 25–52.

Marenin, O. 1982. 'Parking tickets and class repression: the concept of policing in critical theories of criminal justice', *Contemporary Crises* 6: 241–6.

1990. 'The police and the coercive nature of the state', in E. Greenberg and T. Mayer (eds.), *Changes in the State: Causes and Consequences*. London: Sage, pp. 115–30.

2004. 'Police training for democracy', *Police Practice and Research* 5: 107–23.

Mark, R., Sir 1978. *Report to the Minister for Administrative Services on the Organisation of Police Resources in the Commonwealth area and Other Related Matters*. Canberra: Australian Government Publishing Service.

Markell, P. 2003. *Bound by Recognition*. Princeton: Princeton University Press.

Marks, M. 1999. 'Changing dilemmas and the dilemmas of change: transforming the public order police in Durban', *Policing and Society* 8: 157–79.

— 2001. *Young Warriors: Youth Politics, Identity and Violence in South Africa.* Johannesburg: University of Witwatersrand Press.

— 2003. 'Shifting gears or slamming on the brakes? A review of police behavioural change in a post-apartheid police unit', *Policing and Society* 13: 235–58.

— 2004a. 'Democratising police organisations from the inside out: police labour relations in Southern Africa', in C. Fields and H. Moore (eds.), *Comparative and International Criminal Justice: Traditional and Non-traditional Systems of Law and Control*, 2nd edn. Prospect Heights, Ill.: Waveland Press.

— 2004b. 'Researching police transformation', *British Journal of Criminology* 44: 866–88.

Marks, M. and Fleming, J. 2004. 'The untold story: the regulation of police labour rights and the quest for police democratisation'. Paper presented at the *International Employment Relations Twelfth Annual Conference*, Capricorn Coast, 5–8 July.

Marmot, M. and Wilkinson, R. (eds.) 1999. *Social Determinants of Health.* Oxford: Oxford University Press.

Marx, G. 1987. 'The interweaving of public and private police in undercover work', in C. Shearing and P. Stenning (eds.), *Private Policing.* London: Sage, pp. 172–93.

— 2000. 'The police as social change agents? The curious case of Poland's transition', in M. Los and A. Zybertowicz (eds.), *Privatising the Police State.* London: Macmillan, pp. 1–5.

Mason, G. 2004. 'UN peacekeeping and the private sector', *IPOA Quarterly* Issue 1: 1, 7

Maxwell, J. C. 2003. 'Update: comparison of drug use in Australia and the United States as seen in the 2001 national household surveys', *Drug and Alcohol Review* 22: 347–57.

May, J. P. and Williams, E. L. Jr. 2002. 'Acceptability of condom availability in a US jail', *AIDS Education and Prevention* 14: 85–91.

McBarnet, D. and Whelan, C. J. 1997. 'Creative compliance and the defeat of legal control: the magic of the orphan subsidiary', in D. Hawkins (ed.), *The Human Face of Law: Essays in Honour of Donald Harris.* Oxford: Clarendon Press, pp. 177–98.

McCabe, S., Wallington, P., Alderson, J., Gostin, L. and Mason, C. 1988. *The Police, Public Order and Civil Liberties.* London: Routledge.

McConville, M., Sanders, A. and Young, R. 1991. *The Case for the Prosecution.* London: Routledge.

McDevitt, J. 2001. *School Security Officers. Final Report.* Washington, D.C.: National Institute of Justice.

McDevitt, J. and Farrell, A. 2004. *Report on Security at the DNC.* Boston: Center for Research on Justice and Policy, Northeastern University.

McGeough, P. 2004. 'Mercenaries flock to fill Iraq vacuum', *The Age*, 2 April.

McIvor, G. 1997. 'Acquisitions drive growth at Securitas', *Financial Times*, 10 February.

McLaughlin, E. and Murji, K. 1998. 'Resistance through representation: 'storylines', advertising and Police Federation campaigns', *Policing and Society* 8: 367–99.

McLaughlin, S. I., Spradling, P., Drociuk, D., Ridzon, R., Pozsik, C. J. and Onorato, I. 2003. 'Extensive transmission of mycobacterium tuberculosis among congregated, HIV-infected prison inmates in South Carolina, United States', *International Journal of Tuberculosis and Lung Disease* 7: 665–72.

McMullen, J. L. 1996. 'The new improved monied police: reform, crime control and the commodification of policing in London', *British Journal of Criminology* 36: 85–108.

Melossi, D. 2001. 'The cultural embeddedness of social control: reflections on the comparison of Italian and North-American cultures concerning punishment', *Theoretical Criminology* 5: 403–24.

Midford, R., Acres, J., Lenton, S., Loxley, W. and Boots, K. 2002. 'Cops, drugs and the community: establishing consultative harm reduction structures in two Western Australian locations', *International Journal of Drug Policy* 13: 181–8.

Miller, P. and Rose, N. 1990. 'Governing economic life'. *Economy and Society*, 19: 1–31.

Milner, L., Mouzos, J. and Makkai, T. 2004. *Drug Use Monitoring in Australia: 2003 Annual Report on Drug Use among Police Detainees*. Canberra: Australian Institute of Criminology.

Minogue, M. 2002. 'Public management and regulatory governance: problems of policy transfer to developing countries'. Working Paper Series No. 32. Centre on Regulation and Competition, University of Manchester.

Minton, A. 2002. *Building Balanced Communities: The US and UK Compared*. London: RICS.

Mirrlees-Black, C. 2001. *Confidence in the Criminal Justice System: Findings from the 2000 British Crime Survey*. London: Home Office.

Monbiot, G. 2003. *Manifesto for a New World Order*. London: The New Press.

Monjardet, D. 1996. *Ce que fait la police: sociologie de la force publique*. Paris: La Découverte.

Moore, S. 1973. 'Law and social change: the semi-autonomous social field as an appropriate subject of study', *Law and Society Review* 7: 719–46.

Morenoff, J. and Sampson, R. 1997. 'Violent crime and the spatial dynamics of neighborhood transition: Chicago, 1970–1990', *Social Forces* 76: 31–64.

Morenoff, J., Sampson, R. and Raudenbush, S. 2001. 'Neighborhood inequality, collective efficacy, and the spatial dynamics of urban violence', *Criminology* 39: 517–59.

Morn, F. 1982. *The Eye That Never Sleeps: A History of the Pinkerton National Detective Agency*. Bloomington: Indiana University Press.

Morone, J. 1997. 'Enemies of the People: The Moral Dimension to Public Health', *Journal of Health Politics, Policy and Law* 22: 993–1020.

Moynihan, D. 1993. 'Defining deviancy down', *American Scholar* 62: 17–30.

Mulcahy, A. 2000. 'Policing history: the official and organizational memory of the Royal Ulster Constabulary', *British Journal of Criminology* 40: 68–87.

Mutter, R., Grimes, R. and Labarthe, D. 1994. 'Evidence of intraprison spread of HIV infection', *Archives of Internal Medicine* 154: 793–5.

Nadelmann, N. 1993. *Cops across Borders: The Internationalization of US Criminal Law Enforcement*. University Park, Penn.: Pennsylvania State University Press.

Nalla, M. 1998. 'Opportunities in the emerging market', *Security Journal* 10: 15–21.

Narayan, S. 1994. 'The West European market for security products and services', *International Security Review, Winter*: 28–9

Nathan, A. 2004. 'Private military firms face Iraq probe', *Sunday Times*, 20 June.

Nathan, S. 2003. Prison Privatisation Report International, No. 53 (October). http://www.psiru.org/justice/PPRI53.htm (accessed 20 November 2004).

   2004. Prison Privatisation Report International, No. 63 (July). http://www.psiru.org/justice/ppri63.htm (accessed 20 November 2004).

National Center for Health Statistics 2003. *Health, United States, 2003, with Chartbook on Trends in the Health of Americans*. Hyattsville, Md: Department of Health and Human Services.

Naylor, R. 2000. *Economic and organized crime: challenges for criminal justice*, Strategic Issue series. Ottawa: Department of Justice.

Neff, J. and Price, J. 2004. 'Contractors in Iraq make costs balloon', *The News and Observer*, 24 October. http://www.newsobserver.com/news/nation_world/blackwater/story/1762376p-8044834c.html (accessed 21 November 2004).

Neild, R. 1999. 'From national security to citizen security: civil society and the evolution of public security debates', International Centre for Human Rights and Democratic Development, Montreal.

Nelken, D. 1995. 'Disclosing/invoking legal culture: an introduction', *Social and Legal Studies* 4: 435–52.

   2002. 'Comparing criminal justice', in M. Maguire, R. Morgan and R. Reiner (eds.), *The Oxford Handbook of Criminology*, 3rd edn. Oxford: Oxford University Press, pp. 175–202.

Neocleous, M. 2000. *The Fabrication of Social Order: A Critical Theory of Police Power*. London: Pluto Press.

New Zealand Department of Corrections 1999. *National Study of Psychiatric Morbidity in New Zealand Prisons: An Investigation of the Prevalence of Psychiatric Disorders among New Zealand Inmates*. Wellington: Department of Corrections.

Nina, D. 2001. 'Popular justice and the "appropriation" of the state monopoly on the definition of justice and order: the case of anti-crime committees', in W. Schärf and D. Nina (eds.), *The Other Law – Non-State Ordering in South Africa*. Cape Town: Juta, pp. 98–117.

Nogalla, D. and Sack, F. 1998. 'Private reconfigurations of police and policing: the case of Germany'. Paper presented at GERN Seminar *Police et Securité: Contrôle Social et l'Interaction Public-Privé*, Hamburg.

Nolan, J. L. Jr. (ed.) 2002. *Drug Courts in Theory and in Practice*. New York: Aldine de Gruyter.

Norris, F. H. and Kaniasty, K. 1994. 'Psychological distress following criminal victimization in the general population: cross-sectional, longitudinal, and prospective analyses', *Journal of Consulting and Clinical Psycholology* 62: 111–23.

Nossal, K. R. 2001. 'Global governance and national interests: regulating transnational security corporations in the post cold-war era', *Melbourne Journal of International Law* 2: 459–76.

Nozick, R. 1974. *Anarchy, State and Utopia*. Oxford: Basil Blackwell.

Nussbaum, M. 2002. 'Patriotism and cosmopolitanism', in J. Cohen (ed.), *For Love of Country?* Boston: Beacon Press.

Nutley, S. and Davies, H. T. O. 2000. 'Making a reality of evidence-based practice: some lessons from the diffusion of innovations', *Public Money and Management* 20 (October–December): 35–42.

O'Donnell, P. 2003. 'Your guide to New York's spycams', *Wired* 11.10. http://www.wired.com (accessed 20 January 2005).

O'Dowd, D. 2002. *Policing Bureaucracy Taskforce. Income Generation Guide.* http://www.policereform.gov.uk/bureaucracy/change_proposal_reports/ Management_Support/Income_Generation_Guide/ (accessed 20 November 2004).

O'Malley, P. 1996. 'Indigenous governance', *Economy and Society* 25: 310–26.
  1997. 'Policing, politics and postmodernity', *Social and Legal Studies* 6: 363–81.
  2002. 'Globalizing risk? Distinguishing styles of "neo-liberal" criminal justice in Australia and the USA', *Criminal Justice* 2: 205–22.

O'Malley, P. and Palmer, D. 1996. 'Post-Keynesian policing', *Economy and Society* 25: 137–55.

O'Neill, B. 2004. 'A new kind of private war', *Spiked-Politics* 16 April. http://www.spiked-online.com/Articles/0000000CA4DD.htm (accessed 20 November 2004).

O'Neill, H., Pouder, R. and Buchholtz, A. 1998. 'Patterns in the diffusion of strategies across organizations: insights from the innovation diffusion literature', *Academy of Management Review* 23: 98–114.

Ocqueteau, F. 1993. 'Legitimation of the private security sector in France', *European Journal of Criminal Policy and Research* 1: 108–22.

Offe, C. 2003. 'The European model of "social" capitalism: can it survive European integration?', *Journal of Political Philosophy* 11: 437–69.

Olson, M. 1965. *The Logic of Collective Action: Public Goods and the Theory of Groups*. Cambridge, Mass.: Harvard University Press.

Oppler, S. 1997. 'Partners against crime: from community to partnership policing'. Occasional Paper No. 16, Institute for Security Studies, Pretoria.

Osborne, D. and Gaebler, T. 1993. *Reinventing Government*. New York: Plume.

Ostrom, E., Burger, J., Field, C. B., Norgaard, R. B. and Policanscky, D. 1999. 'Sustainability – revisiting the commons: local lessons, global challenges' *Science* 284: 278–82.

Paoli, L. 2002. 'The paradoxes of organized crime', *Crime, Law and Social Change* 37: 51–97.

Parker, C. 2002. *The Open Corporation: Effective Self-regulation and Democracy*. Cambridge: Cambridge University Press.

Parker, C. and Braithwaite, J. 2003. 'Regulation', in P. Cane and M. Tushnet (eds.), *The Oxford Handbook of Legal Studies*. Oxford: Oxford University Press, pp. 119–45.

Perrow, C. 1984. *Normal Accidents*. New York: Basic Books.

Pettit, K., Kingsley, G. and Coulton, C. 2003. *Neighborhoods and Health: Building Evidence for Local Policy*. Washington, D.C.: The Urban Institute.

Pillay, C. 2000. 'Independent pathologists at UDW student's autopsy', Mercury and South African Press Association, News section, 18 January.

Pitman, G. 1998. 'Police minister and commissioner relationships'. Ph.D. thesis, Griffith University.

Policy Co-ordination and Advisory Services 2003. 'Toward a ten year review: synthesis report on implementation of government programmes'. Discussion document. Presidency Office of the Government of South Africa, Cape Town.

Portes, A. 1998. 'Social capital: its origins and applications in modern sociology', *Annual Review of Sociology* 24: 1–24.

Post, D. and Johnson, D. 1998. 'Chaos prevailing on every continent: towards a new theory of decentralized decision-making in complex systems', *Chicago-Kent Law Review* 73: 1055–99.

Potterat, J., Rothenberg, R. and Muth, S. 1999. 'Network structural dynamics and infectious disease propagation', *International Journal of STD and AIDS* 10: 182–5.

Prenzler, T. and Sarre, R. 1998. *Regulating Private Security in Australia*. Trends and Issues in Crime and Criminal Justice No. 98. Canberra: Australian Institute of Criminology.

2002. 'The policing complex', in A. Graycar and P. Grabosky (eds.), *The Cambridge Handbook of Australian Criminology*. Cambridge: Cambridge University Press, pp. 52–72.

Priest, D. and Flaherty, M. 'Under fire, security firms form an alliance'. http://www.washingtonpost.com/ac2/wp-dyn/A59516-2004Apr7?language=printer (accessed 21 November 2004).

Public Order Police (SAPS) 2000. 'Debriefing of crowd management incident: University of Durban Westville on 16 May 2000'. Public Order Police, Pretoria.

Putnam, R. 2000. *Bowling Alone: The Collapse and Revival of American Community*. New York: Simon & Schuster.

Pyle, D. 1995. *Cutting the Costs of Crime*. London: Institute of Economic Affairs.

Quirk, M 2004. 'Private military contractors', *The Atlantic Online*, September. http://www.theatlantic.com/doc/prem/200409/quirk/ (accessed 21 November 2004).

Raab, J. and Milward, H. B. 2003. 'Dark networks as problems', *Journal of Public Administration Research and Theory* 13: 413–39.

Ramsey, M. (ed.) 2003. *Prisoners' Drug Use and Treatment: Seven Research Studies*. London: Home Office Research, Development and Statistics Directorate.

Redrat 2004. http://www.redrat.net/BUSH_WAR/mercenaries/#mercs (accessed 19 November 2004).

Reilly, D., Scantleton, J. and Didcott, P. 2002. 'Magistrates' early referral into treatment (MERIT): preliminary findings of a 12-month court diversion trial for drug offenders.', *Drug and Alcohol Review* 21: 393–6.

Reiner, R. 1991. *Chief Constables: Bobbies, Bosses or Bureaucrats?* Oxford: Oxford University Press.

1992. *The Politics of the Police.* London: Harvester Wheatsheaf.

Reus-Smit, C. 2004. *American Power and World Order.* Cambridge: Polity Press.

Reuss-Ianni, E. 1983. *Two Cultures of Policing.* New Brunswick, N.J.: Transaction Publishers.

Richardson, J. (ed.) 2000. *Police and Private Security: What the Future Holds.* Ottawa: Canadian Association of Chiefs of Police.

Richie, B., Freudenberg, N. and Page, J. 2001. 'Reintegrating women leaving jail into urban communities: a description of a model program', *Journal of Urban Health* 78: 290–303.

Rigakos, G. 2002. *The New Parapolice: Risk Markets and Commodified Social Control.* Toronto: University of Toronto Press.

Rigakos, G. and Greener, D. 2000. 'Bubbles of governance: private policing and the law in Canada', *Canadian Journal of Law and Society* 15: 145–84.

Rigakos, G. and Papanicolau, G. 2003. 'The political economy of Greek policing: between neo-liberalism and the sovereign state', *Policing and Society* 13: 271–304.

Robertson, J. E. 2003. 'Rape among incarcerated men: sex, coercion and STDs', *AIDS Patient Care and STDs* 17: 423–31.

Roche, D. 2002. 'Restorative justice and the regulatory state in South African townships', *British Journal of Criminology* 42: 514–33.

Rogers, E. 1995. *Diffusion of Innovations.* New York: The Free Press.

Romney, M. 2004. *Turnaround: Crisis, Leadership, and the Olympic Games.* Washington, D.C.: Henry Regnery.

Rose, N. 1996. 'The death of the social: refiguring the territory of government', *Economy and Society* 25: 327–56.

1999. *The Powers of Freedom.* Cambridge: Cambridge University Press.

Rose, N. and Miller, P. 1992. 'Political power beyond the state: problematics of government', *British Journal of Sociology* 43: 173–205.

Ross, C. and Mirowsky, J. 2001. 'Neighborhood disadvantage, disorder, and health', *Journal of Health and Social Behavior* 42: 258–76.

Rothbard, M. 1985. *For a New Liberty: The Libertarian Manifesto.* New York: Libertarian Review Foundation.

Rowley, T. 1997. 'Moving beyond dyadic ties: a network theory of stakeholder influences', *Academy of Management Review* 22: 887–910.

Runciman, D. 2003. 'The concept of the state: the sovereignty of a fiction', in Q. Skinner and B. Stråth (eds.), *States and Citizens: History, Theory, Prospects.* Cambridge: Cambridge University Press, pp. 28–38.

Ryan, P. 2000. *NSW Police: Future Directions 2001–2005.* Sydney: NSWPS.

Sadiq, R. 1995. 'Rethinking development strategy in Africa: the imperatives and prospects of human centred development', *Africa Development Review* 7: 14–45.

Said, E. 1978. *Orientalism.* New York: Pantheon Books.

Sampson, R. 2002. 'Transcending tradition: new directions in community research, Chicago style', *Criminology* 40: 213–31.

Sampson, R. and Morenoff, J. 2000. 'Public health and safety in context: lessons from community-level theory on social capital', in B. Smedley and S.

Syme (eds.), *Promoting Health: Intervention Strategies from Social and Behavioral Research*. Washington, D.C.: National Academy Press, pp. 366–89.

Sampson, R. and S. Raudenbush 1997. 'Neighborhoods and violent crime: a multilevel study of collective efficacy', *Science* 277: 918–25.

1999. 'Systematic social observation of public spaces: a new look at disorder in urban neighborhoods', *American Journal of Sociology* 105: 603–51.

Sampson, R., Morenoff, J. and Earls, F. 1999. 'Beyond social capital: spatial dynamics of collective efficacy for children', *American Sociological Review* 64: 633–60.

Samuelson, P. 1954. 'The pure theory of public expenditure', *Review of Economics and Statistics* 36: 387–9.

Sanders, J. 2000. 'Racial and ethnic minorities in San Diego, United States', *Policing and Society* 10: 131–41.

Savelsberg, J. 1999. 'Cultures of punishment: USA–Germany'. Paper presented at the Annual Meeting of the American Society of Criminology, Toronto.

Schärf, W. 1997. 'Reintegrating militarised youths (street gangs and self-defence units) into the mainstream in South Africa: from hunters to game-keepers'. Paper presented at the *Urban Childhood Conference*, Toronto, June.

2000. 'Community justice and community policing in post-apartheid South Africa'. Paper presented at the *International Workshop on the Rule of Law in Development: Citizen Security, Rights and Life Choices in Law in Middle Income Countries*, Institute for Development Studies, University of Sussex, June.

Schmitt, C. 1985 (1922). *Political Theology: Four Chapters on the Concept of Sovereignty*. Cambridge, Mass.: MIT Press.

Scott, C. 2002. 'Private regulation of the public sector: a neglected facet of contemporary governance', *Journal of Law and Society* 29: 56–76.

2003. 'Speaking softly without big sticks: meta-regulation and public sector audit', *Law and Policy* 25: 203–19.

2004. 'Regulation in the age of governance: the rise of the (post-) regulatory state', in J. Jordana and D. Levi-Faur (eds.), *Politics of Regulation*. London: Edgar, pp. 145–74.

Scraton, P. (ed.) 1987. *Law, Order and the Authoritarian State*. Milton Keynes: Open University Press.

Sebald, W. 2003. *The Natural History of Destruction*. New York: Random House.

Sekhonyane, M. and Louw, A. 2002. *Violent Justice: Vigilantism and the State's Response*. Monograph No. 72. Pretoria: Institute for Security Studies.

Seldon, A. 1990. *Capitalism*. Oxford: Basil Blackwell.

Sennett, R. 2003. *Respect in a World of Inequality*. New York: W. W. Norton.

Shaw, M. 1994. 'Point of order: policing the transition', in S. Friedman and D. Atkinson (eds.), *South African Review 7. The Small Miracle: South Africa's Negotiated Settlement*. Johannesburg: Ravan Press, pp. 182–206.

1999. 'The most critical and unresolved issue associated with community policing', in S. Einstein and M. Amir (eds.), *Policing, Security and Democracy: Special Aspects of Democratic Policing*. Huntsville, Tex.: Office of International Criminal Justice.

2002. *Crime and Policing in Post-Apartheid South Africa: Transforming Under Fire*. Cape Town: David Phillip.

Shearing, C. 1995. 'Transforming the culture of policing: thoughts from South Africa', *Australian and New Zealand Journal of Criminology 28* (special issue): 54–6.

1997. 'Towards democratic policing: rethinking strategies of transformation', in *Policing in Emerging Democracies: Workshop Papers and Highlights*. Washington, D.C.: National Institute of Justice, pp. 29–38.

1999. 'The most critical and unresolved issue associated with community policing', in S. Einstein and M. Amir (eds.), *Policing, Security and Democracy: Special Aspects of Democratic Policing*. Huntsville, Tex.: Office of International Criminal Justice, pp. 254–6.

2001a. 'A nodal conception of governance: thoughts on a policing commission', *Policing and Society* 11: 259–72.

2001b. 'Punishment and the changing face of governance', *Punishment and Society* 3: 203–20.

2001c. 'Transforming security: a South African experiment', in H. Strang and J. Braithwaite (eds.), *Restorative Justice and Civil Society*. Cambridge: Cambridge University Press, pp. 14–34.

2004. 'Thoughts on sovereignty', *Policing and Society* 14: 5–12.

Shearing, C. and Berg, J. in press. 'Plural policing in South Africa', in T. Jones and T. Newburn (eds.), *Plural Policing in Comparative Perspective*. London: Routledge.

Shearing, C. and Ericson, R. 1991. 'Culture as figurative action', *British Journal of Sociology* 42: 481–506.

Shearing, C. and Johnston, L. 2003. *Governing Security: Explorations in Policing and Justice*. London: Routledge.

2005. 'Justice in the risk society', *Australian and New Zealand Journal of Criminology* 38: 25–38.

Shearing, C. and Kempa, M. 2000. 'The role of "private security" in transitional democracies', in M. Shaw (ed.), *Seminar Report: Crime and Policing in Transitional Societies*. Johannesburg: Konrad Adenauer Stifting, pp. 205–14.

Shearing, C. and Stenning, P. 1981. 'Modern private security: its growth and implications', *Crime and Justice* 3: 193–245.

1983. 'Private security: its implications for social control', *Social Problems* 30: 125–38.

1985. 'From the Panopticon to Disney World: the development of discipline', in A. Doob and E. Greenspan (eds.), *Perspectives in Criminal Law*. Toronto: Canada Law Books, pp. 335–49.

1987. *Private Policing*. Newbury Park, Calif.: Sage.

Shearing, C. and Wood, J. 2000. 'Reflections on the governance of security: a normative enquiry', *Police Practice* 1: 457–76.

2003a. 'Governing security for common goods', *International Journal of the Sociology of Law* 31: 205–25.

2003b. 'Nodal governance, democracy and the new "denizens"', *Journal of Law and Society* 30: 400–19.

Shearing, C., Wood, J. and Font, E. 2004. 'Nodal governance and restorative justice'. Unpublished paper, Regulatory Institutions Network, Australian National University.

Sheptycki, J. (ed.) 2000. *Issues in Transnational Policing*. London: Routledge.

Shewan, D., Macpherson, A., Reid, M. and Davies, J. 1995. 'Patterns of injecting and sharing in a Scottish prison', *Drug and Alcohol Dependence* 39: 237–43.

Short, J. 1984. 'The social fabric at risk: toward the social transformation of risk analysis', *American Sociological Review* 49: 711–25.

Sibbald, B. 2002. 'Methadone maintenance expands inside federal prisons', *Canadian Medical Association Journal* 167: 1154.

Sidwell, C., Best, D. and Strang, J. 1999. 'Cost of drug use and criminal involvement before and during methadone treatment', *Journal of Clinical Forensic Medicine* 6: 225–7.

Siegrist, J. and Marmot, M. 2004. 'Health inequalities and the psychosocial environment – two scientific challenges', *Social Science and Medicine* 58: 1463–73.

Simmons, J. and Dodd, T. (eds.) 2003. *Crime in England and Wales 2002/3*, Statistical Bulletin 07/03. London: Home Office.

Simon, J. 1997. 'Governing through crime', in L. Friedman and G. Fisher (eds.), *The Crime Conundrum: Essays in Criminal Justice*. Boulder, Colo.: Westview Press, pp. 171–89.

Singer, P. 2003. *Corporate Warriors: The Rise of the Privatized Military Industry*. Ithaca: Cornell University Press.

2004a. 'Should humanitarians use private military services?', *Humanitarian Affairs Review* 4: 14–17. http://www.humanitarian-review.org/upload/pdf/SingerEnglisFinal.pdf (accessed 21 November 2004).

2004b. 'The Iraq war was the "first privatized war": private military firms in today's wars', *Fresh Air*, 9 July (interview with Terry Gross). http://www.agitprop.org.au/nowar/20030709_gross_privatised_war.php (accessed 21 November 2004).

Skogan, W. 1990. *Disorder and Decline*. New York: The Free Press.

Slack, D. 2004. 'Hub police seek to curb pay abuses', *Boston Globe*, 11 October.

Smith, A. 1998 (1776). *Wealth of Nations*. Oxford: Oxford University Press.

Smith, A. D. 2001. *Nationalism*. Cambridge: Polity Press.

Smith, D. 1987. *The Everyday World as Problematic: A Feminist Sociology*. Toronto: University of Toronto Press.

Smith, J. 2004. 'Training for DNC personnel', *Boston Globe*, 9 May.

Smith, K., Wiggers, J., Considine, R., Daly, J. and Collins, T. 2001. 'Police knowledge and attitudes regarding crime, the responsible service of alcohol and a proactive alcohol policing strategy', *Drug and Alcohol Review* 20: 181–92.

Snyder, L. 1996. 'Technology transfer through cautious eyes', *Journal of Communication* 46: 183–92.

Solomon, L., Flynn, C., Muck, K. and Vertefeuille, J. 2004. 'Prevalence of HIV, syphilis, hepatitis B, and hepatitis C among entrants to Maryland correctional facilities', *Journal of Urban Health* 81: 25–37.

South, N. 1988. *Policing for Profit*. London: Sage.

Sozzo, M. 2000. 'Hacia la superación de la táctica de la sospecha? Notas sobre política de prevención del delito e institución policial. Detenciones, facultades y prácticas policiales en la Ciudad de Buenos Aires', CELS-CED, Buenos Aires.

1981. 'The political economy of policing', in D. Greenburg (ed.), *Crime and Capitalism: Readings in Marxist Criminology*. Palo Alto, Calif.: Mayfield.

1987. 'Security and control in capitalist societies: the fetishism of security and the secret thereof', in J. Lowman, R. Menzies and T. Palys (eds.), *Transcarceration: Essays in the Sociology of Social Control*. Aldershot: Gower, pp. 43–58.

Sretrirutchai, S., Silapapojakul, K., Palittapongarnpim, P., Phongdara, A. and Vuddhakul, V. 2002. 'Tuberculosis in Thai prisons: magnitude, transmission and drug susceptibility', *International Journal of Tuberculosis and Lung Disease* 6: 208–14.

Stenning, P. 2000. 'Powers and accountability of the private police', *European Journal of Criminal Policy and Research* 8: 325–52.

Stenson, K. and Edwards, A. 2004. 'Policy transfer in local crime control: beyond naïve emulation', in T. Newburn and R. Sparks (eds.), *Criminal Justice and Political Cultures: National and International Dimensions of Crime Control*. Cullompton, Devon: Willan pp. 209–33.

Stern, V. 2001. 'Problems in prisons worldwide, with a particular focus on Russia', *Annals of the New York Academy of Sciences* 953: 113–19.

Stiglitz, J. 2003. *The Roaring Nineties: A New History of the World's Most Prosperous Decade*. New York: W. W. Norton.

Stone, C. and Ward, H. 2000. 'Democratic policing: a framework for action', *Policing and Society* 10: 11–46.

Strang, H. and Braithwaite, J. (eds.) 2001. *Restorative Justice and Civil Society*. New York: Cambridge University Press.

Strathdee, S. and Vlahov, D. 2001. 'The effectiveness of needle exchange programs: a review of the science and policy', *AIDScience* 1: 1–31.

Struckman-Johnson, C. and Struckman-Johnson, D. 2002. 'Sexual coercion reported by women in three midwestern prisons', *Journal of Sex Research* 39: 217–27.

Sutton, A. and Cherney, A. 2002. 'Prevention without politics? The cyclical progress of crime prevention in an Australian state', *Criminal Justice* 2: 325–44.

Swol, K. 1998. *Private Security and Public Policing in Canada*, Juristat 18. Ottawa: Statistics Canada, Canadian Centre for Justice Statistics.

Taussig, M. 1997. *The Magic of the State*. London: Routledge.

Taylor, A., Goldberg, D., Emslie, J., Wrench, J., Gruer, L., Cameron, S., Black, J., Davis, B., McGregor, J. and Follett, E. 1995. 'Outbreak of HIV infection in a Scottish prison', *British Medical Journal* 310: 289–92.

Taylor, R. 2002. 'Justice denied: political violence in Kwazulu-Natal after 1994', *African Affairs* 101: 473–508.

Thacher, D. 2004. 'The rich get richer and the poor get robbed: inequality in US criminal victimization, 1974–2000', *Journal of Quantitative Criminology* 20: 89–116.

The Center for Public Integrity 2004. 'Kellogg, Brown & Root (Halliburton)'. http://www.publicintegrity.org/wow/bio.aspx?act=pro&ddlC=31 (accessed 19 November 2004).

Tonry, M. 2001. 'Symbol, substance and severity in Western penal policies', *Punishment and Society* 3: 517–36.

Trebucq, A. 1999. 'Tuberculosis in prisons', *Lancet* 353: 2244–5.

Tshehla, B. 2002. 'Non-state justice in the post apartheid South Africa – a scan of Khaylelitsha', *African Sociological Review* 6: 47–70.

Tully, J. 1995. *Strange Multiplicity: Constitutionalism in an Age of Diversity*. Cambridge: Cambridge University Press.

Unger, R. 1996. *What Should Legal Analysis Become*. London: Verso.

United Nations Development Programme (UNDP) 1994. *Human Development Report 1994*. New York: Oxford University Press.

United Nations Economic and Social Council Commission on Human Rights 2003. Sub-Commission on the Promotion and Protection of Human Rights. Fifty-fifth Session. Agenda Item 4. 'Economic, social and cultural rights: norms on the responsibilities of transnational corporations and other business enterprises with regard to human rights', 26 August.

United Nations Office on Drugs and Crime 2004. *The Seventh United Nations Survey on Crime Trends and the Operations of Criminal Justice Systems (1998–2000)*. http://www.unodc.org/unodc/en/crime_cicp_survey_seventh. html#responses (accessed 17 June 2004).

van der Spuy, E. 2004. 'South African policing studies in the making', in B. Dixon and E. van der Spuy (eds.), *Justice Gained? Crime and Crime Control in South Africa's Transition*. Cape Town: University of Cape Town Press, pp. 193–226.

van der Spuy, E. in press. 'International assistance and local pressures in the reform of policing: the case of the Eastern Cape', *Society in Transition*.

Van Maanen, J. 1973. 'Observations on the making of policemen', *Human Organization* 32: 407–18.

van Zyl Smit, D. 1999. 'Criminological ideas and the South African tradition', *British Journal of Criminology* 39: 198–215.

2004. 'Swimming against the tide: controlling the size of the prison population in the new South Africa', in B. Dixon and E. van der Spuy (eds.), *Justice Gained? Crime and Crime Control in South Africa's Transition*. Cape Town: University of Cape Town Press, pp. 227–58.

van Zyl Smit, D. and van der Spuy, E. 2004. 'Importing criminological ideas in a new democracy: recent South African experiences', in T. Newburn and R. Sparks (eds.), *Criminal Justice and Political Cultures: National and International Dimensions of Crime Control*. Cullompton, Devon: Willan, pp. 184–208.

Varghese, B. and Peterman, T. A. 2001. 'Cost-effectiveness of HIV counseling and testing in US prisons', *Journal of Urban Health* 78: 304–12.

Vaughan. D. 1996. *The Challenger Disaster*. Chicago: University of Chicago Press.

Vera Institute of Justice 2003. 'Measuring progress toward safety and justice: a global guide to the design of performance indicators across the justice sector', Vera Institute of Justice, New York. http://www.vera. org/publication_pdf/207_404.pdf (accessed 23 February 2005).

Victoria Police 2003. *Delivering a Safer Victoria Business Plan 2003–2004*. Melbourne: Victoria Police.

Von Hirsch, A. and Shearing, C. 2000. 'Exclusion from public space', in A. Von Hirsch, D. Garland and A. Wakefield (eds.), *Ethical and Social Perspectives on Situational Crime Prevention*. Oxford: Hart Publishing, pp. 77–96.

Von Zielbauer, P. 2003. 'City creates post-jail plan for inmates'. *New York Times*, 20 September.

Vostanis, P. 2004. 'The impact, psychological sequelae and management of trauma affecting children', *Current Opinion in Psychiatry* 17: 269–73.

Waddington, P. A. J. 1999. 'Police (canteen) subculture', *British Journal of Criminology* 39: 287–309.

Wæver, O. 1995. 'Securitization and desecuritization', in R. Lipschutz (ed.), *On Security*. New York: Columbia University Press, pp. 46–86.

Waghorne, M. 1999. 'Public sector trade unions in the face of privatisation', *Development in Practice* 9: 557–68.

Wakefield, A. 2003. *Selling Security: The Private Policing of Public Space*. Cullompton, Devon: Willan.

Walden, K. 1982. *Visions of Order: The Canadian Mounties in Symbol and Myth*. Toronto: Butterworth.

Waldron, J. 1993. *Liberal Rights: Collected Papers 1981–1991*. Cambridge: Cambridge University Press.

Walker, N. 2000. *Policing in a Changing Constitutional Order*. London: Sweet and Maxwell.

2002. 'Policing and the supranational', *Policing and Society* 12: 307–22.

Walker, N. 2003 'The Pattern of transnational policing' in T. Newburn (ed.), *Handbook of Policing*. Cullompton, Devon: Willan, pp. 111–35.

Walker, R. 1997. 'The subject of security', in K. Krause and M. Williams (eds.), *Critical Security Studies*. London: University College London Press, pp. 61–83.

Washo, B. 1984. 'Effecting planned change within a police organisation', *The Police Chief* 51 (November): 33–5.

Wasserman, S. and Faust, K. 1994. *Social Network Analysis*. Cambridge: Cambridge University Press.

Watkins, R. 2004a. 'Victoria Police Organized Crime Strategy Project: "Organized Crime Template"', Victoria Police, Melbourne.

2004b. 'Victoria Police Organized Crime Strategy Project: "Responding to organized crime – Case study"' Victoria Police, Melbourne.

Watkins, R. and Wood, J. 2004. 'Understanding organized crime: a model and analytical tool'. Paper presented at Organized Crime Strategy Workshop, Melbourne.

Weber, M. 1958 (1919). 'Politics as a vocation', in H. Gerth and C. Mills (eds.), *From Max Weber: Essays in Sociology*. New York: Oxford University Press, pp. 77–128.

1978. 'Political communities', in G. Roth and C. Wittich (eds.), *Economy and Society*. Berkeley: University of California Press, pp. 901–40.

Webster, A. 1994. 'Bridging institutions: the role of contract research organisations in technology transfer', *Science and Public Policy* 21: 89–97.

Webster, C. 2001. 'Gated cities of tomorrow', *Town Planning Review* 72: 149–69.

2002. 'Property rights and the public realm: gates, green belts, and Gemeinschaft', *Environment and Planning B: Planning and Design* 29: 397–412.

Weick, K. 2001. *Making Sense of the Organization*. Malden, Mass.: Blackwell.

Weisburd, D., Mastrofski, S., McNally, A., Greenspan, R. and Willis, J. 2003. 'Reforming to preserve: Compstat and strategic problem solving in American policing', *Criminology and Public Policy* 2: 421–56.

Welsh, W. and Zajac, G. 2004. 'A census of prison-based drug treatment programs: implications for programming, policy, and evaluation.' *Crime and Delinquency* 50: 108–34.

Wejnert, B. 2002. 'Integrating models of diffusion of innovations: a conceptual framework', *Annual Review of Sociology* 28: 297–326.

Westley, W. 1970. *Violence and the Police*. Cambridge, Mass.: MIT Press.

Wexler, D. B. 1990. *Therapeutic Jurisprudence: The Law as a Therapeutic Agent*. Durham, N.C.: Carolina Academic Press.

White, M. D. 2002. 'Identifying situational predictors of police shootings using multivariate analysis', *Policing* 25: 726–51.

WHO 2003. *International Migration, Health and Human Rights*. Geneva: World Health Organization.

WHO Regional Office for Europe 2001. *HIV in Prisons: A Reader with Particular Relevance to the Newly Independent States*. Berne: WHO Regional Office for Europe.

WHO Regional Office for Europe and Pompidou Group of the Council of Europe 2001. *Prisons, Drugs and Society: A Consensus Statement on Principles, Policies and Practices*. Berne: WHO Regional Office for Europe and the Council of Europe.

Williams, F. 2004. *Rethinking Families*. London: Calouste Gulbenkian Foundation.

Wilson, J. 2004. 'Private security firms call for more firepower in combat zone', *Guardian*, 17 April.

Wolfe, D. and Malinowska-Sempruch, K. 2004. *Illicit Drug Policies and the Global HIV Epidemic: Effects of UN and National Government Approaches*. New York: Open Society Institute.

Wolfe, M., Xu, F., Patel, P., O'Cain, M., Schillinger, J., St Louis, M. and Finelli, L. 2001. 'An outbreak of syphilis in Alabama prisons: correctional health policy and communicable disease control', *American Journal of Public Health* 91: 1220–5.

Wood, [Justice] J. 1997. *Final Report of Royal Commission into New South Wales Police Service*. Sydney: RCNSWPS.

Wood, J. 2000. 'Reinventing governance: a study of transformations in the Ontario Provincial Police'. Ph.D. thesis, Centre of Criminology, University of Toronto.

2004a. 'Cultural change in the governance of security', *Policing and Society* 14: 31–48.

Wood, J. 2004b. 'New regulatory challenges: the case of organized crime'. Paper presented to the serious Non-Compliance Advisory Group. Australian Tax Office, 13 October.

Wood, J. and Cardia, N. in press. 'Plural policing in Brazil', in T. Jones and T. Newburn (eds.), *Plural Policing in Comparative Perspective*. London: Routledge.

Wood, J. and Font, E. 2003. 'Building peace and reforming policing in Argentina: opportunities and challenges for shantytowns'. Paper presented at *In Search of Security: An International Conference on Policing and Security*, Montreal, 19–22 February.

2004. 'Is "community policing" a desirable export? On crafting the global constabulary ethic'. Paper presented at the workshop on *Constabulary Ethics and the Spirt of Transnational Policing*. Oñati, Spain, 12–13 July.

Wood, J. and Shearing, C. 1999. 'Reinventing intellectuals', *Canadian Journal of Criminology* 41 (April): 311–20.

in press. *Imagining Security*. Cullompton, Devon: Willan.

Woodward, B. 2004. *Plan of Attack*. New York: Simon & Schuster.

World Tribune.com 2004. 'Private military companies paying bucks for elite soldiers in Iraq'. http://216.26.163.62/2004/me_iraq_10_15.html (accessed 21 November 2004).

Young, J. 1999. *The Exclusive Society*. London: Sage.

Zachariah, R., Harries, A., Chantulo, A., Yadidi, A., Nkhoma, W. and Maganga, O. 2002. 'Sexually transmitted infections among prison inmates in a rural district of Malawi', *Transactions of the Royal Society of Tropical Medicine and Hygiene* 96: 617–19.

Zedner, L. 1995. 'In pursuit of the vernacular: comparing law and order discourse in Britain and Germany', *Social and Legal Studies* 4: 517–34.

2000. 'The pursuit of security', in T. Hope and R. Sparks (eds.), *Crime, Risk and Insecurity*. London: Routledge, pp. 200–14.

2003. 'Too much security?', *International Journal of the Sociology of Law* 31: 155–84.

Index

mixed economy of 33, 111–12, 137,
148–9; *see also* peace committees;
popular justice in South Africa;
private security sector
of night-time economy 132–3
power struggles, *see* power relations
as public good 119–20
public/private divide in 111, 115–18
rationed response 119
reassurance policing 134–6
resources 17, 96–104
response to terrorism 55
in South Africa, *see* South Africa
policy, impact on police 146
political actors 91–2
political capital 98–9
popular justice in South Africa 153, 154–7,
158; *see also* peace committees
positivism 223, 224
power
police abuse of 170
use by the weak 29
power relations 87, 246
and policing 4–5, 104–5; minimizing
105–9; police resources 96–104;
stakeholders 91–6
presentational strategies 57
'prisoner's dilemma' 121
prisons, *see* imprisonment
private governments 11–13, 26
private property 12
enclosure of 125–6
exclusion from 127–9
and security as club good 122–3, 124–5
private security sector 169, 171–2
and Australian policing 95–6
as club good 121, 122–3, 124–5, 126
military services industry 40, 41–3, 44–6
and night-time economy 133
public/private divide in 111, 115–18
in shopping centres 127–8
size of 112; *see also* peace committees;
popular justice in South Africa;
transnational commercial security
private/public divide in policing 111,
115–18
privatization 87
Project iThemba 210
property crime 122–3, 124–5
public choice economics 169
public goods 50, 118–20, 131, 183–92
public interest 29–30
Public Order Police unit 142, 147
public spaces, exclusion from 129–31,
132

public/private divide in policing 111,
115–18
punishment
health consequences of 199–200
see also imprisonment
punishment mentality 221–2, 223,
224
pure public goods 118

quasi-public spaces 126–9

reactive policing 82
reassurance policing 134–6
reciprocity 187
referral 204
regulation
meta-regulation 245
of policing 105–9
regulatory state 23–6
repressive state apparatus 173
resource allocation strategies 57
resources
of police 17, 96–104
of the weak 30–2
responsive regulation pyramid 108
restorative justice 156–7, 237
risk analysis 54
risk management 55, 136
risk mentality 221–2
risk-based thought 35
risks 53, 54, 83
Rose, N. 25
rule of law 152–3
Rumsfeld, D. 47

Sadiq, R. 151
Salt Lake City Olympics 66–9, 75–8,
79–85
Sampson, R. 207
Samuelson, P. 118
Savas, E. 23
Schärf, W. 143
Securicor 37
Securitas 37
Security 21 project 175–9
security
concept of 9, 36
constitutive dimension of 189–92
impact on health 196–201, 216;
enhancing benefits of imprisonment
202–3; integrating police and
health work 203–5; reducing
imprisonment 201–2
instrumental dimension of 184–5, 191
mapping 234–5